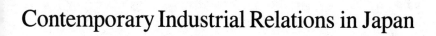

Contemporary Industrial Relations in Japan

Contemporary Industrial Relations in Japan

Edited by
Taishiro Shirai

UNIVERSITY OF WISCONSIN PRESS

Published 1983

The University of Wisconsin Press
114 North Murray Street
Madison, Wisconsin 53715

The University of Wisconsin Press, Ltd.
1 Gower Street
London WC1E 6HA, England
Distributed in Japan by the Japan Institute of Labor.
7-6 Shibakoen 1-chome, Minato-ku
Tokyo, Japan

First printing

Printed in the United States of America

For LC CIP information see the colophon

ISBN 0-299-09280-1

Contributors

Tadashi A. Hanami
Law School, Sophia University, Tokyo

Kazuo Koike
Kyoto Institute of Economics, Kyoto University, Kyoto

Kazutoshi Kōshiro
Faculty of Economics, Yokohama National University, Yokohama

Yasuhiko Matsuda
Faculty of Economics, Yokohama National University, Yokohama

Norikuni Naitō
College of Economics, Rikkyo University, Tokyo

Haruo Shimada
Faculty of Economics, Keio University, Tokyo

Taishiro Shirai
Faculty of Business Administration, Hosei University, Tokyo

Shigeyoshi Tokunaga
Faculty of Economics, Tohoku University, Sendai

Kōichirō Yamaguchi
Law School, Sophia University, Tokyo

Contents

Figures

Tables

Foreword

This book meets a long-standing need in the field of international comparative study. Here for the first time a group of Japanese scholars has undertaken to produce in English a comprehensive analysis of industrial relations in contemporary Japan as it compares to other advanced industrial societies. The few scholarly works on the subject available in English heretofore have been the research output of non-Japanese writers or collaborations between Japanese and non-Japanese. In contrast, this volume presents the results of long years of study initiated and executed by Japanese industrial relations experts themselves. As a result, it takes up a number of aspects of the questions studied which usually either escape the attention of non-Japanese observers or do not receive the emphasis which the Japanese themselves believe they should be accorded. It goes much further in these respects than, for example, the widely read 1973 collaborative volume, *Workers and Employers in Japan,* edited by Kazuo Okochi, Bernard Karsh, and the writer of this Foreword.

The appearance of this contribution, under the leadership of Taishiro Shirai, is most timely and welcome. In the past decade Japan has witnessed dramatic changes in its economy and society, and Japan's position in the industrial world has undergone a transformation of most significant proportions. It is fitting in these circumstances that a fresh and careful portrayal of the industrial relations system in Japan, especially in comparison with Western countries, has now been published. Professor Shirai, it should be noted, also played a key role in the preparation and writing of the 1973 volume, and thus serves as a link with the earlier efforts.

The book is especially welcome because it goes a long way toward restoring analytical balance to a subject which in the recent past has been considerably distorted and stereotyped in the treatments given it not only by the mass media and popular literature written outside of Japan (and often in Japan itself), but also even by some writers considered leading Western experts about Japan. This restoration of balance is long overdue. Of late, in the West, there has been a flood of books, articles, television programs, and the like which, in a euphoric way, have probed the "mysteries" of the present-day industrial society of Japan. Most have inevitably sought the explanation of Japan's "miraculous" economic growth of the post-World War II period in the "unique" nature of that nation's labor-management relations. Often there has been confusion of cause and effect in these treatments, but what is worse have been the presentation of half-truths, the preoccupation with unusual "exotic" facts, and the assumption of the perpetuation of static conditions derived from an agrarian feudal Japan of long ago. In reading these reports, expert Japanese analysts often wonder what country is being described with such certainty.

Each chapter in this volume attempts to clarify and interpret the actual situation, I believe quite successfully. The efforts of the authors, individually and collectively, contribute to placing the development of Japanese labor-management relations well within the common experience of mankind everywhere in the industrial world. They emphasize the universal rather than the peculiar. As elsewhere, in Japan there are failures as well as successes, unresolved dilemmas as well as definitive solutions, conflicts as well as harmonies, lessons to be learned as well as to be avoided. There is neither a "worker's paradise" nor an atmosphere of abject servility.

On the personal side, it has been my good fortune to have had close associations with the contributors to this volume for many years. My friendship and colleagueship with Professor Shirai run back a quarter of a century and that with most of the others almost as long. Over these years we have had the most fruitful of intellectual exchanges through frequent visits with one another in Japan and the United States. The nine contributors are certainly among the most distinguished industrial relations scholars in Japan. All have had intense study experience abroad as well as outstanding academic and practical achievements at home. Each has earned an international reputation as a professional analyst. This volume, thus, has the benefit of each contributor's long-time efforts to construct a framework for cross-national comparative analysis. It is not a sudden outcome of recent events; rather, it has emerged from reflection and study over several decades of professional scholarship. Schooled in sophisticated research method and technique, the group represents the first postwar generation of Japanese scholars to interpret systematically the development of industrial relations in Japan's modern era. Together they have carried forward to higher levels of analysis and understanding what their predecessors and teachers often alone and in isolation had been attempting ever since it became apparent that Japan was becoming a fully industrialized society, among the most economically advanced in the world. In a sense, then, this work represents an internationalization of Japanese intellectual endeavor, which heretofore often was seen, even by non-Japanese analysts, as parochial, distant, and difficult to comprehend.

Space does not permit a full recounting of all the international involvements of the authors. For the past 30 years, Professor Shirai has been among

the foremost scholars in Japan concerned with interpreting Japanese industrial relations from an international perspective. A student of the eminent and
pioneering scholar, Dr. Kazuo Okochi, at Tokyo University, Professor Shirai
initiated his comparative research by participating in the Japan Labor Study
Group, which in the early 1960s undertook an extensive tour of the United
States and Western Europe, meeting with unionists, management, and government officials. I was privileged to be a part of that group and, as a result,
also to invite Professor Shirai to spend a year at the Institute of Labor and
Industrial Relations of the University of Illinois, where he was a Visiting
Research Scholar under the auspices of the joint research and exchange
program of that university and Keio University in Tokyo. At the time,
Professor Shirai held the post of chief of the research staff of the Japan
Institute of Labor, to which I will refer further. Professor Kōshiro also was
to participate soon afterward in the Keio-Illinois program, with a year in
Champaign-Urbana. Professors Matsuda, Koike, Shimada, and Shirai spent
extensive periods studying at the University of Wisconsin in Madison. Dean
Hanami initiated his foreign study with a year at the New York School of
Industrial and Labor Relations of Cornell University, and like the others has
engaged in long-term research in Europe and California. Professors Koike,
Naitō, Yamaguchi, and Tokunaga among them have carried out research for
extended periods in the United Kingdom, West Germany, and Italy. It was
with great pride that we at the Wisconsin Industrial Relations Research
Institute awarded a doctoral degree to Professor Shimada and a masters to
Professor Matsuda. The professional studies of all the contributors have
taken them to most of the quarters of the globe, and each has become an
invaluable resource in cross-national communicatons for Japan throughout
the world.

The genesis and execution of this book owe much to the Japan Institute of
Labor, which undoubtedly is the most important center by far in the world,
let alone in Japan itself, for the study of the Japanese industrial relations
system in comparison with that of other countries. The Institute, located in
Tokyo, came into being in 1959 as the result of far-sighted leadership in the
field of industrial relations. Supported by government funding, it has represented a national recognition of the critical importance of objective study of
industrial relations for the new democratic Japan. As an autonomous institution, it afforded a concentration of human, financial, and physical resources,
which no one Japanese university or government agency could bring together
by itself, in order to attain the critical mass of interdisciplinary and scholarly
endeavor required for the dramatically changing industrial relations scene of
that country. Under the wise leadership of such intellectual giants as Tamon
Maeda, Ichirō Nakayama, Kazuo Ōkochi, Shingo Kaite, and Mikio Sumiya,
among others, the Institute has flourished and gained unrivaled international

stature for its unbiased and systematic study of Japanese industrial relations. Until Professor Shirai joined the faculty of Hosei University, he served for several years as the Institute's first chief researcher, responsible for such key publications as the monthly English-language *Japan Labor Bulletin* and Japan's leading industrial relations periodical, *The Monthly Journal of the Japan Institute of Labor* (in Japanese), as well as a steady stream of monographs and other publications, in Japanese and English. All of the contributors to this volume have been and remain associated with the Institute. Dean Hanami and Professor Kōshiro succeeded Professor Shirai in leading the Institute's research activities, while they and the others all served (and still do) as research associates of the Institute. They, and their colleagues at the Institute, over the years have established the study of industrial relations as a major field throughout Japan. All have gone on to prominent academic and administrative careers in the field of industrial relations in universities and public service positions, such as serving as members of Japan's tripartite labor relations commissions. All are key members of the Japan Industrial Relations Research Association, housed at the Japan Institute of Labor, an affiliate of the International Industrial Relations Association and a counterpart of the Industrial Relations Research Associations in the United States, Western European countries, and numerous other nations. It is fair to say that, had there never been a Japan Institute of Labor, this book would probably not have seen the light of day. From the Institute have come not only the intellectual ferment that made serious systematic study of Japanese industrial relations possible but also the important currents and streams of thought which have critically influenced the course of public policy toward industrial relations in postwar Japan.

In bringing together the work of this group of scholars, the book was intended to be a highly integrative effort. Again, I was fortunate to observe the gestation of the ideas that led to the eventual publication of the 15 essays. About five years ago I had the privilege of attending the initial planning meetings for the book. Here was a group of closely associated professional colleagues, each of whom had concentrated upon the study of certain particular aspects of industrial relations yet was thoroughly familiar with the others' specializations and with the overall data and analytical approaches. It was abundantly clear to the group that the non-Japanese world did not have a deep and accurate understanding of important dimensions of the industrial relations system in Japan as a whole. Yet, it was also their mutual realization that Japanese analysts themselves had the responsibility of bringing such an understanding to those outside Japan, too-long accepting of simple-minded stereotypes, incomplete information, and disturbing misapprehensions. In their meetings, under the aegis of the Japan Institute of Labor, these scholars grappled with the problems of what was important to stress and what was necessary to clarify and demystify — all in terms of the needs of foreigners seriously willing to consider the case of Japan afresh.

One of the earliest decisions was that each scholar would write his contribution directly in English rather than depend upon having it translated from the Japanese, with the risk of losing accuracy and subtlety. While all the contributors had some experience in writing and publishing in English (as well as prolifically in Japanese, I should add), each recognized that this was a most formidable undertaking. However, the task itself was so important that they resolved not to flinch from this burden, onerous as it was. In the process of gathering and drafting the material, they met regularly to learn from one another, to integrate their findings (in English), to eliminate overlap, and to air and express their differences. To make explicit that there were differences of opinion was considered highly important, since it was felt among all of them that disagreement in intellectual interpretation was as widespread in the Japanese academic community as elsewhere and that even for the professional Japanese analysts much remained unexplored and unknown. Early on, the group decided, in addition to drawing on its own resources for clarity and consistency in writing style, to turn to Barbara D. Dennis of the University of Wisconsin-Madison for editorial assistance. Mrs. Dennis, who served as technical editor for the 1973 volume, had more than two decades of experience in dealing with Japanese industrial relations materials and was well known personally to most members of the group. Of key importance in the production of the volume was the continual communication between Mrs. Dennis and members of the group, especially Professors Shirai, Koike, Shimada, and Kōshiro, who served as the principal coordinators of the chapters. Drafts and redrafts crossed the Pacific many times. Professor Robert E. Cole, of the University of Michigan, and I had the privilege of offering advice on substantive content throughout this process.

This collaborative effort has attempted to produce a set of closely related chapters. Working from a common outline, it consciously avoids ending up as a series of disjointed and scattered contributions. Each chapter indeed should be read with the others in mind. The authors are well aware of the fact that space, time, and language limitations would not allow the most comprehensive and integrative presentation that might have been possible. Their aim was to distill the main characteristics of each major feature, with stress upon international comparisons. Much detail has been left to footnotes and references. None of the contributors, I am certain, feels fully satisfied with the final outcome on this score; but no doubt each hopes that the chapters, individually and together, lay the basis for further elaboration in English. Moreover, the reactions to the book, it is anticipated, will serve to bring forth further scholarly efforts to examine these topics, for publication in Japanese as well as English. Indeed, launching this process of international communication, interchange, and reflection may prove to be the most important outcome of this volume.

The world, let alone Japan, owes a great debt to Professor Shirai and his collaborators for making this work available. Finally, we have an authoritative indigenous interpretation of the contemporary industrial relations experience in Japan, an interpretation which can fit more readily than its predecessors with the experiences of other countries. The book goes far to clear up many of the misconceptions that have marred our understanding of key institutions of Japanese industrial society. More important, the work opens up areas that have been hardly treated in English before, as for example the Japanese appraisal of Western literature on industrial relations, labor relations in the vast small and medium-sized firm sector, in government enterprises and the civil service, internal processes of enterprise unions, current Marxist interpretation of industrial relations in Japan, the function of the law in the labor relations field, the structure and strategy of collective bargaining, and the labor movement in politics. At times the authors may seem to take the position of defending Japan's industrial relations system. It should be borne in mind, however, that their principal objective is to hold the Japanese experience up to close scrutiny for comparison with that of other industrial societies. From this perspective, the relevance and importance of analyzing Japanese industrial relations holds its greatest meaning.

SOLOMON B. LEVINE

University of Wisconsin-Madison
January, 1983

Preface

The Japanese industrial relations system has increasingly been attracting the attention of Western labor specialists, both academicians and practitioners, for almost two decades—an interest that is quite understandable in view of the extraordinary economic growth of Japan and its tremendous expansion in world markets during that period. These developments, in part, stimulated the writing of this book. Primarily, however, we—a group of native specialists in either labor law or labor economics—were motivated by a common desire to make available a new book in English on the major aspects of industrial relations in contemporary Japan that would provide non-Japanese readers with the information necessary to develop a sound understanding of how the system actually functions. Our focus, for the most part, is on the 1970s.

Today Japan is the second largest economy in the non-Communist world in terms of gross national product and among the richest in GNP per capita. Its exports, such as steel, automobiles, electronic systems and components, and ships, are technologically excellent and command a continually enlarging share in the world market because of their competitive prices as well as their reputation for reliable quality. The success of the Japanese economy was demonstrated not only in the period of rapid growth up to the early 1970s, but also in the succeeding period of uncertainties brought on by the oil crisis in the fall of 1973. Because of the paucity of natural resources and a heavy dependence on imported oil, the Japanese economy should be the one in the world most vulnerable to such external disruptions. However, Japan managed to find her way out of the crisis, maintaining nearly full employment with moderate inflation, compared with that of other industrialized nations. Impressed by the remarkably successful performance of the Japanese economy, Western observers, particularly labor specialists, have sought the secret of Japan's success; many believe they have found one of the principal keys in her industrial relations system.

No doubt they are right. The industrial relations system is crucial in the evolution and actual performance of the Japanese economy, and how it operates is equally crucial to an understanding of that evolution and performance. I would venture to say that the functioning of this system is perhaps more important in Japan than in other industrialized societies simply because the only asset the Japanese economy has is her human resources, and the industrial relations system has contributed greatly to the development and utilization of those resources in a most efficient manner. Therefore, the increasing attention among non-Japanese people to our system should be highly welcome, as it certainly promotes sophisticated cross-cultural understanding. However, we feel there are some problems that we should try to address here.

One result of this increased attention has been the accumulation of a large body of literature, written in English, on Japan's industrial relations system. As referred to in the following chapters, especially chapter 1, there are a number of books and articles which certainly provide readers with accurate and detailed knowledge of our system. They include several important works in which insightful observations and analysis of the subject stimulated lively discussions among Japanese scholars and policy-makers about the need to re-examine and re-evaluate the industrial relations system of their own country. However, some Western labor specialists have formulated and promulgated notions about the distinctive characteristics of Japanese industrial relations that have become established as stereotypes and have tended to circumscribe the further development of research as well as to constrain a balanced understanding of the system. Typical of these stereotyped notions are lifelong employment, the length-of-service reward system, and enterprise unionism. These three "pillars," as they were called in the 1973 report of the Organization for Economic Cooperation and Development, supposedly constitute the major elements of Japanese industrial relations. This notion reflects reality and certainly does identify very significant aspects of the Japanese industrial relations scene. The trouble is, however, that these "pillars" have come to be taken for granted as if they represented the entire system, and leading observers have failed to understand that these practices and institutions have developed within a limited segment of the Japanese labor market during a limited period of the country's industrializing history.

The distinctive peculiarities of the Japanese system that are implied by these notions were largely attributed to the nation's cultural tradition. It goes without saying that cultural factors play a most significant role in formulating the industrial relations system of any nation. It is particularly so in a country such as Japan, with her homogeneous culture and traditions developed by a single race on isolated islands in the Far East. However, an overemphasis on the cultural tradition as *the* determinant of industrial relations practices and institutions may lead to a failure to pay due regard to the changes, modifications, and adjustments that a system has to make in the historical developmental process in order to meet and solve the problems posed by the dynamism of industrialization. Moreover, overemphasizing the culturalist interpretation is likely to hinder foreign scholars in any further efforts at scientific analysis because, once established, such an interpretation tends to become a fixed and authentic premise which the new observers accept uncritically before they start their cross-cultural study of Japanese industrial relations.

Western students in general are not to blame for this overemphasis on cultural determinants. Rather, the Japanese scholars and practitioners who supplied them with information are largely responsible. No doubt each national system of industrial relations has its own peculiarities, but the easiest way of explaining or interpreting the phenomena to foreigners is to utilize the culturalist approach. Western students, in turn, are generally inclined to expect and accept this interpretation. When they are taught that such-and-such system derived from the cultural legacy of premodern Japan with its vertically structured, hierarchical, group-oriented society, most of them are satisfied with the explanation, which appears to be self-evident as they witness the actual behavior of the Japanese, strikingly different from what they are accustomed to seeing among people in their homelands. Thus they may not explore further to find out what the traditional culture really means and how and why it adapted to and became compatible with the common requirements of industrialization.

Another reason for the persistent and surprisingly broad popularity of these stereotypes is that the great majority of the Japanese people, like most of the non-Japanese, still believe that any industrial relations institution, system, or practice in Western societies is advanced, modern, democratic, efficient, and reasonable compared to that of Japan. Using as yardsticks the Western models, as they see them or think they see them, they criticize their own practices and institutions as backward, feudalistic, inefficient, irrational, undemocratic, and so on. It is impossible for them to imagine that any of the Japanese institutions which developed later than those of advanced Western societies could claim to be a functional alternative and, under certain circumstances, as rational, efficient, and democratic—or even more so—than their Western counterparts, so that they would be applicable in certain situations in other industrialized or industrializing countries. This feeling, so prevalent among the Japanese, is supported by the Marxist interpretation of the Japanese industrial relations systems, which still enjoys surprisingly broad popularity among academicians as well as union leaders. According to the traditional Marxist interpretation, all of the unique features of Japanese industrial relations are true evidence of its backwardness and the undeveloped stage of its industrial democracy; they should be replaced by Western models as soon as possible in order for Japan to reach the level of advanced industrial societies. For example, the so-called lifelong employment and in-plant training system are seen by Marxists as a capitalist policy designed to subjugate workers by discriminating between the regular and the temporary employees and to prevent free mobility in a modern and open labor market. Also, in their view, seniority-based wages are designed to hold down the general wage level as well as to force workers to be heavily dependent upon continued employment in a particular company. Enterprise unions, they argue further, are intrinsically company unions and, therefore, should be replaced by Western-style industrial unions.

Such emphasis on the "backwardness" of Japanese industrial relations is certainly not totally groundless. This is the major reason that we have included the chapter "A Marxist Interpretation of Japanese Industrial Relations" in this book. There are some Western observers of the Japanese industrial relations scene who concur in this evaluation even though they are not Marxists.

However, most of the contributors of the following chapters do not share this critical assessment of the Japanese industrial relations system, although they are keenly aware of its defects and shortcomings—in particular of the immaturity of the parties in their attempts to live up to the standards of advanced industrial democracy. At the same time, they do not necessarily support the very favorable evaluation of the system rendered by some other Western observers, such as those in the 1973 OECD report, who emphasize the amicable and cooperative relationships between Japanese employers and employees, virtues also attributed to cultural factors unique to Japanese society. Most of the writers of the chapters in this volume try, instead, to explain the characteristics of the Japanese industrial relations system in light of policies and counterpolicies deliberately or involuntarily taken to meet specific needs or purposes under the conditions and constraints at a particular stage of this nation's industrializing process under particular circumstances.

The purposes of the actors in Japanese industrial relations can hardly be different from those of their counterparts in Western industrialized societies. Employers want to earn the largest possible profit in competitive markets. Unions want to secure and improve the terms and conditions of employment of their members as efficiently as possible. The government takes either an oppressive or a liberal policy toward the labor movement as it sees fit in a given situation. It also seeks to play an adequate role in adjusting conflicts between the interest groups.

The established system and practices as they operate in contemporary Japan are the outcome of a process during which the parties repeatedly acted and interacted, sometimes through peaceful negotiations and other times through bitter struggle, until they reached a series of compromises on the various issues involved. If a system enjoys the long-standing support of the people concerned, it must have a raison d'être which is accepted as permissible, reasonable, and justifiable by the actors. In short, the seemingly peculiar practices or system of Japanese industrial relations can be largely explained by the same logic that Western scholars use in analyzing their own system and practices, without being heavily dependent on culturalist interpretations. Thus the alleged "distinctive characteristics peculiar to Japan" may be seen as less particularistic but more universal in that they might well function in other national settings under similar circumstances.

If this is the case, at least some notable aspects of the allegedly "backward" Japanese industrial relations system may turn out to be more modern and functionally efficient in meeting and solving the problems any highly industrialized nation has to face—development and utilization of manpower resources, their distribution and reallocation, technological change and job security of workers, collective bargaining and inflation, the traditional structure of collective bargaining and plant-wide negotiations, workers' participation in decisions within the enterprise, discrepancies between the views of union leaders and rank-and-file members, and so on.

In any case, it is our hope that this book will provide the foreign audience with enough relevant information to facilitate a more balanced understanding than before of the whole complex of the industrial relations system in contemporary Japan.

We do not claim, however, that all the chapters support the interpretation described above. Rather, one of the features of this volume is the apparent inconsistency among the views expressed by the contributors, particularly differences between the economists and the lawyers, the latter being more inclined than the former to emphasize the cultural distinctiveness of Japanese society and the behavior of the people. Even among the economists there is sharp dispute. We thought it was fair and necessary to have a chapter on the Marxist interpretation of Japanese industrial relations systems because, as referred to above, that viewpoint is still very important among social scientists, especially in the field of labor, and it does play a significant role in the policy-making of some leading labor unions. As is further elaborated in chapter 1, it was one of the purposes of this volume to disclose disagreement among scholars in the alleged "consensus society" of Japan.

On behalf of all of the contributors, I would like to express our deepest appreciation to the Japan Institute of Labor and its staff, under the presidency of the late Dr. Nakayama Ichirō,* for their generous financial support and administrative assistance in preparing and publishing this book. We regret, however, that the delay of the publication made it impossible to present a copy to Dr. Nakayama, who passed away on April 9, 1980.

The gratitude of all the contributors is due to two American professors, Solomon B. Levine, University of Wisconsin, and Robert E. Cole, University of Michigan, who occasionally participated in our discussions, read some of the manuscripts, and gave us valuable comments and advice.

---

*Japanese personal names are given throughout in standard Japanese order—surname first, given name last—except when the named individuals are referred to as authors of English-language works.

Of utmost importance to our project was the assistance of Barbara D. Dennis, University of Wisconsin, who kindly undertook the difficult task of editing manuscripts written in English by Japanese, which often required a lot of patience, imagination, and insightful understanding on her part. Without her excellent work of highest professional quality, this book would be less readable. She was also very tolerant of the delays in receiving the manuscripts, and we hope that it did not disturb her schedule of other commitments. Jane Dennis-Collins provided editorial assistance and typed the manuscripts. On behalf of all of the contributors, I express our heartfelt appreciation for their work on the book.

TAISHIRO SHIRAI
Professor, Hosei University
Faculty of Business Administration

Contemporary Industrial Relations in Japan

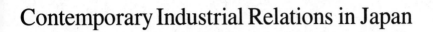

Abbreviations

CKKT   *Chingin Kōzō Kihon Tōkei Chōsa* (Basic Survey of the Wage Structure), compiled by the Japan Ministry of Labor

EC   European Community

ILO   International Labor Organization

LPELR   Local Public Enterprise Labor Relations (Law/Commission)

MKTC   *Maigetsu Kinrō Tōkei Chōsa* (Monthly Labor Statistics Survey), compiled by the Japan Ministry of Labor

NES   *New Earnings Survey*, compiled by the Great Britain Department of Employment and Productivity

OECD   Organization for Economic Cooperation and Development

PCNE   Public Corporation and National Enterprise

PCNELR   Public Corporation and National Enterprise Labor Relations (Law/Commission)

RKKC   *Rōdō Kumiai Kihon Chōsa* (Basic Survey of Trade Unions), compiled by the Japan Ministry of Labor

SEI   *Structure of Earnings in Industry*, compiled by the European Community

1 *Haruo Shimada*

Japanese Industrial Relations—
A New General Model?
A Survey of the English-Language Literature

Introduction

Deep dissatisfaction with the poor economic performance of advanced industrialized nations in the West in recent years led a writer for *The Economist* (Macrae 1980), reporting on a survey of Japan, to assert that the key to understanding Japan's economic leap, the most dramatic in world history, was to be found in her successful enterprise organizations where "the working force plans hourly for greater output tomorrow." Macrae labeled the concept "enterprising" and contrasted it with the disastrous "bureaucratic" organizations where "most people are concerned to avoid any bothersome disturbance tomorrow." He attributed Japan's postwar success particularly to the range of activities that it had retained in the enterprising category rather than allowing them to be swamped in the ever-fattening bureaucratic category, as some of the advanced Western nations have done. He described vividly, as an example of the enterprising spirit, a usual scene in a Japanese factory where skilled engineers "swarm" over the assembly lines at the end of the day shift to check and arrange better conditions for increasing production the next day.

However, an essential question remains to be answered: Why are Japanese workers, often in sharp contrast to their Western counterparts, so earnest and dedicated in their efforts to increase the productivity of their companies?

3

Former U.S. Secretary of Labor and Ambassador to Japan James Hodgson confessed "Japan for me was an unsettling experience. On the other side of the world, the world of work is indeed other-worldly" (Hodgson 1978). He pointed out, for example, that Japanese workers seek "group harmony" instead of "individual justice," they strive to "fit in" rather than "stand out," and they work for "consensus," discarding the "adversary posture."

Is the Japanese world of work really so different? A popular publication of the Organization for Economic Cooperation and Development (OECD 1977), which attempted an analysis of Japanese industrial relations, concluded that the uniqueness of Japan was not so much in its allegedly peculiar institutions such as lifetime employment, seniority wages, and enterprise unionism as in what the report calls "the fourth pillar"—in essence, the "social norms within the enterprise." The report suggested that this consists of such elements as a view of the enterprise as a community, a set of vertical relationships and reciprocal obligations, and a consensual system of decision-making; it maintained that it is this unique cultural asset that keeps the Japanese work organizations operating successfully and productively.

These recent essays and reports all point in the same direction—that there is an increasingly keen interest among Western observers in Japanese work organizations and industrial relations. Why is there such a strong interest today? At one time the Japanese industrial relations system was to some degree a focus of Westerners' curiosity about things exotic, because Japan presented a unique case of successful industrial development among Asian countries. However, their interest now is quite different. It is very serious and policy-oriented, reflecting the economic realities confronting Western industrialized nations at the present time. Stagnant and even partially declining productivity since the early 1970s is the most serious symptom of the currently ailing American economy (Fellner 1979). It has been attributed in part to a failure to motivate workers and to increase their productivity. In Britain and some West European nations, necessary industrial adjustments are hindered in part by the "antique inflexibility" (Dore 1973, p. 420) of trade unions, and thus potential gains in aggregate productivity are thwarted. The flexible mobility of resources and economic efficiency were sacrificed to a large extent as workers made significant gains in the protection of their job rights and their income security.

In contrast, Japanese enterprise organizations and industrial relations appear to assure flexible organizational adaptability to changes in external conditions and efficient allocation of resources while at the same time maintaining high morale and commitment on the part of workers. In view of this intriguing contrast, it would not be surprising if Western observers were strongly tempted to seek useful clues and lessons from the Japanese experiences. Vogel (1979), for example, bluntly recommends that it is now time for

America to look to Japan to find out how to improve the performance of her productive and social organizations. The aforementioned OECD report suggests that there are certainly valuable lessons that Western countries can learn from the Japanese experience. Dore (1973) speculates, though somewhat wryly, that British industrial relations may well be moving toward a pattern more like the Japanese, which subtly implies that Britain could get some useful tips from Japan in the prospective course toward convergence.

Now, the critical question before us is whether we Japanese have a clear-cut model of our industrial relations to present to the world. What are the perceptions of Japanese industrial relations, and what are the realities? Are they identical, or are they different? Are there any informational gaps that we would fill by our own research efforts?

This survey of the literature in the field of Japanese industrial relations will be presented with a hope of finding answers, or at least of giving some insights into the questions. I am confining my focus only to the English-language literature because our book is written for an audience of primarily English-language readers. The purpose of my survey is to equip such readers with a minimal knowledge of earlier works in the field.

Japanese industrial relations indeed have been constantly a focus of foreigners' attention in the past. However, particular points of interest, the methodology of the inquiries, and the implications drawn from the researchers' observations have varied considerably, depending upon academic and policy interests, types and funding of research activities, and the domestic as well as the international economic, social, and political climate at the time. Keeping this varying nature of the evolutionary process in mind, I shall review selected works in the field, which may be categorized into four broadly defined streams of research. These four streams, which correspond roughly to stages of research development—though with exceptions—are examined and discussed in terms of their major findings, implications, methodology, and social background.

The Development of Literature on Japanese Industrial Relations

During the past few decades, we have seen a remarkable number of research studies of Japanese industrial relations reported in English-language books and articles. The purpose of this chapter is to review the development of this literature in order to acquaint readers with some of the important works in the field. I must add quickly, however, that this review has some limitations. One is that the choice of books and articles to be discussed is highly selective and arbitrary. Another is that I concentrate on only a few and discuss them in some depth as representative examples rather than referring briefly to a large number of studies. Still another is that only the

English-language literature is covered explicitly; the Japanese-language literature is dealt with only implicitly. But despite these limits, the sample selected for discussion in this chapter will reasonably represent the major streams of the English-language literature and to some extent will reflect the underlying currents of Japanese thought on their own industrial relations.

I have chosen to categorize and describe these works in four broadly defined streams, rather than in chronological order, because it both makes the presentation more convenient and will, I hope, give the reader a clearer picture of the evolution of knowledge in this field. The ebbs and flows of these streams have been influenced not only by changes in academic interest, but also by the interaction of a host of other factors such as the broad economic and political climate, the policy interests of foreign as well as domestic observers, and the various phases in the development of research methodology.

I identify these four streams as (1) the classical culturalist approach, (2) the descriptive institutional approach, (3) the functional analysis approach, and (4) the neoculturalist synthesis.

These four categories could be viewed as successive stages of research development. Some of the pathbreaking works in the classical culturalist category appeared in the late 1950s, and during the following decade—a period of vigorous growth of the Japanese economy—an atmosphere prevailed in which this approach, which stresses Japanese cultural uniqueness, attracted the attention of foreign observers and also gained the approval of both practitioners and scholars in Japan. This pioneering stage was followed immediately by one in which a series of studies appeared that emphasized the structure and institutions of industrial relations. Thanks to their extensive descriptions, rich factual information was made available on employment, wages, unions, collective bargaining, labor-management relations, and related topics. In the late 1960s and early 1970s, many provocative research findings, the results of more rigorous and systematic empirical analysis, were published, emphasizing the functional equivalence that existed behind the seeming differences in organizational behavior and challenging the alleged preoccupation with Japan's cultural uniqueness in industrial relations. In still more recent years, especially since the mid-1970s, a new stream of thought seems to have emerged and gained considerable popularity among both Western and Japanese specialists. We call this new approach "neoculturalist synthesis."

It seems not unreasonable to regard these four streams as representing four successive stages in the development of thought during the postwar period. However, we should bear in mind that the development process has not been such that the newer approach replaced the preceding one. To the contrary, each newer approach simply added more dimensions to the stock of knowledge while leaving the older approaches as they were. For example, even in recent years the classical culturalist approach still enjoys broad popularity, alongside the others. This kind of evolutionary process in research should be kept in mind as I discuss each of the streams in turn.

The Classical Culturalist Approach

Westerners' interest in Japanese social relations was at first largely anthropological or, in a somewhat broader sense, cultural, as exemplified by Benedict's early (1946) and well-known classical contribution. Among the pioneering works by Westerners in the industrial relations field, a subcategory of social relations, was one by Abegglen (1958) which evoked remarkably broad repercussions among both Western scholars and the Japanese. This early work was a tightly organized report of Abegglen's field survey of a limited number of large Japanese plants.

Abegglen's basic motivation for his research was to discover how Western industrial technology fitted into a non-Western context with a different social heritage. The organizational arrangements and practices he found in Japanese factories were markedly different from those that are regarded as common in American plants. Above all, he stressed two distinctive features, one having to do with employment and the other with wages. He described the employment practice as an established arrangement where an employer does not discharge an employee even temporarily, and in return the worker, at the time he is first employed, commits himself to that company for the remainder of his working life. Wages, according to Abegglen, are determined by the degree of a worker's commitment, not by his position or productivity. In sum, he characterized labor relations in Japanese factories as being analogous to family relations and advanced a hypothesis that this is a consistent and logical outgrowth of Japan's preindustrial social organization. In other words, in explaining industrial relations in Japanese factories, he emphasized the role of anthropological continuity and cultural legacies carried over from Japan's preindustrial society.

At the time of his interview research in the mid-1950s, Abegglen did not fully appreciate the economic effectiveness or efficiency associated with the Japanese factory organization. In fact, he pointed repeatedly to the immobility of the work force, the lack of cost consciousness, the lack of a relationship between wages and skill, and other characteristics—all implying a noneconomic and somewhat irrational behavior of organizations. What was striking to him, however, was the fact that modern technology was absorbed and digested in the Japanese industrial organization without altering the basic organizational character of Japan's feudal society.

Whatever his interest or intent, Abegglen's concept of Japanese labor-management relations appeared so appealing that it apparently had an enormous influence on anyone who was seeking to understand Japanese industrial relations. Thus, in the monumental collaborative work by Kerr and other eminent scholars (1960) on comparative industrial relations worldwide, the lifetime-commitment concept was already incorporated as a distinctive feature of Japanese employment, and was on its way to becoming the stereotype.

Although the impact of Abegglen's book should not be underestimated, he was, of course, not solely responsible for the rapid diffusion and public acceptance of this stereotypical concept of Japanese industrial relations. In my view, there were other important factors that coincidentally operated in the 1960s to help establish and disseminate the stereotype.

One is the fact that Japanese business leaders and employers began to regain confidence in their management policies as a result of their remarkably successful business and economic performance in the 1960s. Employers became increasingly convinced that their Japanese-style labor-management practices were valuable assets rather than deterrents in the growth of efficient corporations. Sakurada Takeshi, a former president of Nikkeiren (Japan Federation of Employers' Associations) often remarked that Japanese business enjoyed "three sacred treasures" in its industrial relations systems—lifetime employment, the *nenkō* (length-of-service reward) wage system, and enterprise unionism. Such an atmosphere certainly was instrumental in advancing acceptance of this particular stereotype in business circles and, in turn, was reflected in foreigners' perceptions of Japanese industrial relations.

For the purpose of reference, let me summarize the popular stereotype of the "three sacred treasures" as follows: Lifetime employment is the system under which the employer provides a worker with security throughout his working life, just as a father recognizes his child as a permanent member of his family; in turn, the worker offers unlimited commitment and loyalty to his employer. This practice assures the employer of a stable and uninterrupted flow of labor services.

The nenkō wage system is a method of determining wages, salaries, and other rewards from employment based primarily on a worker's length of service, but partly on his age and education. With this system, a worker is assured of sufficient earnings to cover his needs over his life cycle. Thus, he is willing to commit himself to the employing firm over a long period of time and also has an incentive to learn on the job.

Enterprise unionism is a type of union organization where employees of the same firm, irrespective of whether they are blue- or white-collar workers, are organized together in a single union. Although such a union differs essentially from the so-called "company union" in that it is organized on the workers' own initiative and by their own free choice, it has a quality favored by employers in that all union members are company employees, so that the employer can expect them to share similar interests with the management and therefore be less prone to strike.

Another factor contributing to the acceptance of the stereotype was the significant change in the views of Japanese scholars. Until around 1960, the time when the Japanese economy began its extraordinarily rapid growth, the majority of the scholars in the industrial relations field believed that the seeming peculiarities of Japanese industrial relations could be attributed simply to the backwardness or immaturity of Japan's capitalist development. This view reflected one of the two competing Marxist interpretations of the development of Japanese capitalism. On one side were those who took the position that Japanese capitalism was basically modernized, while on the other were those who maintained that it was semifeudal. Many scholars of the Marxist tradition who specialized in labor problems were in the latter group.[1]

Those who adopted this latter position quite naturally concentrated on the characteristics of workers who were still closely tied to rural backgrounds (Ōkōchi 1958b). Therefore, interesting topics for them were, for example, the cyclical mobility patterns of workers between urban factories and their rural families; the transplanting of rural social relations into urban factories, allegedly the sociological basis for an enterprise community; the age-wage profiles with a low wage rate for an unskilled new recruit just out of a rural farmer's household, etc. From such a perspective, all of the conspicuous labor practices such as lifetime commitment within a closed enterprise community, the length-of-service reward system, and weak enterprise unions were seen as evidence that Japanese capitalism was backward and semifeudal.

However, the tide changed markedly around the beginning of the 1960s, as the number of scholars taking the view that the unique Japanese labor practices improved rather than hindered labor productivity began to increase. Many of them traced the origins of these practices back to social relations in Japan's largely agrarian preindustrial society. Formally, and up to this point in the analysis, this view resembles the Marxist interpretation. However, these scholars drew quite different implications, attaching a positive meaning to the peculiar labor practices, while the Marxists regarded them simply as deterrents to modernization. Nakayama (1975), for example, repeatedly emphasized the usefulness of the special assets of Japanese industrial relations, such as a common interest and mutual trust, in finding a Japanese-style solution to labor conflicts. His argument is based upon the recognition that Japanese industrial relations are strongly characterized by and based on the family-like enterprise community. The popularity of such a view among Japanese scholars certainly lends strong support to an Abegglen-like stereotype.

All components of the stereotype are, of course, not necessarily wrong. There are elements, though oversimplified and somewhat exaggerated in the stereotype, that do exist in reality in more moderate and diversified forms. However, the stereotype tends to overshadow facts that do not conform with it and to discourage alternative interpretations. The danger is especially real when information is generally lacking and there is no other evidence that can be used to evaluate its validity. In such a situation, the stereotype assumes the role of "reality."[2]

The stereotype is quite popular not only among those foreigners who are inclined to be interested in and expect to see something exotic in Japan, but also among the Japanese who wish to emphasize the harmony and consensus in Japanese society. A widely read book by a perceptive anthropologist, Nakane (1970), for example, fulfilled such desires marvelously by offering an intriguing anthropological theorization of what she claims is the "vertical" structure of social relations in Japanese society. Reflecting popular interest and preconceptions, the culturalist interpretation persists. A leading labor lawyer (Hanami 1979b), for example, emphasized what he regarded as cultural influences that, in effect, create particularly Japanese-style interpretations within a legal system that originated in the West and was transplanted to Japanese soil—interpretations quite apart from the original spirit and meaning of the laws in their original context.

The Descriptive Institutional Approach

The second category of research is what might be characterized as the descriptive institutional approach. In this group I place studies in which a large amount of heterogeneous information is gathered and the structure and operation of various institutions are analyzed inductively through examination of the collected data. This method might be called a problem-centered approach to industrial relations. Studies in this category have contributed significantly to our knowledge during the past two decades. Thanks to the continuous efforts of a number of scholars and researchers, we now have a large stock of descriptive information on almost all facets of Japanese industrial relations.

The major advance in the descriptive institutional approach to Japanese industrial relations was made by Levine (1958) in a book published the same year as Abegglen's. Levine examined carefully and in detail the structure and operation of management systems, the trade union movement, collective bargaining, labor disputes, and government regulation of industrial relations. This book was the most comprehensive report on Japanese industrial relations systems ever written until that time in a Western language. It did not have as strong an appeal as Abegglen's sweeping generalizations, in spite of its reliable and accurate descriptions and its cautious and balanced assessment of the universal and particular elements of the structural and behavioral characteristics observable in Japanese industrial relations in the mid-1950s. Nevertheless, Levine's contribution provided a significant point of departure and a basic framework for the institutional study of industrial relations.

Along somewhat the same lines, Cook (1966) enriched knowledge of the structure and functioning of Japanese trade unions in a book that systematically describes the structure and activities of enterprise unions and industry-wide federations of unions, the organizational structure and policies of the major national centers, and the relationship between unions and political parties. In short, her book is a good introduction to Japanese trade unionism of the early postwar period. Levine (1967) presented an updated and considerably more descriptive analysis of collective bargaining than was included in his earlier book in an article in which he discussed its structure, process, and scope. Shirai (1965) described the historical development of collective bargaining, and in another article (Shirai 1975) he discussed the Japanese enterprise union as a decision-making mechanism. A comprehensive factual review of the evolution of Japanese industrial relations is provided by Shirai and Shimada (1978) in a lengthy article on the economic and organizational rationale of Japanese enterprise unions and the employment system from the perspective of Japan's economic development.

In a book on selected aspects of the structure and operation of the labor market, Evans (1971) provided intriguing and informative comparisons between the United States and Japan. His topics include labor market institutions, employment and manpower problems, aggregate wage patterns, wage differentials, and low-wage industries. A concise and yet quite informative report on Japanese labor market and manpower policies can be found in OECD (1973), which was issued as one of the series on manpower policies of selected OECD member countries. The report summarized the views of both Japanese authorities and foreign observers on the institutional and structural characteristics of the Japanese labor market, the employment systems and practices, as well as the major issues of manpower policy. Nishikawa (1980) presented 14 articles by Japanese university scholars and government economists on various aspects of the labor market. Some of the papers are theoretical, but most are descriptive and policy-oriented analyses. All except one by Nishikawa and Shimada were originally published elsewhere and in Japanese. This book greatly enriched the supply of information available in English on the operation of the Japanese labor market and related policy issues. Sumiya (1963) provided rich background information on the historical evolution of the Japanese labor market structure, analyzed in the context of Japan's long-term economic development—the context in which her labor movement and labor-management relations also evolved.

Let me now refer to two other significant publications by Japanese authors, each a collection of articles. One is the set of papers by Tsuda, Shirai, Sumiya, Minemura, and Nakayama that appeared in the July 1965 issue of the *British Journal of Industrial Relations* covering such aspects of Japan's industrial relations as the wage structure, collective bargaining, technological change and industrial relations, the role of government, and the modernization of the industrial relations system. The other is a book, edited by Ōkōchi, Karsh, and Levine (1973), that was compiled especially to provide accurate and instructive descriptions of various elements of Japanese industrial relations. The book includes a chapter on the concept of the national industrial relations system by Karsh and Levine and a historical and contemporary overview of institutional arrangements by Sumiya, as well as chapters on the legal framework by Ariizumi, the labor market by Ujihara, management by Okamoto, workers' spontaneous organizations by Kawada, collective bargaining by Shirai, labor disputes by Fujita, wages and benefits by Funahashi, personnel administration by Tsuda, and social security by Takahashi.

These publications may be regarded as show-window demonstrations of the views of leading Japanese scholars, and they do have some common features. One is that each author writes on his topic in the somewhat pedantic fashion of an authority. Although all the papers are quite informative, there appears to have been little discussion among the authors themselves, nor are there many provocative arguments directed to the English-reading audience. Except for a few of the papers, all were written originally in Japanese and in the Japanese heuristic style; then they were translated into English. Indeed, these two memorable collections may be viewed as direct predecessors of our present effort. As I will describe later, however, with our book we intend to go beyond this traditional pattern, not to produce just another updated version of these authoritative works.

Before moving on to the next category, let me mention a few more books on some auxiliary areas of industrial relations. Yoshino (1968) offered useful background information on the nature of Japanese management, its historical development, structure, policies, major problems, etc. Vogel (1963) successfully conveyed a realistic picture of the lives of Japanese families in a suburban city, which is very useful for readers seeking to understand the life-style of Japanese workers during the early phase of rapid postwar economic growth. A classic work by Lockwood (1968) and a more recent analysis by Ohkawa and Rosovsky (1973) provide important detail on the historical process of Japanese economic development. Yamamura (1967) studied economic policies in the postwar period of economic growth, and Minami (1971b) presented an insightful analysis of what he considered to be the turning point in the Japanese economic development process.

There are a number of other valuable contributions on various aspects of Japanese industrial relations and related topics, but space limitations preclude my referring to all of them. My review in this chapter inevitably is highly selective and sketchy, and my intention is to indicate to the reader that ample descriptive information is now available on Japanese industrial relations, broadly defined.

The Functional Analysis Approach

At the same time that the descriptive institutional studies of industrial relations were being published, a series of important works appeared that analyzed Japanese industrial relations and the labor market on the basis of a clearly defined theory and using a refined and systematic methodology. Many of the studies in this category came out in a cluster during the late 1960s and early 1970s, and others have appeared from time to time since then. I identify this category as "functional analysis," but before reviewing specific examples, let me make some comments on the nature and background of this approach.

By the functional analysis approach, I mean a kind of deductive analysis that relies on solid theoretical concepts, such as market competition in economics, conflict and conflict resolution in sociology, or power in political science. Developed on the basis of some unquestionable theoretical axioms, these concepts are deemed value-free. Functional analysis requires certain methodological and analytical procedures that usually follow such steps as specification of theoretical models and of working hypotheses, collection of relevant data and hypothesis-testing before eventually arriving at evaluation and qualification of the initial theoretical propositions. This approach apparently is much more rigorous and powerful in deriving certain conclusions and policy implications from observed facts than the impressionistic method of descriptive studies in which the researcher simply collects data and evaluates them largely by using his own intuitive judgment. Functional analysis has been applied most vigorously and with remarkable success by many social scientists in American academic circles during the postwar era, and it was a natural consequence of this flourishing development that some American scholars would use this methodology in studies of Japanese industrial relations. The prevalence and far-reaching influence of this approach are not unrelated to the fact that the postwar prosperity of the United States made money and places available to bring together scholars from all over the world and to foster major centers of social research.

The functional analysis approach, however, seems to have an inevitable methodological bias; that is, the technique has an unavoidable inclination to imply a universal commonality or convergence. It is more or less typical in functional analysis in any of the social sciences, whether it is economics, sociology, political science, or social psychology, to assume a general conceptual world in which the single set of analytical concepts is always valid and capable of explaining any observed phenomena with which the discipline is considered compatible. Think of examples such as the concept of the market in economics, conflict in sociology, or power in political science. Economists believe even before they begin an analysis that the market mechanism is a universally valid concept, regardless of different outlooks or institutional arrangements within various economies. To them, the different behavior of individuals or organizations is simply a different form of their economically optimal choices. Similarly, sociologists believe that confrontation and conflict always exist, explicitly or implicitly, in any society. A relatively new and fashionable multidisciplinary approach is not likely to change the situation; it will probably simply confirm the good old convergence thesis in an inflated multidimensional framework.

Let us begin with examples of economic analysis. One of the early studies that made a noteworthy contribution in this area was that by Taira (1970).[3] Skillfully applying the analytical tools of economics, he demonstrates convincingly that Japanese labor market institutions are basically the consequence of optimal economic choices of employers and workers under the given labor market conditions during the process of industrialization. His criticism, naturally, was directed toward the classical culturalist interpretation represented by Abegglen (1958).

The major point of Taira's critique was that the seemingly paternalistic labor-management system in the Japanese factory had its origin not in the feudal relations of the preindustrial society, but rather in the rational economic calculus of employers during the phase of modern industrial growth. By documenting carefully that the paternalistic system emerged as late as World War I as a rational reaction of employers in major corporations in their attempt to cope with a chronic shortage of skilled workers and their high turnover rates and low commitment, he disputed Abegglen's hypothesis and argued that if it were true, industrial paternalism should have existed from the beginning of Japan's industrialization. He contended that there was no evidence that it did. He contended further, based on his statistical analysis, that from the earliest stage of industrialization, the Japanese labor market has been flexible enough for neoclassical economic analysis to apply quite well. In sum, he demonstrated persuasively that the peculiar character of Japanese industrial relations is not so much a carry-over from the feudal society as it is a rational economic choice of employers.

More recent theories and methodologies in microeconomics have also been used in analyzing the economic rationale of Japanese labor market institutions and practices. Utilizing human capital theory (Becker 1964, Oi 1962), Kuratani (1973) attempted to demonstrate theoretically that labor practices of the types known as lifetime commitment and the length-of-service reward system are the results of optimal choices of employers and workers. Along similar lines, Hashimoto (1979) examined both theoretically and empirically the microeconomic rationale associated with the bonus-pay system and the Japanese internal labor market. Tan (1980) analyzed the Japanese age-wage profiles across firms of different sizes, focusing on the relation between technological progress and the development of human capital. Alongside these theoretical developments were the efforts being made to construct a comparative data base with which to make more rigorous and precise comparative studies. The work by Shimada (1974, 1981) is an attempt along these lines; it is a comparative examination of age-wage profiles in the United States and Japan. These studies are only a small portion of the research in this area that is increasing and enriching our understanding.

Using the research methods of social psychology, Whitehill and Takezawa (1968) present one of the early examples of a study that employed full-fledged questionnaire surveys of workers' perceptions and attitudes in a comparative analysis of the United States and Japan. Although the study relied on the discipline of social psychology, the analysis took into account influences of a number of organizational and institutional variables when evaluating the similarities and differences in workers' responses in two countries that have quite different histories and cultures.

The questionnaire surveys were conducted with about 2,000 respondents equally divided between the two nations and representing comparable populations. The analysis covered such topics as motivation, employment commitment, status, rewards, and role-sharing. The survey results seem to indicate that although American and Japanese workers share various attitudes and perceptions, they differ in terms of relative degree. For example, Japanese workers were found to have greater loyalty and commitment to their company, to feel greater employment security, to enjoy closer mutual involvement with their fellow workers, etc., than their American counterparts. In short, the survey results suggest that the quantitative measures reveal a tendency for Japanese workers to be more deeply involved in the company community than are American workers.

Cole (1971a) made a significant contribution in this area with his field surveys using the "participant observation" method. He actually worked for a few months as an unskilled worker in two Japanese factories—a small diecasting factory in the central city and a medium-sized auto parts plant in a suburb—in order to observe at close hand the actions and attitudes of workers and the informal rules on the shop floor; he also lived in one of the small apartment houses in a lower-class workers' community in order to share the family-life atmosphere of Japanese blue-collar workers. On the basis of the rich data obtained from this participant observation and from his documentary research he reported a number of interesting findings.

He pointed out, for instance, that nenkō wages are in fact quite instrumental in increasing workers' incentives and satisfaction and in decreasing alienation by providing continuous and predictable rewards. This system simply supplies efficiencies of a different kind, compared to the Western concept. The seemingly rigid employment system, according to his observation, actually contains a considerable degree of internal flexibility: for example, forcing workers to quit "voluntarily" in cases of de facto dismissals. Workers are very sensitive to promotions and advancements, which suggests that among themselves they are highly competitive. The apparent harmonious and egalitarian solidarity within groups is in fact maintained by careful maneuvers of management and even of the union itself to suppress potential conflict. In other words, Cole described relations quite unlike the "family-like" harmony alleged or assumed to exist by classical culturalists and some of the descriptive institutionalists. He discovered in almost every aspect of factory life elements of rational calculation, competition, conflict, and power politics that take different forms under the different institutional settings of Japanese industrial society. These are what he defined as "functional equivalents," a concept which implies that differing behavioral patterns and institutional arrangements have common functional outcomes. His findings supported this concept, while providing powerful criticism of the mystifying generalizations of the classical culturalists.

A highly sophisticated analysis of the work organizations in Japanese factories from the viewpoint of the sociology of complex organizations was presented by Marsh and Mannari (1976). In their study, they sought the key to understanding and explaining Japan's remarkable economic success in the effectiveness of work organizations. Their specific objective was to examine the validity of the conventional and popular notion that they call the "paternalism–lifetime commitment hypothesis." As their research sites they chose three factories in different industries and employing workers of different types—an electrical appliance manufacturing plant with 1,200 workers, a shipbuilding yard employing 800 workers, and a sake brewery that had 70 employees. Their data came from extensive questionnaire surveys of workers, supplementary observations, and documentary research.

In order to test their primary hypothesis with a rigorous sociological methodology, they constructed a variety of composite indices by quantifying the workers' responses to their questionnaire to meet the requirements of a number of specific hypotheses arising from the central question. These hypotheses were then tested using multiple regression techniques. Relevant subtopics analyzed in this way included job satisfaction, values, attitudes toward pay and promotion, identification with the company, organizational cohesiveness, paternalism, conflicts, mobility, and performance. After integrating these separate analyses, the authors concluded that at a fairly modernized stage of industrialization, as in contemporary Japan, the performance and attitudes of workers were more a function of structural and functional variables—sex, status, job satisfaction, and knowledge of organizational procedures—which they share with Western workers, than of such organizational variables as paternalism, company, and lifetime commitment, which are more distinctly Japanese. In short, the authors emphasized that performance in Japanese and Western firms appears to be based on the same sources, and thus they concluded that the convergence hypothesis is not refuted by the culturalist approach.

Cole's (1979) book was an eclectic report of his quantitative analysis of large-scale interview surveys in Detroit and Yokohama, together with results of his field surveys of selected plants (particularly the Toyota Auto Body Co.) and his documentary research that focused on the effectiveness of the so-called quality control (QC) circle activities. It provides interesting findings on the question whether Japanese industrial relations display greater peculiarity than commonality. Although Cole fully acknowledged Japan's unique organizational arrangements in the workshops as well as the influences of a different historical background, he presented rather striking results that sharply counter the culturalist allegations. For example, he used rather carefully controlled comparative data on Detroit and Yokohama workers to support his findings that both the inter- and intrafirm mobility of Japanese workers is much lower than that of American workers, thus contradicting the common belief that the internal labor market of a Japanese firm is much more flexible than that of its Western counterpart.[4] Another impressive finding—this one contrary to the popular supposition that the Japanese are much more committed to their work than are Americans—is that the work commitment scores of Detroit workers appear to be even higher than those of Yokohama workers.

In general, Cole's results appear to reconfirm the validity of the convergence hypothesis. What his findings mean is that the behavioral patterns of American and Japanese workers and the quality of the workers themselves are not so different as the culturalists imply, when these factors are examined in a well-controlled quantitative analysis. In other words, workers in the two countries may be said to have many behavioral patterns and traits in common, contrary to the assertion of the culturalists who unduly exaggerate behavioral differences that are attributed to differing cultures.

A more significant contribution of Cole's work, in my view, is that it eloquently suggests the need to develop better and more reliable data with which to make meaningful comparisons and evaluations. His data undoubtedly are better and more conducive to generalization than are most of the sets used in the preceding studies.[5] However, as his forthright qualifications suggest, unresolved problems become even more obvious as the data become more reliable. The implication is, therefore, that many of the previous comparative studies have been heavily impressionistic rather than being based on genuine empirical analysis. Cole's analysis reveals persuasively what needs to be done in future research in order to make the comparative study of industrial relations more scientific.

Although my review of functional analyses of Japanese industrial relations has been only partial and quite selective, I hope that the reader can deduce that the research has finally reached the stage of rigorous application of the most advanced and sophisticated theory and empirical analytic methodology. Yet, in order to evaluate properly the implications of the studies of Japanese industrial relations made during the past two decades, it is useful to comment on the broader economic and political environments in which the "convergence hypothesis" has come to be fashionable.

During the 1950s and 1960s, the United States enjoyed an overwhelming superiority in the world both politically and economically as the leading nation of the non-Communist bloc, challenged only by the Communist bloc. Under these circumstances, it was perhaps inevitable that the worldwide research project on comparative industrial relations organized by Kerr and his colleagues (1960), centering upon the academic interest in the "convergence vs. divergence hypothesis," was interpreted subsequently with highly politicized connotations. The question was whether, with the irreversible progress of industrialization, the industrial relations systems of various nations, including Communist countries, would converge to the pattern represented most typically by American industrial relations.[6] In terms of methodology, what was attempted in this project was, in effect, a multidisciplinary consolidation of functional analyses on a global scale; this was called the "interdisciplinary" approach to comparative industrial relations. And perhaps because of a built-in methodological bias in the research, if not a political bias, the conclusion was that there was a worldwide trend of convergence toward an American-type industrialized society.

As is apparent in our review of some of the examples, comparative studies of Japanese and American industrial relations have flourished since then. Whatever the intentions of the researchers in these subsequent functional studies, the influence of this giant project was so great that the results of later research often tended to be interpreted in terms of the major conclusion of the Kerr et al. study, namely, convergence toward the American pattern.[7] An interesting example is Galenson (1976). He analyzed the operation of the Japanese labor market and industrial relations system and concluded, in effect, that Japanese unions have not generated the strength necessary to represent workers' demands properly or to protect their interests, and that they have failed to secure the workers' due share of the gains from economic growth. A view of this kind apparently assumes that American or Anglo-Saxon trade unionism is almost the sole ideal type and dismisses some differing but important attributes that make Japanese-type unions effective.

This trend probably was an inevitable result of the influence of the overwhelming economic and political power of the United States, extending even as far as academic circles. If this was indeed the case, it is not surprising that this universal concentration on convergence toward the American model ultimately weakened and the focus of interest shifted—or at least became plural—with the recent decline in the relative power of the United States vis-à-vis other advanced nations. It seems that recent functional analyses are finally divorced from the old convergence thesis and are seeking a more general conceptual framework in which Japan's industrial relations system is now considered to be an important basic model that is worthy of examination and analysis rather than only an exotic special case and an object of curiosity.

The Neoculturalist Synthesis

In spite of the impressive development of functional analysis as applied to Japanese industrial relations with its massive and well-organized data, refined theory, and methodological rigor, the Japanese audience is still dissatisfied and, in a sense, unfulfilled. Even though functional analysis theory is supposedly complete and the methodology of empirical analysis is presumably flawless, Japanese readers remain not quite persuaded. They feel intuitively that something is lacking in the glittering functional analysis—something that is perhaps essential to an understanding of Japanese industrial relations although they are not quite able to identify what it is.

I would speculate that this dissatisfaction felt by the Japanese audience relates to two factors. One has to do with the fundamental assumptions underlying the basic theories of functional analysis: for example, economic optimization and market competition in economics, social stratification and conflict in sociology, power relations in political science. Insofar as these concepts are regarded as abstract axioms, they may be universally valid. However, once these concepts are treated as *the* theoretical basis for empirical analysis, analysts often tend to use them without properly taking into account influences of a myriad of intervening variables characterizing Japanese industrial relations—and doing so is a difficult if not impossible task. Thus, the results arrived at finally, and the implications of the results, leave the Japanese audience dissatisfied.

The other factor is the change in the relative power of the Japanese economy vis-à-vis the American and other economies. A decade ago the Japanese accepted and were quite satisfied with the dictum that Japan would follow a course of development toward the American pattern of industrial relations. They no longer are. They are aware that Japan has followed a somewhat different path from that of the United States to attain her current prosperity, and they not only feel intuitively, but they also perhaps wish to think, that the predictions of the convergence thesis are out of date and that the future rational course for Japan would be and should be somewhat different from the course of the United States, which they perceive as relatively declining.

During the past several years, there has been renewed and increasingly keen interest among foreign observers in the genuinely Japanese type of development, particularly in her productive organizations. As mentioned in the introduction to this survey, a number of works along these lines have recently appeared, ranging from an essay based on casual observations to more serious research studies. A relatively early and outstanding example of serious research of this type is Dore (1973). Although still at a quite immature stage methodologically, his investigation seems to suggest a potentially fertile direction for academic as well as policy interest. Let me therefore introduce his work in some detail.

Dore's monograph is a research report produced out of a comprehensive field survey of four large plants in the electric-appliance industry in Britain and Japan. The notable characteristic of the report is that, unlike the aforementioned sophisticated functional analyses, it is written in a manner almost completely free from overt theoretical assumptions and methodological constraints. Instead, the whole book is filled with vivid yet precise and factual descriptions of his day-to-day observations of the lives of the workers in the selected factories; the only exception is some speculative arguments in the final few chapters. Another notable feature of his treatment is that he tries to place the findings of his field survey in diverse and much broader contexts, encompassing the family, politics, and even education. He also tries to identify the historical roots of the type of industrial relations he found in the Hitachi factories by documenting the thinking and practices of labor and management during the prewar days, and even going as far back as the Tokugawa era.

Since his study is not welded in a rigid framework of analytical models and his observations are not necessarily set forth in a systematic scheme, at first glance the book may appear to readers—particularly those relatively uninformed about Japan—as a descent from the heights of refined analysis achieved by the functional analysts. However, when those readers scrutinize each of the descriptions, they will surely recognize that every statement captures not only the apparent perspectives, but also small differences in connotation and the subtleties behind them, with remarkable precision and sensitivity. Given the author's extraordinary competence in the Japanese language and his profound commitment to and experiences with Japanese society, his careful and sensible descriptions are highly insightful and suggestive. Although the way he presents his observations is rather impressionistic, this was perhaps the most effective way to express his ideas unequivocally and without interruption. After giving fact-sheet information about the factories, he describes in detail the employment practices of both blue-collar and managerial workers, the pay systems, the structure of unions, and labor-management relations, in each case comparing Britain and Japan. Such descriptions are not necessarily unique to this book, but his subtleties are novel and outstanding. Once his observations go beyond the usual depictions of the basic institutions to get deeper into the enterprise community and small work groups and to extend to such externalities as the family, politics, education, and the general attitudes of the people, readers may absorb a lively and comprehensive picture of industrial relations as they operate in a real world. The phrase Dore uses to characterize what he has described is "welfare corporatism."

After having presented these detailed descriptions, the author plunges on to offer a rather dubious prediction. He bases it on what he sees as possible trends of change in both Japan and Britain—that various aspects of British industrial relations appear to be drifting toward the Japanese pattern, while no substantial alterations in Japanese industrial relations are anticipated in the immediate future, although there undoubtedly have been some in the recent past. This trend might be interpreted as a kind of "convergence." He also speculates, on the basis of a rather careful documentary survey of the historical development of Japanese industrial relations, that the major explanation of why the Japanese pattern differed so much from the British model can be found in what Dore calls Japan's "late development."[8] For him, these considerations also support his prediction of convergence toward the Japanese pattern. It is undeniable that his speculation appears rather far-fetched and is not necessarily convincing. However, it is very interesting to observe that a highly talented researcher, after having made thorough comparative field surveys relatively free from disciplinary or methodological constraints, arrives at a convergence thesis of this type.

Another important work that deserves attenton is Rohlen (1974). This book is a significant contribution to the study of industrial relations in Japan because it describes for the first time, and in great detail, the life and work of employees in a typical white-collar organization—a bank. This study complements the Cole (1971a) book on blue-collar workers; together they provide readers with a complete picture of the two major categories of Japanese workers. The reason that Rohlen's study is particularly relevant here is the fact that he intentionally attempted to refrain from beginning with any theoretical presuppositions. He stated explicitly that his research strategy was to examine the data "without the intent of proving one particular explanation." His objective was to "explore, illustrate and interpret the vocabularies of daily, particular reality as found in the company's organization and as given in the explanations and actions" of bank workers (Rohlen 1974, p.

269). He worked along with them for 11 months as a participant-observer, and his elaborate descriptions of their lives are evidence that he was quite successful in achieving his research objective. He vividly describes various aspects of the work and life of the bank employees from the standpoint of an individual worker or a group of workers, both inside and outside the office— from their daily work to special occasions such as ceremonies and songs; from their ideologies to the employment practices, rewards, and promotions; from small-group activities to the operation of formal organizations; from a bachelor's life in a dormitory to the family life of married employees; and from human relations in the office to outside recreation-group activities. Ample anecdotal examples drawn from his on-the-spot observations of actual events, such as quits, company activities, and the personal affairs of various workers, convey to the reader a realistic picture of the atmosphere in the office and the broader enterprise community. This was precisely the author's intention. In conclusion, he emphasizes that "what must be avoided is the false assumption that a functional analysis is a complete analysis," and he asserts that in order to advance understanding of organizations beyond "the present boundaries created by the functional and historical perspectives," we have to consider them in cultural terms by means of careful and sensitive field work which "illuminates the character of immediate reality in each case" in their own vocabulary and understanding, and not ours (Rohlen 1974, pp. 279–80).

This approach has strengths as well as weaknesses. It is strong in that the description is so elaborate and real that the reader feels almost as if he is right on the spot and, consequently, he can comprehend the many clues and ideas that suggest further thought and investigation. On the other hand, quite ironically and precisely because of its nature, the description tends to be merely description, however insightful and suggestive it might be, and it is incapable of providing simple and unambiguous conclusions. This is the innate weakness of this approach.

However, it is important that this approach attempts to describe reality as accurately and as faithfully as possible while at the same time trying to be as free as possible from a priori theoretical presumptions and methodological restraints. Viewed from the present stage of "advanced" research methodology, such an approach may easily be criticized as too naive and primitive. Description, without a solid theoretical framework as a guide, may well appear to be merely a collection of casual rather than scientific observations. However, note that this approach arose *after* the flourishing development of functional analysis, perhaps as a reaction to it. This might imply that some scholars, knowing full well the virtues and advantages of functional analysis, were dissatisfied or disenchanted with it and dared to adopt this alternative approach. It is for this reason that I categorize these recent works as a "neoculturalist synthesis," to emphasize that they attempt to integrate cultural and other factors while recognizing both the advantages and shortcomings of functional analysis. However, this may be my own wishful thinking. It may be an overstatement to say now that these works eventually would lead to the development of a new stream of thought. In view of their methodological immaturity—for instance, their statements are untestable and their research not replicable—there may indeed be some grounds for these concerns. Notwithstanding, it seems to me that there is something worth pursuing in the direction to which these recent works point.

The remarkable sales of the book by Vogel (1979) are interesting in this connection. The Japanese version sold nearly 500,000 copies within a year after it was published, unprecedented for a nonfiction book by a foreign writer. The reasons for these record-breaking sales are said to be the extraordinary nervousness of the Japanese about what foreigners have to say about them, and the perfect timing of its publication—right before the 1979 Tokyo Economic Summit Conference. However, to me it seems that a more significant reason for the book's success is that it gratified that previously unfulfilled desire of the Japanese that I described earlier. Vogel praised the strength and viability of Japanese social and industrial organizations in a way the Japanese wanted to hear, although he provided no theoretical explanations for why the organizations operate as they do or how they came into existence. The book simply described the tremendous growth during the past 30 years, on the one hand, and, on the other, the operation of several major economic and social organizations that existed and developed during that period. The factual description is largely eclectic and is neither functional nor cultural, unlike its predecessors. It might be called the "let-the-facts-tell" approach which, however, turned out to be remarkably successful. The significance of the book, if any, is its emphasis on the need to understand the importance of organizations in Japanese society. In this respect, a number of recent publications—Dore (1973), Rohlen (1974), OECD (1977), and Macrae (1980)—all make essentially the same assertion. This reinforcing interaction between Japanese intuition and foreigners' interest in work organizations seems to point to some fertile and meaningful areas for research. Unfortunately, however, thus far there has been no convincing theorizing in this potentially promising sphere.

Concluding Observations

The preceding survey of the literature was presented with two purposes in mind. One was to select and review some of the books and articles in the field of Japanese industrial relations that were written in English to acquaint the English-reading audience with a portion of the basic literature in the field.

The other was to provide a context within which the contribution of our volume can be properly placed and evaluated, a task which will be carried out more explicitly in the final chapter of this book.

In concluding this introductory survey chapter, let me make a few qualifying comments.

First, limiting the survey to the English-language literature poses special difficulties for interpretation. Needless to say, it is only a small subset of the entire stock of literature on Japanese industrial relations. For Japanese writers, there are no compelling academic reasons to express their thoughts in English except for the marginal one of broader communication. In other words, what we have to take into account is that there exists a large and rich body of literature that has been developed and accumulated according to its own logic, regardless of whether or which part of it is written in the English language, and that none of the literature written in Japanese has been dealt with explicitly in my survey.

A similar problem applies with regard to the work of foreign writers. In the broad field of industrial relations research in the writers' respective countries and/or in their respective disciplinary fields, topics related to Japanese industrial relations usually enjoy only a small or marginal focus. Theoretical, methodological, and policy interests motivating the writers stem from sources in their own fields as well as from an interest in Japan. In other words, their research often develops from their interest in particular issues in their own industrial relations or their disciplinary fields and focuses on Japan as a point of reference. This means that, in order to understand what these studies of Japanese industrial relations really mean, we need also to have some knowledge of the broader background from which they emerged. Unfortunately, none of these background factors was analyzed in my review, except only very implicitly at some points.

What these limitations amount to is that it is extremely difficult to discern logical threads of development in the one, limited, English-language subsection that I have considered, since it is dominated for the most part by developments within broader background contexts which, unfortunately, are not covered in this survey.

Second, in spite of this difficulty, my review nevertheless suggests that some distinctive and meaningful streams of thought are discernible. Those streams are the classical culturalist approach, the descriptive institutional approach, the functional analysis approach, and the neoculturalist synthesis. Quite naturally, the development patterns of such streams are influenced by combinations among a host of background factors that include the economic and political position of the United States in the world and its consequence for policy and academic interest, the rapid growth of the Japanese industrial economy and its impact on Japanese industrialists and scholars, changes in the relative position of Japan's economic strength vis-à-vis other advanced industrialized countries and the consequent impact on the interest of foreign observers as well as the Japanese themselves, the influences of Marxist ideology in Japanese academic circles, and the development of theories and methodologies of social research in the United States and elsewhere. An interesting trend that seems to be emerging recently from the historical interactions of these factors deserves special attention. The new focus is on trying to distinguish Japan's own logic of development in industrial relations, with the intent of identifying elements possibly transferable to Western advanced nations. This trend may be described as a "search for a new general model of industrial relations through Japanese experiences." Although the trend seems to lead in meaningful directions, it has not quite developed to the stage of demonstrating convincing theoretical or empirical evidence.

And so, it is in this context that we offer our new book. We are convinced that it does contribute to the stock of knowledge available in the English-language literature in at least the following ways:

It adds to and enriches the previously rather scarce information in such areas as the public sector, small firms, and female workers. It also adds valuable information on such important subjects as collective bargaining, negotiations and the determination of wage patterns, and the structure and functions of internal labor markets, all of which deserve very careful examination for proper understanding.

Quite unlike writers in earlier works of this kind, the authors in this book frankly express diverse and frequently contrary views on some of the same subjects. A notable example is the issue of the legitimacy and strength of Japanese enterprise unionism. This difference of opinion among the authors indicates that there is a richness in the Japanese literature that is usually not well reflected in the English-language literature, and, at the same time, it delineates the complex reality of the Japanese industrial relations system that the heterogeneous views represent.

Above all, we hope that the most significant contribution of the present volume will be to provoke new and perceptive ideas within the English-language literature, namely, what I summarized as a "search for a new general model of industrial relations." In particular, in chapter 2 Koike proposes a theoretical hypothesis, relying on his concept of the internalization of labor markets, which purports to explain why Japanese blue-collar workers are highly committed, motivated, and productive. Shirai, in chapter 5, argues persuasively the importance and necessity of constructing a new yardstick—an alternative to the conventional Anglo-American type and one that takes Japanese experience into account—with which to measure the legitimacy, strength, and achievements of unions in contemporary industrial societies. On the basis of his thorough examination of the collective bargaining experiences of Japanese unions, Kōshiro (chapter 9) suggests a new model of enterprise-wide collective bargaining that yields economically rational outcomes.

These works basically share the focus that has been attracting increasing attention among foreign observers in recent years—namely, the efficient work organizations in Japanese industrial relations. These efforts may be interpreted as an attempt to provide theoretical insights into this subject. That Japanese work organizations are efficient is probably undebatable. However, it would be a mistake to draw the conclusion hastily that the efficient operation of the internalized labor markets of individual firms means that the labor market as a whole is operating properly in allocating the labor force and distributing labor incomes. It is in this latter dimension that the roles of unions and labor market institutions and policies need to be examined carefully. Many important areas remain to be analyzed empirically before interested readers can acquire a well-balanced understanding of industrial relations in contemporary Japan.

Notes

1 See a brief summary of these developments in Sumiya 1981. For an intriguing reinterpretation of these two Marxist positions on capitalism, see Yasuba 1975.

2 There are many writings stressing the viability of Japanese industrial society that strongly imply the cultural uniqueness of the Japanese people, but neglect other aspects and viewpoints (e.g., Ballon 1969b).

3 Since Taira's 1970 book is a compilation of rewritten versions of many of his articles that were published beginning in the early 1960s, I count his works as early contributions.

4 This finding should be interpreted with caution, however, because Japanese workers are likely to be much less conscious about their jobs or occupations than their American counterparts, and thus would tend to report their intrafirm transfers less frequently even if the actual frequency of job transfers of the two groups were the same.

5 The Cole data set has advantages in that it covers a broader population than a group of workers within a few selected plants and that it is constructed in such a way that rather rigorous cross-national comparisons are possible.

6 See Cochrane 1976 for the background and process of developing the large-scale collaborative study of comparative industrial relations by Kerr et al. 1960.

7 See Dunlop et al. 1975 for the original authors' reconsideration of the convergence thesis.

8 Although the "late development effect" is an interesting point, Dore's impressionistic presentation still does not address the theoretical questions of why and

how effective and productive work organizations have been fostered within Japanese enterprises. Koike (chapter 2 of this volume) aptly points to a weakness of Dore's work: the shallow analysis or, put more bluntly, the lack of analysis of the process of career formation of workers within the highly structured internal labor market.

Internal Labor Markets:
Workers in Large Firms

Two theses that seem to run counter to what might be termed the "majority opinion" about Japanese industrial relations are presented and developed in this chapter:

1. Blue-collar workers in large Japanese firms share important skill and work-career characteristics with white-collar workers in Western Europe.

2. The system under which Japanese workers gain their skills enables them to perform a wide range of jobs, and thus is the cornerstone of both internal labor markets and industrial relations in Japan.

Although the assessments vary, the majority opinion in the West as well as in Japan holds that the so-called "three pillars" of Japanese industrial relations—seniority wages, lifetime commitment, and enterprise unionism—are peculiar to Japan. This type of industrial relations is evaluated positively by Western scholars (e.g., OECD 1977) but negatively by the Japanese.[1] The first thesis questions whether the "three pillars" are typical only of Japan, and in the first section the argument is developed that there are similarities with the career characteristics of some workers, particularly those in white-collar occupations, in the West.

The second thesis introduces an alternative explanation of Japanese industrial relations. Although the majority opinion tends to emphasize an "unlimited supply of labor," "technological transfer" from the West, or a cultural tradition such as "familism," it is unlikely that these variables can explain similarities between the working careers of blue-collar workers in large Japanese firms and Western white-collar workers. Rather, a focus on the ways in which workers acquire skills for a wide range of jobs might not only aid in identifying the similarities with systems in other countries, but also be crucial to an understanding of the Japanese industrial relations system itself. Ronald Dore's (1973) study, which avoids any stereotypical framework, makes this point, calling it "a wider range of progression," but he does not observe how job skills are acquired to enable workers to enjoy this "wider range." This could be one of the reasons that his book, though detailed and far more analytical than any of the others, has not yet succeeded in gaining wide acceptance. The main part of this chapter deals with the second thesis.

Intensive "White-Collarization"

Let us begin with seniority wages, the first of the "three pillars" that supposedly make the Japanese industrial relations system unique. Fortunately, the recent availability of the European Communities' (EC) survey, *The Structure of Earnings in Industry* (SEI) and the *New Earnings Survey* (NES) in the United Kingdom, when combined with the very detailed Japanese statistics, make possible international comparisons of wages by age and length of service. In addition, a rough U.S.-Japan comparison can be presented using the less detailed data from the *U.S. Census of Population*.

Figure 2.1 displays age-wage profiles for France, Germany, and Japan. Since one of the well-known features of Japanese wage profiles is the variance by size of firm, the graph includes blue-collar wages in both large firms (1,000 or more employees) and the smallest firms (10–99 employees). The EC figures are averages for all establishments with ten or more employees, wages by age and by size of firm being unavailable. From figure 2.1 we see that (1) the profiles of Japanese blue-collar workers are distinctly different from those of French and German blue-collar workers; the Japanese slopes, even for the smallest firms, are far steeper than those of the other two countries, and seem to provide support for the majority opinion. But (2) when we compare the Japanese profile for large firms to the Western white-collar rather than the blue-collar profiles, we perceive a similarity, as Japan's is located between those of France and Germany. If Japanese wages can be called "seniority wages," then French and German white-collar salaries would also have to be called "seniority wages." (3) A minor difference is the sharp drop in wages of the oldest age group in Japan; this will be discussed later. Figure 2.2, which compares the wage profiles of the United Kingdom and Japan, comes close to confirming the findings from figure 2.1.

A somewhat different story is told by the comparison of the U.S. and Japanese wage profiles in figure 2.3. Unlike the findings in the EC and Japan

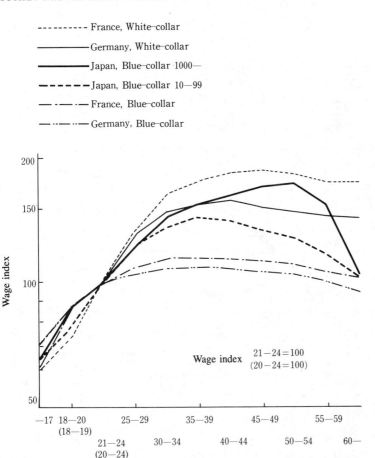

- - - - - - - - France, White-collar

——————Germany, White-collar

——————Japan, Blue-collar 1000—

- - - - - - Japan, Blue-collar 10—99

— - — - — France, Blue-collar

— ·· — ·· — Germany, Blue-collar

Figure 2.1. Wages by Age, Manufacturing Industries, Male Workers: France, Germany, and Japan, 1970s. Japanese statistics are monthly earnings for firms with 1,000+ and 10–99 employees, respectively; European Community data for white-collar workers are monthly earnings, and for the blue-collar group, they are gross hourly earnings. Numbers in parentheses refer to the Japanese age classification. *Source*: For Japan, CKKT 1976; for the EC countries, SEI 1972.

comparison, the Japanese profiles—even the one for large firms—are not steeper than that of American blue-collar workers, in terms of the ratio of the highest to the lowest. A minor difference is that the peak age is 35–44 in the United States, while it is 45–54 in Japan; consequently, the slope until workers reach their middle thirties seems slightly steeper in the United States than in Japan. Thus, as a rough estimate, it would be difficult to deny that

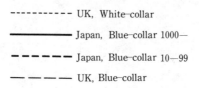

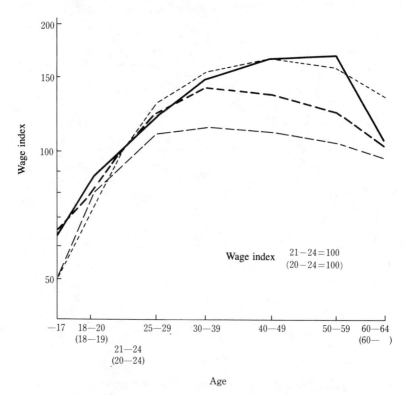

Figure 2.2. Wages by Age, Male Workers: United Kingdom and Japan, 1975-76. The U.K. statistics are gross hourly earnings for all industries and services; statistics for Japan are monthly earnings for manufacturing for industries with 1,000+ and 10-99 employees, respectively. Wage data classified for manual or nonmanual workers are not available in Japan for service sectors. *Source*: For Japan, CKKT 1976; for the United Kingdom, NES 1975, Part F, Table 169.

the blue-collar wage profiles of the two countries are quite similar, but conclusive remarks have to be reserved. According to a comparative survey using more detailed data (Shimada 1974), the Japanese profiles seem to be somewhat steeper than their U.S. counterparts, even for blue-collar workers. However, it is clear that U.S. blue-collar workers have a steeper profile than those of comparable European workers. Therefore, it can be concluded that

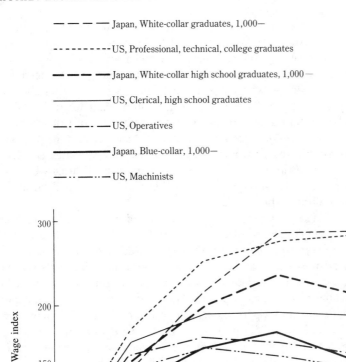

— — — — Japan, White-collar graduates, 1,000—

- - - - - - - - - US, Professional, technical, college graduates

━ ━ ━ ━ Japan, White-collar high school graduates, 1,000—

———————— US, Clerical, high school graduates

—·—·— US, Operatives

━━━━━━ Japan, Blue-collar, 1,000—

—··——···— US, Machinists

Figure 2.3. Wages by Age, Male Workers: United States, 1960, and Japan, 1976. Japanese data are monthly earnings for manufacturing industries with over 1,000 employees; U.S. data are yearly earnings for all industries and services. Number in parentheses refers to the Japanese age classification. *Source*: For Japan, CKKT 1976; for the United States, Department of Commerce, Bureau of the Census 1960.

the age-wage profiles for large firms are *not* peculiar to Japan; seniority wages can also be found among white-collar workers in EC countries and even to some extent among American blue-collar workers.

The second "pillar" of Japanese industrial relations is lifetime commitment. Whether this is unique to Japan can also be examined by comparing the statistics, referred to above, for the United Kingdom, the EC countries, and Japan. Figures are available on the distribution of workers by length of service, though, except for Japan, not broken down by size of firm. From figure 2.4, it can be seen that Japanese blue-collar workers in large firms probably do not enjoy more stable employment than European white-collar workers. The percentage with ten or more years of service is only slightly less for Japanese blue-collar workers in large firms than for white-collar workers in both France and Germany. Only the percentage of British white-collar workers with ten or more years of service is smaller than the percentage of Japanese blue-collar workers in large firms with equivalent service, partly because the British survey includes workers in small firms with less than ten employees. Thus, the findings for France, Germany, and Japan, at least, could confirm the first thesis.

The United States-Japan comparison is presented in figure 2.5, which is relevant to all employees irrespective of size of firm. From this figure, two findings seem worthy of note: the United States leads Japan (1) in terms of the percentage of workers with less than one year of service, and also (2) in terms of the proportion of workers with the longest service. Finding (1) might reflect the pervasive custom in the United States of layoff according to seniority and seems to support the majority opinion. Finding (2), however, obviously contradicts it. If a portion of the Japanese workforce could be called "permanently employed," then at least some part of the American workforce would also have to be termed "permanently employed."

The third "pillar" of the Japanese industrial relations system is enterprise unionism which, according to the majority opinion, implies two features: (1) the basic unit of union organization is enterprise- or plant-wide, and (2) the relationship between management and an enterprise union is cooperative and harmonious.

To begin our examination of feature (2), we can use the number of working days lost through industrial disputes per a given number of workers as an indication of the degree of harmony in union-management relationships. Figure 2.6, based on International Labor Office (ILO) statistics, displays these figures for the United States, the United Kingdom, Italy, France, Germany, Sweden, and Japan. By this measure, Japan appears to have distinctly more harmonious industrial relations than the United States or Italy, but not more harmonious when compared to the other countries. The figures for France, as well as for the United Kingdom until the end of the 1960s, are approximately equal to Japan's, while the numbers of man-days lost through industrial disputes in Sweden and Germany were much lower.

If we examine workers' organizations in the West in some detail, we can also find feature (1), enterprise- or plant-wide labor unions. The majority of American local unions in the industrial sector are plant-wide, irrespective of occupation, although statistical evidence to support this statement is not yet

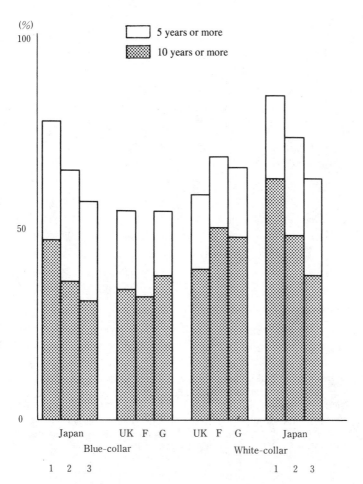

Figure 2.4. Length of Service, Male Workers: United Kingdom, France, Germany, and Japan, 1970s. Data for Japan, France, and Germany are for manufacturing industries. The U.K. data are for all sectors. The numbers below the graphs for Japan indicate size of firm: 1 = 1,000+ employees; 2 = 100–999; 3 = 10–99. *Source*: For Japan, CKKT 1976; for France and Germany, SEI 1972; for the United Kingdom, NES 1975.

conclusive.[2] Shop-steward committees in the United Kingdom are noteworthy as informal union organizations. They are the core of union activities in contemporary British industrial relations, they usually are plant-wide in scope, and they represent blue-collar workers regardless of occupation or union affiliation. In addition to the employee organizations already noted, there are those under the so-called participative systems, particularly in the EC coun-

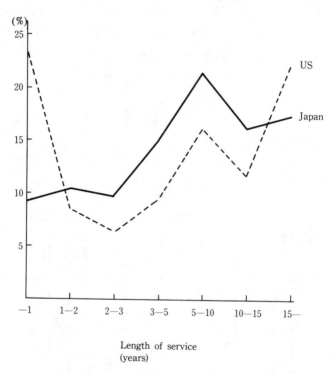

Length of service
(years)

Figure 2.5. Distribution of Male Workers by Length of Service: United States, 1966, and Japan, 1962. *Source*: For Japan, Prime Minister's Office, Bureau of Statistics 1962; for the United States, Hamel 1967. For Japan, CKKT also provides data on the distribution of workers by length of service; however, workers in firms with fewer than 10 employees are not included. The data in *Employment Status Survey* (Prime Minister's Office, Bureau of Statistics 1962) are nearly equivalent to those in *Job Tenure of Workers* (Hamel 1967), but are available only for 1962.

tries. The *Betriebsräte* (works councils) in Germany and the *comités d'entreprise* (enterprise committees) in France, representing both white- and blue-collar workers, seem to be similar to Japanese enterprise unions in organization as well as in operation, in that they have a voice in negotiating wages, working conditions, and fringe benefits.[3] Further discussion of this feature is left to chapter 5, where the topic is the theory of enterprise unionism.

A derivative of the three pillars, what Dore (1973) calls "welfare corporatism," is also pertinent to this discussion. The notion that large Japanese firms are extremely concerned about their employees' welfare and express this concern by providing an array of fringe benefits has been widely disseminated. The reason that the firms provide these benefits, according to these

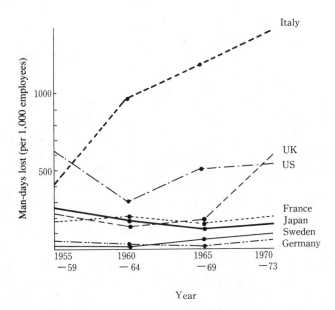

Figure 2.6. Man-Days Lost through Industrial Disputes: United States, United Kingdom, Italy, France, Germany, Sweden, and Japan, 1955–73. The data are for average man-days lost per year per 1,000 employees during each 5-year period. The definition of "strike" varies in the statistics of the various countries, although the variation has little effect on the summary results. The inclusion or exclusion of the smallest strikes (fewer than 10 participants or less than 10 days' duration) in the statistics of various countries accounts for most of the difference between definitions. *Source*: ILO Yearbook 1955–73.

observers, is to encourage the employees' identification with the employer and thereby to promote harmony and cooperation. Since we have already raised doubts about the three pillars of Japanese industrial relations, upon which "welfare corporatism" depends, and since there has been a remarkable proliferation of fringe benefits in the West, this derivative also needs to be examined. Fortunately, an integrated survey of labor costs in the EC countries has been published every three years since 1966 and statistics are available as well for the United States and Japan, enabling us to make an international comparison of benefits.

Problems exist with any international comparison, the principal one being differences in definition. For example, since the definition employed in the EC surveys is "labor costs" rather than fringe benefits, we need a different and more restrictive definition—payments other than wages and salaries that firms make to their employees for meeting living costs. Thus we exclude training and recruitment costs. Even with this more precise definition, there are differences from country to country that reflect shop-floor customs; for example, premium payments for overtime work are included in fringe benefits in the West, but not in Japan, and the semiannual bonuses[4] that comprise a large part of Japanese compensation are normally omitted from Japanese fringe benefits, although bonuses are counted as additional benefits in the West. In our definition, both the overtime premium and the semiannual bonuses are excluded. In addition, in contemporary society, the variety and coverage of fringe benefits is extensive—from monetary payments such as family allowances and retirement payments[5] to benefits in kind such as canteens, heat, clothing, housing, and medical and cultural facilities. Since most components of fringe benefits depend upon the customs of a particular country, it is extremely difficult to compare them across international boundaries. Nor is there any common classification. The only possible distinction that can be made here is to designate which are contributions required by law and which are not. Among the former are a firm's social security-type contributions to health, unemployment and industrial accident funds, for example, as well as those under old-age-pension plans. These are not true fringe benefits, but they, too, have to be considered here. What we mean by "true" fringe benefits are any benefits in addition to employee wages and to these payments into social security systems. The nonstatutory payments are the genuine fringe benefits—any benefits that are supplementary to social security contributions, benefits in kind, and other company expenditures for medical and cultural facilities. Thus we can obtain a ratio (a) of company payments for fringe benefits to total labor costs, and a ratio (b) of statutory contributions to total labor costs.

The most interesting finding in figure 2.7 is that Japan's ratio (a) is similar to those for white-collar workers in the EC countries. The Japanese ratio of 9.1 percent for all workers in establishments with 30 employees or more is similar to most EC ratios for white-collar workers: 10.6 percent for the Netherlands, 9.1 percent for the United Kingdom, 8.7 percent for France, 8.1 percent for Denmark, and 7.5 percent for Germany. The 4.6 percent for Belgium and 1.6 percent for Italy are two exceptions. In contrast, most of the ratios for blue-collar workers in the EC countries are far lower than Japan's; the only exception is the Netherlands—8.6 percent. In other words, the difference in ratio (a) between blue- and white-collar workers in the EC countries is remarkable. In contrast, little variation exists in Japanese fringe benefits by occupation. This finding again implies the " white-collarization" of blue-collar workers. In any industrialized country, the number of white-collar workers commonly increases far more rapidly than the number of blue-collar male workers, and it seems that the benefits that originate in the white-collar group spread to blue-collar workers. Thus, presumably we can say that this development in the Japanese fringe benefit system may provide a precedent for the expansion of blue-collar benefits in other industrial countries.

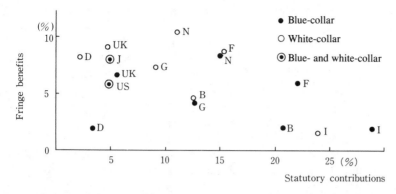

Figure 2.7. Ratios of Firms' Expenditures for Fringe Benefits and for Statutory Contributions to Total Labor Costs, Manufacturing Industries: European Community Countries, United States, and Japan. The data are for 1969 in most of the EC countries, 1973 in the United Kingdom and Denmark, and 1968 in Japan and the United States. B = Belgium; D = Denmark; F = France; G = West Germany; I = Italy; J = Japan; N = The Netherlands; UK = United Kingdom; US = United States. *Source*: For Japan, Rōdōshō, Tōkei Jōhōbu 1968; for the EC countries, Economic Community 1972–75 and 1974; for the United States, Bauman 1970.

Two additional points need to be noted with regard to the content of fringe benefits in Japan, although no data for international comparisons are available. (1) A firm's expenditure for worker housing would be far higher in Japan than in other countries, partly because many firms have to recruit workers from remote areas in order to meet the rapidly increasing labor demand, and partly because the housing shortage is more serious in urban areas of Japan than in similar areas of other industrialized countries. (2) Although more workers presently are in the younger age groups in Japan than in the West, in the coming decades this pattern will change, and the movement of these young workers into older age-categories will necessitate an increase in retirement payments, thus pushing the fringe benefit ratio higher.

Japan's ratio (b) apparently is less than those of the West except for the United Kingdom, Denmark, and the United States. The first two countries as well as other Scandinavian nations have systems that are more dependent on direct contributions from individuals than from firms, and the United States is well known for her less developed social security plans. Does this indicate that the Japanese social security system is lagging behind, since the contribution systems in Japan are most similar to those in Germany? The answer is clearly no, for if we compare the content of the various systems in the industrialized countries, we find that Japan's old-age-pension system is one of the most favorable in the world in terms of the payment level. Although there is not enough space here to explore the differences among systems in detail, the following three points should be made: (1) The bulk of a firm's social security contribution in any industrialized country is for old-age pensions. Because a smaller percentage of Japanese workers are in the aged categories, as mentioned above, the ratio of pension contributions to total labor costs in Japan is still lower than those in the West. Moreover, because the old-age-pension system was late in starting in Japan, originating in 1942, and because it takes a long time, say 30 years, to accumulate sufficient reserves so that all workers may receive pensions adequate for their needs, some retired workers are not yet satisfactorily covered by the system. Both factors contribute to Japan's lower ratio. For the same reasons, the ratio will necessarily increase as the workforce ages, even if the systems are not improved and extended. (2) Family allowances in Japan are only a small part of total social security payments, while in France and Italy in particular they comprise another main portion of the benefits. (3) Firms generally contribute more to social security in France and Italy than in Japan; as noted above, the Japanese system is similar to Germany's. In short, Japanese firms are not more eager than employers in other industrialized countries to contribute to their employees' welfare, and Japan's social security systems are as well developed as those in the West.

In summary, we can conclude that the three pillars of Japanese industrial relations are not peculiar to Japan. Rather, we suggest that blue-collar workers in large Japanese firms are "white-collarized." Why is this so? To answer this question, it is necessary to have some insight into the career during which the Japanese worker acquires his skills.

Wide-Ranging and Flexible Mobility of Workers within a Plant

The conventional wisdom has been that most blue-collar employees of large firms in Japan enter the firm directly from senior high school and that they normally remain with that firm until they reach retirement age. The facts, as revealed in figure 2.8, contradict this common concept. The figure, which graphs the rates of separation in a year by age and by size of firm, tells us, first, that even in the largest firms with 1,000 or more employees, where "lifetime commitment" is said to prevail, the separation rate in a year exceeds 20 percent until workers reach their mid-twenties. Apparently a majority of the younger workers move to other firms within five years after starting to work. Of course, we are speaking of the *average*; some workers may change jobs frequently, and some may stay with the firm that originally hired them. Although an international comparison is impossible because separation rates by age are not available in the West, it is reasonable to conclude that the separation rate for young Japanese blue-collar workers is

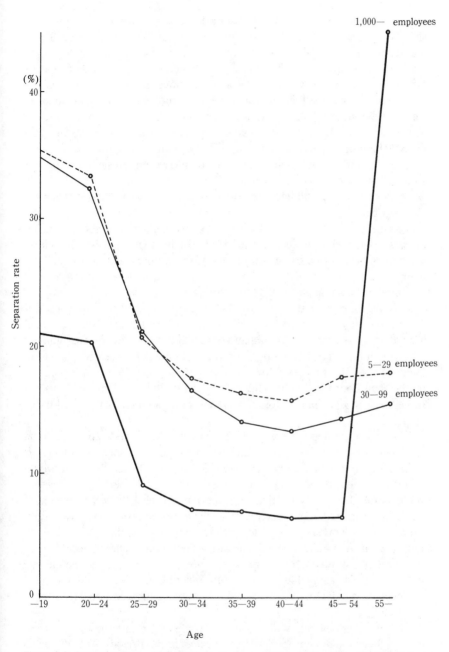

Figure 2.8. Separation Rates, Male Workers, by Age and Size of Firm, Manufacturing Indus-tries: Japan, 1970. Separation rate data by age have been available since 1952, but statistics on separation rates by age and size of firm are for the years 1964–70. Although the figure uses 1970 data, a similar pattern prevailed throughout the period. *Source*: Rōdōshō, Tōkei Jōhōbu 1970.

far higher than has been widely assumed. Second, separation rates drop sharply at ages 25-29. This pattern is common for firms of all sizes. Thus, the separation rates of workers in their thirties and forties, even in the smallest firms, are lower than those of younger workers in large firms. In other words, younger workers in large firms move more frequently than do older workers in small firms who have been thought to be quite mobile. Third, differences by size of firm are obviously large for each age group. The most stable workers, needless to say, are those aged 30–50 in large firms, where the separation rate is 6 or 7 percent in a prosperous year and 4 or 5 percent in a slack one. This level of turnover represents the factual evidence for what has been called "lifetime commitment." Fourth, after workers reach their middle fifties, their separation rate in large firms rises abruptly because of compulsory retirement in those firms. This last point, one of the problems in contemporary Japanese industrial relations, will be discussed later. Here we can summarize by saying that Japanese blue-collar workers in large firms move from firm to firm in their youth and that, after their middle twenties, they tend to stay with a firm. How, then, do they acquire the skills that will serve them throughout their careers?

A young man who starts to work in a large firm in most instances will have completed his senior secondary education, which is heavily oriented toward general education rather than vocational training. His first assignment will be to a formal training program for, say, a couple of weeks or months at the most—too short a period for him to acquire any job skills that he can use on the shop floor. Apprenticeship training is rare in large firms, and even in small ones it is available for only a few occupations, such as tailors or carpenters.

On-the-job training now plays the major role in workers' skill acquisition and development in large firms and has had that role since World War I, when it began to replace apprenticeship training. This type of training would be most efficient if the skills a worker could acquire in performing one job could be used not only on that job, but also on the next job to which he would be promoted. Consequently, a sequence of job progression was established in each workshop, since the jobs there were most likely to be closely related from the standpoint of skill acquisition and accumulation. For an understanding of how the system operates now, some insight into the internal mobility on the shop floor is of prime importance. Because no statistical evidence is available, it is necessary to rely on observations from field research.

The observations below are based in large part on interviews with local union officials and shop stewards, conducted in the period 1972–75, in 13 plants—eight in manufacturing and five in chemicals. All are unionized, and all employ more than 1,500 workers. However, nearly two dozen workshops with various technologies are included: non-mass-production machine and assembly shops, mass-production machine and assembly shops, main production departments, and some maintenance shops in process industries. Because of the variety of technologies used in these shops, open-ended interviews are necessary; otherwise there is a danger of missing or misinterpreting crucial distinctions or similarities in the actual operating systems of the various workshops that might appear to be different because they employ different technologies. Detailed results of this investigation are reported in Koike (1977); some cases are highlighted here.[6]

Let us observe a work group in a blast furnace department of a giant integrated iron and steel plant. There are three large blast furnaces, each of which is operated by four work groups in three shifts. Each group, consisting of about a dozen workers, has to cover approximately ten positions. Two features of the deployment system are remarkable: (1) job assignments are made in an egalitarian way, and (2) there is a wide range of mobility within a cluster of workshops performing similar functions.

Every half-day, workers rotate jobs, regardless of seniority. The system appears to be very different from any in the United States where the job ladders are rigid and promotions are based strictly on seniority. Some critics may question the feasibility of the system. How can workers rotate jobs in such an egalitarian way? Do the jobs require the same or equal skills, or does each job not require any skills at all, unlike similar jobs in the United States? Even in the Japanese workshops, some jobs require more skill than others, and some can be performed by green new recruits. When the operation of the system is observed in more detail, it is recognized that in practice the system is less egalitarian than it first appears. A young recruit who joins a work group following formal training is usually backed up by the subforeman for a period of time—say, several months. Even after that, he is instructed and attended by a senior worker who occupies the next position in the rotation sequence. Under this system (feature 1), a worker obviously can acquire the skill to perform all the jobs more quickly than his U.S. counterpart, which enables feature (2) to operate.

One or two workers are exchanged yearly among the three blast furnace workshops. Since the furnaces were built in different years, they vary slightly in the degree of automation and, accordingly, in the way they operate. Therefore, it would enlarge a worker's experience to move to other furnace shops. In addition, the worker normally also moves to the maintenance workshop which services all three blast furnaces, and this experience affords him a good opportunity to learn the blast furnace mechanism which, in turn, contributes to his skill in operating any blast furnace. As a consequence, within ten years or so, a worker will have had experience in more than 30 positions. This is what is meant by "a wide range of mobility within a cluster of workshops performing similar functions" (feature 2). The case described above is not exceptional. According to a 1971 union survey of job-rotation systems in 79 workshops of eight plants of the largest Japanese firm, jobs in nearly 20 percent of them were rotated regularly; almost all jobs were rotated, though not regularly, in 18 percent; and some jobs were rotated in 30 percent of the shops.[7] Three of the seven blast furnace workshops surveyed had a system of regular job rotation, and another two rotated nearly all jobs, although irregularly.

An automobile assembly line is the usual example of a mass-production workshop. At two assembly lines visited, again it was found that the workers moved from one position to another until they had had experience on all jobs in the shop. One feature of Japanese automobile assembly lines is said to be that temporary workers perform some of the same jobs as the regular workers. However, the rotation system is confined to the regular workers, which results in very different career patterns for workers in each group. And it is the regular workers who are in the majority, although the ratio of temporary to regular workers varies with labor market conditions; the tighter the market, the larger the ratio.

In one case, mobility was found to be neither regular nor orderly, but depended on minor changes in production and in the composition of the workforce, such as absences or the number of new recruits in the group. Even though this mobility was irregular, in practice it was those workers who had had experience in almost all jobs in the workshop who tended to be appointed as subforemen. In another plant, the mobility systems were more orderly, and the workers exchanged positions every three months or so. A large table on the wall, which listed the jobs in which each worker had had experience, clearly showed that the longer the service, the more jobs a worker had performed.

Why is there such mobility? On an automobile assembly line, as an extreme case of a mass-production shop, changes in production inevitably occur—and more frequently than is usually imagined. The product mix varies with demand because several types of cars may be assembled on one line in Japanese automobile plants. The composition of the workforce also varies, because of absences, retirements, or the number of new recruits; sometimes experienced workers are in the majority, and at other times there are more new and inexperienced workers. Therefore, in order to maintain the production flow, minor changes in deployment are necessary, and these can be more efficiently accomplished if a certain number of workers who can perform most jobs on the assembly line are readily available. The regular workers in a Japanese auto plant are trained to fulfill this need.

Adaptations to changing production needs are necessary in mass-production industries in any country, but the methods used are different. An American assembly-line worker apparently stays in his job because the pay for each job is the same and the local union has the vested right to protect workers from transfers they do not want. Thus, in order to adjust to changing needs, a few workers are trained separately to perform almost any job on the line, and they fill in as relief men when needed. Japanese regular workers on assembly lines can be said to be the equivalent of U.S. relief men. In other words, the Japanese automobile assembly line can make use of any regular worker as a relief man with no increase in the total workforce, unlike its U.S. counterpart.

Take as another example a workshop in a large plant where heavy electrical machinery is built. About 35 workers in this workshop erect medium-sized switchboards. There are seven types of switchboards of this size, each of which is made by one of seven subgroups in the workshop. A remarkable feature is that the composition of the subgroups is reshuffled yearly, so that all the workers in the workshop in a period of, say, ten years will have had experience in making all seven types of switchboards. In addition, these workers tend to move to two similar related workshops that produce larger or smaller switchboards. As a result, they are trained to deal with all the types and sizes of switchboards that this plant can produce.

Throughout workshops of various types, whether in process, mass-production, or non-mass-production industries, it is recognized that there is wide-ranging and flexible mobility between similar, related workshops within a plant. How this process is regulated highlights another feature of Japanese industrial relations—that neither the managerial staff nor the local union regulates mobility within a workshop or within a cluster of similar related workshops. Our survey revealed that management does not even have an accurate record of which workers are deployed on which jobs, nor does the union try to regulate the rotation, although it does handle a rare grievance if one is filed. In each of the cases surveyed, the workshop foreman and subforeman made the work-assignment and job-rotation decisions.

An easy interpretation of why the system functions as it does might be that the union is weak at the shop-floor level, leaving the foreman, as first-line management, a free hand to exercise favoritism or to maximize production by encouraging competition among the workers. The validity of this interpretation depends on whether or not the foreman actually has a free hand in assigning workers. In all cases surveyed, it was found that shop-floor practice restricts the foreman's discretion, though the extent of the restriction varies. In some instances, the foreman assigns workers according to the custom of the work group; in an extreme case assignment is decided by discussion within the group. In other instances, a foreman has considerable freedom of choice. Generally speaking, however, egalitarian methods of deployment, some of which have been described above, in practice limit the foreman's discretion.

Yet practice is no more than practice. The question might be raised as to why it is so prevalent. Why do foremen not deviate from it? Here it should be noted that the foreman in Japanese labor markets is much more involved than his Western counterpart in a worker's career. He is not only the first-line supervisor, but is also one of the most senior members of the work group. This leads to the presumption that the work group might be a kind of "semiautonomous group." Since the members work together every day and share common career goals, a high degree of solidarity develops, enabling them to handle issues by themselves, independent of outsiders—the managerial staff or local union officials, for example. Yet this work team is not an established formal group, but is restricted in nature. It exists only with higher management's tacit consent, and management intervenes on occasion. When there is rival or dual unionism, as is often found during periods of intense industrial relations warfare in Japan, management does dare to "invade" the autonomy of the work groups and to take over the assignment of workers, favoring members of one group or the other, in order to reduce if not eliminate union rivalry and warfare.

A final question might be: Why does management usually give its tacit consent to work-group autonomy? As suggested above, it is mainly because this system greatly reduces the cost of adjustment to changes in both production and workforce composition. Such changes often require some variations in assignment or even some minor redesigning of jobs. Under the system described above, a worker can perform jobs in workshops other than the one to which he happens to be assigned. This, along with the custom that allows flexible allocation of the workforce, makes it easier to modify the assignment of workers. In addition, long-service workers who have had experience in a variety of jobs have grasped the total production process, thus making them more adaptable when jobs have to be redesigned. It should be stressed again that changes in production processes do occur more frequently than might be imagined—even daily on a minor scale, as Japan's high rate of economic growth demands constant changes from the industry level down to the work organization. Thus, it would be impractical for management to try to regulate daily adjustments, and therefore it prefers to leave those issues in the hands of the small, relatively independent work groups. The implications of this practice will be developed more fully in the final section of this chapter.

Temporary Transfer and Layoff

Large industrial plants everywhere find it necessary to adjust their work-forces with changes in product demand and manufacturing methods. Some workshops decline in importance, while others need to expand. Temporary transfer is one of the methods the Japanese employ to accomplish an adjustment beyond a cluster of similar and related workshops. Although temporary transfer is almost universally used, it occurs far more frequently in machinery industries where variation in employment accompanies changes in the amount of production and far less in chemicals where there are fewer employment fluctuations. Large firms are apt to have both temporarily growing and declining workshops, between which temporary transfers are made. Thus the number of layoffs is remarkably reduced. Plant-wide seniority as it applies to layoffs in the United States has the same general effect. However, the difference between the two countries is large: plant-wide seniority is seldom seen in U.S. process industries where the internal training system is similar to Japan's. Rather, it is mostly favored by smaller U.S. firms where skill differences by workshop are not so large (U.S. Dept. of Labor 1970, p. 14).

As might be expected, a temporary transfer in Japan can be made even between remote workshops where the required skills are dissimilar. Although this system contributes substantially to employment security, it affords a worker little opportunity for developing skills, whereas transfer among workshops performing related work provides them with better opportunities to expand their skills and, in addition, facilitates the firm's capacity to adjust to changing needs. Permanent transfers are infrequent, but on occasion they are made to a division doing similar work at another of a firm's plants.

Unlike the practice with regard to mobility within a workshop or among similar workshops, the plant-level union has a voice in most cases of transfer, although union effectiveness in this regard varies from case to case. The variation depends also upon the effect of the transfer upon the worker. The union impact is least where transfer is between less remote workshops and is greatest where the transfer is permanent. In other words, the more unfavorable the transfer is to the worker or workers, the stronger the union voice becomes.

To be effective, union regulation of transfer must be concerned with the following issues: (a) how many workers are to be transferred, (b) from which workshop to which workshop, (c) for how long, (d) on what conditions, and (e) who will be transferred. Issue (a), the number of workers to be transferred, depends upon the amount of production in the workshop. In most cases, the monthly production schedule is one of the topics on which there is union-management consultation, although the union's impact on the ultimate production decision varies. Issue (a) as well as issue (b) are usually handled in local negotiations. Issues (c) and (d) are most clearly union-regulated; by long-standing agreement, the maximum period of transfer in most cases is set at three months, and the original wage rate is usually guaranteed during the transfer period. Since Japanese workers lack seniority, issue (e), who is to be transferred, is least subject to union influence. Many local unions have the formal right to make sure that those who are designated for transfer are willing to accept the new assignments. However, without explicit rules such as seniority, some room for a foreman's discretion remains. Only in a few instances is some type of rotation system employed as shop-floor practice.

Thus, the transfer system provides further evidence of semiautonomous work groups. Japanese local unions do have a voice in regulating conditions that lie beyond the work group as well as the production schedule in the workshop, and they may be effective in restricting a foreman's discretion within a work group.

One of the myths concerning Japanese industrial relations is the so-called "lifetime commitment." To be sure, layoffs were comparatively rare during the period from the mid-1950s to the early 1970s when the rate of growth of the economy was relatively high. But experience during the recession of the mid-1970s demonstrates that layoffs do occur and that their number in response to decreases in production is no less than in the West. Table 2.1 presents figures on the elasticity of employment and labor input to output for manufacturing industries in various countries since 1973. It clearly shows that (1) in the countries surveyed, the elasticity of labor input to output is far larger than that of employment—that is, adjustment to decreases in output is accomplished by decreasing the number of hours worked rather than by decreasing total employment; and (2) the size of the adjustment in both hours of work and total employment in Japan is approximately the same as that in other countries except the United States, where both figures are much higher. Therefore, we cannot say that all Japanese workers enjoy "lifetime commitment." Conclusive remarks with regard to workers in large firms must be reserved, however, for there are no data by size of firm on which to base international comparisons.

Table 2.1

Elasticity of Employment and of Labor Input to Output in Manufacturing Industries: Japan, the United States, the United Kingdom, Germany, and France, 1974–75

Nov. 1973 until . . .	Elasticity of Employment					Elasticity of Labor Input				
	Japan	U.S.	U.K.	Germany	France	Japan	U.S.	U.K.	Germany	France
June 1974	.09	.43	—	—	—	.32	3.00	—	—	—
Sept. 1974	.13	.26	.04	.19	—	.69	1.23	.58	.33	—
Dec. 1974	.19	.79	.16	.32	.07	.59	1.14	.46	.52	.60
Mar. 1975	.25	.87	.34	.36	.18	.85	1.14	.81	.91	.64
June 1975	.38	.85	.43	—	.23	.66	1.07	.82	—	.66
Sept. 1975	.49	.97	.58	—	—	.86	1.20	.91	—	—
Dec. 1975	.51	—	—	—	—	.89	—	—	—	—

Source: Shimada, 1976. Shimada's calculations are based primarily on ILO statistics.

A layoff is a severe blow for a Japanese worker. For him, unlike his American counterpart, there is no prospect of being recalled since there is no seniority system. Who shall be laid off, therefore, is a crucial question. In order to avoid serious disputes, managements usually advertise for volunteers, offering an additional increment in severance pay as an inducement. Prior to the mid-1950s when layoffs were more common, if the number of volunteers did not meet the quota, managements would make the additional selections, usually choosing older workers (45 years of age or older), those with poor attendance records, and those who were "less efficient." The last item, in particular, tended to be used to lay off active union members such as shop stewards. Needless to say, trade unions strongly opposed these layoffs. Even the weakest unions struck, sometimes for several months, though usually in vain. These strikes were so costly to managements that they have since become very cautious in their selection of the workers to be laid off. During the recession of the mid-1970s, they again advertised for volunteers, but the conditions under which workers would be laid off had been previously negotiated with the union. The focus still was on older workers, the group most vulnerable to layoff. An international comparison of unemployment by age group indicates that Japanese unemployment tends to be concentrated among older workers, whereas a relatively larger proportion of younger workers are apt to be unemployed in European countries and in the United States in particular (Shinozuka and Ishihara 1977). The conclusion has to be, then, that older workers in Japan have less employment security than their counterparts in the West.

The government as yet has no effective policy for dealing with this problem. Its general policy on unemployment works well. Unemployment benefits are part of the social security system, shorter-hours benefits are available when industries suffer from a recession, and there are incentives to encourage firms to hire older workers. But neither legislation nor custom protects older workers from layoff. On the one hand, this may reflect the competitiveness of the Japanese industrial relations system, but it may also be a defect in the system.

The older worker problem is compounded by the compulsory retirement system. In large Japanese firms, workers have to "retire" when they are in their late fifties, a requirement established a half-century ago when not many of them survived to that age. In the modern world, workers in their fifties are still able to work, and many of them need jobs in order to support their families. In practice, they do not retire. Rather, they are compelled to leave the large firms and to find alternative employment in small firms. As it is not easy to locate jobs that fit their skills in these small firms, they often have to settle for employment in unskilled work at much lower pay, where the skills they have acquired during their long careers in large firms are largely unused. Thus, the sharp drop in the wage profile of older workers is explained.

There is no doubt that the number of older workers in the Japanese labor force will increase, bringing about a change in the age distribution. To counter the distress of this increasing number of workers, it is of prime importance that the retirement age in large firms be raised to, say, 65 years. If workers are able to remain in the workshops, more effective use can be made of their skills, and the sharp drop in their wage profiles can be avoided.

Career Patterns—Japan and the West

A description of the working career of employees of large Japanese firms will give the reader a notion of what might be called a "career type." Rarely is a worker confined to only one job during his working life with a company. Rather, he would have a series of closely related jobs, and this series would determine the breadth of his skill and how much his wages would increase. Career types can be distinguished by their extent and structure—whether they are external or internal, whether or not they have a high ceiling, and whether a ceiling occurs early or late in the career. The features that are found among Japanese workers in large firms are work careers within the firms (internal) that have late and high ceilings—here called the "internal promotion type" of career pattern. This is the essence of what we identify as "white-collarization." Once the content of "white-collarization" is clarified, we can explain the "three pillars" of Japanese industrial relations.

One pillar, seniority wages, implies a set of features: (a) a positive slope in age-wage profiles; (b) wage rates determined separately from jobs being performed; and (c) no significant differentials in basic wages according to workshop or occupation. Feature (b) means that each wage rate is determined primarily by length of service, but partially by merit-rating, although the basic rates are negotiated by the local union. This feature is common for all blue-collar workers of the internal-promotion type, regardless of industry. Consequently, a worker's compensation increases roughly in accordance with his length of service, but at a decreasing rate and including some individual merit differentials. This creates the positive slope in age-wage profiles, feature (a). Feature (c) obtains because wage rates are set mainly by length of service and, because workers are of a common career type regardless of workshop, there is no reason for large differentials by workshop or, accordingly, by occupation. If there is any premium pay for heavy or dirty work, it comprises only a very small part of total compensation.

Although these features may appear unusual, they fit very well with the flexible operation of Japanese internal labor markets. Because the wage rate is determined separately from the job performed, workers can move flexibly from job to job within the workshops, and because there are only minor differentials in basic wages among workshops, frequent transfers do not cause disruptions. A worker's wage profile can be said to coincide in general with the improvement in his career—that is, the longer his service, the more jobs he can command. The existence of merit-rating is an indication of some lack of union influence, on the one hand, but on the other it works to narrow the gap between skill and seniority wages to some extent.

This description of career types and wage determination also explains why Japanese blue-collar workers in large firms have as stable employment as white-collar workers in the West. Staying with the firm never implies staying on the same job. Instead, flexibility and frequent internal mobility over a wide range of jobs is the rule, thus giving workers an opportunity not only to acquire a range of skills, but also to understand the total production process. Even though engineers, who are white-collar workers, are assigned the task of developing more efficient ways of carrying out production, the white-collarized blue-collar workers are also capable, indeed eager, to improve the handling of their jobs. This capability provides the very foundation of small-group activities on the shop floor, and it is this small-group activity that has attracted attention as the source of Japanese productivity. A frequent explanation of these activities is in terms of these workers' loyalty to their companies. However, without their technological background—that is, their having developed skills over a wide range of jobs—Japanese industry never would have been as successful as it is in improving methods of performing jobs over such a long period.

This skill and knowledge on the part of the workers also make it easier for a firm to introduce change. Adjustments to minor changes have been described above, but the same worker traits are equally desirable when major changes are made, such as the introduction of new equipment to increase output. The availability of a workforce with a wide range of skills can reduce the difficulties facing a firm when introducing new machines because the workers have developed the ability to understand the total production mechanism. Thus managements see no reason to modify the system. From the workers' point of view, since the longer their service, the more extensive their skills and the higher their wages, they too see no reason to change or abandon it.

By this reasoning, it is also possible to clarify the rationale for enterprise unionism. It is clear that workers are most concerned about their careers or the mobility through which they acquire their skills. As shown above, their careers tend to develop on the shop floor of a firm so that some specificity is inevitable. Therefore, no workers' organization can regulate these issues more effectively than one at the enterprise level or on the shop floor. Thus, it is reasonable that Japanese workers have chosen enterprise unions to protect their interests.

The majority opinion also suggests that Japanese workers have a greater identification with their firms than do workers in the West. Once a worker's interest in his career opportunities is clarified, as it has been above, it follows that he will be convinced that his benefits and welfare depend upon the economic position of his firm. The more prosperous it is and the more rapidly it grows, the better his opportunities to develop skills, the more stable his employment, and the faster he will be promoted to a better job. A worker may not be really "loyal" to his firm, as the majority opinion implies, but he realizes that his prospects for future benefits are closely linked to how well his firm operates in the larger economy.

It is reasonable to presume that the Japanese industrial relations system and enterprise unionism contribute to the rapid growth not only of the firm but also of the total economy of Japan. As Japan's economy (like those of most of the EC countries) depends on foreign trade far more than does that of the United States, the ability to compete in world markets is crucial if she is to sustain her national welfare. The needed machinery and raw materials can be imported, but human capital from other countries is difficult to secure except on a minor scale. Therefore, if Japan is to maintain her ability to compete in international markets, she must rely heavily on developing the human capital of her own people to the fullest possible extent. The skills in and the knowledge of a wide range of jobs that blue-collar workers in large firms acquire fulfill this need for human capital development and can be said to be a vital contribution to the growth of the economy.

One result of the system is smaller wage differentials among workers in large firms. First, as stated above, no significant differentials exist among departments or occupations for blue-collar workers because the internal-promotion career type is common to most departments. Second, differentials between blue- and white-collar workers, as well as according to the amount of formal education completed, are narrower in Japan than in the West (see fig. 2.9), partly because of greater social mobility in Japan and partly because they have in common the internal-promotion type of career pattern. This could be why Japanese enterprise unions have been successful in organizing both blue- and white-collar workers in the same plant-wide union since World War II. The same reasoning could be applied in explaining why blue- and white-collar workers in the mining industry are in separate unions; blue-collar miners do not have internal-promotion career patterns.

The relative power of each party to the union-management relationship is another aspect of the distribution issue. Enterprise unions, the subject of chapter 5, do not yet have as firmly vested rights as do unions in the United

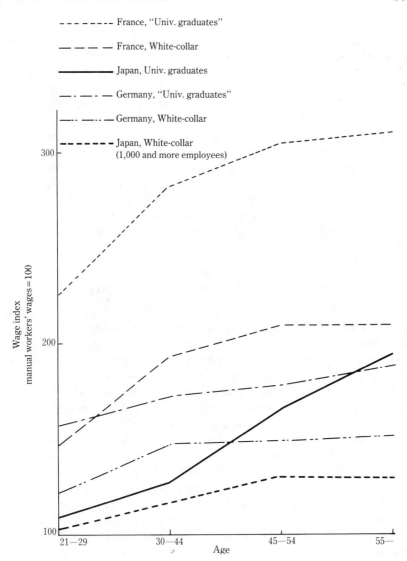

- - - - - - - France, "Univ. graduates"

— — — — France, White-collar

————— Japan, Univ. graduates

—·—·— Germany, "Univ. graduates"

—··—··— Germany, White-collar

- - - - - Japan, White-collar (1,000 and more employees)

Figure 2.9. Wage Differentials between Male White- and Blue-Collar Workers in Manufacturing Industries: France and Germany, 1972, Japan, 1976. Japanese data on which this figure is based are for firms with 1,000+ employees, while those for France and Germany are for firms with 10+ employees. Wages of "university graduates" in France and Germany are averages of "Leistungsgruppe [qualification groups] 1B and 2"; these groups are 26.8 and 32.7 percent, respectively, of male white-collar employees in the two countries. Individuals in qualification groups 1B and 2 are defined as those who "have undergone technical, administrative, legal, commercial, or financial training, normally evidenced by a university degree, or . . . recognized as equivalent." The percentages for these groups are similar to the Japanese figure of 30.4 percent. *Source*: For Japan, CKKT 1976; for France and Germany, SEI 1972.

States and the United Kingdom. However, the semiautonomous work group on the shop floor, including the foreman and subforeman, seems to have the power to deal with issues within the group independent of either management or the union. In practice, members of the work group apparently participate in decision-making to a considerable degree.

Yet there are defects in the industrial relations system. Undoubtedly one of them is the unfavorable situation in which older workers find themselves when they are forced to retire. This problem has been long neglected, in part because in the past there were fewer older workers and in part because they were thought to be well compensated because of their length of service. The number of older workers will increase in the next two decades, and large-scale policy measures will be needed if their plight is to be alleviated. Another defect that is frequently cited by those who express the majority opinion is the large differentials in wages by size of firm, the subject of chapter 4.

Why the Internal-Promotion Career Pattern?

The final question to be addressed is that of the factors that gave rise to the phenomenon of "white-collarization," or the establishment of the internal-promotion career type. A first step toward answering this question would be to determine to what extent and where the pattern exists, as well as where it does not; this might reveal key variables. Needless to say, there is no statistical survey that could provide the answers. Fortunately, there are some indirect indicators for postwar Japan: the statistics on average length of service with a particular company and of experience in an occupation by size of firm that are recorded in the Ministry of Labor's *Chingin Kōzō Kihon Tokei Chōsa* [Basic survey of the wage structure], hereafter cited as CKKT. A comparison of average length of service and of experience in an occupation yields the desired indicators, assuming that, if an occupation is of the internal-promotion type, (a) both length of service and of experience would be extensive, and (b) they would be similar in duration. In the following discussion, item (a) is specified as more than five years of both service and experience. Item (b) is specified in two ways: (1) a strict measure, requiring that average length of service with the company equals or exceeds the amount of work experience, and (2) a broader measure that includes occupations where the difference between total work experience and length of service is less than one year.

Figure 2.10 shows the percentages, by both the strict measure (1) and the less restrictive measure (2), of all male occupations that were of the internal-promotion type in 1961, the year for which the statistics have the broadest coverage. From this figure, we can conclude, first, that the internal-promotion career is characteristic of large firms; in any industry, the larger the firm, the higher the percentage by either measure. Second, there are some differences by industry. Almost all occupations in chemicals are of the internal-promotion type, even by the strict measure; the lowest percentages are in the machinery industry. Third, even in the machinery industry, more than 50 percent of the occupations are of the internal-promotion type by the less restrictive measure. The only exception is transportion equipment; there, so many of the ship-building occupations have such long service (some exceeding a dozen years) that experience is apt to be longer than service by more than one year. Thus we can conclude that the internal-promotion career prevails in large firms in almost all industries.

Time-series data are available for the years 1955–61 and for 1964–69 and are summarized in figure 2.11. As the available statistics for some years are limited in coverage, the observations here have to be confined to three major industry groups—chemicals, machinery, and non-heavy manufacturing. The strict definition employed in figure 2.10 is again used in the figure for the 1955–61 data; for the 1964-69 statistics, the number of occupations in which workers have more than seven years' average service in the same company is compared to the number of occupations where workers have five to nine years of job experience, exclusive of company. The latter is the broadest measure employed and cannot be compared with the other, but both support the findings in figure 2.10. In any year surveyed, the larger the firm, the greater the probability of finding the internal-promotion career pattern. Even in the machinery industry, 90 percent of the firms are in this category in 1969, using the broadest measure. Figure 2.11 also indicates that this career type was expanding from the mid-1950s through the 1960s when labor markets were becoming increasingly tight and technology was changing rapidly.

Available evidence from case studies in the United States, the United Kingdom, Japan, and other sources is assembled in table 2.2. The table shows, first, that the internal-promotion career type usually is found among both production workers in process industries and male white-collar workers in all three countries. Second, its use is most prevalent in Japan and least in the United Kingdom, with the United States somewhere in between.

It follows from this difference that a worker's career type can differ even if the technology is given. It is unlikely that there is a large variation in the technology of the same industries among these countries. Indeed, career type is not merely the product of technology; it also depends upon the social system. Suppose technology—say, a set of machines—requires a particular quality and quantity of work. Yet there is freedom in the way in which a given amount and type of work is divided into various job assignments, and in how these jobs are combined in sequence into various career streams. The

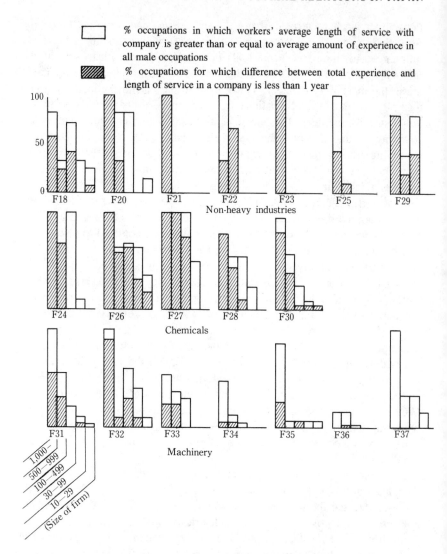

Figure 2.10. Percentage of Male Occupations of the Internal-Promotion Type, by Industry and Size of Firm in Manufacturing Industries: Japan, 1961. The industry key is: F18 = food; F20 = textile; F21 = apparel; F22 = wood; F23 = furniture; F25 = printing and publishing; F29 = leather; F24 = pulp and paper; F26 = chemicals; F27 = petroleum and coal products; F28 = rubber; F30 = stone, clay, glass; F31 = iron and steel; F32 = primary metals; F33 = fabricated metal products; F34 = machinery; F35 = electrical equipment; F36 = transportation equipment; F37 = instruments. *Source:* CKKT 1961.

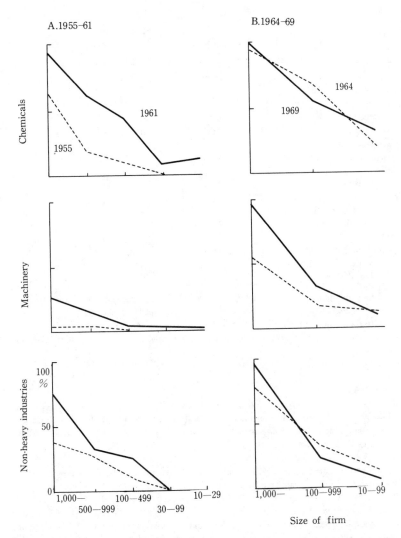

Figure 2.11. Changes in the Percentage of Male Occupations of the Internal-Promotion Type, by Industry, Japan, 1955-61 and 1964-69. *Source:* CKKT for the years cited.

forming of career patterns in effect determines the specific processes through which worker skills are developed and thus the investment in human capital is made. Unlike physical capital, human capital cannot be easily converted because it is embodied in a particular human being. And if trade unions support a system in which the human capital of members is developed, then the system becomes even more stable. Because one objective of trade unions

Table 2.2
Major Career Types of Male Workers in Large Firms, by Industry:
Japan, the United States, and the United Kingdom, 1977

	Japan	U.S.	U.K.
Machinery industry			
Non-mass-production type			
Machinery	A[ab]	B, C[a]	B, C, D[c]
Heavy electrical machinery	A[a]	B[a]	C, D[d]
Mass-production type			
Light electrical appliances	A[a]		
Auto	A[a]	D, B[ae]	C, D[f]
Process industry			
Steel			
Production workers	A[ag]	A[ah]	A[i]
Maintenance workers	A[ag]	A[ah]	C[i]
Chemicals			
Production workers	A[a]	A[j]	A[k]
Maintenance workers	A[a]	A[aj]	C[k]
White-collar workers	A[a]	A[a]	A[l]

A=internal-promotion type; B=less internalized type; C=craft type; and D=laborer's type.

[a]Based on the writer's field work, most of which is represented in Koike 1977.

[b]Kōshiro Kazutoshi, "Sangyō Kikai" [Industrial machinery], in Ōkōchi, ed. 1965.

[c]Based on the writer's field work covering three cases in Manchester, England in 1969, and Lupton 1962.

[d]Hazama 1971.

[e]Guest 1954.

[f]Turner 1966.

[g]Based on case studies in Ōkōchi, ed. 1965, and Inoue 1969.

[h]Although other information is available, the best descriptions can be found in Bureau of National Affairs, Inc., *Fair Employment Practice Cases*, in particular *U.S. v. U.S. Steel Corp.*, 5 FEP Cases 1253 (N.D. Ala. 1973).

[i]Knowles et al. 1958, and Scott 1956.

[j]Far more information is available for this industry than for any other. The following are the best sources. For pulp and paper see Brooks and Gamm 1955, and *Watkins v. Scott Paper Co.*, 6 FEP Cases 511 (S.D. Ala. 1973), *Hicks v. Crown Zellerbach Corp.*, 2 FEP Cases 433 (E.P. La. 1970) and *Stevenson v. International Paper Co.*, 5 FEP Cases 499 (S.D. Ala. 1972). For petroleum see King and Risher 1969. For rubber and tires see Northrup et al. 1970 (part 5) and *Johnson v. Goodyear Tire and Rubber Co.*, 349 F.Supp. 3, 5 FEP Cases 32 (S.D. Tex. 1972) and 491 F.2d 1342, 7 FEP Cases 627 (5th Circ. 1974).

[k]Lerner et al. 1969.

[l]Based on the writer's interview.

is to protect the jobs of their members, they have a vested interest in any training process through which members acquire skills. A craft union is a prime example of an organization that effectively regulates skill training through apprenticeship. Once a system of human capital formation has been established with trade-union backing, it tends to become institutionalized and will survive for a long period of time.

From table 2.2 we can see that the existence of the internal-promotion career for blue-collar workers seems to vary inversely with the craft-union tradition. Craft unions appear to be strongest in the United Kingdom, relatively strong in the United States, and least pervasive in Japan; they also appear to be weak or nonexistent in process industries and in white-collar employment in all three countries. Where the craft-union tradition prevails, one rarely finds a system of the internal-promotion type. But how and why it exists in particular segments of industry and in particular work situations in Japan as well as elsewhere, such as process industries and white-collar employment, have yet to be explained.

Let us begin with the finding that the internal-promotion career type of blue-collar employment is mainly confined to large firms in Japan and to process industries in the United States and the United Kingdom. These industrial subdivisions share two common features: vast fixed capital and prospects for long-term employment based on their monopolistic status in their product markets. Other researchers have determined that the longer the job tenure of workers with specific skills, the greater the returns to firms employing them (Becker 1964, 1975; Oi 1962), but the connection between vast fixed capital and the internal-promotion type of system needs to be explored. A large amount of fixed capital seems to require either a high degree of technology and, therefore, a highly skilled workforce, a fluid production system, or both. In such a situation, particularly in a process industry, which fits the above description, any trouble in one section—say, a job not being covered—affects production throughout the system. Therefore it is essential to have available workers who know the jobs and understand the system, since the most effective way to avoid delays is to have workers who thoroughly understand the total operation and production process so that they will be quickly aware of trouble and will be able to deal with it. The internal-promotion system seems to be the least expensive way to secure and train workers with these requisite skills. Needless to say, male white-collar workers share with their blue-collar counterparts this same need to be able to understand the plant's total operation.

When these two sets of forces are considered in historical perspective, a tentative hypothesis is suggested. Let us start by assuming, as do most Japanese institutional economists, that there are two major stages in the process of industrialization and that large monopolistic firms prevail in the second stage, but not in the first. Each stage has its individual set of complex systems—technological, economic, and social, including an industrial relations system. Second, change in each system occurs at different rates; a technological system will change most rapidly, while a social system will be the slowest to adjust.

During the first stages of industrial development, craft unionism, with its relevant technology, prevailed in most countries. As is well known, Japan's industrialization began at the end of the nineteenth century, at the time that the most prosperous period for craftsmen and their relevant technology was about to decline and large monopolistic firms were beginning to emerge. There was not enough time for Japan to have developed a large number of craftsmen, powerful craft unions, and the requisite technology. With the second stage following so closely after the first, it was neither difficult nor costly for the country to abandon the craft technology and production system, its methods of training and deploying workers, and its industrial relations system. This transition was eased by the absence of powerful craft unions. A new way of training and deploying workers, better suited to the new technology, was easily developed after World War I, and over the years the internal-promotion pattern was adopted by an ever-widening range of firms and industries. In contrast, in societies where the first stage of industrial development began earlier, lasted longer, and was more prosperous, and where the transition to the second stage was less abrupt, it proved too costly to abandon the former system and to substitute another one; rather, these societies preferred simply to adapt their well-established systems to the new technology.[8]

In a sense, an internal-promotion system is more compatible than any other with the monopolistic stage of industrialization. Thus, the practice of promotion from within seems to be spreading, blue-collar wages are becoming more like white-collar salaries, and the variety and amount of fringe benefits seem to be increasing for blue-collar workers even in European countries. It would be reasonable to say that, among the developed nations, the tendency toward what we have called the "white-collarization" of blue-collar workers has been taking place most intensively in Japan.

A final word of caution is warranted. This "white-collarization" thus far extends to only a small segment of the total Japanese workforce—less than a third by a rough estimate. It is still not available to most workers—the employees of small and medium-sized firms, the subject of chapter 4.

Notes

1   There have been many articles and documents, too many to be listed here; most of them are written in Japanese.
2   Koike (1977) insists that it is likely that nearly 80 percent of union members in U.S. manufacturing industries belong to plant-wide local unions.
3   The evidence for these statements is provided in case studies that Koike (1978b) conducted in Germany, Sweden, and France.
4   These semiannual bonuses, in total, comprise nearly one-third of the yearly earnings for a worker in a large firm and a quarter or a fifth for a worker in a small firm. An individual worker's bonus is generally a certain proportion of his

basic wage rate; thus, under the definition of fringe benefits being employed here, it is reasonable to exclude these bonuses. The payment of semiannual bonuses to all workers is not a custom that has prevailed since the beginning of Japan's industrialization. Prior to World War II, only white-collar workers received them.

5 In most cases, a retirement payment is a lump sum paid to a worker when he retires or leaves a company's workforce for another reason. The size of the payment differs according to the reason for the separation—the highest sum being paid in cases of retirement. The payment is higher when a worker is laid off than when he quits. In recent years, increasing proportions of the retirement payment have been converted to private pensions for retiring workers. In practical terms, these retirement payments, whether they are lump sums or private pensions, are the functional equivalent of the supplementary private old-age-pension plans in the West. Readers should note that they are completely different from old-age pensions as part of a social security system.

6 The concluding chapter of this book has been translated into English in Koike 1978a.

7 See Shinnittetsu Rōsō Kyōgikai [Japan Federation of Steel Unions], *Chōsa Jihō* [Bulletin] (August 1971) and Koike 1977.

8 This interpretation is somewhat similar to Dore's (1973) "latecomer theory," though the differences are far from minor. First, he based his theory on "welfare corporatism" rather than on workers' skill acquisition and careers which, in my opinion, are crucial. Without an insight into skills and careers, it would be difficult to explain why welfare corporatism dominates and is confined to large firms. Second, his theory does not recognize the two major stages in the historical development of industrialization. Consequently, all latecomers must have very favorable opportunities, which is unlikely.

3 Kazutoshi Kōshiro

The Quality of Working Life in Japanese Factories

Maintaining the morale of blue-collar workers has become increasingly difficult in most advanced industrial societies.* So it is in Japan where the problem of the quality of working life (QWL) has been discussed since the early 1960s.[1] A number of different criteria for defining the quality of working life have been suggested. Richard Walton (1975) proposed "eight major conceptual categories": (1) adequate and fair compensation; (2) safe and healthy working conditions; (3) immediate opportunity to use and develop human capacities; (4) opportunity for continued growth and security; (5) social integration in the work organization; (6) constitutionalism in the work organization; (7) work and total life space; and (8) the social relevance of work life (pp. 91–97). Neal Herrick and Michael Maccoby (1975) suggested that "four principles of humanization of work are presented: security, equity, individuation, and workplace democracy" (p. 63). The International Council for the Quality of Working Life, in its definition, confined the concept to the

*The original draft of this chapter was presented to the Sixth Japan-Germany Cultural Exchange Seminar, "Humanization of Work in Japan and in the Federal Republic of Germany—Macroeconomic, Microeconomic and Social Fundamentals," 3–6 October 1977, at David-Hausemann Haus, Düsseldorf. The author is grateful to Prof. Dr. Willy Kraus for his generous permission to reproduce it here.

"humanization and democratization of work" rather than including "security" and "equity" as Herrick and Maccoby did.[2]

Combining these definitions and criteria, we can distinguish three dimensions of the quality of working life: (1) extension of industrial democracy to the plant and shop-floor levels; (2) measures to deal with increasing worker dissatisfaction, alienation, and defiance in the workplace; and (3) improvement of wages and other conditions of work. In the context of a study of the Japanese industrial relations system, the first two are of particular interest; however, the third aspect will be briefly considered in order to provide useful background information for foreign readers.

In this chapter, I shall first describe worker satisfaction (or dissatisfaction) in Japanese factories, then proceed to a discussion of innovations in work organizations and production techniques, and of the significant features of the whole system as they affect an individual's work life within the Japanese lifetime employment system. In the conclusion, some assessment will be made of the quality of working life in Japan and possible future lines of development will be considered.

Indices of Worker Satisfaction at the Plant Level

Increasing absenteeism and labor turnover, and particularly an excessive quit rate, can be considered major indices of worker dissatisfaction. Charles Levinson (1974, p. 46) of the International Chemical Workers Federation (ICF), for example, says that the "sickness" rate of workers at Swedish Volvo, which reached 10 percent, and a worker turnover rate of 25 percent forced the company to maintain a permanent labor surplus and to introduce self-management on the assembly lines.[3]

Whether similar situations could be found in Japanese factories would be of major interest to colleagues in other countries. To pursue this question, the author undertook case studies in four Japanese manufacturing establishments; an automobile (passenger car) assembly plant, a steel plant, a shipyard, and a textile mill. Figures from these cases will illustrate the situation in Japan better than could general statistics.

Low Absenteeism

A strikingly low level of absenteeism is observed in Japan. In the four establishments studied, more than 90 percent of the firms' blue-collar workers had regular attendance records in 1976. If we set aside absences because of paid vacations and leaves, the real absentee rates were only about 1 or 2 percent (table 3.1).

Table 3.1
Average Attendance and Absence
Rates for Blue-Collar Workers, 1976, 1977
(percentage)

Plant	Attendance Rate	Absentee Rate	Paid Vacations and Leaves
Automobile	96.0	0.9	3.1
Shipyard	90.3	2.3	7.4
Shipyard[a]	90.0	1.7	8.3
Steel[a]	92.2	0.2	7.6
Textile[b]	96.5	1.0	2.5

Source: The personnel affairs department of each plant surveyed.

[a]Averages in January–June 1977. The figures for the auto plant are for fiscal 1976. The others are averages for the year 1976. The rate of paid vacations usually increases in summer and December, and the attendance ratio in the steel plant is overstated to that extent. However, attendance has been increasing in all cases in recent years because of the economic recession, a tendency that can be observed in the two figures for the shipyard. Figures for the steel plant are for shift workers.

[b]The extraordinarily high rate of attendance in the textile plant is mostly attributable to the relatively short length of service of young female workers, whose paid vacations are considerably less than those of male workers in other plants.

One reason for the low rates lies in traditional Japanese work practices, with workers tending to take their paid vacations in small segments because of an illness or another unexpected event. This does not necessarily mean that workers are not allowed sick leave. Rather, they simply prefer to take fully paid vacation days in case of illness because, otherwise, they would have to be satisfied with sick-leave pay, which is only 60 percent of "standard earnings."[4] However, even when the rates of genuine absence and paid vacations are combined, the attendance rate still remains quite high in the four establishments studied and seems to be representative of the general tendency in most large Japanese factories.

Absence rates do in fact fluctuate on a monthly basis and year by year, reflecting business cycles and institutional changes. Table 3.2 illustrates the fluctuations in the shipyard case. The real absentee rates increased in the early 1970s, but have been decreasing remarkably since the oil crisis of 1973. Introduction of a five-day workweek every two weeks in this shipyard in January 1972 and of the five-day workweek throughout the year in April 1973 also seems to have had a considerable effect in reducing absences. Another contributing factor is that workers realize that there are a limited number of job opportunities during a recession, and they prefer not to risk losing their jobs because of frequent absences—discharge being one penalty

Table 3.2
Monthly Rates of Genuine Absence in a Shipyard, 1968–77
(percentage)

Month	1968	1969	1970	1971	1972	1973	1974	1975	1976	1977
Jan.	1.9	2.2	2.9	2.9	1.8	2.4	2.1	1.7	1.6	1.3
Feb.	1.9	2.6	3.3	3.5	2.0	2.6	2.2	1.8	1.8	1.4
Mar.	2.6	2.8	3.4	3.9	2.4	2.6	2.3	2.1	1.9	1.5
Apr.	2.8	2.8	3.3	3.5	2.7	2.8	2.2	2.0	2.0	1.7
May	2.8	3.1	3.6	3.4	3.1	3.2	2.3	2.0	1.8	1.9
June	3.0	3.4	4.1	3.9	3.2	3.2	2.5	2.5	2.1	2.1
July	3.7	4.3	4.7	4.5	3.9	4.3	3.2	2.6	2.5	NA
Aug.	4.4	4.7	5.2	5.2	4.6	5.3	3.8	2.9	2.9	NA
Sept.	4.2	4.0	5.3	4.2	4.2	4.6	3.5	2.8	2.7	NA
Oct.	4.4	4.3	5.2	5.0	4.0	4.4	3.5	2.9	2.6	NA
Nov.	4.1	4.5	4.8	4.4	4.1	4.5	3.7	3.3	2.7	NA
Dec.	5.0	6.5	5.9	5.5	5.7	5.5	3.9	3.9	2.8	NA
Average	3.4	3.8	4.3	4.2	3.5	3.8	2.9	2.5	2.3	NA

Source: The personnel affairs department of the shipyard surveyed.
NA: Data not available.

for excessive absenteeism. Thus there has been a notable decrease in the absentee rates in recent years.

Labor Turnover (Quit Rate)

Another index of worker satisfaction is the rate of labor turnover or separation (especially quits). The average monthly rate of separation in manufacturing in Japan has been about 1 to 2 percent, which is about half the rate in the United States (table 3.3). This low rate seems to reflect the influence of the "lifetime commitment" system in Japan, where workers are believed to have a strong propensity to remain with the same company until they retire at age 55 or 60.

The separation rate in official statistics is not adequate, by itself, to identify the extent of worker satisfaction or dissatisfaction and the causes of separation. Information obtained at the shipyard is more meaningful. Out of 3,859 blue-collar workers employed in December 1975, 284, or 7.4 percent, separated in 1976. This separation rate is less than half the national average (1.5 percent times 12 months results in a national average of 18 percent a year). The general tendency in the Japanese labor market seems to be, the larger the firm, the lower the separation rate. Table 3.4 shows the breakdown of causes of separation at the shipyard.

From this table, we can see a few distinctive features of the Japanese employment system: (1) No workers were laid off in spite of increasing

Table 3.3
Monthly Separation Rates[a] of Workers in Manufacturing Industries:
Japan and United States, 1955-80
(percentage)

Year	Japan	U.S.			
		Total	Quit	Layoff	Others[b]
1955	1.8	3.3	1.6	1.2	0.5
1960	2.1	4.3	1.3	2.4	0.6
1965	2.3	4.1	1.9	1.4	0.8
1970	2.3	4.1	1.2	2.2	0.7
1973	2.0	4.6	2.7	0.9	1.0
1974	1.9	4.8	2.3	1.5	1.0
1975	1.7	4.1	1.4	2.1	0.6
1976	1.5	3.8	1.7	1.3	0.8
1977	1.5	3.8	1.8	1.1	0.9
1978	1.4	3.9	2.1	0.9	0.9
1979	1.4	4.0	2.0	1.1	0.9
1980	1.4	4.0	1.5	1.7	0.8

Source: For Japan, MKTC; establishments with more than 30 employees are surveyed. For the United States, *Monthly Labor Review.*

[a]The separation rate is the percentage ratio calculated as: decreased number of employees during a given month divided by number of employees at end of the previous month, where "decreased number of employees during a given month" is defined as those who were dismissed or discharged, retired, or were transferred to other plants of the same company, and those who did not receive pay during the month because of labor disputes or suspensions. However, official statistics are not classified by reasons for separation.

[b]"Others" include those who were discharged, on military leave, and a miscellaneous group (retirement on company pensions, death, permanent disability) as well as intrafirm transfers between plants. See U.S. Department of Labor, Bureau of Labor Statistics (1954), pp. 57–58.

Table 3.4
Reasons for Separation of Manual Workers
at a Shipyard, 1976

Reasons for Separation	N	%
Company policy		
Retirement	108	38.0
Termination of extended employment after age 55	24	8.5
Death (Non-work-related)	14	4.9
(Work-related)	2	0.7
Transfer to other plant	1	0.4
Subtotal	149	52.5
Voluntary	135	47.5
Total	284	100.0

Source: The personnel affairs department of the shipyard surveyed.

redundancy. The shipyard was reducing the number of employees through attrition and transfer to other plants or related subsidiaries, a portion of which is reflected in the table statistics. (2) The proportion accounted for by retirement and its equivalent (expiration of extended employment after age 55) is significant, although it varies year by year and in different firms or plants. (3) Disciplinary discharges are not explicitly classified because Japanese firms usually issue a warning or a recommendation that a worker quit voluntarily to those who are absent frequently or for a prolonged period or who deserve to be discharged for other reasons (Cole 1971a, p. 119). In this shipyard, about a third of the voluntary separations can in fact be classified as "discharges." (4) About a tenth of the voluntary separations may well be classified as quits because of dissatisfaction with pay or other working conditions.[5]

Increasing Propensity to Remain in the Same Plant or Company

As the relatively low rate of voluntary separation suggests, the propensity to stay in the same plant or company has been strong among Japanese blue-collar as well as white-collar workers. This propensity has intensified in the past few years. Table 3.5 shows the change in separation rates in the steel plant surveyed before and after the 1973 oil crisis.

The same picture might better be painted in another way. Although the rate of separation as a whole is currently low, it had tended to be a little higher during the boom period of the late 1960s and early 1970s (Cole,

Table 3.5
Change in Separation Rates[a] in a Steel Plant,
by Reasons for Separation, 1970–76
(percentage)

	Reasons			
Fiscal Year	Retirement at Age 55	Involuntary[b]	Voluntary[c]	Total
1970	1.3	0.3	2.4	4.0
1971	1.5	0.3	1.7	3.5
1972	1.8	0.2	2.0	4.0
1973	1.3	0.4	2.0	3.7
1974	1.7	0.3	1.1	3.1
1975	1.8	0.3	0.8	2.9
1976	1.8	0.3	0.6	2.7

Source: The personnel affairs department of the steel plant surveyed.

[a]The rates are figured as follows: number of separations in the fiscal year divided by number of blue-collar workers at the beginning of each fiscal year.

[b]Expiration of extended sick leave, death, marriage, etc.

[c]Quit for various reasons and "hidden" discharges.

Table 3.6
Blue-Collar Workers Remaining in the Same Plant
after One Year of Service, 1968–76
(percentage)

Year	Textile	Auto	Steel
1968	NA	66	NA
1969	81.2	68	NA
1970	NA	75	90.4
1971	NA	81	92.8
1972	NA	90	98.0
1973	85.9	91	83.8
1974	NA	82	90.9
1975	86.9	81	91.9
1976	NA	NA	98.2

Source: The personnel affairs departments of the plants surveyed.
NA: Data not available.

1971a, pp. 122–27). Before the oil crisis, less than 20 percent of the textile workers, a little less than 40 percent of the automobile workers, and slightly more than 50 percent of the shipbuilding workers were still employed in the same plant after five years of service. Even in the steel plant, where the workers have had the strongest tendency to remain in one location, about a fourth of the blue-collar workers had quit by their fifth year of service. Table 3.6 shows the rising rates of settled employment in the textile, auto, and steel plants after one year of employment.

It would be impossible for any company to eliminate all causes of worker dissatisfaction, part of which is resolved through voluntary separations or labor disputes, or is temporarily mitigated by absenteeism under a free industrial relations system. However, one goal of personnel management in a free market economy is to minimize absenteeism, the quit rate, and labor disputes by various devices that involve both labor and management, such as joint consultation, worker participation in management at the plant and shop-floor levels, and collective bargaining. The statistics cited above seem to demonstrate that the managements in the establishments surveyed have succeeded in achieving this goal to a considerable extent. Whether such achievements have really improved the quality of working life at the plant level will be examined in the following sections.

Innovations in Work Organizations and Production Techniques

The worsening labor shortage in the 1960s and early 1970s prompted many companies to introduce mechanization and automation as replacements for dirty or hazardous work, and the increasing criticism of industrial pollution around 1970 compelled many of them to take steps to reduce dust, odors, smoke, and noise, thus improving work environments. Measures to deal with the monotony of work resulting from mechanization, such as quality control (QC), zero defects (ZD), and other group activities to enhance worker autonomy and self-development, have prevailed since about 1965.

Replacement of Hard and Dirty Work with Machinery

Pressures from the labor shortage and from market competition prior to the liberalization of international trade in the late 1960s, and from the need later to cope with the rising prices of oil and other resources, stimulated rapid rationalization and the modernization of plants and equipment.

Auto.—The general manager of the auto assembly plant told the author that, because the labor shortage prevented the company from increasing output by hiring extra workers, it had to turn to investing in machines and equipment if it wished to increase production. If the company could replace the addition of one man to its workforce with a machine costing ¥10 million, then it preferred to invest in the machine. The two-shift system made ¥20 million the break-even point for capital investment. The same situation prevailed in the steel plant, where the three-shift system with four crew units increased the break-even point to ¥40 million.

In the auto assembly plant, multispot welders, machine bags, and robot welders have been introduced to process automatically 87–90 percent of the approximately 3,000 welding spots on a passenger car. The tin-plating facilities, where the working conditions are unpleasant, have been reduced to a third of their previous number. On the assembly lines, major production processes are now centrally controlled by computers at a rate of one and one-half minutes per car. Interestingly enough, various models—four-door sedans, hardtops, station wagons—and colors are mixed on any one line in an effort to relieve worker monotony as they repeat the same tasks over and over again, although the fact that the models are different may require additional attention from the workers. The only workplaces in the plant where the tasks still are difficult and require endurance are those where soldering is performed, and these workers are rotated every four or five years. Soldering jobs are essential for workers who wish to become skilled sheet-metal workers.

Shipyard.—In the shipyard, computers are utilized in all stages of the production, from design to process control. Numerical control drafting machines make blueprints that are transferred by electroprint marking to the steel plates which, in turn, are cut by automatic machines and gas cutters. The pieces are press-fabricated and carried to the assembly shop where they are assembled into large blocks, using automatic welders and two-stage roller conveyors on sliding floors and under sliding roofs. Hull blocks are fitted with pipes, valves, etc. (early outfitting), and the units are assembled in a large building berth. The block-assembly method, early outfitting, and automatic welding techniques all help in building high-quality vessels rapidly and economically. At the same time, these new techniques replace noisy riveting and relieve many workers from having to perform dangerous tasks in high places.

Steel.—Steel-making formerly was one of the hardest, hottest, and most physically taxing jobs in industry. Today processes are so highly computerized and automated that most key jobs are carried out in air-conditioned panel-pits. Even crane operators and ingot-buggy operators in the slabbing mill are inside the air-conditioned operation room protected from the heat. The table of job-grading in the slabbing mill, based on job evaluation, is surprising. Table 3.7 shows the results of job evaluations of the three key jobs in the slabbing mill, in which each factor is graded in five ranks (from A, the lowest, to E, the highest).

While "knowledge," "skill," and "mental load" are graded highly in these jobs, "physical load" is given a "B" grade in all three. A plant personnel officer says that, when all the jobs in this plant are considered, only 10 percent of the total workforce is in job classifications where the grades for "knowledge" and "skill" are "B and C." These jobs may well be classified as "monotonous," although they are closely linked with the lines of progression to more highly skilled jobs. In this respect, work in steel mills requires more knowledge and judgment than work on belt-conveyor lines.

Table 3.7
Examples of Job Evaluations in a Steel Slabbing Mill, 1977

	Job		
Job Grading and Rating	Chief Slabbing Roll Operator	General Roll Operator	Roll Operator
Factors			
Knowledge	E	D	C
Skill	E	D	D
Responsibility	D	C	B
Mental load	D	D	D
Physical load	B	B	B
Environment	C	C	C
Points	322	219	183
Rating (job grade)[a]	22	19	18

Source: The personnel affairs department of the steel plant surveyed.

[a]Ratings are on a scale from E (highest) to A (lowest). There are 22 job grades, rated by a point system. However, the actual classification ranges from the 10th to the 22nd grades.

Textiles.—In the textile plant, the spinning and weaving processes are highly mechanized and standardized. Work at the automatic winders, located at the end of the spinning process, and at the automatic spoolers at the beginning of the weaving process, are recognized as simple and monotonous, although the work environment has improved so significantly that it is difficult to imagine what the conditions in textile plants were like before World War II, when many young female workers were infected and died from tuberculosis.

Work at the spinning frames and automatic looms, however, requires the skill and experience to judge what is wrong with the machine, materials, or operation so that the number of scratches and defects can be minimized. The work environment for looming is the most unpleasant in the plant, because of the high humidity and ear-splitting noise. At first workers tend to dislike this assignment, but once they understand the challenging nature of the work, they seem to get greater satisfaction from it than from other jobs.

In short, modern production techniques have reduced hard and dirty work to a considerable extent and created semi-intellectual jobs on the one hand, but on the other, such techniques have increased the monotony and the danger of accidents on quite a few jobs. However, this does not mean that blue-collar work has become enjoyable at any place, nor does it mean that monotony or the threat of accidents will paralyze the production system. The truth seems to be somewhere in between. Thus, managements took steps to introduce innovations into workers' lives in the plant through such initiatives as improvements in working conditions, job enrichment, continuing education, and the so-called QC (quality control), ZD (zero defects), ZA (zero accidents), and VT (vital team) programs.

Increased investment to prevent and/or reduce industrial pollution has resulted in remarkably improved work environments. In the case of the steel plant, it is said that it costs the company more than ¥10,000 per ton of finished steel products to combat pollution. The principal air pollutants used to be iron ore and coal dust as well as fumes and smoke laden with nitrogen dioxide, sulphur dioxide, and carbon monoxide and dioxide. Today, dust and malodorous fumes are minimal. Water is completely recycled; none is discharged into the ocean. Strong governmental regulations as well as company self-regulation of industrial pollution have benefited workers in all industries.

Trade unions also have been urging stricter control of industrial pollution for better sanitation and safety. For example, the union at the steel plant revised its target for reducing dust from 5 milligrams per cubic meter to 3 milligrams per cubic meter in 1976. The union also sets several targets for combating occupational diseases such as lumbago, hearing loss, silicosis, chrome poisoning, and gas poisoning.

Industrial Safety

The number, frequency, and severity of industrial accidents have been decreasing in all industries, including the manufacturing industries.

Among the plants surveyed, the shipyard had no recorded fatal accidents between 1968 and 1973; it had one in 1974 and two in both 1975 and 1976. The severity rate fluctuated each year and once dropped to 0.09 in 1967, but climbed again to 1.21 in 1975 and 1.44 in 1976. The frequency rate, however, showed a remarkable and steady decrease from the high of 76.34 in 1967 to 14.19 in 1976.

In the steel plant one regular worker and three subcontract workers suffered fatal accidents in 1975. From January to August 1976, only one subcontract worker was killed in an accident. The frequency rate for regular workers was 0.53, whereas for subcontract workers it was 0.69 in 1975. The rates dropped to 0.25 and 0.64, respectively, in the first eight months of 1976.[6]

In an effort to reduce industrial accidents, particularly among subcontract workers, a law was enacted in 1964 to require parent companies to assume the responsibility for the industrial safety of subcontract workers, and new, more comprehensive legislation, the Labor Safety and Hygiene Law, was enacted in 1972, stipulating further responsibility for parent companies (Articles 29 to 32).

Employers have sought to improve working conditions and to reduce industrial accidents by introducing improved methods of performing work, more safety clothes and shoes, safety organizations among rank-and-file workgroups, and intensified safety education as well as by encouraging workers to participate in voluntary activities to prevent accidents.

Trade unions, too, have tackled this problem, not only at the national level, but also at the industry and plant levels. Expert committees for industrial safety and sanitation were established at joint consultation conferences between labor and management in shipbuilding, iron and steel, automobile, and other major industries. Safety patrol teams have been organized to visit plants periodically.

The enterprise union at the steel plant launched a "zero accidents" (ZA) movement in 1972, creating union safety organizations at the plants (union headquarters and branch levels) and in small groups at the shop-floor level. The ZA patrols visit every facility two or three times a year to ensure that safety standards are equal among facilities. The union also encourages the setting of particular targets for safety improvement in each plant. The tenth of each month is "safety day," when joint union–management meetings are held to examine the results. Similar activities can be found in each of the other plants surveyed.

One of the greatest contributions by the trade unions in the field of industrial safety is their drive for supplementary compensation for work accidents over and above the legal requirement. The Workmen's Accident Compensation Insurance Law of 1947, as amended in 1971, stipulates that employers should compensate an injured worker for 60 percent of average normal wages until he or she recovers, as well as paying full medical expenses.[7] If a worker dies as a result of an industrial accident, the survivors receive pensions. A worker who suffers a permanent disability also receives a pension. The amounts of disability and survivors' pensions depend upon the gravity of the injury (disability) or the number of survivors.

Beginning around 1967, trade unions began to demand supplementary benefits beyond the compensation required by law. Unions are particularly eager to obtain an additional lump-sum payment for survivors. According to a 1973 survery by Dōmei (Japanese Confederation of Labor 1974, p. 50), 57.4 percent of affiliated enterprise unions had obtained provisions for a lump-sum death benefit of more than ¥5 million; 7.4 percent of them had achieved the provision of a death benefit of more than ¥10 million. Now the benefit exceeds ¥13 million ($48,507 at ¥268/dollar) in most large enterprises (Takezawa and Asazawa 1977, p. 36).

Job Enrichment

Job enlargement or enrichment can be a means of enhancing workers' morale, relieving them from the monotony of repeating a simple, tedious task. Among the cases studied by the author, the steel plant is far ahead of the others. It has also been reported that in a shipyard other than the one surveyed, 98 jobs were integrated into 36 enlarged jobs (Takezawa and Asazawa 1977, p. 45). However, it seems that management in Japan is not very interested in enlarging jobs, for several reasons, the most important of which is that the traditional system of progression within job clusters, coupled with the lifetime employment system, has made it customary practice for workers to be trained on the job. During the training process, workers are required to undertake various tasks within a job cluster or shop. In this sense, jobs in Japanese factories have already been enlarged to a considerable extent, and thus there is no urgent need to implant the Western idea of job enlargement, which emerged out of the traditional craft system with its strict job demarcations.

Second, worker morale has not yet deteriorated in Japan, as previously demonstrated by the low absentee rate and the declining quit rate. This topic was discussed when the Volvo representatives visited Japan to talk with the managements of the Japanese auto industry. Stimulated by the discussion of job enrichment, some of the subsidiary parts producers of one automobile company experimented with Volvo's "island" method and found it quite effective. However, the parent company remains unconvinced of the value of the Volvo system because of its slight impact upon productivity and the required increase in the initial inventory of parts.[8]

Quite a few employers now realize, however, that the reasons for trying job enlargement are increasing in number and importance. (1) Changing demand for products requires the flexibility to rearrange the workforce, particularly given the restrictions on management's freedom to discharge employees. (2) The reliance on attrition to reduce manpower tends to result in an increase in the size of the middle-aged workforce, and efforts are needed to sustain their morale. (3) Young workers with 12 years of education would be dissatisfied with simple, monotonous work.

In the steel plant, an experiment to integrate three jobs at the blast furnaces into a single job, "blast furnaceman," has been under way since February 1977. Formerly, *romaekō* (furnace dischargers), *sōrokō* (furnace operators), and *romae seibi* (furnace maintenance men) were separate positions. However, in order to improve the quality of furnace operation (reduce fuel consumption, stabilize the quality of raw materials, increase heat stability and gas circulation within furnaces, increase the temperature of the blast, etc.), it was necessary to reorganize and integrate the three jobs; manpower savings were also desired. Twenty-six of 44 "blast furnacemen" did not have any prior experience in operating blast furnaces, which requires understanding the operation of a computerized panel. Thus, they had to learn FORTRAN as well as how to decipher figures and pictures on the TV screen showing conditions of heat, gas circulation, and melted materials inside the furnace, to regulate these conditions by operating keys on the panel board, and to give appropriate instructions from time to time; therefore, intensive off-the-job training was undertaken. About a third of the candidates did not complete the retraining.

Before implementing the reorganization, the management proposed the plan to the union, and details were negotiated. The superintendent of the blast furnaces stressed the need to motivate educated young workers. It was considered unfair that some workers happened to have been assigned as furnace dischargers or furnace maintenance men at the time of hiring and had to remain at those jobs without being given any opportunity to learn furnace operation. Since they have to work where the heat is intense, their working conditions are worse than those of operators, who are protected in an air-conditioned panel room. However, the mental tensions involved in dealing with furnaces by remote control may be greater for the operators.

Continuing Education and Training

An integral part of the Japanese employment system is continuing education and training.[9] Employees of large firms are expected to work for the same company until they retire, and employers expect to receive a return on

Table 3.8
Worker Development Training Courses at a Steel Plant, 1977

	Trainees				
Content	Middle Management	Foremen and Subforemen	Ordinary Blue-Collar Workers	Shop as a Whole	Total
General training	61	59	70	17	207
	(10.6)	(10.3)	(12.2)	(3.0)	(36.1)
Technical training	115	38	136	78	367
	(20.0)	(6.6)	(23.7)	(13.6)	(63.9)
Total	176	97	206	95	574
	(30.6)	(16.9)	(35.9)	(16.6)	(100.0)

Source: The personnel affairs department of the steel plant surveyed.
Note: Figures in parentheses represent the percentage of workers at each occupational level receiving training.

Table 3.9
Major Subjects for the Worker Development
Training Courses at a Steel Plant, 1977

Subjects	Percentage of All Sections (Mills) Which Selected the Subject
Engineering and technical subjects	82.5
Industrial engineering, quality control techniques	49.2
Computers and related subjects	12.7
Rationalization of tasks	20.6
Shop management	25.4
Problem resolution	14.3
Safety	12.7
Work environment	31.8
Other	20.6

Source: The personnel affairs department of the steel plant surveyed.

their investment in the human capital of these workers in whom they have made a substantial training investment (Oi 1962; Becker 1964/1975).

In the steel plant, there were 574 courses for worker development listed in 1977, as compared to 478 the previous year. The content of the courses is shown in tables 3.8 and 3.9.

About a fifth of the courses are conducted during working hours, while 40 percent are offered after hours. Sometimes workers take their training at a residential facility. Most interesting are the courses for foreman candidates. These courses are divided into several specific subjects, such as blast furnaces, steel-making, slabbing, sheet-rolling, or cold strip, and candidates from all of the company's plants go to a particular training institute for four months. During this period, schooling in basic metallurgy, chemistry, and other subjects continues from 8 A.M. to 4:30 P.M. Examinations are given at least once a week. Most of the candidates are in their thirties or forties. The high quality of the textbooks as well as their number (a stack more than a foot high) is surprising.

Education during working life is not limited to skilled male workers. In the textile plant, young women who have completed nine years of compulsory education have access to study in the evening senior high school for four years, if they choose; after completing this schooling, most prefer to quit their jobs to marry or to go to other jobs.

One of the most notable developments in worker education in the past decade is workers' voluntary participation in quality control classes. The classrooms of the steel plant's training institute were fully occupied by participants who were studying in their off-time, between shifts.

Quality Control, Zero Defects, and Other Small-Group Activities

Quality control (QC) groups were introduced in Japan around 1960 and the zero defects (ZD) movement began in 1965; both are modeled on American techniques. The recession in 1965 and the impact of the liberalization of international trade and direct foreign investment on Japan in the late 1960s and early 1970s generated a "crisis consciousness" among employers and workers. Among the establishments studied, the shipyard introduced QC groups in 1966, the same year the steel plant began a ZD movement.

The basic idea behind QC, as explained by the company, is "activities to improve managerial efficiency, the quality of products, and working conditions as well as methods of performing work, with the participation of all employees of the shipyard."[10] In promoting these activities, management encourages the participants to stress clear-cut objectives, to improve communication and cooperation among employees, and to utilize the techniques of scientific management. It is expected that through such activities the quality of products will be improved, a more human and interesting atmosphere in each workshop will be created, and self-development and mutual education among workers will be enhanced.

In the beginning, more than 1,400 QC groups were organized in the shipyard; these were integrated into 994 groups by 1977. A great many proposals for improvement came from these groups—37,040, or 6.4 per employee, during the second half of fiscal 1967. These figures had decreased to 8,092, or 1.4 proposals per employee, by the first half of fiscal 1976.

An example of how a QC group program operates is the following: The production norms for plate cutting by gas cutters were raised from 16 meters per hour (m/h) to 19.5 m/h and the target was set at 20 m/h. Foremen take a leading role in the work group's acceptance of the norms. They have a dual status: not only do they supervise the blue-collar workers in each workshop, but at the same time they belong to the same union as their subordinates. Therefore, they in fact act as chief negotiators for the work groups under their supervision when new work norms are set by the workshop superintendent. They usually can judge from their experience whether the norms will be accepted by their subordinates, but before making any substantial changes in the norms or methods of work, they sound out the opinions and feelings of the workers. Communication and understanding among the people involved have become all the more important because of the QC groups.

At the steel plant, ZD movements were inaugurated first as a device to improve the product yield rate and to reduce industrial accidents. Meanwhile, there were also significant effects in terms of worker spontaneity and group cohesiveness. For example, in the slabbing mill, there are 28 groups among the regular workers, and each sets its goals for a specific period—usually three months, but occasionally one year. Sometimes subcontract workers are involved in groups.

Achievements are reported to the foreman, the superintendent of each workshop, and finally to the chairman of the ZD headquarters (deputy general manager of the plant, in charge of technology). The reports are screened on the basis of a schedule of point ratings and are graded for one of three awards—special, ¥1,200 per person involved; excellent, ¥800 per person; and good, ¥500 per person. During a recent quarter, the slabbing mill had 28 awards (one special, 12 excellent, and 15 good) with a total prize of ¥871,000. Twice a year the money is spent for recreational activities for all employees in the mill.

For example, a group of 20 roll hands in the slabbing mill contrived an instrument to prevent roll-cooling water from falling on the slabs while they were being rolled. The device contributed to improving the yield rate of rolled products. A young worker was elected as the leader of the team and received the honor of reporting the achievement to the general manager and other top executives of the plant. The process leading to the achievement was recorded on slides to be shown to the public.

Similar small-group activities are promoted under various names in various factories, and they might be considered an indigenous component of "welfare corporatism" which flourishes in the lifetime commitment system.[11]

Work Life in the Factory

In discussing "humane organization of work in the plants," it would certainly be inappropriate not to make mention of the total structure of work life in a Japanese factory, which is based on "lifetime commitment" (Abegglen 1958) or "career employment" (OECD 1977, p. 15). The whole system of employment in large enterprises might well be characterized as "humane organization," although it cannot benefit those outside the system.

Several books on Japanese industrial relations, written in English, have described this system (Cole 1971a, Dore 1973), and it is referred to in other chapters of this volume. Although the system will not be described in detail here, it seems desirable to mention it briefly as it applies to the theme of this chapter.

The Structure of Job Clusters

The smallest formal work group on the shop floor is called *kumi* or *han* and is headed by a subforeman (*kumichō, gochō, hanchō,* or *kōchō*). The group usually consists of 10–20 workers and coincides with a job cluster in which workers are expected to rise from the bottom (unskilled) to supervisory positions. In that sense, it is a microcosm in which workers have to spend their day-to-day working lives—one that is cohesive and has the power to determine a worker's future.

For example, in the steel slabbing mill, there are three sections; the head of each, called a *kakarichō,* is usually an engineer with a university degree. Within each section there are foremen, the highest rank normally available to manual workers. In this plant, they are not eligible for union membership. In the second slabbing section, there are five foremen, one for each shift crew (three shifts of four crews) and one for the day-only shift. There are six *kōchō tan'i* (subforeman units), each of which consists of all workers in the four shift crews; thus there are four kōchō in each subforeman unit except for the day-only SISCO shift, which has only one foreman (fig. 3.1).

The salient features of the nenkō system (which emphasizes age and years of service—assuming the older the person, the greater his knowledge and experience) are implicit in table 3.10.

Table 3.10
Membership of a Basic Work Unit at a Steel Plant, 1977

Name[a]	Position	Monthly Basic Wage (¥)	Monthly Job Wage (¥)	Age	Years of Service	Rank
C	Subforeman	120,370	79,911	48	27	6
E	Bōsun	93,020	57,833	42	18	6
P	1st Hand	81,130	54,941	34	15	7
Q	2nd Hand	46,400	51,581	21	2	8

Source: The personnel affairs department of the steel plant surveyed.
[a]From table 3.11.

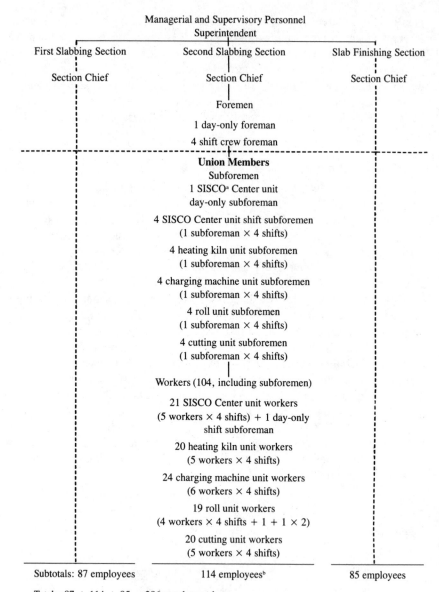

Managerial and Supervisory Personnel
Superintendent

First Slabbing Section   Second Slabbing Section   Slab Finishing Section

Section Chief   Section Chief   Section Chief

Foremen

1 day-only foreman

4 shift crew foreman

Union Members
Subforemen
1 SISCO[a] Center unit
day-only subforeman

4 SISCO Center unit shift subforemen
(1 subforeman × 4 shifts)

4 heating kiln unit subforemen
(1 subforeman × 4 shifts)

4 charging machine unit subforemen
(1 subforeman × 4 shifts)

4 roll unit subforemen
(1 subforeman × 4 shifts)

4 cutting unit subforemen
(1 subforeman × 4 shifts)

Workers (104, including subforemen)

21 SISCO Center unit workers
(5 workers × 4 shifts) + 1 day-only
shift subforeman

20 heating kiln unit workers
(5 workers × 4 shifts)

24 charging machine unit workers
(6 workers × 4 shifts)

19 roll unit workers
(4 workers × 4 shifts + 1 + 1 × 2)

20 cutting unit workers
(5 workers × 4 shifts)

Subtotals: 87 employees   114 employees[b]   85 employees

Totals: 87 + 114 + 85 = 286 regular workers
286 + 416 subcontract workers (6 companies) = 702 total employees

Figure 3.1 Organization of a Steel Slabbing Mill.
[a]Steel Ingot and Slab Control Center.
[b]Includes the superintendent and three workers on the safety staff. These figures represent the negotiated manning in the mill and differ from the actual working members at a particular date; these are listed in table 3.11.

Table 3.11
Membership of a Job Cluster: A Steel Slab Rolling Unit, FY 1977

Name	Age	Years of Service	Rank	Supervisory Position	Basic Wage (¥)	Job Wage (¥)	Total[a] (¥)
A	51	24(27)[b]	6	B	111,570	61,584	218,166
B	49	24(25)	6	SF	113,630	67,407	233,345
C	48	27(21)	6	SF	120,370	79,911	250,018
D	43	24(19)	6	SF	112,170	79,911	246,552
E	42	18(24)	6	B	93,020	57,833	193,532
F	40	21(19)	6	B	99,030	61,584	205,897
G	39	20(19)	7		91,530	54,941	186,451
H	39	21(18)	7		95,720	54,941	192,342
I	38	19(19)	7		89,740	54,941	184,371
J	37	19(18)	6	DSF	92,230	73,659	210,292
K	37	19(18)	6	SF	98,720	79,911	228,558
L	36	17(19)	7		87,550	54,941	183,289
M	36	21(15)	6		93,750	61,584	190,568
N	35	13(22)	7		79,110	54,941	172,504
O	34	18(16)	6		83,340	56,192	179,530
P	34	15(19)	7		81,130	54,941	174,775
Q	21	2(19)	8		46,400	51,581	124,335
R	19	0(19)	9		41,210	50,018	115,801

Source: The personnel affairs department of the steel plant surveyed.

SF = Subforeman; DSF = Deputy Subforeman; B = Bōsun (an informal position next to DSF).

[a]Total = basic wage + job wage + job premium + production bonus + shift allowances = straight-time monthly wages. Overtime allowances, midnight allowances, other allowances (which averaged ¥27,535 for 9.8 hours in June 1977 for blue-collar workers) and the semiannual bonuses are excluded.

[b]The figures in parentheses show age at the time of entry into the firm.

1. The 18-worker unit is essentially a consolidation of four basic cells of four workers each on the same shift plus two other workers. Here, the basic wages are determined by (a) the hiring wage rate set by education level and age at time of entry, which are specified by the collective bargaining agreement with the enterprise union; (b) the annual increment by merit rating, the range of which is determined by the collective bargaining agreement; and (c) the wage increase negotiated every April. Thus, the order of basic wages generally reflects the order of age and years of service. As the years pass, however, an able and industrious person can be promoted faster than older fellow workers: for example, compare K with G and H in table 3.11.

It should be emphasized that the subforeman unit (a combination of four shift crews) or the basic cell (a single subforeman unit on one shift) is a job cluster within which workers expect to be promoted to higher positions. Although no definite rule for promotion exists, the superintendent of the slabbing mill noted that only 15 percent of the workers had been promoted to higher positions outside of the subforeman unit in the past seven years. All other promotions had taken place within the subforeman unit.

2. From the figures in parentheses in table 3.11, it is obvious that all but five of the workers (A, B, C, E, and N) entered the firm right after leaving high school (M and O entered after leaving junior high school; the others after senior high school). In general, "halfway" workers, that is, workers recruited in mid-career, are at a disadvantage in terms of the basic wage rate: for example, E (halfway) vs. F, or N (halfway) vs. O. However, it was not unusual before and during the war for workers to be hired as regular employees after completing military service. Moreover, as the years pass, the pay differentials at time of hiring tend to diminish, reflecting merit and industriousness.

3. Despite the emphasis on age and years of service as a principle of wage-determination, the merit principle is also important. The art of adjusting the two principles is essential in maintaining the nenkō system.

4. Egalitarianism is also an important element in dealing with workers. The job wage rate is determined strictly by job evaluation. Thus, six workers (G, H, I, L, N, and P) have job wage ratings of ¥54,941 although their basic wages differ. Furthermore, among the older workers, three of four subforemen have a job wage rate of ¥79,911 and are in the sixth rank. (The first rank is for department managers, the second for deputy managers, the third for senior section chiefs or workshop superintendents, the fourth for section chiefs, the fifth for foremen, and on down to the ninth for new entrants.) At the same time, a deputy subforeman and three *bōsun* are also in the sixth rank, which means that although they are still bōsun, an unofficial title, they are qualified in terms of ability and potential to be promoted to subforeman when there is a vacancy. To be promoted from the seventh rank to the sixth, a written test as well as a merit rating and interviews are required. To advance to the fifth rank, candidates must present a paper.

As Fred Emery and Einar Thorsrud suggest, one way to enhance the quality of working life is to modify a system of strict job-wages or payment by results to one embodying "qualification wages" that provides pay not for the job the workers perform, but for the potential abilities they possess. Periodic increments for years of service are also recommended by Emery and Thorsrud.[12] These "reforms" have long been practiced by Japanese firms, as illustrated above.

However, one defect in the nenkō system is the dual structure of employment. For example, apart from the regular workers in the slabbing mill, there are 416 subcontract workers whose jobs are supplementary, such as scraping cracks on the surface of rolled slabs. Generally speaking, the proportion of subcontract workers to total employees in the iron and steel industry is about 45 percent; in some modern plants, this figure exceeds 60 percent (Niinuma

1977, p. 5). These workers are employed by subcontractors and are usually organized in separate enterprise unions of their own, although in some cases they are unorganized. The cleavage between regular and subcontract workers seems unfair; nevertheless, it should be noted that quite a few workers who retire from parent companies at age 55 are then employed by these "related" or "cooperating" companies.[13] In this sense, the dual structure is an indispensable supplement to the "lifetime commitment" system.

Subcontract workers are also employed extensively in the shipbuilding industry. In 1970, there were 76,348 subcontract workers, accounting for 32.6 percent of the total workforce. By 1975, the number had declined to 73,508, or 28.7 percent of the total (Japan, Tsūshō Sangyōshō, 1976). The construction and chemical industries are others that employ substantial numbers of subcontract workers. Although many subcontracting firms supply parts for other industries, only those industries mentioned above employ subcontract workers. As buffers against business fluctuations, the automobile industry, for example, depends heavily on outsourcing and hires seasonal temporary workers, and the electrical appliance industry uses female part-time workers. Generally speaking, the workforce in most industries consists of an upper one-third of regular workers who enjoy job security, good wages, and safe working conditions. The remaining two-thirds of the workforce are relatively poorly paid, have less job security, and are more subject to work-related accidents.

Fringe Benefits

Last but not least, fringe benefits are contributing a great deal to the quality of working life in Japan. Monthly wages and salaries constitute only about 60 percent of total labor costs in the surveyed shipyard (table 3.12), and a similar situation could likely be found in other plants.

Table 3.12
Total Labor Costs, Wages and Salaries, and Fringe Benefits
at a Shipyard (Monthly Average per Employee), 1976

Items	1 October 1975 to 31 March 1976		1 April 1976 to 30 September 1976	
	¥	%	¥	%
Monthly wages and salaries	185,104	58.5	212,727	59.1
Bonus	73,606	23.3	77,861	21.6
Compassionate payments	969	0.3	708	0.2
Commuter fees	4,125	1.3	4,879	1.4
Lump-sum retirement payments	20,335	6.4	23,990	6.7
Fringe benefits not required by law	11,917	3.8	16,346	4.5
Fringe benefits required by law	20,351	6.4	23,307	6.5
Total	316,407	100.0	359,818	100.0

Source: The personnel affairs department of the shipyard surveyed.

Among the legally required fringe benefits, the largest is the employers' contribution to the health insurance accounts. The premium is 8 percent of the monthly standard earnings in this firm, of which employers in large enterprises usually pay 60 percent. Required contributions to the welfare (old-age) pension fund are increasing and now constitute about a third of the fringe benefits required by law. The premium for male workers currently is 10.6 percent of standard monthly earnings. In some large companies, the employer assumes the burden for 70 percent of the premium. The employment (unemployment) insurance premium is 1.3 percent of the total payroll, including bonuses and allowances, of which employers contribute 0.8 percent.

The costs for worker's accident compensation are also considerable, particularly in hazardous industries, because merit ratings are applied on the basis of the standard premium. In the steel plant, the premium was 0.59 percent of the total payroll. This item accounted for 14.2 percent of the legal fringe benefits at the shipyard and 7.5 percent at the steel plant (table 3.13).

Among the fringe benefits not required by law, most of which are negotiated with each enterprise union, the major costs are for dormitories and company houses, housing loans, lunchrooms and cafeterias, hospitals and clinics, and sports and recreation facilities. At the same time, the cost of the lump-sum retirement payment has been increasing. Workers with 35 years of service at the steel plant were entitled to receive ¥10,308,000 ($38,463 at ¥268/dollar) under the 1976 agreement.[14]

Table 3.13
Legally Required Fringe Benefits at a Steel Plant
and Shipyard (Monthly Average per Employee), 1976

Items	Steel Plant FY 1976		Shipyard First Half of FY 1976	
	¥	%	¥	%
Health insurance	9,201	43.0	9,872	42.4
Welfare pension	8,172	38.2	7,462	32.0
Employment insurance[a]	2,199	10.3	2,352	10.1
Workmen's accident compensation	1,609	7.5	3,321	14.2
Children's allowance[b]	229	1.0	222	1.0
Others[c]	1	—	78	0.3
Total	21,411	100.0	23,307	100.0

Source: The personnel affairs department of the plants surveyed.

[a]In 1975, the name of the policy was changed from "unemployment insurance" to "employment insurance" to cover additional active manpower development programs.

[b]For fiscal year 1976, the premium set by order of the Minister of Health and Welfare was 1.2 per mill (0.12 percent) of the standard earnings stipulated by the Health Insurance Law.

[c]Off-duty compensation stipulated by the Labor Standards Law.

Conclusion

Japanese manual workers are still well disciplined, and there has been little evidence of their becoming unmanageable in terms of either the absentee rate or the quit rate. Nonetheless, since around 1965, Japanese employers have been eager to forestall problems related to the quality of working life. Workers are well aware that well-paying jobs are scarce under the dualistic system of employment, and this perception has been reinforced since the industrial reorganization in the late 1960s and the continuing decline in production and economic slowdown following the 1973 oil crisis.

Most measures proposed to deal with the quality of working life have been practiced or experimented with by many major Japanese firms. Yet the traditional system of "lifetime commitment" seems to embody respect for human relations among employees, to enhance the cohesiveness of work groups, and thus to integrate workers into the value system of the particular enterprise. On the other side of the coin, it also tends to eliminate, through self-selection, highly individualistic personalities from the communal society and to segregate "strangers" or the unqualified.[15]

The mechanization of production processes and the modernization of work organizations under the continued pressure of a labor shortage over the past two decades, and the increased pressure to combat industrial pollution, have resulted in a tremendous improvement in work environments. But the improvements require substantial capital investments that will earn returns only by increasing efficiency through various measures such as QC and ZD movements.

Trade unions have played an indispensable participative role in increasing economic growth. They have not demanded strict control over job demarcation, but rather have concentrated their activities on improving safety, wages and other conditions of work, and fringe benefits. The influence of intensive communication, negotiation, and joint consultation at the shop-floor level cannot be disregarded.

One of the most desirable reforms affecting the quality of working life in Japan would be the extension of "welfare corporatism" to those workers who have been denied the privileges enjoyed by the "elitist half." Several unions have attempted reforms in this respect by extending membership in the mutual benefit health insurance associations to retired employees or extending trade union membership to those who are transferred to subsidiary or "related" companies.

Hasty criticism of the dualistic employment system would not serve to stimulate positive reforms. There can be no free enterprise that has no buffer against business fluctuations. At the same time, the system of dual employment itself, supported by "related" subsidiaries, is an integral part of the "lifetime employment" system. Further innovations in this respect would be most welcome in the future development of the quality of working life in Japan. It would be impossible, however, to resolve this problem for individual enterprises without more positive financial, monetary, and other public policies at the macroeconomic level.

Notes

1 A series of dramatic experiments to humanize work organizations was first inaugurated in Japan at Sony's Atsugi plant in the early 1960s. The first change was to eliminate the checking by lunchroom cashiers of the prices paid for food, on the premise that workers would be honest in paying the full amount owed. This belief in workers' honesty and enthusiasm for self-development was the starting point for a series of other changes. For example, the checking of daily starting and quitting times and the keeping of time-records were abolished and replaced with self-control by each work group (called a "cell"). The unique philosophy of the general manager of the plant, Kobayashi Shigeru, was that he had great respect for workers' initiative to derive satisfaction from their jobs. He was strongly critical of Taylorism and other forms of scientific management, but praised the personnel policies of Texas Instruments. For some details, see Kobayashi 1966. The success of Sony's Atsugi experiments received wide publicity, and similar innovations were introduced by many companies in the latter half of the 1960s.

2 International Council for the Quality of Working Life 1973, p. 4. Both Walton, and Herrick and Maccoby, were quoted by the Japan QWL Committee 1974, pp. 10–15. See also the undated paper by Delamotte and Walker, pp. 3–14.

3 Overall absenteeism at a British electrical appliance factory was between 12.6 and 13.6 percent (Dore 1973, p. 26).

4 Paid sick leave in addition to paid vacations is not common in Japan, although paid compassionate leaves, paid menstruation leaves for female workers, and unpaid maternity leaves are usually granted. Some companies allow special paid sick leaves for workers infected by epidemics that require compulsory quarantine.

   Article 45 of the Health Insurance Law of 1922 guarantees 60 percent "standard earnings" for six months; there is a three-day waiting period. In case of serious illness, such as tuberculosis, designated by the Minister of Health and Welfare, the benefit period shall be extended to 18 months (Article 47). Most health insurance associations in large companies grant additional monetary benefits (usually an additional 10 percent) and an extended benefit period.

5 It is very difficult to generalize on this point. In the automobile plant, it is estimated that about a fourth of total separations were "quits because of dissatisfactions."

6 "X" Seitetsujo Rōdō Kumiai Dai 49 Kai Teiki Taikai Gijiroku [Proceedings of the 49th annual assembly of the enterprise union at the "X" Steel Plant], October 10, 1976, pp. 122–123. The following statistics give a general picture

of differentials in accident rates between two groups of companies in the iron and steel industry:

Fatal Injuries in the Iron and Steel Industry

Year	Parent Firms	Subcontracting Firms	Total
1965	48	88	136
1966	48	80	128
1967	65	102	167
1968	47	178	225
1969	57	125	182
1970	68	191	259

Source: Tanaka 1971, p. 47 quoting Japan Iron and Steel Federation, *Summary of Safety Administration in the Iron and Steel Industry.*

7   The maximum period for compensation while recovering from an injury is three years, after which the injured party can receive "a long-term-injury compensation benefit." The compensation level of the long-term benefit is 50% of the regular benefit and is paid in the form of an annual pension.

8   Interview with the general manager of the auto assembly plant, July 18, 1977.

9   Since the hiring of skilled workers from outside the plant is alien to the lifetime employment system, Japanese firms must continually train and retrain their career workers; "using slack time to carry out training" is a common practice. See OECD 1977, pp. 16–17.

10   Document No. 16 of the Shipbuilding Yard.

11   Dore (1973) defines "welfare corporatism" as follows: "factory and company based trade union and bargaining structure, enterprise welfare and security, greater stability of employment and integration of manual workers as 'full members' of the enterprise, greater bureaucratization and a cooperative or corporate ideology" (p. 370). The OECD Study Group (1977) also took particular note of the strong group orientation of Japanese workers and "social norms within the enterprise" (pp. 27–30).

12   Emery and Thorsrud are quoted in Japan QWL Committee 1974, p. 26.

13   These are standard euphemisms for subcontractors. See Niinuma 1977, p. 29. For a case of an electrical appliance company (Hitachi), see Dore 1973, p. 202.

14   Enterprise union of "X" Steel Plant, *Kikan Yakuin Handobukku* (Handbook for Union Officials), September 1976, p. 123.

15   Some academicians and journalists who are sympathetic with the New Left ideology are very critical of the personnel and labor policies of giant firms such as Toyota and Shinnittetsu (Japan Steel Corporation). They even criticize Sony's new approach, labeling it a sophisticated method of exploiting workers. See Nakaoka 1971a, pp. 210–12, 228–34, 259, and 1971b, pp. 212–14; Kamata 1973, which is a diary of a seasonal worker at a Toyota plant; and Fukada 1971, which criticizes company policies and the attitudes of the enterprise union from the viewpoint of a subcontract worker.

4 *Kazuo Koike*

Workers in Small Firms and Women in Industry

A somewhat sophisticated explanation of the high growth rate of the Japanese economy emphasizes its dependence on the availability of a vast corps of workers in small firms who are paid far lower wages and have poorer working conditions than workers in the large firms. This explanation asserts that the large enterprises make use of the lower wages paid in small firms in various ways: not only do they subcontract the manufacture of components of their products to these firms, but they also directly subcontract for labor from small firms, some of which even are located on the premises of the larger "host" corporation.[1] There is another important effect of such an alliance. When the large firm has to reduce production and, therefore, its workforce for one reason or another, it is the employees of the subcontracting firms who are laid off first, rather than the regular employees of the large enterprise who enjoy the so-called "lifetime commitment." Thus the conclusion is that the Japanese economy was able to grow as rapidly as it did only at the expense of a large number of employees of these small firms. Since the analysis of the "majority opinion" with regard to workers in large enterprises in chapter 2 indicates that that opinion was more of a legend than a reflection of reality, the reliability of the prevailing explanation of the role of workers in small firms also needs to be examined.

Wage Differentials by Size of Firm

Let us begin by finding out what proportion of the labor force is employed by small firms. The best survey of workers by size of enterprise and by employment status is the *Employment Status Survey* (originally published as *Shūgyō Kōzō Kihon Chōsa*) issued by the Prime Minister's Office every three years since 1956. According to the 1974 survey, 70 percent of Japan's total labor force of 51,341,000 are employees and the other 30 percent are self-employed. As in other industrialized countries, the self-employed portion of the labor force in agriculture and forestry has been declining; in 1974 it was only 12 percent of the total labor force. However, the number of self-employed nonagricultural workers was increasing, so that the relative portion of the self-employed in the total labor force remained stable at 30 percent. The latter group plays a key role in the operation of labor markets in the smallest firms and will be examined in a later section of this chapter.

The employee segment of the total labor force is divided into three main groups. One-third are women workers, the subject of the last section of this chapter. Another 28 percent are male workers in large firms with more than 500 employees, including public corporations; this group is analyzed in chapters 2 and 10. The remaining 40 percent, the largest group, are male workers in the smaller firms; on these, the first two sections of this chapter focus.

Although apparently a majority of male workers are employed in small firms, this group is far from homogeneous, as figure 4.1 reveals. Age–wage profiles, reflecting the degree of skill, differentiate three types of workers in small firms. First, there are the white-collar workers whose wages increase roughly according to age and whose age–wage profile is similar in both slope and level to that of blue-collar workers in large firms, suggesting that this subgroup has the internal-promotion type of career pattern described in chapter 2. Second, there are the blue-collar workers whose wages rise very little after they are about 35 years old, although their wage increases before then. The third group is composed of laborers, whose wages are stable until middle age irrespective of size of firm after which they decline somewhat. No statistics are available on the size of each subgroup, but it can be reasonably assumed that the blue-collar subgroup is the largest. This subgroup is also important, in that these workers are the ones most utilized by large firms—because they seem to have the skills that enable them to substitute for regular workers.

The wages of the blue-collar subgroup need to be examined in some detail. When length of service—internal experience within a given firm—is added as a new variable (see figure 4.2), the wage profile confirms the findings from figure 4.1; the wage slope rarely rises after these workers reach their mid-

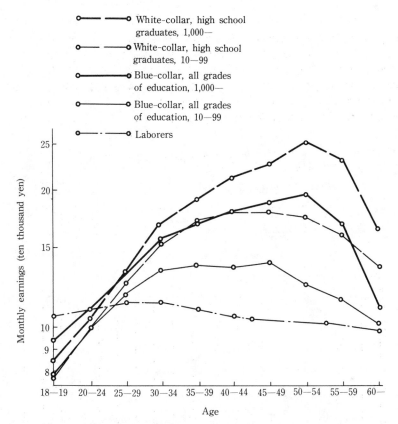

Figure 4.1. Age-Wage Profiles, Male Workers, by Size of Firm and Grade of Education, Manufacturing Industries: 1975. *Source*: CKKT 1975; Rōdōshō, Tōkei Jōhōbu 1975.

thirties in age, even after ten years of service. In other words, the main source of wage differentials between blue-collar workers in large and small firms comes when they are middle-aged and after ten or more years of service. The pattern raises questions: Why do these differentials appear at that age? Why don't the wages of this subgroup increase with length of service? A first step in finding the answers to these questions would be to compare the differentials with those in Western countries, for the prevailing opinion is that the diffusion in Japan is unusually large.

Unfortunately, data on wage differentials by age and size of firm are not available for countries other than Japan, but the 1972 European Community (EC) survey does provide statistics on average wages by size of firm, by sex, and by white- or blue-collar employment. Figure 4.3 is based on this information, and reveals that for male blue-collar workers, Japanese wage differ-

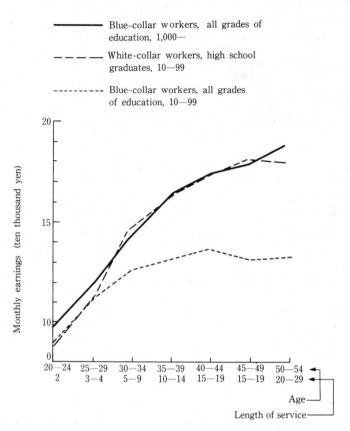

Figure 4.2. Wages of Workers, by Age and Length of Service, Manufacturing Industries: 1974. *Source*: CKKT 1974.

entials by size of firm are no larger than those of France and that the difference between Germany and Japan is small. Even for white-collar workers, the differential in Japan for the smallest firms is nearly 15 percent, which is a smaller differential than that which exists for blue-collar workers in both France and Japan. Although the lack of comparable data precludes any firm conclusion, what evidence there is indicates that Japanese wage differentials by size of firm are not strikingly different from those in France and Germany.

Thus, wage differentials by size of firm appear to be crucially dependent on age and length of service, and when these variables are controlled, some interesting interindustry comparisons emerge. From figure 4.4 we see that differentials of more than 20 percent exist for blue-collar workers only in manufacturing, not in other industrial sectors nor for white-collar employees even in manufacturing. Since blue-collar employees of small manufacturing

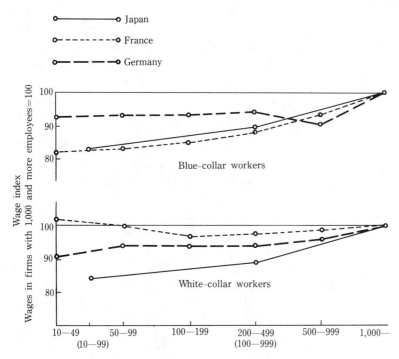

Figure 4.3. Wage Differentials, Male Workers, by Size of Firm, Manufacturing Industries: Japan, France, and Germany, 1970s. Numbers in parentheses refer to Japanese firm size classification. *Source*: For Japan, CKKT 1975; for France and Germany, SEI 1972.

firms are obviously not of the white-collar type, as are male employees in wholesale and retail trade and in the service industries, we may suspect that the wage differentials are due to some characteristics of these blue-collar workers, and we need to turn our attention to identifying these characteristics.

The most common explanation of Japanese wage differentials by size of firm is based on the labor market. It applies the so-called "Lewis Model" to the Japanese situation which suggests that vast wage differentials occur when labor supply greatly exceeds demand. The conclusion based on this model applied to Japan is that there was an "unlimited supply of labor" until about 1960 and that it was mostly this element that created the differentials.[2] Although space is not available to discuss the Lewis Model in detail, it should be noted that three important factors were missing from analyses of the Japanese situation. In the first place, the rate of growth in real wages was greater in Japan than in the West during the first half of the twentieth century.

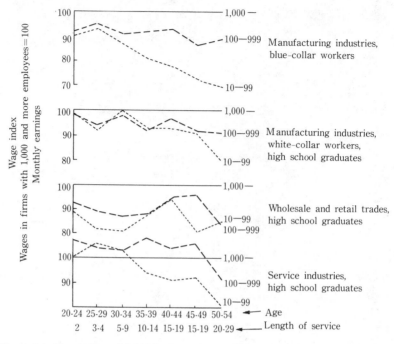

Figure 4.4. Wage Differentials, Male Workers, by Size of Firm and Industry: 1974. *Source*: CKKT 1974.

In particular, during the World War I era, real wages increased 5–6 percent a year, which implies a substantial labor shortage rather than an "unlimited supply." Second, there was a severe labor shortage during World War II. Third, industry and employment suffered a disastrous breakdown following Japan's defeat in World War II. In short, the "unlimited supply of labor" explanation distinctly underestimates the actual state of the Japanese economy prior to 1960.

Another explanation of wage differentials also relies on labor market conditions—the "Reder hypothesis" (Reder 1955) that suggests that the tighter the labor market, the smaller the differentials. The validity of this explanation can be assessed by examining figure 4.5, which displays wage differentials by size of firm and by age and length of service for the period 1954–76. The figure shows first that until 1964 wage differentials decreased rapidly; their decrease coincided exactly with the ever-tightening labor market. Second, from 1964 to 1973, when the labor shortage was at its height, the differentials rarely decreased and actually became slightly larger, particularly for younger workers. Thus the hypothesis is supported by the first finding but not by the second.

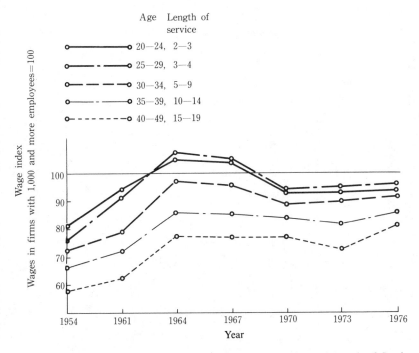

Figure 4.5. Changes in Wage Differentials by Size of Firm, Age, and Length of Service, Manufacturing Industries: 1954–76. The years selected were those when the size of the survey was greatest. *Source*: CKKT 1954–76.

Still another popular explanation of wage differentials is based on the variance in productivity. It argues that variations in productivity result in differences among the ability of firms to pay and, therefore, in wage rates. This reasoning relies on two assumptions: (1) that both large and small firms produce similar goods and compete in the same product markets, and (2) that the wages a firm pays are directly related to its ability to pay. Empirical studies do not support assumption (1); in most industries surveyed, the products of small firms in general are different from those of large firms (Koike 1962). And it would be difficult to presume that a firm with a greater ability to pay would actually pay higher wages unless it was obliged to do so.

Figure 4.6 shows differences in union organization by size of firm, which is the basis for yet another theory of why wages are higher in large companies than in small ones. The argument here is that workers in small firms have difficulty in forming unions because of the enterprise union tradition and the small number of potential members in each firm, and that the lower wages are the result of the absence or weakness of trade unions in these

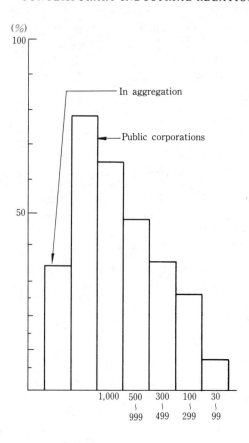

Size of firm

Figure 4.6. Ratios of Trade Union Membership to Employees, by Size of Firm: 1971. *Source*: For number of employees, Prime Minister's Office, Bureau of Statistics 1971; for the number of union members, RKKC 1971.

firms. It is evident from the figure that the smaller the firm, the lower the ratio of union members to total number of employees—less than 10 percent in firms with 30–99 employees and only a negligible amount in firms with fewer than 30 employees. A similar pattern probably prevails in the West, although data are lacking (Bain and Price 1972). A firm in which the workers are represented by a trade union may pay higher wages than one where there is no union, but the difference would be slight, and it would be difficult to conclude that differentials of more than 20 percent are due to union activities. If they are, then Japanese unions would be the most powerful in the world.

The Careers of Workers in Small Firms

None of the various hypotheses explored above offers a valid explanation of wage differentials between workers in large and small firms, particularly the differentials that have existed since the mid-1960s. Since these differentials are most pronounced in the wage slopes, presumably they reflect differences in the skills that workers develop during their working careers. Thus, it is necessary to explore exactly what the career of a worker in a small plant consists of and to compare it with the career of a worker in a large enterprise.

Figure 2.8 showed that young workers in small plants move from one firm to another so frequently that the annual separation rates are more than 30 percent. Although these rates drop to about 15 percent when these workers are in their thirties and forties, they are still about 10 percentage points higher than the rate of Japanese workers in large enterprises. This mobility is not unlike that of blue-collar workers in the West, in terms of distribution of workers with longer service, as shown in figure 2.4. This high rate of turnover suggests that there are differences between the ways workers acquire their skills in small plants and under the internal-promotion type system in large plants. It would seem that in the small plants the workers may acquire a kind of general skill from experience in several different firms.

Yet a very different profile is obtained from the results of a recent questionnaire survey of 420 firms ranging in size from 30 employees to slightly more than 300 (Koike 1981, ch. 1). One of the questions in the survey asked for an estimate of the percentage of the present workforce that was trained externally—here defined as workers who had more than three years' experience in their present occupations but at another company. These results are displayed in figure 4.7. In 63 percent of the firms, the proportion is less than 10 percent, and the larger the firm, the less the workforce will have been trained externally. The answer to the question about which type of workers the managements prefer—those trained internally or externally—is that, overwhelmingly, they prefer to train their workers themselves.

How, then, do these small firms train their workers? Chapter 2 describes how workers in large firms acquire a wide range of skills, first by rotating jobs within one workshop and later, after several years of service, by moving to other, technologically similar workshops. In this way, the range of a worker's experience and skill is enlarged. Whether or not this is the pattern for workers in small firms needs to be determined.

Two questions in the survey are relevant: (1) "Do workers change their positions within a workshop, at times or regularly?" (2) "Have the long-service workers had experience in most jobs in their workshop?" The answers to both questions show very similar tendencies (see figure 4.8). The larger

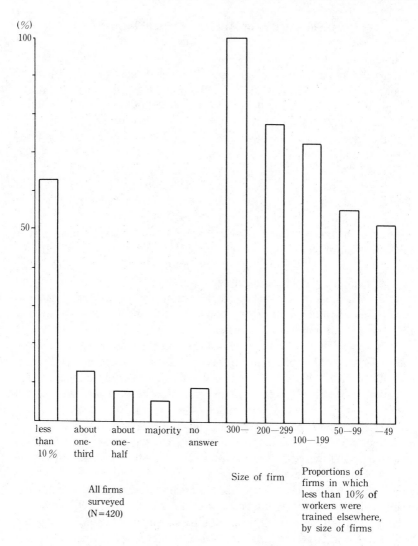

Figure 4.7. Ratios of Workers with More Than Three Years of Experience in the Same Occupation in Other Firms, Manufacturing Industries: 1978. *Source*: Koike 1981.

the firm, the greater the internal mobility; 75 percent of the firms with more than 300 employees do provide such mobility, as do 35–45 percent of the smallest firms. More detailed results indicate, however, that most of the intraworkshop mobility is "at times" rather than "regularly," irrespective of firm size. The implication of this finding might be that this form of skill training is neither as deliberate nor as well organized as it is in large firms.

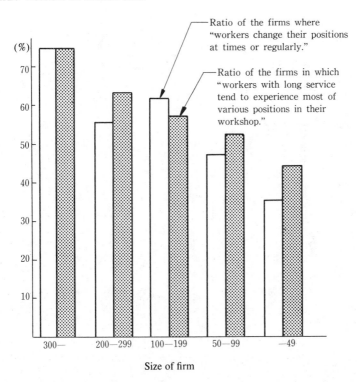

Figure 4.8. Mobility within a Workshop: Ratios of Firms in Which Male Blue-Collar Workers Move within a Workshop, Manufacturing Industries. *Source*: Koike 1981.

Figure 4.9 tells a similar story about mobility among workshops. Again, the larger the firm, the greater the probability that workers will be rotated among similar workshops, and the proportions for firms of various sizes are about the same as for mobility within a workshop. Too, most of this type of mobility is "at times" rather than "regularly." It occurs mainly between "familiar shops," closely related in technology, and it is a practice which enlarges a worker's experience. Thus, it can be concluded that internal training prevails in more than half of the small firms surveyed and that it is preferred by most of them.

This internal training in small firms still might differ from that in large enterprises. Taking into account that the survey indicated that the larger the firm, the higher the quality of internal training, it may be safe to say that large companies with 1,000 or more employees have developed a more comprehensive system of skills training. Thus, we might infer that the working career of a blue-collar employee of a large firm includes a wider range of technologically related positions than may be available to similar

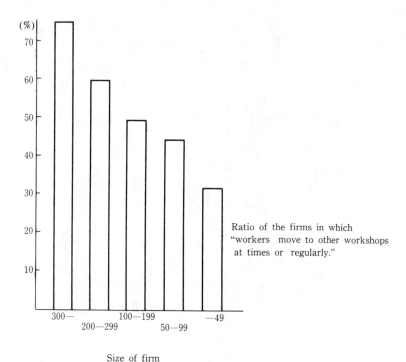

Figure 4.9. Interworkshop Mobility within a Firm: Ratios of Firms in Which Male Blue-Collar Workers Move to Other Workshops, Manufacturing Industries. *Source:* Koike 1981.

employees of small firms. This, then, may be the principal reason that the wages of workers in small firms increase very little after ten years of service, so that there exist large wage differentials according to the size of the firm.

If the difference in skills between workers in large and small firms can be attributed to differences in the variety of jobs available for internal training, most of the questions concerning the relationship of workers in large and small plants can be explained. Subcontract workers at plants of large corporations can compete with regular workers at those plants for lower-grade jobs, but they have not had the opportunity to develop the skills required for higher-grade positions. There is little difference in wages between these two groups competing for lower-grade jobs, for the regular workers in these jobs have fewer years of experience and their pay accordingly is lower. Empirical studies indicate that subcontract workers are rarely found alongside regular workers in higher-grade jobs in large firms, and in cases where an egalitarian system of deployment is practiced, the two groups seldom overlap. The division of labor between the two groups seems to depend for the most part upon skill differences.

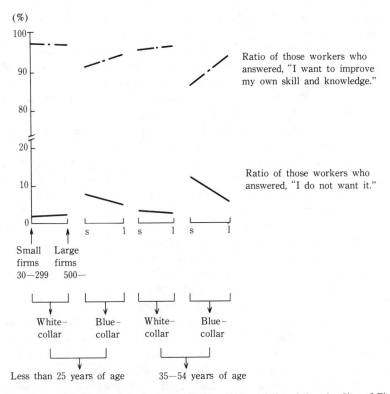

Figure 4.10. Male Workers' Aspirations to Improve Skill and Knowledge, by Size of Firm, Age, and Occupation, All Industries. *Source*: Rōdōshō, Tōkei Jōhōbu 1972.

This difference in skill level by size of firm does not imply that workers in small firms have few opportunities to develop skills. They do have opportunities to develop skills on their own, but not as many as are available to regular workers in large firms. Nor does it mean that their aspirations are not as high as those of employees of the large companies. In figure 4.10 are the results of a nationwide attitude survey by the Ministry of Labor in which workers were asked the same questions irrespective of size of firm. From this information, we can compare the attitudes of workers in large and small companies. One of the questions had to do with whether or not they wished to improve their skill and knowledge. An overwhelming majority responded that they did; a negligible number gave negative answers. Only among blue-collar workers was there a slight difference in the level of aspirations, with employees of small firms expressing slightly lower aspirations than did workers employed by large enterprises. This difference might be attributed in part to the less developed career patterns in small firms. There was no difference in the level of aspirations among white-collar workers by size of firm.

The discussion so far has been confined to workers in firms with more than 30 employees. Nearly one-third of the labor force, however, works in even smaller businesses, and three-fifths of these workers are male. Generally it has been argued that they are the source of the recorded lower wages and poorer working conditions, but careful investigation reveals that there is a career pattern here that often leads to the ownership of a small business. The most detailed and reliable assemblage of statistics on employment structure, the *Employment Status Survey*, which has been compiled every three years since 1956, includes figures, by size of firm, on the number of workers who have moved from the employee sector to self-employment. An analysis of the trend (Koike 1981) reaches the following conclusions: (1) There is a stream of employees of the smallest firms who move on to the ownership of the smallest businesses, and this stream decreased very little between 1959 and 1971. (2) The ratio of workers who became business-owners during their careers to the number of male employees is inversely correlated with the size of the firm by which the worker who moved was employed. Nearly half of the workers in the smallest firms with 10 or less employees become self-employed, about a third from firms with 10–29 employees do so, and only a few from the larger firms are ever business-owners.

A number of implications can be drawn from this mobility. First, an employee of the smallest firm does not always end his career as an employee; his chances of becoming an owner of a small business are good, and this can compensate for his low wages while he is an employee. Second, while he is employed by the very small firm at low wages, he is, in effect, training to be an owner, and trainees in any case receive low wages. Third, and most important, this stream from employee to owner could augment the competitiveness of Japanese industrial society. Supported by this stream, neither the size of the nonagricultural self-employed sector nor that of the smallest business sector has declined very much in recent decades.

If workers' organizations existed in the small firms, undoubtedly they would be useful in providing a voice for the employees and in promoting their welfare. But, as figure 4.6 indicates, there are few trade unions in this sector in Japan, a characteristic common also in the West. However, in many European countries the labor relations law authorizes so-called worker participation in management, and its use is spreading. The Betriebsräte (works councils) in Germany and the comités d'enterprise (enterprise committees) in France are examples. The fact that worker participation is authorized by law does not necessarily mean that it will be widely used, and although statistical evidence is lacking, worker participation appears to be found more frequently in large firms than in small ones. But the mere existence of such a law would do more than its absence in promoting some type of worker participation.

There are no such laws in Japan, a fact that leads one to consider whether or not they would be desirable.

Although trade-union membership is far less in small firms than in large ones, there is an inverse and partially compensating relationship between size of firm and the number of employees belonging to some other type of employee organization, as shown in figure 4.11. Field research discloses that these organizations began as recreational or friendly associations (*shimboku-kai*) that included, as well, members of the managerial staff except company directors. Now, a substantial number of them, if not all, consult with man-

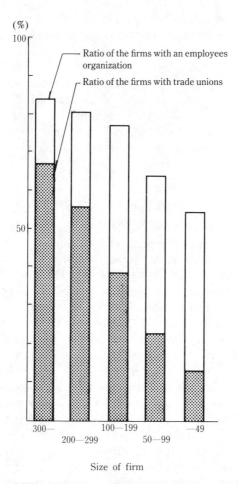

Figure 4.11. Ratios of Firms in Which an Employee Organization Exists, by Size of Firm, Manufacturing Industries. *Source*: Koike 1981.

agement or even negotiate wages and working conditions (Koike 1981, ch. 5). Even though they may not have the power of trade unions, some of them do perform equivalent functions. If membership in these employee organizations is added to that of trade unions, the proportion of organized workers in small firms rises to more than 50 percent. The existence of the voluntary associations raises the issue of whether or not worker participation laws are really needed. On the one hand, such a law would provide a basis upon which these associations could extend their operations and effectiveness, but on the other hand the result might be friction between the associations and existing trade unions. Because of the enterprise union tradition, there could be no distinction between the two types of workers' organization.

But what workers in the smallest firms appear to need most is encouragement to initiate their own small businesses. Financial aid is crucial. The amount of financing needed has been increasing year by year, as the price of land in urban areas rises, and it is not easy for workers in the smallest firms to accumulate the necessary capital by themselves out of their earnings as employees. There are public corporations that loan money to small businesses at interest rates below those charged by private finance companies. However, the size of the stream of workers moving from employee status to ownership calls for an expansion of the public financial-aid system.

Women Workers in Industry

Not much attention has been paid to women workers in Japan since the rapid growth of the total economy and the accompanying relative decline in importance of the textile industry which employed a substantial portion of the female labor force. This apathy has enabled the traditional image of women workers to survive. What might be labeled the "lag-behind" hypothesis suggests that when economic growth is especially rapid, a part of industrial society inevitably is left behind. In this instance, it is working women. Most Japanese housewives, according to this hypothesis, remain in their homes, and even if they do work outside the home, it is at wages far lower than those of males, so that the differentials in Japan between male and female wages are greater than those prevailing in the West. This phenomenon has rarely been examined, although a quantity of data is available in International Labor Office (ILO) publications and recent European Community (EC) documents.

Figure 4.12 displays the labor force participation rates of women in France, the United Kingdom, West Germany, and Japan for the period around 1970. It suggests the following interpretation: (1) Apart from the percentages for the teen years, which simply reflect differences in school attendance among the countries, the rates for Japan peak at two points—a sharp peak at ages

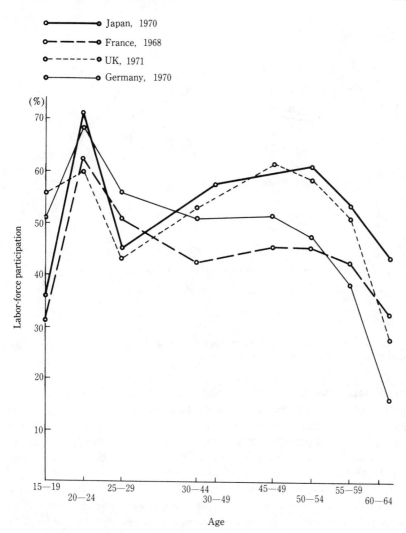

Figure 4.12. Female Labor-Force Participation Rates: Japan, 1970, France, 1968, the United Kingdom, 1971, and Germany, 1970. *Source*: ILO Yearbook 1968, 1970, 1971.

20–24 and a broad peak beginning at about age 35 and continuing into the fifties. There is a decided drop in labor force participation when women are in their late twenties, the usual time for marriage and child-bearing, but it is particularly pronounced for Japan. Neither France nor Germany has the broad peak at middle age, and although the United Kingdom has two peaks not unlike Japan's, the participation rate in the early twenties is less than Japan's. The one-peak pattern of France and Germany is similar to that of

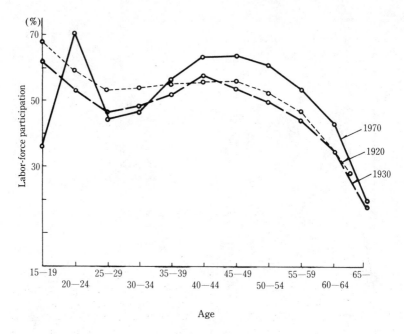

Figure 4.13. Female Labor-Force Participation Rates: Japan, 1920, 1930, 1970. *Source*: Prime Minister's Office, Bureau of Statistics 1920, 1930, 1970.

prewar Japan (see fig. 4.13). The present pattern may imply that Japanese women are more committed to the world of work now than at any time previously. (2) There are more working women in the oldest age group in Japan than in the other countries. (3) In aggregate, of the four countries Japan clearly has a larger proportion of women in the labor force, a fact which contradicts the "lag-behind" hypothesis.

Two questions come to mind. What if we compare Japan with the United States and Sweden, both notable for their high rates of female labor force participation? Could the high ratio of Japanese women in the labor force be due to a higher proportion in the self-employed sector in Japan than elsewhere? It is not unusual in any country for a larger proportion of women to be in the self-employed sector, but the ratio in Japan is slightly higher than in the West. Figure 4.14 shows U.S. rates for 1970 and 1975 and the total rate for Japan as well as that for "all-cities" in 1970. By excluding the agricultural sector, the all-cities rate is comparable to the U.S. figures in terms of the proportion of the self-employed. It is clear from the figure, first, that the participation of American women in the labor force increased between 1970 and 1975 by nearly 10 percentage points—even more among the youngest women. The only exception to this trend is in the 50-years-of-age and

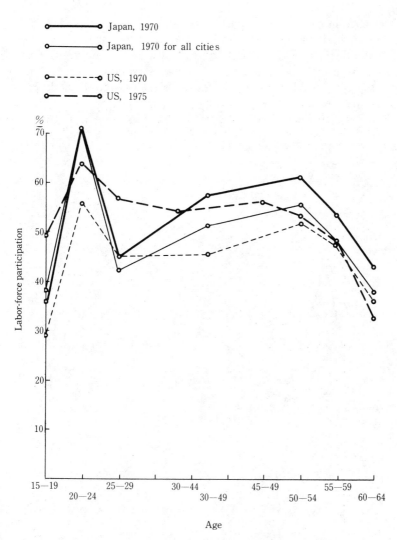

Figure 4.14. Female Labor-Force Participation Rates: Japan and the United States, 1970, 1975. *Source*: ILO Yearbook 1972,1977.

older categories. Second, it is true that the larger the proportion of self-employed, the higher the labor force participation rate among women, particularly older women. Japan's 1970 rate of total female labor force participation is higher than the all-cities rates after about age 35. Third, even Japan's all-cities rates exceed those of the United States for 1970. Fourth, the recent remarkable increase in female labor force participation in the United States has resulted in their rates equaling or surpassing Japan's rates in some age categories. A similar tendency can be identified in the Japan–Sweden comparison in figure 4.15. The labor force participation rate of Swedish women in 1970 is generally lower than that of Japanese women in cities, but the increase in participation between 1970 and 1975 was so great that the Swedish rates now exceed Japan's.

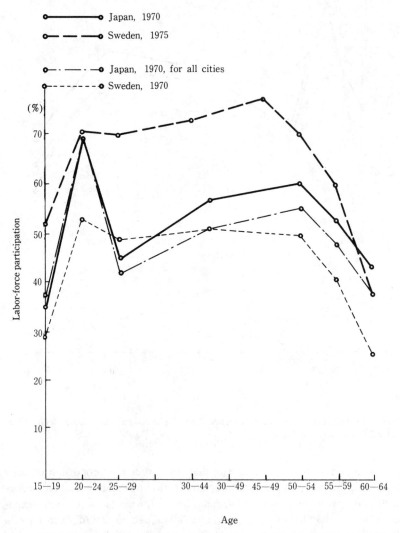

Figure 4.15. Female Labor-Force Participation Rates: Japan and Sweden, 1970, 1975. *Source*: ILO Yearbook 1972, 1977.

A more detailed analysis, however, reveals several "lag-behind" aspects in the Japanese case. When the ratios of female to total employment by occupation in Japan and in the West are compared (see fig. 4.16), two of the percentages are noteworthy—those for professional and technical, and for administrative employees, both occupations that are considered attractive in terms of wages and working conditions. Japan's percentage of women in professional and technical jobs is comparable to those of Western countries, but the proportion of women in administrative positions in Japan is smaller. Even though the number of women in administrative jobs is relatively small in any country, Japan's percentage might be a "lag-behind" aspect of her industrial society. It also should be noted that more Japanese women are in production occupations and fewer in clerical work, as compared with Western countries. In Japan there are few typing jobs owing to the great number of characters in the Japanese language.

Figure 4.17 suggests one of the reasons that fewer Japanese women are in administrative positions. Based on the 1972 EC survey as well as Japan's CKKT, the figure shows the distribution of women workers by length of service. As explained in chapter 2, the statistics are similar enough that they are readily comparable. In Japan, the percentage of women workers with ten years or more of service is less than in any country in the West except the Netherlands. This finding holds for both blue- and white-collar workers, although the difference between Japan and the West is particularly apparent in the white-collar group. The percentages of women with ten or more years of service are higher among white-collar than among blue-collar employees in all of the Western countries, but not in Japan. If white-collar skills are developed on the job, a premise developed in chapter 2, then these workers would have to have longer service to qualify for administrative jobs. This distribution of women workers by length of service does not imply that there are fewer older women in the Japanese labor force. According to the surveys cited above, 55 percent of the working women in manufacturing industries in Japan are 35 years of age or older; except for Germany, there are more younger women in manufacturing jobs in the EC countries.

These two features of the female labor force in Japan—more older women workers and fewer women with ten or more years of service—explain why the age–wage profiles are more horizontal for Japan than for the EC countries. Figure 4.18 clearly shows that the wages of Japanese middle-aged female workers are even lower than the wages of young women in their early twenties. This is not so in France and Germany. For white-collar workers, Japan's profile is less positive than those of the other two countries. But it should be reiterated here that, as demonstrated in chapter 2, the differential in wages between white- and blue-collar male workers in Japan is less than those in the EC countries, and figure 4.19 tells us that the finding holds for

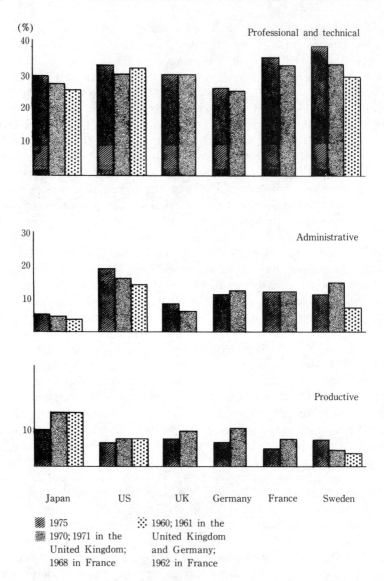

Figure 4.16. Ratios of Female Employees by Occupation, All Industries: Japan, 1960, 1970, 1975; the United States, 1960, 1970, 1975; the United Kingdom, 1971, 1975; Germany, 1970, 1975; France, 1968, 1975; and Sweden, 1960, 1970, 1975. *Source*: ILO Yearbook 1968, 1972, 1977.

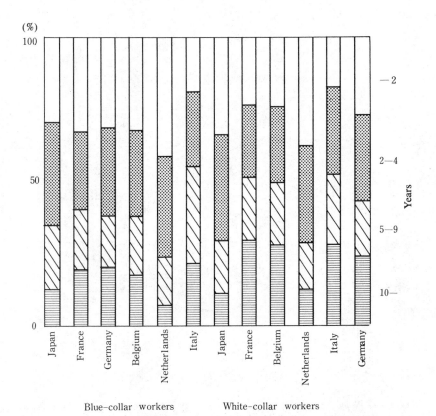

Figure 4.17. Distribution of Female Employees by Length of Service, Manufacturing Industries: Japan, 1973, and the European Community, 1972. *Source*: For Japan, CKKT 1973; for the EC countries, SEI 1972.

Japanese women workers as well. The differentials are smaller than in France, Italy, and Germany, although the difference between Japan and Germany is slight.

What are the effects of all the features described above on wage differentials by sex, which are usually considered to be indicators of discrimination in labor markets? It has long been claimed that the differentials for Japanese women are the largest among industrialized nations. The measures, however, depended solely on *average* differentials by sex, irrespective of job experience, which would be indicated by length of service or age. Since the variance in employment distribution by age and length of service has been demonstrated, it would be useful to observe women's wages by age and, if possible, by length of service in the West. The 1972 EC survey provided

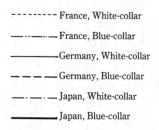

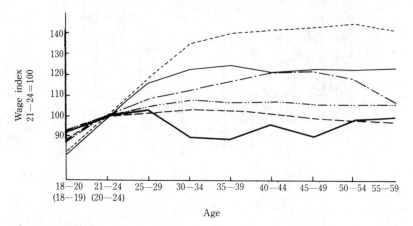

Figure 4.18. Wage Differentials by Age, Female Workers, Manufacturing Industries: Japan, 1973, France and Germany, 1972. Numbers in parentheses refer to Japanese age classifications. *Source:* For Japan, CKKT 1973; for France and Germany, SEI 1972.

wages by age statistics for the first time for West European industrialized countries; they are compared with the Japanese statistics in figure 4.20. From the figure it can be seen that wage differentials for Japanese women in their twenties are not larger than those in the United Kingdom and Germany. However, they are much greater for middle-aged women workers in Japan than in any of the four EC countries. The same trends appear for the white-collar group. Wage differentials in Japan, Germany, the United Kingdom, and France are about the same for women workers in their twenties; only Germany's wages for women are slightly closer to men's wages at about age 30. The great gap occurs in wage differentials during middle age. Thus we can understand why the *average* wage differential by sex is so large for Japan. The greater number of middle-aged women in the labor force and the larger differential between their wages and those of middle-aged men together contribute to the larger average differential.

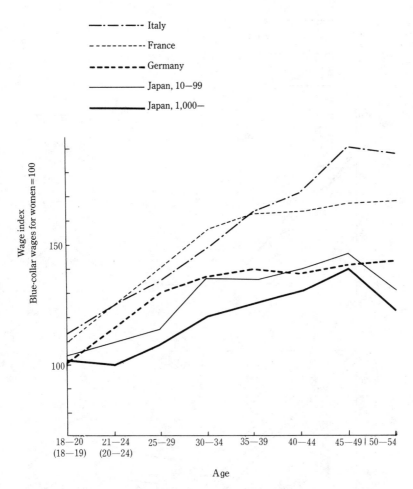

Figure 4.19. Female Wage Differentials by Occupation, Manufacturing Industries: Japan, 1973, Italy, France, and Germany, 1972. Figures in parentheses refer to Japanese age classification. *Source*: For Japan, CKKT 1973; for the EC countries, SEI 1972.

One critical question remains: Why are wage differentials by sex greater for women in middle age but not when they are in their twenties? The observations above as well as factors discussed in chapter 2 suggest several reasons. In part, the gap could be due to the shorter length of service of Japanese middle-aged women workers. The distributions just cited indicate that there are more women in the over-30 age group in the labor force in Japan, and also that there are fewer women workers with ten or more years of experience than in the EC countries. Since the principal way of developing

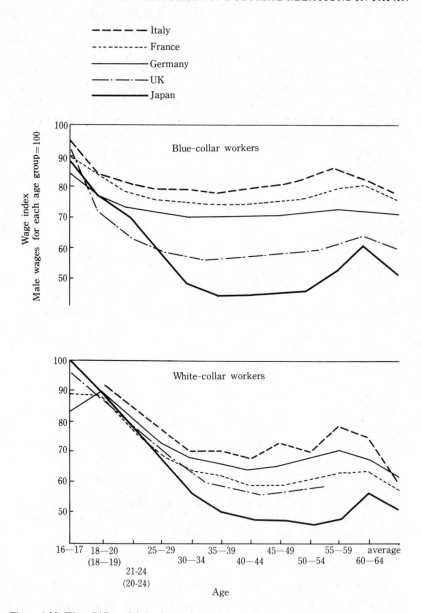

Figure 4.20. Wage Differentials by Sex and Age, Manufacturing Industries: Japan, 1976, Italy, France, and Germany, 1972; and the United Kingdom, 1975. Figures in parentheses refer to the Japanese age classification. The U.K. figures are for all industries. *Source*: For Japan, CKKT 1976; for the EC countries, SEI 1972; for the United Kingdom, NES 1975.

skills in Japan is on-the-job training, it follows that a shorter length of service would result in lower wages.

Another contributing factor might be the age–wage profiles of Japanese male workers, which have a more positive slope in middle age than do those of their European counterparts. These profiles are the product of the widespread adoption of the internal-promotion system for male workers, which emphasizes length of service. Thus we can say that the important role of length of service in skill development, eventual promotion, and wages leads to a widening of the differential between male and female wages when workers reach middle age. The shorter length of service of Japanese women workers limits their ability to acquire skills, while the longer service of male workers affords them more opportunities.

Notes

1 These workers are called *shagaikō*, which literally means "workers outside the firm." This does not imply that they actually work at some place other than at the plant of the larger corporation, but rather that they do not have a *direct* employment relationship with that corporation. These workers are employees of a small firm that contracts to supply labor to the larger enterprise. "Outside workers" are found most frequently at new plants of large corporations.

2 The "Lewis Model" differentiates two stages in economic development; the one with "unlimited supply of labor" where the wages of less-skilled workers cannot increase, and the other with "limited supply of labor" where the wages of less-skilled workers tend to increase with a greater speed than that of the skilled. It is crucial, therefore, to examine wage differentials. This concept is based on a famous paper by W. A. Lewis, "Economic Development with Unlimited Supplies of Labour," *Manchester School of Economics and Social Studies*, May 1954, 22:139–191. In application to Japan, Minami's 1968 and 1971a, 1971b, studies are representative of the majority opinion; Taira (1970) denies that there has been an "unlimited supply of labor" in modern Japan.

A Theory of Enterprise Unionism

Enterprise Unions: Company Union or Independent Agent?

The purpose of this chapter is to provide non-Japanese audiences with a more objective and integrated interpretation of Japanese enterprise unionism than has been previously available in Western-language studies. Enterprise unionism has attracted increasing attention from foreigners who see it as an important contributor to the remarkable economic growth of Japan following World War II, particularly between 1955 and 1974. After the 1973 oil crisis, Japan, like other industrialized economies, faced difficulties that seemed almost insurmountable because of her heavy dependence on imported energy and other resources. However, Japan managed to weather the difficult situation and to find a way out of it, and enterprise unionism was credited with facilitating the adjustment of the Japanese economy to changing circumstances. Moreover, as the competitive strength of Japanese industry in international markets increased, and as Japan seemed to be gaining more than its due share, some criticism of enterprise unionism began to emerge; that is, some foreign observers of Japanese industrial relations began to question whether enterprise unions were really bona fide unions, or, more bluntly, whether they were not what Americans would call "company unions." A 1977 report of the Organization for Economic Cooperation and Development (OECD), which in general speaks favorably of enterprise unionism as one of the three pillars of the Japanese industrial relations system, describes it somewhat indecisively as follows:

> In Western eyes an enterprise union tends to be suspect, as likely to be too dependent on management. But the Japanese enterprise union owes its development not to employers but to historical chance and to the life-time employment system, which led workers to identify with their working group and to lack interest in what happened in other enterprises. Even though union officials normally remain employees of the enterprise throughout their terms of office (and have a good chance of promotion within the enterprise), the Japanese enterprise union could not be said to be dominated by management. (pp. 22–23)

The report does not explain how the union's dependence on management and union officers' retention of their employee status can be congruent with freedom from domination by management.

Walter Galenson (1976, pp. 630–34) is more frank and sharp in his criticism of Japan's enterprise unionism. For him, the enterprise union is a primitive form of workers' organization, still in the process of becoming a "multi-employer union 'proper'." Because it is not a fully developed workers' organization, the enterprise union has "serious drawbacks in economic power" arising from its submissiveness to management control, which is inevitable because of the lack of professional leadership at the local union level.

This criticism of enterprise unionism has also been quite prevalent among Japanese scholars as well as the unionists themselves. It can hardly be denied that the behavior of at least a considerable number of Japanese enterprise unions closely resembles that of company unions. Also, one can easily point out many defects and weaknesses associated with enterprise unionism which are not shared by unions in other industrialized countries.

With due regard to all these reservations, however, in this chapter we attempt to provide a better and more realistic understanding of enterprise unionism. Our analysis is based on the following central theses: (1) Enterprise unionism is a legitimate form of workers' organization in Japan and it is the one of Japanese workers' own choosing. For the overwhelming majority of Japanese workers, alternative forms of organization are neither acceptable nor workable. (2) Enterprise unions certainly are vulnerable to infringing maneuvers by employers. On the whole, however, they have been successful in maintaining their independence and autonomy in representing the interests of employees; they are bona fide unions, not company unions. (3) In view of their relatively short history, their achievements have been very significant, and their record cannot be evaluated as poor when compared with that of unions in Western countries. (4) Japanese enterprise unionism will remain viable in the forseeable future. However, the unions will have to face serious challenges which may impel them to adjust by moving toward a more consolidated structure for the Japanese labor movement as a whole.

Characteristics of Enterprise Unions

Enterprise unions have the following characteristics: (1) Membership is limited to the regular employees of a particular enterprise. Other workers not regularly employed in the same plant or firm (temporary and part-time workers) are not eligible for membership. (2) In general, both blue- and white-collar workers are organized in a single union. (3) Union officers are elected from among the regular employees of the enterprise, and during their tenure in office, they usually retain their employee status but are paid by the union. (4) About 72 percent of the enterprise unions are affiliated with some type of federation outside the enterprise, but since most of these federations are loosely organized national industrial unions, sovereignty is retained almost exclusively at the local enterprise-union level.

Solomon B. Levine (1958) rightly characterized the enterprise union as follows:

In appearance, the enterprise union resembles the local of an industrial union, or an "intermediate" organization like the Ford or General Motors departments of the United Automobile Workers in the United States. However, the similarity ends about there. The essential distinction between the enterprise union and the local industrial union is that the former is a unit in and of itself; it is not merely an administrative component of a national union nor is it simply an "inside" independent company-wide union. (pp. 90–91).

As Levine notes, enterprise unions do resemble most locals of industrial unions in the United States. Their notable common characteristics are: (1) the unions are organized at local plants; (2) there are few professional union functionaries at this level; and (3) collective bargaining is normally conducted between a union or unions and a particular firm or one of its plants.

There are, however, some basic differences between locals of American industrial unions and Japanese enterprise unions: (1) Although most of the latter are affiliated with industry-wide federations of enterprise unions, the power or authority of the federation to control or regulate constituent unions is quite limited. For example, enterprise unions, as a rule, have complete autonomy to make decisions: they may change their constitutions, elect their own officers, determine the amount of union dues, and call or terminate strikes. (2) Although various categories of employees, blue- and white-collar alike, usually join together in a single enterprise union, there are almost no arrangements for sectional representation, such as by "bargaining units," within a union's organization. (3) In American industrial unions, many of the local agreements are the result of local collective bargaining within the framework of a national or master agreement negotiated between a national union or its intermediate organization and the respective corporations in an industry. Any such national agreement involving a Japanese union federation and a company is rare. According to a Ministry of Labor survey in 1974 (Chūō Rōdō Iinkai, Jimukyoku 1974a), officials of a higher organization participate in the collective bargaining of only 5 percent (72 unions) of the 1,362 unions surveyed. The percentage declines as the size of the local union increases; the larger the enterprise union, the greater the degree of its autonomy in all its activities, including collective bargaining.

Japanese enterprise unions bear a close resemblance to another type of workers' organization within a plant—the works councils in some Western countries. Perhaps West Germany's works councils (Betriebsräte) would be the best example. One important function that enterprise unions and the Betriebsräte in West Germany have in common is so-called joint consultation. Most enterprise unions engage in joint consultation with their respective managements apart from collective bargaining.[1]

The joint consultation system in Japan serves mainly as a channel for management to inform and consult with labor about the current business status of the enterprise to which they both belong, any problems and their possible solutions, management programs or plans for future investment, plant location or relocation, manpower adjustments required by the introduction of a new technology, and the possible impact of such technologies on employment and working conditions. Employees are usually very eager to have information on current business conditions of their enterprise and its future prospects, since their employment and income security derive from the viability and competitiveness of that enterprise. Japanese management in general is willing to provide such information to the union through the joint consultation system in order to secure labor–management cooperation and industrial peace.

Matters on which there is joint consultation are not confined to production and management questions. They include issues in the area of personnel administration, such as recruitment, placement, transfer, work schedules, training and retraining, vacations, and discipline. Social concerns—employees' welfare facilities and services, industrial safety, sanitary conditions, environmental problems, and the like—also are discussed. Furthermore, there often is joint consultation on such basic working conditions as wages, hours, holidays and vacations, discharge and other methods for reducing the workforce, and the compulsory retirement age, all of which are proper subjects for negotiation at the bargaining table. It is an established practice that as long as these issues are being discussed during joint consultation, unions will not exercise their right to strike over them. In this regard, the joint consultation systems of enterprise unions and the Betriebsräte are similar in the way they operate.

However, there are basic differences between the German Betriebsräte and enterprise unions in Japan. Unlike the Betriebsräte, enterprise unions are not organizations required by law, but are voluntary associations of workers and, as such, are labor unions. The Betriebsräte are financed by the employers, but an enterprise union is financially independent. In addition, the Betriebsräte handle intraplant issues that are not covered in collective bargaining conducted outside the enterprise by an industrial union and a regional employers' organization; an enterprise union, in contrast, bargains by and for itself. While the Betriebsräte have no right to strike, the enterprise union is free to strike, if necessary, or to use other job actions in an effort to resolve disputes with an employer.

The characteristics of enterprise unions as contrasted with unions and other worker organizations in some Western societies may be simply stated: The enterprise union in Japan, as a single organization of employees of a particular firm, functions in two ways. As the workers' organization it confronts and resists the employer in order to protect the employees' interests when they conflict with those of the employer. It also cooperates with the employer in promoting the mutual interests of the parties in a particular enterprise.

These two functions are, by definition, contradictory and might often lead enterprise unions in opposite directions. An enterprise union can be militant when there is a conflict of interest between the employer and employees. It can be docile when cooperation with management is the union's preferred policy alternative. Which direction an enterprise union tends to take may be determined by such variables as the ideology of the leadership, the reaction of the rank and file, the composition of the labor force in the enterprise in terms of occupation, sex, age, etc., the labor policy of the management, and the nature of issues involved in the labor–management dispute.

The Historical Facts

Before beginning an explanation of the rationale of enterprise unionism, it should be emphasized that the enterprise union has been the predominant form of workers' organization in Japan since the end of World War II; an overwhelming majority of organized workers are members of unions of this type. According to RKKC for 1975, for example, more than 90 percent of all unions in Japan were enterprise unions and 80 percent of all union members were affiliated with enterprise unions. As table 5.1 shows, these proportions have not varied much over the years.

Alternative forms of labor organizations, such as craft or industrial unions, have shown no notable increase as a proportion of the total number of

Table 5.1
Distribution of Unions and Their Membership among Different
Forms of Organization, 1964 and 1975[a]

Forms of Organization	1964		1975	
	No. of Unions	No. of Members	No. of Unions	No. of Members
All Forms	27,138	9,799,653	33,424	12,590,400
	(100.0)	(100.0)	(100.0)	(100.0)
Enterprise unions	25,414	8,320,665	31,294	10,382,225
	(93.6)	(84.9)	(93.6)	(82.5)
Craft unions	424	63,976	451	140,563
	(1.6)	(0.7)	(1.6)	(1.1)
Industrial unions	836	1,004,547	1,107	1,663,856
	(3.1)	(13.1)	(3.1)	(13.2)
Others[b]	464	410,465	571	403,756
	(1.7)	(1.7)	(1.7)	(3.2)

Source: RKKC 1964, 1975.
Note: Percentages of unions in parentheses. Unionized workers represent approximately 35% of total employed workers in 1964, and approximately 32% in 1975.

[a]This survey is conducted every year, but the distribution of unions and their membership among different forms of organization was covered by the survey only for selected years.

[b]"Others" include "general unions" which in Japan are unions of workers in small firms or establishments organized irrespective of the trade, industry, and enterprise to which they belong.

Japanese unions, although the increase in the number of members of industrial unions in recent years is not negligible. The fact that the overwhelming majority of organized workers in Japan choose enterprise unions indicates that this form of union organization has been what most workers want. No other than this simple interpretation is consistent with historical development.

The origins of the enterprise unions have been traced to different historical circumstances. Some Japanese scholars have claimed that they were prompted by the American Occupation, one of whose basic policies, pursuant to the Potsdam Declaration, was to encourage a free trade union movement in Japan. Occupation officials often did urge the Japanese government to promote the immediate formation of labor unions at both the national and local levels; the Japanese, in response, found that the easiest and quickest way of forming unions was to organize workers at the plant or enterprise level. Thus, it is true that the policy of the American Occupation contributed greatly to the rapid formation of unions immediately after the war. However, this theory fails to explain why Japanese workers, once organized at the plant or enterprise level, did not move further to form a more consolidated and centralized organization than an enterprise union despite motivation to follow the model of American-type industrial unionism. It also fails to explain why

Japanese workers continued to choose the enterprise union as the most suitable form of workers' organization after the Occupation ended.

Other scholars have insisted that enterprise unionism developed because it was the form most favored by the Communists, who played the leading role in the radical leftist labor movement right after the war (Kawada 1973, pp. 227–28). They base their theory on two factors: not only did enterprise unionism conform to the principle of union organization advocated by the World Federation of Trade Unions—that is, "one single union in one plant"— but it also would counter and perhaps eliminate the power of prewar right-wing union leaders whose stronghold was in unions outside of enterprises. However, in view of the vastly decreased influence of the Communists in the Japanese union movement since 1948, this argument can hardly be maintained.

Another explanation is that enterprise unionism may have been an outgrowth of Sangyō Hōkokukai (Sampō), a wartime patriotic labor organization designed by the government to ensure industrial peace and workers' dedication to the war effort. An enterprise union is essentially the same thing as Sampō, some labor specialists insist, because both organizations consist of employees of a particular enterprise created by a directive of the highest authority—the national government in Sampō's case and the Supreme Commander for Allied Powers (SCAP) in the case of enterprise unions. It cannot be denied that the legacy of Sampō is noticeable in the structure of enterprise unions as well as in the fact that joining an enterprise union is not a voluntary act for many Japanese workers. However, this explanation also is not entirely adequate, since it grossly devaluates the spontaneity of the impulse that led Japanese workers to form and maintain their unions.

One might still argue that at least one of the reasons that enterprise unions have been chosen by the overwhelming majority of Japanese unionists is that it is the only form that employers would tolerate. It is true that Japanese employers in general have opposed the intrusion of "outsiders" into their enterprises or plants and have favored an enterprise union formed by their own employees exclusively. Some leaders of employers' organizations openly appraise enterprise unionism as a real asset of the Japanese industrial relations system. It is also true that Japanese workers, by forming an enterprise union rather than one of any other type, could lessen or even avoid employer resistance, which otherwise might be fierce and possibly destructive. However, this interpretation also fails to explain why it is that even groups of militant workers imbued with radical leftist ideologies choose the enterprise union as the most efficient type of organization to ensure membership solidarity. In addition, workers are legally protected in their right to form organizations of their own choosing, and it is an unfair labor practice, under the Trade Union Law, for an employer to interfere; thus workers are assured that they may choose any form of organization they wish—even one opposed by their employer. The question remains: If Japanese workers have a legally protected right to choose any type of organization, why do not the overwhelming majority make use of it?

Historical fact that refutes the above-cited explanations is that enterprise unionism emerged not after World War II, but in the period between World Wars I and II. In the 1920s there was a tendency among workers in large firms to organize unions within the confines of the particular enterprise or establishment where they were employed (Komatsu 1971). For example, unions were formed in such state-owned enterprises as arsenals, naval shipyards, the tobacco monopoly, and municipal street railways as well as in large private firms in the mining, steel, machinery, engineering, shipbuilding, copper refining, and textile industries and in electricity and city gas supply. Unlike their postwar counterparts, these prewar enterprise unions consisted exclusively of blue-collar workers. The difference in rewards and status between blue- and white-collar workers at that time was too great for the two categories of workers to be organized in a single union.

The explanation of why these blue-collar workers tended to organize themselves on the basis of their enterprise or establishment is that the large firms already had developed a complex internal labor market with an industrial reward system that was the prototype of what is called the nenkō system in postwar Japan. Organizations of this type were called "vertical unions," in contrast to "horizontal unions," where membership was not limited to employees of a particular employer. The horizontal unions found it difficult to intrude into the large firms and to organize the employees. It is estimated that in the early 1930s nearly half of all union members were in vertical enterprise unions; peak total membership was about 420,000. However, most of them were forced to dissolve before World War II and were reorganized into Sampō. After the war, they revived quickly as enterprise unions.

The Rationale of Enterprise Unionism

Internal Labor Markets of Large Enterprises

Why have enterprise unions persisted as the predominant form of labor organization in Japan? Although foreign scholars well versed in Japanese industrial relations have shown a great deal of interest in the breadth as well as the function of enterprise unions, they have not attempted to explain the phenomenon.

For most of them, the enterprise union is accepted either as given or as something that could be construed as a legacy of a typically Japanese culture. Even Robert E. Cole (1971a, pp. 227-28), a keen observer of the actual operation of enterprise unions at the workplace, listed only a few factors which may have contributed to the development of this particular form of labor organization in Japan: the impact of the labor policy of the Occupation Forces, the economic instability of workers in the period right after the war, the legacy of the wartime Sampō, and the cultural legacy of the corporate group.[2] Ronald Dore (1973), who also made a penetrating study of the Japanese industrial relations system at the factory level and whose observations of enterprise unionism are extremely perceptive, attempts to rationalize enterprise unions as follows:

Given the strength of enterprise consciousness and the absence of a market-based wage system, it was inevitable that when powerful unions developed they have been enterprise unions. They played a powerful role in entrenching the system (a) by being able to demand and fight for security of employment, and (b) by their very existence reinforcing enterprise consciousness. (p.400)

However, as pointed out elsewhere, the enterprise-union form is not confined to powerful unions, but is adopted by almost all unions regardless of strength. Also, the enterprise consciousness of employees and the "absence of market-based wages" certainly are contributing factors, but they alone do not provide an adequate answer.

It is to be expected that foreign observers would find it difficult to explain enterprise unionism. Even in Japanese academic circles, there is no established and universally accepted theory. However, a growing number of scholars are trying to find the basic rationale of enterprise unionism in the employment practices already described, developed particularly among large enterprises: long-term employment (often misnamed "lifetime employment"); in-plant training; an industrial reward system based largely on seniority; and employee welfare plans financed by the respective enterprises. Therefore, in their effort to explain enterprise unionism, these scholars are applying and further developing the "internal labor market" hypothesis.[3]

Since employment practices of the type described above are almost universal in the large firms, an enterprise union becomes the logical form of organization for Japanese workers because they find their common interests as industrial workers within a particular enterprise. Their basic conditions of employment—wages, working hours, fringe benefits, welfare facilities, and employment security—tend to be more or less determined by the industrial characteristics of a particular enterprise, such as technology, the structure and composition of the labor force, the skills required of employees, an in-plant training system, the market and budgetary situation, the personnel policies of management, etc. Under such circumstances, the workers' feelings of solidarity based on their common interests are shared first and foremost with the colleagues with whom they work at the shop-floor, plant, and enterprise levels.

Thus, it is to be expected that Japanese workers would organize an enterprise union to represent them and to protect their primary common interests. For them, it is only the enterprise union that they are willing to support because it is the only one in which they have confidence and on which they are willing to rely. Japanese workers feel that outsiders, such as professional union leaders, do not have sufficient knowledge and experience to handle their concerns in structured internal labor markets. They do not question the functional effectiveness of enterprise unions in dealing with such matters as the wage level as well as the amount of the semiannual bonuses relative to the ability of the enterprise to pay, the internal wage structure, the so-called *chingin taikei* (factors that comprise the total amount of wages), overtime rates, shift allowances, welfare facilities, industrial safety and sanitary conditions, transfer, discharge, etc., all of which are determined specifically by the actual working conditions and practices at the level of the enterprise, plant, and shop. In spite of some of the deficiencies of enterprise unions, most Japanese workers do not choose an alternative form of unionism.

Historical and Cultural Factors

The internal labor market hypothesis proposed above as an explanation of enterprise unionism may give rise to two questions: (1) Other countries also have large firms with internal labor markets. Why don't they have enterprise unions? (2) Why do Japanese workers in medium-sized and small enterprises, where internal labor markets are much less structured than in the large enterprises, also tend to organize themselves primarily into enterprise unions?

The internal labor market hypothesis does not provide a complete rationale for enterprise unionism in Japan. Historical and cultural factors also must be taken into account. As an answer to the first question, it should be pointed out that although Japan was a latecomer among industrialized nations, internal labor markets had developed within her large enterprises, including government establishments, long before a free labor union movement gained legitimacy and strength. In other advanced countries, this seems not to have been the case, although the evolutionary course of both industrialization and the labor movement has varied. In countries where traditional craft or industrial unionism was firmly established, it was apparently difficult to adapt the union structures to cope with the labor problems that arise with the internalization of labor markets. In some countries, the emphasis in collective bargaining has shifted from the national or industry level to the enterprise or shop level in recent years, as works councils and other arrangements for workers' participation in management have developed. These changes may well be seen as a process for adjusting the organizational structures of unions to the internalization of labor markets. In Japan, the lack of a tradition of craft or industrial unions contributed to the development of enterprise unionism.

The cultural factor which led the Japanese workers to organize themselves into enterprise unions is their "enterprise consciousness," which Dore (1973) rightly emphasizes. As he explains, for most Japanese workers employed in large enterprises, the firm to which they belong is not simply a place where they work for money, but is a community with which they strongly identify. It is at their workplace that they communicate and feel solidarity with each other, and these two factors serve as the natural basis for their organization. For most Japanese workers, trades, occupations, or living quarters are not a foundation on which a stable union organization could develop.

Enterprise Unions in Medium-Sized and Small Enterprises

The reasons that workers in medium-sized and small enterprises also tend to organize themselves primarily into enterprise unions are similar to those that apply in large enterprises.

1. Some characteristically Japanese employment practices are found even among medium-sized and small firms. For example, long-term employment, in-plant training, seniority wages, fringe benefits, and employee welfare schemes that are enterprise-specific are shared in various degrees, so that the labor markets in these sectors are also more or less internalized. Inasmuch as this is particularly true of the medium-sized enterprises, workers tend to form associations primarily on the basis of the plant or enterprise where they work.

2. For workers in medium-sized and small enterprises, the workplace is where they feel the need for solidarity to protect their common interests as employees; the enterprise union appears to them as the easiest and most workable form of worker organization, provided that they can themselves supply the leadership and finances.

3. Because of the relatively short history of both Japanese industrialization and her labor movement, market-oriented unions, such as craft, industrial, and general unions, exist for only a very few occupations and industries. Despite the efforts of these industrial and general unions to organize workers in medium-sized and small enterprises, they have for the most part failed to maintain constant memberships. One of the factors that discourages workers in such firms from joining industrial or general unions is that these unions are strongly ideology-oriented, either leftist or rightist. Most workers prefer not to have their unions involved in ideological movements which may well lead to organizational strife and divisiveness; instead, they choose to form an enterprise union.

Other Forms of Union Organization in Japan

As table 5.1 shows, there are worker organizations other than enterprise unions in Japan. Although their share both in number of unions and in membership is far smaller than that of enterprise unions, they are far from insignificant. Among them, Kaiin (All Japan Seamen's Union) is the only Western-style industrial union as well as being one of the most powerful unions in Japan. Organized as early as 1920 as an industrial union, it has maintained this organizational form for several reasons, among them, that (1) seamen are trained not by particular enterprises, but by either a national institution or on the job aboard ship, and (2) sailors move frequently from ship to ship, so that their labor market is too open to be internalized. The shipping industry is the only one in Japan to have national, industry-wide bargaining. Other industrial unions are mostly local, catering, as a rule, to employees of medium-sized or small enterprises. Workers in a small firm find it difficult to form and maintain an enterprise union, because of their small numbers and high mobility.

Craft or occupational unions are composed mostly of workers with special skills—carpenters, plasterers, machine operators, and electricians in the construction industry, taxi and truck drivers, and so on. In the construction and transport industries, the employing firms usually are small in size and do not have in-plant training facilities. The common feature of workers in these fields is that their skills are developed either through traditional apprenticeships in the occupation, through public occupational training facilities, or through some individual effort to acquire the skill and knowledge necessary to pass the governmental examination and get the required licenses. Accordingly, their labor markets are external and their mobility is relatively high— thus the rationale for labor organizations not of the enterprise union form. However, these unions have grown very slowly; their high mortality rate keeps them in a minority position in the Japanese labor movement.

The Functional Characteristics of Enterprise Unionism

Are They Bona Fide Unions?

As mentioned earlier, some foreign observers suspect that Japanese enterprise unions are what Americans would call "company unions," or at least a primitive form of labor organization still in the process of becoming a multi-employer union proper, and suffering from deficiencies in economic power. We should first differentiate a weak union from a bona fide union: the latter may be weak, depending upon the yardstick by which its strength is measured. Nor can the bona fides of a union be arbitrarily linked to its form of organization.

The minimum requirement for a union to be "bona fide," we think, is for it to exist and function independently and autonomously in representing the interests of its members. Galenson (1976) denies that enterprise unions are independent and emphasizes their submissiveness to management or the employer, particularly because there are no professional union leaders at the local level. It is true that even full-time union officials, who are on the union's payroll, retain their employee status while they hold union offices; their term of office is usually one or two years, and their turnover rate as officers seems to be rather high, although no comparable data are available for other countries. It is also true that because officers are elected from employee ranks—quite often from among workers holding lower supervisory positions—there are cases where management tries to exert some influence on the union elections, although legally such interference is an unfair labor practice, strictly forbidden by the Trade Union Law. Thus enterprise unions in general are more susceptible and vulnerable to management's interference than are other forms of unions, as Galenson rightly points out.

However, the enterprise union is not the only example of a union organization lacking professional leadership. Locals of American industrial unions rarely have professional leaders, in the strict sense of the word. Also, shop stewards and committeemen in England and the United States and the *Vertrauensleute* in West Germany are not professional union functionaries. They retain their employee status, and in many cases they are even paid by management while they are on union business. If these local unions in other countries are considered to be independent, why should the case not be the same for enterprise unions?

As a matter of fact, most enterprise unions scrupulously maintain their autonomy by means of certain characteristics in their government and administration. The following contrasts can be cited between enterprise unions in Japan and unions in the United States.

First, the executive officers of Japanese enterprise unions have far less discretion in decision-making than their American counterparts, for almost without exception, their authority and power are limited by the union constitution. The president and secretary-treasurer are just two more members of the executive committee, and in the Japanese union world it would be out of the question for the president, in his capacity as an executive officer, to preside at the union convention, which is the highest legislative body of the organization. Executive officers usually find themselves in a kind of defensive position at the convention.

Second, in large unions there are two levels at which legislative action is taken—at an annual union convention and through an interim legislative body, the name of which varies from union to union; it can be called the central committee, the delegates' meeting, or the secretary's meeting. Most of the latter groups meet every two or three months. These legislative bodies and their frequent meetings are designed to ensure union members' control of their executives and functionaries, very often at the sacrifice of administrative efficiency (see chapter 6).

Third, as Dore (1973) rightly states, more effective vigilance by the rank and file is possible in enterprise unions than in national or industrial unions in other countries, because the union officials are not as far removed from the rank-and-file members and are in close communication with them.[4]

Thus, the claim that the enterprise union is not bona fide cannot easily be justified by its structural characteristics.

The Functional Weakness of Enterprise Unions

Here we apply another touchstone of union "authenticity." Do enterprise unions pursue the legitimate purposes of bona fide unions as fully as their constituencies expect? Do they raise wages as much, shorten the workweek as much, or improve the job security of members as much as the members might wish?

Before undertaking any cross-national comparison of union achievements—both at certain times and in different areas—we must consider the historical development, surrounding political, economic, social, and cultural constraints, and particular policy goals that labor movements in the respective countries have established in trying to meet the expectations of workers. Undoubtedly, the Japanese labor movement set a high priority on the abolition of status discrimination among the different categories of employees with regard to wages and employment security.

In the "status society" of prewar Japan with its legacy of feudalism, blue-collar workers as well as low-grade and nonelite white-collar workers were placed in a subordinate position in the employee hierarchy of an enterprise. These workers were bitter about such discriminatory treatment, so that it became one of the most popular and enthusiastically promoted targets of the union movement right after the war to demand that status discrimination be abolished; the slogan was "democratization of management." That goal was achieved. The status system with its traditional discriminative titles such as *shokuin* (salaried white-collar) and *kōin* (daily-paid blue-collar) was abolished; differentials among employees of different status and category for wages, fringe benefits, and other welfare facilities, were drastically narrowed. For example, unions successfully demanded semiannual bonuses for every regular employee, irrespective of category. In prewar days, blue-collar and low-status white-collar workers did receive a lump sum of money twice a year in addition to their regular pay, but this payment was totally different from the semiannual bonuses (a kind of profit-sharing) that high-status white-collar employees with advanced educational backgrounds received as one of their privileges. More important is the fact that the wage differentials between blue- and white-collar workers as well as between different categories of the latter have been remarkably narrowed by the unions' wage policy in collective bargaining. Japan is one industrial society where blue-collar workers have widely achieved salary status.[5]

The same tendencies exist with regard to fringe benefits and welfare services, such as retirement allowances, company housing, recreational facilities, mess-halls, etc. In Japanese plants, for instance, one can observe blue- and white-collar workers and management people lunching together at the factory mess-hall and also wearing the same kind of work-clothes, supplied by the company. Such achievements owe much to the enterprise unions with their strong egalitarian orientation (Shirai and Shimada 1978).

Wage increases attained by *shuntō*, the united drive for higher wages, or "Spring Offensive," during the ten years prior to 1975 were roughly twice the size of those won by union workers in other advanced countries; as table 5.2 shows, wage differentials between Japan and other selected countries have narrowed, and in some cases Japan's hourly wage rate is now higher. Needless to say, the rapid and continuous wage increases cannot be attributed only to union strength; an increasingly tight labor market as well as the continuous growth of productivity also had their effects on wage levels. It is quite difficult to identify how much of the wage increase was the result of

Table 5.2

Comparison of Nominal Wages: Blue-Collar Hourly Rate
in Manufacturing Industries, 1960–75

Wage Rate[a]	Japan	U.S.	U.K.	West Germany	France
1960					
Wage rate	0.26	2.26	0.79	0.63	0.43
Differential	100	869	304	242	165
1965					
Wage rate	0.45	2.61	1.01	1.03	0.61
Differential	100	580	224	229	136
1970					
Wage rate	0.94	3.36	1.30	1.63	0.84
Differential	100	357	138	173	89
1975					
Wage rate	2.84	4.80	2.57	3.70	2.19
Differential	100	169	90	130	77

Sources: For Japan, MKTC; for United Kingdom, Great Britain, Department of Employment *Gazette*; for United States, W. Germany, and France, ILO Yearbook, for the years selected.
Note: The exchange rate to the U.S. dollar is that at the end of every year. The wage rate in the United Kingdom is for October in 1960, 1965, and 1970, but for April 1975.
[a]Rate is in U.S. dollar equivalent.

union strength, but at least one cannot deny that the unions' united drives have provided the initiative for general wage increases and have contributed to the diffusion and standardization of the annual increases. It is also true that the wage increases by the Spring Offensive varied markedly, both in amount and in rate (see table 5.3), showing the flexibility of enterprise unionism to adapt to a changed economic environment. The reason for this flexibility will be discussed later.

As for the average number of hours worked weekly in manufacturing industries, Japan is now placed among countries with the shortest workweek, according to International Labor Office statistics. Notable is the fact that the decline in the number of hours worked and the rate of decrease between 1965 and 1975 were most remarkable for Japan as compared with other countries, as table 5.4 shows, although after 1975 the number of hours worked weekly increased again, to 40.2 in 1976, to 40.3 in 1977, to 40.6 in 1978, and to 42.7 in 1979. Again, the reduction in the length of the workweek cannot be attributed only to the unions' demand and their strength. Rather, it should be pointed out that the achievements of the Japanese labor movement in terms of the five-day week as well as of extended paid vacations are poorer than those achieved by unions in other industrialized countries. These factors explain in part why the total annual hours of work of Japanese workers are far greater—about 200 more—than those of workers in other highly industrialized Western countries. In 1977, only 23.1 percent of all workers surveyed by the Ministry of Labor regularly enjoyed a five-day workweek, although another 48.8 percent had a five-day week one to three times a month. As for paid vacations, few collective agreements gave workers longer vacations than the legal minimum requirement of 20 days for those with 15 years or more of service. As a matter of fact, Japanese workers in general are less concerned about fewer hours and longer vacations than about wages. Leisure is still not a value for the overwhelming majority of them, except for the younger generations. Most adult male workers would not take the full vacation to which they are entitled, despite the urging of their unions to do so. This attitude toward leisure is due in part to the traditional work-oriented value system, but largely to the high cost of leisure, the poor condition of housing in excessively overpopulated urban areas, the needs of their children for higher education, and insufficient manning at the workplace.

For fringe benefits and social security, it is difficult to find a common yardstick to calculate and compare what various countries have attained so far. An accurate evaluation for each country cannot be made without considering the historical development of relevant systems and practices, the institutional design of social security plans, the age composition of the population and labor force, and legal and supplemental arrangements which as a whole

Table 5.3
Negotiated Wage Increases in Shuntō, Japanese Labor's
Spring Offensive: 1956–78

Year	Wage Increase (¥)	Wage Increase Rate (%)	Coefficient of Variation	Rate of Productivity Increase in Manufacturing Industries (%)
1956	1,063	6.3	0.29	13.9
1957	1,518	8.6	0.20	7.2
1958	1,050	5.6	0.29	-0.4
1959	1,281	6.5	0.20	13.1
1960	1,792	8.7	0.17	12.7
1961	2,970	13.8	0.14	10.2
1962	2,515	10.7	0.13	2.9
1963	2,237	9.1	0.16	9.7
1964	3,305	12.4	0.10	12.2
1965	3,150	10.6	0.16	3.5
1966	3,403	10.6	0.12	13.0
1967	4,371	12.5	0.07	16.5
1968	5,296	13.6	0.07	13.8
1969	6,865	15.8	0.07	13.6
1970	9,166	18.5	0.06	10.4
1971	9,727	16.9	0.07	4.4
1972	10,138	15.3	0.08	11.1
1973	15,159	20.1	0.05	17.5
1974	28,981	32.9	0.07	-0.5
1975	15,279	13.1	0.16	-3.9
1976	11,596	8.8	0.10	12.3
1977	12,536	8.8	0.07	5.1
1978	9,218	5.9	.20	8.0
1979	9,959	6.0	0.10	12.0
1980	11,679	6.7	0.06	NA

Sources: For the rate of productivity: Surveys conducted by the Nihon Seisansei Hombu, Labor Division. For wage increases, their rate, and coefficients: see Rōdōshō 1956–78, 1979a, 1980.
Note: Figures of 1955–59 are averages of 72–84 major private firms; for 1960–73 they are unweighted averages of 157–63 major private firms; while for 1974–76 they are unweighted averages of 265 major private firms.
   The rate of wage increase is the percentage of the average negotiated monthly wage increase per worker relative to the average monthly regular wage just prior to the wage negotiations.
   The coefficient of variation used here is defined as: (wage increase of a firm at the third quartile − wage increase of a firm at the first quartile) ÷ (median of wage increases).
   Since the announced negotiated wage increase for the iron and steel industry in 1973 was specifically for a worker aged 35 with 12 years of service, it may not be treated, rigorously speaking, on an equal basis with the average wage increase of various categories of workers in other industries. The average wage increase of all industries excluding the iron and steel industry in 1973 was ¥9,955, the rate of wage increase was 15.1 percent, and the coefficient of variation 0.11. NA: Data not available.

Table 5.4

Changes in Weekly Hours Worked in Manufacturing, 1965-79

Year	Japan	U.S.	U.K.	West Germany	France
1965	44.3	41.2	46.1	44.1	45.6
1966	44.5	41.4	45.0	43.7	45.9
1967	44.8	40.6	45.3	42.0	45.4
1968	44.5	40.7	45.8	43.0	45.3
1969	43.8	40.6	45.7	43.8	45.4
1970	43.2	39.8	44.9	43.8	44.8
1971	42.5	39.9	43.6	43.0	44.5
1972	42.3	40.6	44.1	42.7	44.0
1973	42.0	40.7	44.7	42.8	43.6
1974	40.0	40.0	44.0	41.9	42.9
1975	38.8	39.4	42.7	40.4	41.7
1976	40.2	40.0	43.5	41.4	41.6
1977	40.3	40.3	43.6	41.7	41.3
1978	40.6	40.7	44.2	41.6	41.1
1979	42.7	40.4	NA	41.9	41.3
Decreased hours 1965–75	5.5	1.8	3.4	3.7	3.9
Rate of decrease (%)	12.4	4.4	7.4	8.4	8.6

Source: ILO Yearbook.

Note: For the United States and West Germany, figures are weekly paid hours; for the United Kingdom, figures are for male workers only.

NA: Data not available.

contribute to the improvement of workers' welfare. This is not the place for attempting such an evaluation, but it might be useful to comment briefly on the cost of social security in Japan. The percentage of the national income devoted to social security expenses in Japan has long been less than that of other advanced countries. This is largely due to two factors: (1) the Japanese population as well as its labor force has been relatively young compared to other countries, and (2) the old-age-pension schemes of Japan have a shorter history than those of other advanced countries, so that disbursements by the system have been less. However, as the Japanese labor force ages, the number of pension recipients is showing a notable increase. Also, the average level of pensions has been improving remarkably since 1973. As a result of these recent changes, it is expected that the proportion of the national income devoted to pension disbursements and other social security expenses will rise in the near future.

With regard to the employment security of Japanese workers, there is a misleading stereotype of "lifetime employment," which implies that the Japanese employer would never discharge workers except in an emergency. This is, of course, an exaggeration. However, it is true that discharge is the last and most difficult decision for a Japanese employer to make when he has to remove redundant or undesirable workers. The American-type layoff is simply impossible for Japanese employers. This employer policy of retaining the workforce as far as possible is due partly to a wish to maintain the human capital accumulated through in-plant training and partly to a paternalistic philosophy, but in large measure it is prompted by the desire to avoid a bitter struggle with the enterprise union concerned. Japanese unions usually are moderate in such industrial actions as strikes and slowdowns in wage disputes, but a mass dismissal often precipitates an acrimonious dispute which sometimes leads to protracted work stoppages that might last for as long as a hundred days. There have been many examples of prolonged strikes in the postwar period, particularly in the late 1950s, when redundancy dismissal took place during the recurrent recessions following the Korean War, as well as during the so-called "energy revolution."

Unions fight against dismissals because employment security is taken for granted as a vested right of regular employees under a long-standing employment practice; thus a dismissal is a sort of betrayal of the employees' trust in management. In an enterprise community, distrust of the employer or of management is fatal to the maintenance of peaceful industrial relations in the long run, so that employers will try to avoid dismissals as far as possible, even at the sacrifice of profits. Enterprise unions, in turn, will cooperate in other methods of adjusting to redundancy, such as curtailment of overtime, reduction in the number of temporary workers, reduction of operations, attrition, and in-plant, interplant, or even interenterprise transfer. They also will be willing to accept the freezing of wage increases, postponement of periodic increments, reduction of the semiannual bonuses, and even wage cuts. If unions have to accept redundancy dismissals, as is often the case during a prolonged recession, unions resist the employer's arbitrary dismissal of certain workers, and in its place establish a system that includes inducing some workers to resign voluntarily, negotiating the number of workers that will be induced to resign, premium severance allowances, the employer's assistance in securing new employment for those workers who resign, and conditions of possible recall. Thus, enterprise unions try to protect the employment security of their members, although in a different way from that of unions in other industrialized countries.

Achieving Union Goals:
Enterprise Unions' Cooperativeness with Employers

According to some non-Japanese observers, Japanese unions rarely strike, and the strikes that do occur usually are of short duration. Also, it is claimed that the strikes by Japanese unions are not intended to damage employers, but just to show the workers' determination to struggle or to embarrass the

Table 5.5
Work Stoppages and Time Lost Due to Industrial Disputes
in Selected Countries, 1958–77

	Canada[a]	France	West Germany[b]	Italy[c]	Japan[d]	Sweden	U.K.[e]	U.S.[f]
Number of industrial disputes								
1958	259	954	NA	1,756	903	10	2,629	3,694
1962	311	1,884	NA	3,532	1,299	10	2,449	3,614
1966	617	1,711	NA	2,387	1,252	26	1,937	4,405
1970	542	3,319	NA	4,162	2,260	134	3,906	5,716
1974	1,216	3,381	NA	5,174	5,211	85	2,922	6,074
1977	803	3,302	NA	3,308	1,712	35	2,703	5,506
Workers involved[g] (in thousands)								
1958	111	1,112	203	1,147	1,279	0.1	524	2,060
1962	74	1,472	79	2,652	1,518	3.5	4,423	1,230
1966	411	3,341	196	1,887	1,132	29.4	544	1,960
1970	262	1,160	184	3,721	1,720	26.7	1,801	3,305
1974	592	1,564	250	7,824	3,621	17.5	1,626	2,778
1977	218	1,920	334	13,803	692	13.1	1,166	2,040
Working days lost (in thousands)								
1958	2,817	1,138	782	2,606	6,052	15	3,462	23,900
1962	1,418	1,901	451	19,045	5,400	5	5,798	18,600
1966	5,178	2,524	27	14,474	2,742	352	2,398	25,400
1970	6,540	1,742	93	20,887	3,915	16	10,980	66,414
1974	9,255	3,380	1,051	19,466	9,603	58	14,750	48,045
1977	3,308	3,666	24	16,566	1,518	87	10,143	35,822

management. Therefore, they are called "demonstrative strikes" (OECD 1977, pp. 25–26).

It is not correct, however, to conclude that Japanese unions rarely strike. Table 5.5 shows that the number of industrial disputes in Japan is as great as it is in France, although the employed labor force is much larger in the former. In addition, the total number of Japanese industrial disputes does not include strikes of less than four hours' duration, which occur quite often. It is true that most strikes by Japanese unions are short as compared with those in the United States, Canada, England, and Australia. However, a short strike is not peculiar only to Japan. If we estimate the average duration of strikes in each country by dividing the number of working days lost by the number of workers involved, we find from the last section of table 5.5 that strikes in France, Germany, Sweden, and Italy are also, in general, of short duration, and long strikes are confined largely to those countries just mentioned (although Australia is not included in the table).

A distinctive feature of the mentality of Japanese unionists, both leaders and the rank and file, which distinguishes strikes by Japanese enterprise

Table 5.5 (continued)
Work Stoppages and Time Lost Due to Industrial Disputes
in Selected Countries, 1958–77

	Canada[a]	France	West Germany[b]	Italy[c]	Japan[d]	Sweden	U.K.[e]	U.S.[f]
Days lost per thousand employees[h]								
1958	631	96	44	278	293	6[d]	163	471
1962	285	151	22	1,800	214	2	258	338
1966	863	180	1	1,307	93	112	103	407
1970	950	114	4	1,560	120	48	488	956
1974	1,135	204	49	1,285	270	17	659	629
1977	NA	NA	NA	NA	NA	NA	NA	NA
Average duration of work stoppage (working days)								
1958	25.4	1.0	3.9	2.3	4.7	150.0	6.6	11.6
1962	19.2	1.3	5.7	7.2	3.6	1.4	1.3	15.1
1966	12.6	0.8	0.1	7.7	2.4	12.0	4.4	13.0
1970	25.0	1.5	0.5	5.6	2.3	5.8	6.1	20.1
1974	15.6	2.2	4.2	2.5	2.6	3.3	9.1	17.3
1977	15.2	1.9	0.7	1.2	2.2	6.6	8.7	17.5

Sources: ILO Yearbook and national publications; U.S. Department of Labor, Bureau of Labor Statistics, 1978.
NA: Data not available.
[a]Figures exclude disputes in which the time lost is less than 10 man-days, and also workers indirectly affected.
[b]Excludes the Saar for 1955–56 and includes West Berlin beginning 1961. Excludes disputes lasting less than one day, except those involving a loss of more than 100 working days.
[c]Excludes strikes in the agriculture sector, political strikes, and workers indirectly affected.
[d]Excludes workers indirectly affected and disputes lasting less than four hours.
[e]Excludes disputes (a) not connected with terms of employment or conditions of labor, and (b) involving fewer than 10 workers or lasting less than one day, unless a loss of more than 100 working days is involved.
[f]The number of stoppages and workers relates to those stoppages beginning in the year. It excludes disputes involving fewer than six workers and those lasting less than one full day or shift.
[g]Workers are counted more than once if they were involved in more than one stoppage during the year.
[h]Per thousand persons with paid hours in nonagricultural industries. Days lost include all stoppages in effect.

unions from those by their counterparts in other advanced countries, is that Japanese unionists are really hesitant to cause any severe damage to the enterprise to which they belong. This is not because of their submissiveness to their employer or to management, but because of their identification with, or a sense of belonging to, their enterprise. If a worker serves a particular enterprise for many years during which he has good prospects for improving his wages, fringe benefits, skills, position, and status, it is quite understandable that he would acquire an interest in and concern about the enterprise; thus both employer and employee come to share a common desire to maintain the enterprise and to keep it prospering as much as possible. The enterprise becomes a kind of community to which employees tend to commit themselves. Under the highly structured internal labor market system in Japan, with its institutional devices for consolidation, such as the nenkō system or what Dore (1971) calls "welfare corporatism," workers' basic interests, particularly in their employment, income security, and opportunities to advance, depend critically on the prosperity of the firm to which they "belong." A strike-minded and militant union leader cannot ignore or override this feeling among union members. If he does and the result is a prolonged strike that causes or threatens to cause severe damage to the enterprise, the consequence may well be the breakup of the union, followed by the formation of a new separate union—called a "second union."[6] This is one of the organizational weaknesses that makes an enterprise union vulnerable to a prolonged strike; it is the reason that the union sometimes appears to be much too cooperative with management.

Another factor that explains why enterprise unions cooperate with management is the process by which managerial elites are formed, their power structure, and a philosophy of personnel management that is particularly characteristic of large corporations in postwar Japan. Largely because of the political and economic reforms effectuated after World War II, such as the dissolution of the zaibatsu (the large industrial and financial complexes) and the dispersion of shareholding, Japan became an industrial society in which the separation of management from the ownership of corporations advanced tremendously. The controlling power of shareholders over managers became almost nominal or ceremonial, which gave the managements an extensive, almost untrammeled, decision-making power in running the businesses. The overwhelming proportion of borrowed capital to total capital—around 85 percent on the average in 1977—resulting from the rapid expansion of business operations during the period of high economic growth helped to entrench the authority and power of management against the control of shareholders.

More significant is the fact that the top executives such as the president, vice-president (unlike their counterparts in the United States, there are only two or three vice-presidents in large Japanese corporations), and other full-time members of the board of directors, with few exceptions, have risen to their high positions through internal promotion within their corporations. A 1977 survey by Keizai Dōyūkai (Japanese Committee for Economic Development), one of the leading national associations of managers, disclosed that out of 2,636 full-time directors surveyed 2,398 (91.0 percent) were named to their positions through internal promotion, while only 64 (2.4 percent) of the full-time directors were owners or shareholders of the firms.

Since the top executives are generally promoted from among rank-and-file employees of the firm, it is to be expected that they once were members of the enterprise union. The survey reveals that out of 134 firms surveyed, 46 have directors who have had experience as an official of the firm's enterprise union. It is highly possible that persons who demonstrate ability and leadership as officers of the enterprise union may be promoted later to high-ranking managerial positions. In such a context, the relationship between the enterprise union and the management of a particular firm would be more cooperative than otherwise.

Even without the experience of being a union member, high-ranking managers tend to regard the rank-and-file employees not as wage earners with conflicting interests, but as one-time or junior colleagues in the same enterprise community with a common interest in the survival and prosperity of that enterprise.

Even if a national industrial federation of enterprise unions comes to play a more direct role in collective bargaining than at present, it seems quite unlikely that the unions' cooperative attitudes toward managements would change radically, since the leaders of national industrial federations in the private sector are generally very sensitive to the need for Japanese industries to be competitive in overseas markets. The overpopulation in this small island country, where only 16 percent of the total land is arable, the unfortunate lack of natural resources, and thus the heavy dependence on imported energy, raw materials, and food to support and improve the welfare of the people make most union leaders—particularly in such basic exporting industries as steel, automobiles, and electrical machinery and appliances—acutely conscious of the competitiveness and productivity of their industries. Most of them believe that in the long run the employment security and improvement of working and living conditions of their members crucially depend on how their industry improves its position in changing world markets. Rank-and-file members usually share this way of thinking. The homogeneity of the Japanese people, the relatively high level of education among workers, the extensive availability of information about the national economy and related matters, and the good communications between management and workers are all factors which tend to make the unions' behavior moderate and cooperative rather than aggressive and discordant.

Also, these concerns may explain at least in part the difference in union behavior between the private and public sectors in Japan. Employees of public corporations, such as the National Railways, also share the feeling of identification with their enterprises, but they are in a position where they do not have to consider seriously the financial loss to the enterprise incurred in strikes or other industrial actions, because public corporations and national enterprises either are relatively free from competition in the market, as compared with private industries, or are able to enjoy continuing governmental financial support to keep them operating.

Enterprise Unionism and Its Future Prospects

Like other types of labor organizations, enterprise unions have both virtues and faults. To summarize: Among their virtues are their contributions to (1) the rapid increase in union organization within a relatively short time, as table 5.6 shows; (2) the enlargement of the scope and subject matter of collective bargaining; (3) the success in the organizing of white-collar workers; (4) sound and stable union finances; (5) good communications between leaders and the rank and file, particularly on the shop floor; (6) easy access

Table 5.6
Union Membership and Organization Ratios, 1945–79

Year	Membership (in thousands)	Organization Ratios (%)	Year	Membership (in thousands)	Organization Ratios (%)
1945	381	3.2	1962	8,971	34.7
1946	4,926	41.5	1963	9,357	34.7
1947	5,692	45.3	1964	9,800	35.0
1948	6,677	53.0	1965	10,147	34.8
1949	6,655	55.8	1966	10,404	34.2
1950	5,774	46.2	1967	10,566	34.1
1951	5,687	42.6	1968	10,863	34.4
1952	5,720	40.3	1969	11,249	35.2
1953	5,927	36.3	1970	11,605	35.4
1954	6,076	35.5	1971	11,798	34.8
1955	6,286	35.6	1972	11,889	34.3
1956	6,463	33.5	1973	12,098	33.1
1957	6,763	33.6	1974	12,462	33.9
1958	6,984	32.7	1975	12,590	34.4
1959	7,211	32.1	1976	12,509	33.7
1960	7,662	32.3	1977	12,437	33.2
1961	8,360	34.5	1978	12,383	32.6
			1979	12,309	31.6

Sources: Union membership data for 1945–46 are obtained from surveys by Kōseishō. The data for 1947 and thereafter are from RKKC.

Note: Membership data prior to 1953 correspond to total union members on the basis of *tan'i kumiai* (union organization corresponding roughly to an establishment); the data for 1953 and thereafter correspond to those accumulated on the basis of *tan'itsu kumiai* (union organization corresponding roughly to an enterprise).

Organization ratios are the percentage of union membership divided by the number of employees, which is taken from Prime Minister's Office, *Employment Status Survey.*

to management in handling day-to-day problems; (7) a single united union within each enterprise as a rule; (8) the flexible adjustment to structural changes in industries; and (9) the establishment of a very appropriate structure for dealing with problems emerging within a plant or enterprise.[7]

On the other hand, they have undeniable faults: they (1) disperse union resources for the total labor movement because of their highly decentralized structure; (2) impede the possible development of a united labor movement; (3) are unwilling to organize unorganized workers, including unemployed workers; (4) lack the will to make an effort to protect the interests of retired workers who had long been union members; (5) suffer from administrative and financial inefficiencies (see chapter 6); (6) are susceptible to employer interference and pressure; and (7) are relatively weak in their bargaining power against employers, including the government.

Union leaders have long been acutely conscious of the weaknesses of enterprise unionism, and have continuously advocated the adoption of industrial unionism as it exists in the United States, West Germany, and other countries in Western Europe. However, there has been almost no change in the predominant position of enterprise unions in the Japanese labor movement over the more than 30 years since the war. To be sure, along with the development of the Spring Offensive has come a notable increase in the authority and control of higher organizations, such as the industrial federations of unions and the so-called national centers, as well as a greater dependence of enterprise unions on such organizations for various services. Industry-wide collective bargaining also has developed in some industries (Shirai 1965). Notwithstanding, union power is still largely decentralized, and the administrative autonomy of enterprise unions remains almost unaffected. Despite the provisions in the constitutions of some national industrial federations which empower them to regulate and control affiliated enterprise unions, it is still quite rare for the former actually to take any step that would force a decision on the latter.

The experience of more than 30 years of enterprise unionism in postwar Japan leads the author to conclude—perhaps somewhat reluctantly—that within the socioeconomic and cultural context of Japanese industrial society, the enterprise union seems to employed workers to be the most acceptable and effective form of union organization.

It might well be said that enterprise unionism has worked as well to meet workers' expectations as have other types of unions in other countries, although, as several surveys of membership attitudes toward unions show, there are quite a few members who are dissatisfied with and critical of union achievements in Japan. However, it seems very unlikely, at least in the foreseeable future, that a radical restructuring of enterprise unionism will become a goal of the labor movement that will command the support of the majority of rank-and-file Japanese unionists. This is not only because, as elsewhere, unions tend to be conservative in making changes in their organizational arrangement and power structure, but because, again as elsewhere, the growing importance of industrial relations problems at the plant and enterprise levels will continue to demand an effective union organization and activity at those levels. In several Western countries, the focus of collective bargaining seems to be moving down from the national or industrial levels to the enterprise, plant, and shop levels. But there also appears to be movement in the opposite direction, to more centralization at the national and industrial levels. However, as a downward movement progresses, unions have to adjust their organizational and power structure to meet the needs and to provide effective representation of workers at the enterprise, plant, and shop levels. Japanese enterprise unions are already established and are functioning effectively to meet these requirements.

There are also tendencies, as well as increasingly intensified needs, in Western countries to organize white-collar, managerial, and supervisory workers, but it seems that the established craft, industrial, and general unions of the West have been facing problems in organizing these workers within their traditional structures. Because Japanese enterprise unions are structurally different, they have been relatively successful in organizing white-collar workers in the same unions with blue-collar workers.

Thus, it seems that enterprise unionism in Japan is not totally out of line with the general orientation of union movements in highly industrialized societies. And depending upon the strategies and methods for developing an industrial labor force and for achieving industrial democracy in developing countries, enterprise unionism may be one of several alternative structures of union organization for these countries to consider.

Notwithstanding, enterprise unionism, with its intrinsic deficiencies, does not have the organizational structure to handle the tasks that are now facing the Japanese labor movement. More coordination among unions is certainly needed to meet new problems and challenges under new circumstances and structural changes. A gradual but steady shift of power and a reallocation of resources from enterprise unions to industrial and national federations would be a practical and realistic solution.

Notes

1 According to another survey by the Ministry of Labor, 70.8 percent of all establishments surveyed, covering 82.3 percent of the workers, have a standing committee for joint consultation. The percentage is higher among larger establishments. For example, 92.6 percent of establishments with more than 5,000 employees have joint-consultation arrangements, covering 95.6 percent of all

workers employed in this category. The percentage is also higher among unionized establishments, where 82.6 percent have joint consultation compared to only 40.3 percent of unorganized establishments (Rōdōshō, Tōkei Jōhōbu, 1977).

2 It should be acknowledged, though, that Cole hints at the internal labor market hypothesis when he says, "the diffusion of the nenkō wage and permanent employment strengthened the functional reasons for the emergence of enterprise unionism" (p. 277).

3 Although the "internal labor market" terminology has only lately been imported from the United States, particularly from the work of Doeringer and Piore (1971), a similar concept has long been used for the analysis of enterprise unionism and other relevant practices of the Japanese industrial relations systems. Some familiar concepts are: enterprise-contained labor market, particularized labor market within an enterprise, vertically segmented labor market within an enterprise, etc. See Ujihara 1955 and Ōkōchi 1958a.

4 Dore (1973, pp. 346-47) comments upon the more extensive communication between union officers and the rank and file within enterprise unions as compared with British unions.

5 Although comparable data are not available, Ministry of Labor time-series surveys on the form of wage and salary payment show that an increasing number of firms are applying the same pay plans—a monthly salary with or without a deduction for absences—to both blue- and white-collar employees. See Rōdōshō, Tōkei Jōhōbu (Ministry of Labor, Department of Statistics and Information), *Chingin Rōdō Jikan Seido Sōgō Chōsa Hōkoku* [Report on the comprehensive survey of wages and working hours], particularly for 1966. The movement of blue-collar workers to a salary status is a natural result of their career patterns within an enterprise becoming very similar to those of white-collar workers, as described by Koike in chapter 2 of this volume. However, it should be noted that there was also somewhat of a reverse trend in pay plans. Largely due to the Labor Standards Law of 1947, white-collar workers at nonmanagerial levels as well as blue-collar workers now get premium pay for overtime work and lose pay for time not worked. Thus, these workers are not "salaried" in the strict sense of the word.

6 Many cases can be cited in which management is involved when a union breaks apart and a second union is formed in the same enterprise. Such management involvement constitutes an unfair labor practice, strictly forbidden by the Trade Union Law.

7 Taira (1977) expresses great appreciation for the functional efficiency of enterprise unions in dealing with in-plant problems. He even insists that an enterprise union is the most relevant and instrumental form of union organization in the advanced stage of capitalism, where the internal labor market becomes the predominant form of labor market.

6 *Norikuni Naitō*

Trade Union Finance and Administration

Objectives of the Analysis

Many Western researchers have studied various aspects of Japanese trade unions, such as their organizational structure, functions, and the external constraints on their activities, but very few scholars—even in Japan itself—have investigated their internal government and administration. This fact may reflect the tendency of the Japanese unions themselves to pay relatively little attention to internal union affairs compared to their concern with collective bargaining and political activities. This tendency has perhaps been inevitable since Japanese unions have enjoyed rapid membership growth, which started immediately after the war, and their major concern during this period has been confined almost entirely to negotiating wage increases. Only recently have Japanese unions begun to pay serious attention to the problem of achieving a balance between popular control and administrative efficiency.

As noted in chapter 5, the 10.3 million enterprise union members in Japan today are dispersed among about 31,000 separate unions, each relatively small in size and organizationally independent. Each has its own internal administration and its own set of rules for electing officers, for financing its activities, and for holding its conferences. The enterprise union organizes only the employees of its own enterprise and tends to emphasize egalitarianism in internal union matters. Three factors above all characterize or con-

145

strain the internal government of Japanese enterprise unions: (1) Since there is usually only one union within a plant or company, the employees seldom have an alternative other than to join it; the unusual case is one where a group of workers has split off to form a second union. (2) Two-thirds of the unions have union-shop agreements; such an agreement in Japan is often considered useful in preventing union splits. (3) Since the size of an enterprise union is determined mainly by the number of employees of the enterprise, it is difficult to evaluate the effectiveness of union administration by using size as a criterion. Thus in order to evaluate that effectiveness it is necessary to pay particular attention to the relation of the union to the members.

The specific objectives of this chapter are: (1) to provide factual information about union officers, conferences, finance, and so on; (2) to investigate the nature of Japanese union government and its derivation; (3) to examine the issue of balance between popular control and administrative efficiency; and (4) to evaluate the internal government of Japanese unions, using British union government as a frame of reference.

Union Fees

Membership contributions in Japan are extremely high—possibly the highest in the world. This very fact would seem to explain many of the peculiar characteristics of Japanese unionism, and it is therefore reasonable to begin our analysis with the financial aspects of union administration.

The average level of monthly contributions and the ratio of contributions to average monthly basic wages are presented in table 6.1 for 345 major unions which together had a membership of 1,685,630 in the private sector in 1977. The average monthly contribution amounted to ¥2,437 per member, which is 1.64 percent of the average monthly wage of ¥148,770 (excluding annual bonuses). The percentages were 1.3 and 1.5, respectively, for 1971 and 1975. Thus, it can be seen that contributions have risen faster than have wages.

About one-third of these unions imposed special levies, which amounted to as much as a monthly contribution, twice a year when the semiannual bonuses are paid to workers. More than half of the unions also have special funds to finance wage offensives. According to the survey, an average union member in Japan makes the equivalent of 14 monthly contributions in a year, which, when totaled, increase the yearly contribution to more than 2 percent of the average basic wage.

Furthermore, trade unions in the public sector, with a total of 3,450,000 members, or about 30 percent of total union membership in Japan, have much higher monthly contributions than the private-sector unions. Although

Table 6.1
Average Contributions per Member for 345 Major Enterprise Unions, 1977

Industry	No. Unions	No. Members	Average Monthly Basic Wage per Member (¥)	Average Monthly Contribution per Member (¥)	Average Percentage of Monthly Basic Wage Contributed
Iron and steel	26	186,132	161,850	1,905	1.18
Engineering	160	154,527	145,249	2,356	1.62
Shipbuilding	20	215,034	149,441	2,184	1.46
Motor bicycle	4	174,600	136,419	2,155	1.58
Chemicals	35	32,801	156,944	2,612	1.66
Textiles	23	131,098	130,881	2,610	1.99
Electrical engineering	21	427,115	135,800	1,635	1.20
Electricity	9	131,098	181,737	4,010	2.21
Food	9	16,019	137,623	2,367	1.72
Mining	5	12,708	200,311	3,761	1.88
Distribution	11	39,847	133,924	2,423	1.81
Naval transport	1	156,775	172,076	4,400	2.56
Miscellaneous	21	2,031	122,868	1,698	1.38
Total	345	1,685,630			
Average			148,770	2,437	1.64

Source: Asia Shakai Mondai Kenkyūjo 1978.

reliable figures for the public sector are not available, it is estimated that the average monthly contribution per member is about ¥4,000, or 2.5 percent of the average monthly wage. Moreover, some public-sector unions require even larger membership contributions, which is not surprising because of the persistent and costly struggles of these unions to obtain the right to strike, a right denied them but universally enjoyed by union members employed by private-sector firms. Thus, most public-sector unions have been compelled to provide a protection benefit fund for victimization, which pays benefits to members discharged for union activity. At any rate, we can estimate roughly that the average monthly contribution per member in Japan is between 2 and 2.5 percent of the average monthly wage.

In contrast, membership fees in British unions are quite low. According to a Trades Union Congress (TUC) survey, the average yearly contribution per member of TUC-affiliated unions in 1974 was £6.99, or "just over 13 pence a week which was less than the cost of half a pint of bitter in the pub. . . . In 1974 the subscription to the union amounted to a mere 0.28 percent of the average weekly male wage of £46.50" (Taylor 1978, pp. 30–31).

The ratio of the contribution to the average wage in Japan is nearly ten times higher than that in Britain. Moreover, the average monthly contribution of ¥2,437 for private-sector unions was the equivalent of about £6.50 at the exchange rate of £1.00 to ¥370 in 1974; that is, the Japanese *monthly* contribution was almost equal to the British *annual* contribution, even though it is well known that British union fees are relatively low. According to the 1977 TUC Report, the average yearly contribution had increased to £8.25 in 1975, but this still does not make any great change in the vast difference between contributions in Japan and Britain. How can we reconcile these differences?

Most Japanese unions have adopted a system of linking the level of contributions to the basic wage in order to provide for an automatic adjustment when wages are increased. This type of adjustment has gained popularity in Japan because the unions have been suffering from the effects of the rapid inflation which has undermined the real value of contributions. In addition, most unions have a checkoff system, highly advantageous because they can automatically collect contributions from all members.

If a correlation existed between the size of members' contributions and the level of union services, there would be little need for further discussion of this point. But it seems unlikely that Japanese unions provide much better services to their members than their British counterparts. Why, then, do Japanese unions demand such high contributions? The answer to this question can be found in the peculiar problems raised by the procedures characteristic of Japanese union governments and methods of administration.

Union Officers

The largest expenditures of Japanese unions are for the salaries of union officers, staff members, and clerks, including their fringe benefits. This one item amounts to between 40 and 50 percent of total union expenditures.

Union officials, however, do not necessarily enjoy high salaries compared with those of their fellow union members. Considering their task, the responsibility, and the amount of time they devote to their work, their remuneration is relatively low. The high total expenditure on union salaries results, therefore, not from the size of individual salaries, but from the large number of union officials drawing salaries. Japanese unions employ far more full-time officials than do unions in other countries, and the ratio of full-time union officers to total members is extraordinarily high when compared to that in other countries.

Table 6.2 shows the ratio of full-time officers, staff members, and clerks to the total memberships of enterprise unions affiliated with industry-wide federations belonging to the International Metalworkers Federation—Japan Council. According to an IMF—JC survey (1978), the average ratio was one official to 572 members. Counting union staff people and clerks, the ratio would become 1:328. Thus, trade unions in the metal and engineering

Table 6.2
Total Union Membership and Number of Full-Time Union Functionaries, 1978

Union Federations	Membership	Officers	Staffs and Clerks	Officers, Staffs, and Clerks	Officer[a]	Members per Officer, Staff, or Clerk[b]
Electrical Engineering	519,694	802	848	1,650	648	315
Motor Car	550,000	1,180	510	1,690	466	325
Iron and Steel	237,911	433	252	685	549	347
Shipbuilding and Heavy Engineering	210,000	433	295	728	485	288
Engineering	310,097	344	470	814	901	381
Total	1,827,702	3,192	2,375	5,567		
Average					572	328

Source: IMF–JC 1978.
Note: Enterprise unions covered by this survey are member unions of five industry-wide union federations affiliated with the IMF–JC.
[a]This is obtained by dividing the first column by the second column.
[b]This is obtained by dividing the first column by the fourth column.

industry have employed one full-time functionary for every 328 members. The figures are representative of the general tendency toward a high proportion of union officials to total union members in Japan.

In contrast, the ratios in other countries are far lower. According to the so-called Donovan report (Great Britain, Royal Commission on Trade Unions and Employers' Associations, 1968):

There are about 3,000 full-time trade union officials in Britain, which represents about one union official for every 3,800 trade union members. Equally reliable figures are not available for all other comparable countries, but the evidence suggests that in the United States the ratio of officers to members is of the order of 1 to 1,400 and in the Federal Republic of Germany as low as 1 to 800. Both Italy and France appear to have twice as many officers per member as we do. (p. 188)

The figures cited are for ten years ago, but Japan's ratio has not changed very much for a number of years. Japanese trade unions themselves have made persistent efforts to increase the number of full-time union functionaries. It would not be surprising if union leaders in Britain, who have become accustomed to a low proportion of full-time officers to members, would interpret this effort as being a full-employment policy of the unionists themselves.

There are, however, vast differences in the definition of a full-time union officer in Japan and in some other countries. In Britain, the definition is limited to officials paid by the union, although British trade unionists are also served by many full-time shop stewards, who are paid by the employer while doing union business in their plants. Boraston et al. (1975) note:

The studies point to a fairly rapid and continuing growth in the number of convener, senior stewards, lay branch secretaries and other lay union officers who are paid by employers and give most or all of their time to union business. . . . In 1974 it is as good a guess as any that the full-time laymen may now outnumber the full-time officers. (p. 193)

It is quite common in some countries to have full-time union representatives who play vital roles in industrial relations at the workplace. In Japan, where the workplace organization is synonymous with the union organizations inside the plant, it is meaningless to distinguish between full-time union representatives engaged in industrial relations at the workplace and the full-time officers of the trade unions: they are identical. Therefore, the most striking aspect of Japanese full-time trade union officers is that they are employees of the company in which their union is organized even though their salaries are paid by the union. At the enterprise union level, almost all full-time officers retain their employee status in the company, and their employee position is formally recognized by the management while they are serving as union officers. If a union officer is defeated in an election or chooses not to run as a candidate in the next election, he can return to his former position in the company under the same conditions he previously enjoyed. He is assured of the same wage as his fellow workers when he returns.

Full-time officers of enterprise unions are, to some extent, comparable with "conveners" or "chief shop stewards" in Britain who can spend all their time on union activities within an establishment. They are also functionally comparable to a "committeeman" in a local union in the United States. To the extent that the full-time officers of a Japanese enterprise union have to perform both as union officials and as workplace representatives, their number inevitably would have to be much greater than the more narrowly defined full-time union officers in other countries. It seems clear in Britain that "it has been possible for the ratio of full-time officers to members to remain roughly stable because there has been a substantial increase in the time given to industrial relations in the plant by shopstewards" (Boraston et al. 1975, p. 193). However, one should recognize these notable characteristics of the Japanese union officer: that he is a union representative elected by the members of the union employed in the plant or company where he himself works. Some officers are given "time off" as full-time union officers by the management when they take part in collective bargaining—a reflection of the employers' strong preference to negotiate only with their own employees rather than with outside professional leaders. The tendency exists for outsiders not to be accepted, not only by employers but also by members of enterprise unions whose membership is restricted to employees of the plant or company. Moreover, it is also common for Japanese industry-wide union federations to have elected, full-time officers who also maintain positions in their companies to which they can return.

The significant difference in trade unionism between Japan and some of the Western countries is found not only in the union organization, but also in the character of their officials. In most cases, Japanese full-time union officers are not professional union officers, unlike their counterparts in the United States and Europe. This is an important characteristic of Japanese trade unions.

Full-time officers have a dual allegiance, one as a union representative and the other as an employee of the company. The widely expressed allegation that Japanese enterprise unions are susceptible to employer intervention appears to be based on the dualist nature of union officers. However, this dualism should not be interpreted to mean that Japanese union officers are less independent than their Western counterparts. They are as independent as conveners or chief shop stewards in Britain or committeemen in the United States, all of whom maintain their employee status while engaging in union activities. Indeed, Japanese union officers are formally recognized by collective agreements to have the freedom to engage fully in union activities within a plant or company during the period of their service with the union, and the management has little to say about their appointments.

It should be recognized that Japanese unions are independent financially. They have to pay the salaries of all full-time representatives who perform the functions of both union officer and workplace representative. Although Japanese union officers play an important role in industrial relations at the workplace, they are not paid by the company (indeed, Japanese law prohibits it) because they are trade union officers and not workplace representatives. The enterprise union that is organized inside the company, therefore, is at a serious disadvantage in this respect compared with unions in other countries. The large size of the contributions required of the members of Japanese unions is the price they pay to maintain their independence.

Costs of Union Meetings

The second largest union expenditure is for various meetings, ranging from those of the central committee and subcommittees to union conferences or delegate meetings. The proportion of total expenditures spent on meetings varies from union to union—it can be as little as 10 percent or as much as 40 percent—but is a significant expense.

Any union, whether in Japan or in other countries, has an executive body and must have a union conference to conduct its organizational activities. For instance, many unions stipulate in their rules that the conference functions as the "supreme government" or "supreme authority for decision-making." It is also common for the rules to provide for the executive to preside over the work of the union between its periodic conferences. These functional and organizational aspects of Japanese unions are no different from those of their Western counterparts. However, the unions do differ considerably in the power balance between their executive committees and the union conferences—or, one could say, between cabinets and parliaments.

The Japanese Trade Union Law requires that union rules provide both for a yearly conference and for the election of officers by ballot if the organization is to qualify as a registered union. Thus every union has either a delegates' conference or a general meeting of all members at least once a year, the type depending upon the size of the union. Many enterprise unions in Japan are small enough to bring all members together for a general meeting. (In this chapter's discussion, the term "conference" will refer to both general and delegates' meetings.) Of course, the more frequently a conference is held, the greater the role it plays as a democratic check by the membership on actions of the officers. Special conferences may be called at the discretion of the central committee or on the demand of a specified proportion of the membership; most special conferences are convened by the executive committee.

A notable feature of Japanese trade unions is that they have more frequent conferences than do some of their Western counterparts. It is not unusual for a union to convene a conference twice or three times a year—for example, an annual conference in the summer and two special conferences, one in the spring and another in the autumn. There are some cases of small unions' calling quarterly conferences.

Most unions stipulate that an annual or special conference is entitled to perform such functions as: (1) approve or criticize the report of the executive committee; (2) make or amend union rules; (3) decide on union policy; (4) elect union officers, including auditors; (5) determine income and expenditures and approve the closing accounts; (6) decide on a strike; (7) approve the collective agreement; (8) expel members from the union; (9) affiliate with or withdraw from the upper organization of unions; or (10) dissolve the union.

In Japan, this provision in the union rules not only stipulates the power of the conference but also requires that all these items should be decided by the conference as a democratic check by the members on the actions and policies of the executive committee. Thus, it is obvious that the executive committee's power is considerably curtailed by the popular control exercised through frequently held conferences.

In addition to the conferences, the large enterprise unions as well as the industry-wide union federations and national centers usually have another decision-making body, called the "central committee" or "general council." "Central committee" is used here as a generic term. In their rules, many unions describe the functions of the central committee as "the authority subsequent to the conference." Its relation to the conference appears to be similar to that of the national executive council or the national executive committee in the case of British trade unions. The central committee usually meets every two months or quarterly. For instance, Shitetsusōren (General Federation of Private Railway Workers' Unions of Japan), which has a membership of 210,000, has a central committee consisting of 135 members elected from nine regional constituencies; its conference is composed of about 600 delegates representing each affiliated union, the number of delegates depending on the size of each union. In this federation, the rules state that the central committee must be convened more than five times a year. These conferences may be considered the intermediate decision-making body. Most unions specify in their rules that the central committee has the authority (1) to formulate plans to carry out the policy resolutions that were approved in the conference, (2) to interpret union rules whenever they are questioned, (3) to select union officials supplementarily under special circumstances, (4) to decide upon a supplementary budget, and (5) to impose special levies on members.

As might be expected, however, in many unions the distribution of power between the conference and the central committee is ambiguous and the functions of the two bodies overlap and interlock. Therefore, it is not unreasonable that many large unions, especially since 1970, have begun to place increasing importance on their central committee relative to special conferences, in the interest of administrative efficiency.

Why then have Japanese unions found it necessary to hold such frequent expensive conferences and meetings of central committees? Shirai (1975) wrote, about frequency of meetings:

It is due to organizational weakness caused by the internal contradictions pervading Japanese enterprise unionism. On the enterprise level, various employee interest groups form coalitions and conflicts with other groups: white-collar versus blue-collar, young versus old, well-educated versus poorly educated, those who are intensely loyal to the firm versus disloyal, those with higher seniority versus those with lower seniority, and so on. In addition, there are divisions based on ideology and political factionalism.

At the industrial-federation and national-center levels, splits frequently occur over such factors as differences between unions in large and small enterprises; conflicts of interest among unions that belong to competing enterprises marketing the same type of commodities or services; incompatibility between unions in the private and public sectors; and confrontations based on loyalty to contending political parties and ideologies. These conflicts often lead to organizational splits and lend a distinctly political coloring to the decision-making process in Japanese unions. Frequently conventions are essential to ameliorating these conflicts through conciliation and compromise, and forming a new consensus. (pp. 167–84)

Even so, a question remains. In Britain, the most bureaucratic and powerful leadership is found in the Transport and General Workers' Union, with its two million members divided into more than ten trade groups. Why then did strong leadership with a powerful and efficient administration not develop in Japan? Shirai pointed out that one of the important factors responsible for the lack of strong leadership, backed by efficient administration, was that the internal government of Japanese unions has been based on a conception of "democracy" as unconditional egalitarianism in rights, opportunities, and rewards. This concept seems to have rapidly engulfed the Japanese population in the feverish movements of social and institutional reforms right after World War II. Its rapid diffusion among the public, particularly workers, in the epochal period of what might be termed a "social democratic revolution" may be interpreted as a massive social reaction against the system of rigid status differentiation that governed prewar Japanese society. At any rate, the ideology of "democracy," which spread quickly and widely throughout the country shortly after the war, in two important respects played a significant role in the development of enterprise unionism: (1) There is no differentiation between white- and blue-collar workers as members of an enterprise union. (2) The pattern of union administration is characterized by what Sidney and Beatrice Webb (1920) once called "primitive democracy," or the idea that "what concerns all should be decided by all." In other words, the latter gives rise to the widely held conviction among union leaders as well as rank-and-file members in Japan that the greater the number of union officers and the more frequent the union meetings, the greater the degree of union democracy. It is for this reason that administrative efficiency seems to have been unduly sacrificed to popular control in Japan.

Administrative Inefficiencies

If union democracy can be defined as rule by the members, then most Japanese trade unions should be considered democratic organizations. In order to confirm this assertion, we can show further evidence of Japanese-style "union democracy." However, it is important to keep in mind that these "democratic" tendencies have aggravated administrative and financial inefficiencies.

In the first place, executive authority is vested collectively in the executive committee, and the power of the president is decidedly limited. The executive committee consists of the president, the vice-president, the chief secretary, and several other members. This body is a standing committee which meets regularly at least once a week to conduct the general business of the union; occasionally, if necessary, it will meet several times during a week. Business decisions can be made only after consultation with all members of the executive committee. This method of collective decision-making by consensus prevails in order to preserve the collective leadership and responsibility of union government; it is a behavior pattern that is very popular not only among the unions, but also among all Japanese people. In such collective decision-making, the distribution of power between the top leader and the individual member necessarily suffers from a certain vagueness.

Although the apex of the hierarchy of union officials is the president, his position is quite different from that of the president of American unions or the general secretary of British unions. Most unions describe, in their rules, the functions and authority of the president as "general management and representative of the union." This abstract provision has been interpreted to mean that the president (1) presides at the executive committee meetings, (2) summons the conference and central committee meetings, and (3) signs his name to the collective agreements and other official documents.

According to this interpretation, the president has no more than the minimum power necessary to transact union business. His constitutional power is no greater than that of the vice-president, the chief secretary, or other executive committee members. He has only one vote and no right to veto. If he wishes to display his leadership, he must do so by persuading the other committee members to agree with his position.

A second notable point is that in most unions all members of the executive committee are elected annually. This is the pattern preferred by Japanese unions, although during the past 15 years some large enterprise unions have extended the terms of office of executive committee members to two years. Moreover, it is not unusual for the officers to be reelected several times in large enterprise unions as well as in industrial federations and national centers.

However, it is quite alien to Japanese unions for the officials, once elected, to remain in office for life. No Japanese union rule gives any officer the privilege of holding office for life or "at the union's pleasure," as in the case of the general secretary of the Transport and General Workers' Union in Britain. Thus, it is possible that Japanese union officials are so constrained by the members through frequent elections that they may not be able to display the best leadership. Yet trade unionists in Japan apparently are reluctant to place full power in the hands of particular individuals. This is the fundamental nature of Japanese union government and explains the almost total absence of professional union leaders and the limited power of the presidents. Japanese workers as well as their leaders certainly would be surprised to hear about the nepotism in the General and Municipal Workers' Union in Britain.

A third piece of evidence of "union democracy" in Japan is that any member is an eligible candidate for election to union office; such is not the British practice. For instance, the *Rules* of the National Union of Railwaymen in Britain state:

> No member shall be eligible for election, or to act, as a delegate to the Annual General Meeting unless he is a benefit member with not less than five consecutive years' membership in the Union at the date of nomination. (1976 ed., p. 8)
>
> Each candidate [for the general secretary] must be a benefit member, [and] have at least ten consecutive years' membership. (1976 ed., p. 22)

By the same token, Japanese unions permit any member to be elected as a conference delegate. Moreover, most unions do not require any qualifications of the candidates for union officers, including the president, vice-president, and chief secretary. Theoretically, any member who hopes to be president can stand as a candidate for this post. It is obvious that this has decreased expertise in union administration. Even in large Japanese unions, we can find amateurism in the leadership. Collective leadership, recurrent elections, and amateurism again demonstrate clearly how Japanese "union democracy" is achieved at the sacrifice of administrative efficiency.

Last, Japanese trade unions frequently publish their own journals, and they are much interested in distributing many kinds of union publications. Their prevailing motto is, "Union journals are stronger organizers than any other device." Although there is no difference between Japan and other countries in the function of union journals as an important medium of communication between the union and its members, Japanese unions have placed greater importance on their journals for the same reason that they have frequent meetings.

Frequency of publication of the union journals for the 125 industrial federations, with an aggregate membership of seven million in 1977, is indeed noteworthy. Of the journals published in 1977, 17 were published weekly, 57 every 10 days or fortnightly, 34 monthly, 7 quarterly or semiannually, and 10 irregularly.[1]

Although reliable figures are not available for other countries, these figures suggest that in Japan the frequency of publication of union journals is considerably greater than in other countries. I could not find any weekly journal in Britain except the *Railway Review*, the journal of the National Union of Railwaymen, when I visited many unions in London and Sheffield in 1968 and 1976.

Most of the 125 union journals were in newspaper format; they ranged from 2 to 8 pages and contained reports, news, and general articles. These journals are directed very broadly to the entire membership: 79 of the unions published a copy for each member, 16 unions published a copy for every 2 members, and 5 unions published a copy for every 3 members. One union with a membership of about 300,000 was mailing a copy of its journal to every member and expected, by this method of distribution, to reach both members and their families. In this journal, there are columns for wives and children.

In addition to their journals, most of the large industrial federations publish a monthly union magazine containing statements on union policy, articles, and research information. Some of them devote pages to poems and novels written by members—Sōhyō (General Council of Trade Unions of Japan), the largest of the four national centers, is proud of its "Sōhyō Literary Award." Moreover, some large unions also put out monthly research bulletins.

Union journals receive much attention at the enterprise union level as well. A large union with several thousand members usually has its own journal in newspaper format, and many small unions send news in printed form to their members several times a week. If a small union employs a full-time clerk, his main task may be to print newsletters by copy-machine and to distribute them to members.

There also are workshop papers, some of them published daily. In some plants a number of workshop organizations publish papers in rotation: workshop A on Monday, B on Tuesday, through E, on Friday. Many enterprise unions as well as national centers have been encouraging the publication of these papers devoted to shop-floor issues because they believe that it contributes to lively trade union activity at that level. The unions expect member interest in union affairs will be stimulated and maintained through the editing of their own papers. But, as one might expect, opposition factions within a union also can use the workshop papers for their own propaganda.

In short, Japanese trade unions at three levels—the enterprise union, the industrial federation, and the national center—have many types of union journals. Even if enterprise unions give more space to their own news than do the journals of the industrial federations and national centers, union journals of all kinds tend to contain similar news. Do rank-and-file members really read them? Probably not, but although trade union officials admit this fact, it is difficult for them to change their attitudes because they have believed that union journals are essential in maintaining communication between union officials and rank-and-file members in order to preserve democratic government.

Conclusion

In the preceding sections we have provided some important factual information on the internal structure that affects the behavior of Japanese unions. The first thing to be said is that the Japanese pattern of union government is to some extent comparable with the earlier type of trade union democracy in Britain, discussed by Sidney and Beatrice Webb. This is quite understandable by reason of the relatively small average size and the large number of Japanese trade unions. These unions are quite different from those of other countries which have centralized union governments and administrative efficiency. Since enterprise unions in the same industry form industrial federations and these federations, in turn, are affiliated with national centers, the internal structure of the upper-level organizations as well closely reflects the governing procedures of the enterprise unions. Most of these upper-level organizations are no more than loose federations governed through the delegates of the affiliated unions.

In practice, however, the government of large unions such as enterprise unions with between 3,000 and 5,000 members, as well as industrial federations and national centers, is quite similar to that of trade unions in other advanced countries. In fact, the tendency for bureaucratization is as apparent among the large unions in Japan as elsewhere.

Although any member is eligible to be a candidate for election to union office, most candidates for positions as members of the executive committee of these large unions, particularly the president, vice-president, and chief secretary, are persons with long careers in the trade union movement. Most of them rise from being activists on the shop floor to higher positions on the ladder of the union office hierarchy. This ladder includes not only the offices within the enterprise union, but also within the regional or district organization of the industrial federation and the local trade councils in large industrial cities and prefectures. Thus, Japanese union officials do not differ greatly from professional union officials as we know them in the United States and Britain, except that they retain their employee status in their companies. Most of them continue their devotion to the trade union movement. Particularly in large unions where election is required every two years, many presidents hold office for a long time—some for more than ten successive years. Although there is no union rule in Japan which provides life tenure for the president, some presidents in large unions have de facto life tenure, although they must be reelected every two years in order to meet their own unions' requirements. But, although the system of frequent meetings and recurrent elections symbolizes the concept of union democracy, it tends to produce weak and unstable leadership.

In the 1970s there emerged new leaders whose ideas were close to the concept of "business unionism," centering upon big business in the metal and engineering industry, and they have exerted a great influence on Japanese trade unionism. Most of the new leaders are highly educated, and have paid more attention than anyone previously to the problems of the internal union structure. In part, this redirection was necessitated by the economic slump following the oil crisis in 1974, which led to a decrease in the number of union members. Research has shown that 185 of 250 large companies in all industries in the private sector reduced their labor forces in the following four years. The average reduction for each company was 1,165 employees or 12.6 percent of the workforce; this implied a similar reduction in the membership of the enterprise unions which are organized within those 185 companies. As one might expect, union income decreased by nearly 10 percent over those four years. At the least, it will become more difficult than in the past to increase member contributions. Obviously, many large enterprise unions and industrial federations will face more seriously than ever before the problem of how to achieve centralization of union government while maintaining a balance between popular control and administrative efficiency.

Notes

1 These figures are derived from Nihon Kikanshi Kyōkai 1977, pp. 22–23.

7 *Tadashi A. Hanami*

The Function of the Law
in Japanese Industrial Relations

With some few exceptions, such as the Factory Law of 1911 and the Labor Dispute Mediation Law of 1926, Japanese labor laws are almost exclusively products of the postwar period. Union organization was stimulated by the strong encouragement of the Allied Occupation and the Japanese government immediately following World War II, and most of the present labor legislation was introduced in this period as a result of government initiatives. This historical event is one of the factors that still prescribes the nature of today's labor laws.

Japanese unions tend to rely heavily on labor legislation. The Dreyer Commission of the International Labor Organization (ILO), which investigated public-sector industrial relations in Japan during the 1960s, stated in its conclusion that the government's "excessive legalism" was one cause of the problems in the public sector (ILO, 1966, p. 496). However, one can find "excessive legalism" in the union movement as well. In the public sector, when unions engage in industrial actions prohibited by the Public Corporation and National Enterprise Labor Relations Law and the National Public Service Law, they always justify their illegal acts by citing the constitutional guarantee of their right to act collectively.

In this chapter we intend to analyze this union reliance on the law and the functions of legal theories and court decisions as they relate to industrial relations in order to examine the cultural impact of Western legal systems in the Japanese context. The present Japanese labor law system is literally a patchwork of pieces that had their origin in several Western national legal systems—American, British, German, and French.[1] Those pieces were introduced more or less arbitrarily into Japan after the war, and now, in the Japanese context, they perform very different functions from the laws on which they were patterned. The author believes that this evolution of the law in Japanese industrial relations, one example of the result of a non-Western society's adoption of Western legislation, illustrates a very interesting cultural phenomenon.

The "Eternal and Inviolable" Right to Organize

One often reads in labor law textbooks in Japan a peculiar contention that the right of workers to organize, guaranteed by Article 28 of the Constitution of Japan of 1946, is "eternal and inviolable." According to most Japanese labor law scholars, this right is sacred and holy—a mythology that can be found in hardly any other civilized country. Article 28 of the Constitution states that the workers' right to bargain and to act collectively, together with their right to organize, are fundamental human rights. Japanese labor lawyers are proud of this constitutional provision, since few countries other than socialist and developing nations recognize as human rights in their constitutions the right to bargain and to act collectively. No Anglo-Saxon country guarantees the right to organize, as distinct from freedom of association, in its constitution or bill of rights. Only a few Western European countries, such as West Germany, France, or Italy, have constitutional guarantees of the right of workers to organize. The right to strike, but not the right to bargain, is acknowledged in France and Italy.

In spite of the fact that, in Japan, the rights of workers are stated explicitly in the Constitution, Japanese lawyers seem unable to agree on how to interpret these guarantees. The majority theory maintains that recognition of the right to organize can be distinguished from freedom of association and means more extensive prerogatives for workers than for ordinary citizens. For instance, the legality of union actions to "secure its position" is usually differentiated by this contention. That is, any pressure on workers to join a union is legal even if it involves some actions that might be interpreted as illegal were they pursued by ordinary citizens. The constitutional right to organize is often interpreted to include certain privileges for the unions—the employers' provision of office space for the union on the company premises, employees' devoting full time to their union offices, or the checkoff of union dues and fees from the members' wages, for example. Such issues are normally regarded elsewhere as subjects for union–management negotiations.

Another example of the broad interpretation of workers' rights is the legality of picketing. So-called mass picketing, which frequently, for all practical purposes, shuts down the flow of traffic through the plant gates, is regarded as legal by the majority theory which contends that the right to act collectively means something more than the freedom to refrain from working and the freedom to persuade others to do so.

Such a broad interpretation of workers' rights, based as it is on constitutional guarantees, apparently only reinforces the unions' reliance on legal arguments, often to the neglect of their own organizing efforts. Furthermore, because the broad interpretation tends inevitably to obscure the scope of legal rights, the unions favor it, thus still further reinforcing their tendency to rely on legal arguments. In addition, since fundamental human rights are declared by Article 11 of the Constitution to be "eternal and inviolable" guarantees, the legal argument in favor of a broad interpretation of the right to organize has led to the further contention that any union privilege once acquired through organizing efforts is inviolable. This argument is often utilized by unions to recover what they may have lost in cases where the leadership has failed or is inept. The declaration in the Constitution that such rights are "eternal and inviolable" is only a legal fiction that had its basis in the neglect and violation of human rights experienced in the prewar period. The Constitution at the same time states that human rights shall be maintained by the people's own endeavor, that the people shall refrain from any abuse of these rights, and that they shall be responsible for utilizing them for the public welfare (Article 12). Individual rights are to be respected to the extent that they do not interfere with the public welfare (Article 13). However, such a logical limit often is conveniently ignored by those who assert their own legal rights.

This general trend in labor law theories certainly played a great role in the early postwar period, when the union movement needed strong support in its organizing efforts after a long period of suffering under the oppression of the military government during the war. But to the extent that good industrial relations requires the establishment of a mutually beneficial understanding between the managements and the unions, the trend was not very desirable. As the unions continued to assert their legal rights and to regard the managements as hostile opponents, unnecessary friction was created between the parties. For instance, in the public sector, the legislation prohibiting all acts of dispute has been one of the major causes of trouble in Japanese industrial relations. Here, the government's reliance on excessive legalism noted in the Dreyer Commission Report, and, at the same time, the unions' stubborn advocacy of an absolute recognition of their right to strike have delayed any practical solution of the issue.

In the following sections, we will discuss the impact of legal arguments on the trade union movement in Japan as they apply to different areas: union security, collective bargaining, disputes, and unfair practices.

The Right to Organize and Union Security

The legal theories concerning union security start with the contention that the right of workers to organize is something more positive than the freedom of association of ordinary citizens. Relying on the German theory of *Organizationszwang* (coercion to organize), most of the theories hold that a freedom to refrain from being organized does not exist. In the context of the trade union movement, the aim of such a legal interpretation is to stimulate the unions' organizing efforts, but it also tends to neglect the rights of the minority that may not agree with the views of the majority and its chosen leadership within the union organization. Direct adoption of the German theory in a different context has resulted in problems within the trade union movement. Since World War II, German union organizations have been in principle independent of political affiliations, but in Japan union organizations still are split more or less along ideological and political lines. There have been cases in which workers were expelled from union membership because of differences in political opinions and, under union-shop agreements, were dismissed by their employers; they then challenged the legality of the dismissals in court. In a typical case, a union, by a majority vote in its general assembly, may pass a resolution to support a certain political party or candidates for a general or local election. A minority of members may not agree with the resolution, do not abide by it, and either refuse to contribute to the political fund or actively support other parties or candidates. The result may be expulsion from the union and consequent dismissal by the employer.

The absence of the rights of the minority from the content of the constitutional right to organize causes yet another problem if a minority group forms another union. The theories relied upon in these cases are more or less confusing and even ridiculous in their actual effects. One theory contends that union-security arrangements have no legal effect if the expelled members have organized another union, since the latter should also enjoy the positive right to organize. Then, one may wonder what the legal effect of dismissal would be if the expelled workers were trying to organize and succeeded only after a court ruling upholding their dismissals. Would the dismissals be illegal retroactively after the workers succeeded in organizing a union? Thus, a second group of theories contends that the legal effect of the dismissal depends on which of the unions is a "genuine" one, worthy of being protected. If the existing union is the genuine one, it would be legal to dismiss the expelled workers, but if the newly organized union is the genuine one, the dismissal is illegal. One may also wonder what the conclusions might be if both unions were "genuine" organizations.

A third theory contends that the legality of union action to secure its position depends on the organization rate of the union in a plant. If a union has organized the majority of the workers in a plant, any union-security agreement it concludes has legal effect. This contention is based on Article 7, Section 1, of the Trade Union Law of 1949, which declares that the discharge or other discriminatory treatment of a worker by reason of his union membership or union activities is an unfair labor practice. The proviso to this article states that it shall not prevent an employer from concluding an agreement with the majority union to require membership as a condition of employment. This provision has nothing to do with the legality of particular union-security agreements, but only permits such agreements, excluding them from the law that governs unfair labor practices. But upholders of the third theory contend, relying on this provision, that only an agreement concluded with the majority union has a legal effect. Theoretically speaking, such an interpretation is not absurd, but its actual effect may well be. What would happen if the majority union that concluded such an agreement lost so many members that it became a minority union?

These theories held by the majority of labor law scholars also find support in most of the court decisions. A number of decisions have held that since the right to organize is guaranteed to every union equally, the legal effect of the union shop ceases to be determinative once the majority union that concluded the union-shop agreement no longer enjoys majority status, or if those workers who seceded from the union have succeeded in organizing another one.

On the whole, the general trend of such legal theories reflects the organizational pattern of the Japanese trade union movement, and when one views how union security actually functions in Japan, one can find some peculiarities in comparison with Western countries. First of all, the only meaningful union-security arrangement is the union shop, since unions are organized on an enterprise basis and employee status is a prerequisite for union membership. The closed shop, which requires union membership as a prerequisite for employment, is possible only in the rare case of Kaiin, the Seamen's Union, the only significant industrial union in Japan. Second, most enterprise unions are organized in such a casual way that new employees of an enterprise join the union without much serious consideration, and where a union is firmly established and recognized by the management, joining it is taken as a matter of course. In such cases it is often more difficult for the newly employed worker to refuse to join than to follow the normal course and join.

In fact, it is not unusual for the union officers to be invited to explain the function of the union and to urge new recruits to join during the company's own orientation courses.

Thus, the theory in law that upholds only the legal effect of a union-shop agreement concluded by a majority union reflects the organizational reality where such agreements are concluded in order to confirm and secure the status of the majority union that is accepted by and has a good relationship with the management. Union-security arrangements in Japan rarely contribute to the expansion of a union organization, but only to the maintenance of its already established status. The legal theory that denies the legal effect of a union-shop agreement concluded by a minority union naturally does not help such unions to expand their organization. Furthermore, those theories that deny the effect of the union shop when a union has split even ignore the important function of union-security agreements in maintaining the status quo in a time of crisis.

As a result, those theories that claim to support the workers' right to organize actually fail to promote the unions' real needs to maintain and to promote their organizational power. This is a rather ironic reality of the labor law that is supposedly "prolabor" and devoted to the union cause.

The Peculiar Distinction between Power and Violence

The majority theory of the constitutional guarantee of the right to act collectively, according to most legal experts, goes beyond the right to strike. Union activities other than the strike tend to be regarded as legal in principle, and the courts often hold that this right permits unions to engage in "positive" actions—something more than the "negative" refusal to work. The attitude of the courts toward violence is the best illustration of this interpretation. For instance, Japanese courts often hold that unions may go beyond peaceful picketing, since something more than freedom of speech and association is guaranteed by the right to act collectively. The result is that it is very difficult to make a clear-cut distinction between legal collective acts and illegal violence, although Article 1, Section 2, of the Trade Union Law states that in no event shall acts of violence be construed as appropriate for trade unions.

The Supreme Court ruled as follows in a case involving violence, threats, and intimidation:

It goes without saying that the union (and consequently, the union officials and union members who comply with the will of the union) may by peaceful means of persuasion, request, orally and in writing, that persons starting work cease to do so, but causing such persons to suspend starting work by means of violence, intimidation, or force must be construed *generally* as illegal. Naturally, *though,* whether an act bringing about the suspension of starting work is to be recognized as illegal or not must be carefully *determined by particularly taking into account the various circumstances* at the time the particular strike or other acts of dispute are being carried out.[2]

The court concluded its decisions on the case in question as follows:

The union started to go on strike demanding better working conditions. A former president of the union and some others who had close connections with the management started to work. The defendants . . . got extremely angry with the dissident group and joined several others who were sitting in front of a truck in order to obstruct its path. . . . Judging from these developments, the conduct of the defendants was, so to speak, a matter of the union's internal affairs. Moreover, they only joined others who had already been trying to prevent the moving of the truck. Thus their conduct does not constitute a forcible obstruction of the business of another.[3]

The Supreme Court upheld a decision of a high court in another case as follows:

The conduct of the defendants occurred *in connection with internal union affairs* during the dispute. Moreover, the victim, being in a responsible executive position, participated in factional activities and was accused and summoned to be heard and examined on charges of betrayal by the central committee of the union . . . and [the defendants] then caught both his arms, held his shoulders and when he tried to escape, restrained him for several minutes, finally persuading him to go to the nearby Hotel Botansō. Having committed no other violence or threats, the conduct of the defendants under the circumstances does not constitute an unlawful arrest of another.[4]

When the author was teaching Japanese industrial relations abroad, he found it almost impossible to make foreign students understand the reasoning of the Japanese courts. First of all, the argument that the defendants' conduct was "a matter of internal union affairs" was hardly persuasive. The students pointed out that, in these cases of conflict among union members, the Supreme Court emphasized that the defendants were incensed by the betrayal of their former associates. They added that, intentionally or not, the court in its judgment gave greater weight to the subjective condition of the defendants than to the objective evidence of violent acts. The students inquired whether criminal conduct was excusable in Japan if a defendant was angry—a very good question indeed. The court ruled in the last case as if the victim, who previously had been trying to escape, suddenly became willing to go along with the defendants, which sounds very unlikely. The Japanese courts often "take into account various circumstances," but in most cases non-Japanese find it very difficult to perceive what these "circumstances" are.

Foreigners ask, for instance, what Japanese courts would say if several *yakuza* (gangsters) apprehended a citizen and, as he was trying to escape, caught him by the arms and brought him, "with his consent," to a hotel.

Upon being told that the courts certainly would find this a crime of unlawful detainment and confinement, they then point out that the Japanese courts give extraordinary privileges to unions when their members perform such acts. In answer to this, most Japanese labor lawyers present their trump card, that is, that the workers' right to act collectively, as guaranteed by the Constitution, is distinct from and goes beyond mere freedom of association.

The two cases mentioned above are not, however, typical of all Supreme Court decisions. In most cases where striking union members prevented others from working by mass picketing or by forcible obstruction, the Supreme Court ruled that the accused were guilty of breaking the law. Lawyers who represent unions are very critical of any court decisions that are unfavorable to labor. They even find fault with the court's arguments in the two cases just cited, pointing out that the court failed to declare the union members' conduct an appropriate act of dispute and only held that their behavior did not constitute criminal conduct, given the circumstances. According to most of them, this was an incorrect interpretation of the law concerning the right to act collectively; obstruction tactics should be recognized as "proper" acts during labor disputes. Many lower court decisions reflect this opinion.

As already mentioned, Article 1, Section 2, of the Trade Union Law states that violence is an improper act of dispute. However, unions' lawyers say that while violence (*bōryoku*) is not proper, power (*jitsuryoku*) is permissible, a viewpoint that has been sustained by a number of lower court decisions. This is a distinction that foreigners find hard to grasp. Literally translated, jitsuryoku means "real power." In a labor relations context, it would describe a situation where, for instance, union members sit down arm-in-arm in front of the entrance to a plant, thus preventing the workers from entering without hitting or kicking them. "Power" in this context is not just psychological or spiritual, but is physical as well. To English-speaking people, to say that physical power does not involve violence is a mere play on words. But it is one of the traditional Japanese ways of thinking to regard a certain kind of human violence as a natural phenomenon that can be distinguished from a human violation, or a physical attack upon a person's body. This concept is related to the idea that human violence, just as a natural calamity, is an act of God if it is carried out as punishment (by God) against an evil. The famous story of the vengeance exacted by the 47 *rōnin* (masterless samurai) for the death of their former Lord is the best illustration of such heavenly punishment. The vengeance itself is an act of violence, but since it is a punishment for the evil deeds of the opponents of the dead lord, it is completely justified in the Japanese mind, and even praiseworthy. The story evokes the emotional sympathy of the audience whenever this most favorite Kabuki drama is performed today.

The arguments in favor of the "real power" of unions rest on feelings of sympathy and on the Japanese "logic" of "heaven's punishment." Similar assumptions underlie the strictures against employers who discipline their employees as well as the union lawyers' criticism of courts that penalize the behavior of union members. These arguments run as follows: "Intervention in union organization is a serious crime; therefore, violence is a proper punishment for those who participate in such crimes," or "Violence is certainly excessive, but the employers should be blamed for their refusal to entertain the proper demands of the innocent union members." This way of thinking is the basis for the two Supreme Court decisions mentioned above. Not only in industrial relations, but also in political movements, it is often emphasized that those who resorted to violence were simply innocent persons who became indignant over the evil deeds of their shameless opponents; thus the violence against them was deserved and was only the punishment of God. This logic of punishment by God acknowledges the absolute authority of self-appointed prosecutors who accuse their opponents of evil, charge and judge them, and carry out their verdicts. Thus, whenever a union is a defendant in court, all it need do is to emphasize the cruelty of the employer and to portray itself as a group of innocent men who were forced to stand up and fight an unscrupulous tyrant. If the union is successful with this appeal, there is a good chance that its violent acts will be regarded as a just judgment against the employer.

The role of this traditional logic in defending the radical activities of political organizations and militant unions is not only ironic and absurd, but it is also harmful. Use of such arguments to justify violent trends among so-called "progressive" groups may well result in their neglecting any real organizing efforts. Quite often violent actions are desperate efforts to hide organizational weakness and, at least in industrial relations, may be taken by minority unions that have lost the support of the workers. It is very symptomatic that the legal theories which insist upon regarding "real power" as proper acts of dispute often try to justify their arguments by pointing out differences between Japanese and Western unions. According to them, Japanese unions are more vulnerable to strike-breakers because of their enterprise-union organization, and Japanese employers are more hostile to unions than their counterparts in the West. Regardless of the appropriateness of such contentions, what they really mean is that, because of their organizational weakness, Japanese unions need more legal protection than do Western unions. The argument concerning the lawfulness of mass picketing is typical in this context. The claim is made that since Japanese employers are hostile toward union organizations and can easily find strike-breakers, the unions are entitled to resort to more violent actions than are Western unions. In the final analysis, it seems to the author that the persistent claim that the Japanese situation is unique only serves to perpetuate the weakness of Japanese union organizations. In spite of the argument that "real power" promotes the unions' cause, it will not result in a stronger union movement; rather, it may be an obstacle to the establishment of sound industrial relationships based on the effective bargaining power of the unions.[5]

The Legal Interpretation of a Strike Vote

Another example of the legalism of the Japanese union movement can be found in attitudes toward the strike vote. Article 5, Section 2, of the Trade Union Law stipulates that the constitution of a union shall include a provision requiring a majority vote by secret ballot of either members or delegates before a strike action may be begun. What the law requires here is only that there must be such a provision in the union rules or constitution before a union qualifies for registration with the Labor Relations Commission and before it may appeal disputes to it. Neither a strike by an unqualified union nor one begun without a secret ballot vote and the majority support of the union membership is illegal. However, union members and even some officers simply misunderstand this provision of the law; many of them think that if a strike is carried out without following the secret-ballot procedure and without the support of a majority of the members, it is illegal. Thus union officers tend to observe what is frequently mistakenly understood to be a legal requirement. This makes them appear to be very law-abiding and respectful of the democratic role of union administration.

However, this "law-abiding" attitude of union officials in Japan is not completely admirable, since they often regard the majority vote as only a legal requirement and disregard its real meaning as support for strike actions. In most Western countries, there are no legal limitations on a union's decision to strike. Rather, unions have their own rules on how such decisions are made, and many have established rules to require at least a majority support for action throughout every stage of a strike, regardless of any legal requirement. For instance, West German unions have provisions requiring at least a majority vote in support of strike actions, and some require a two-thirds vote. Union rules in Germany often require that another vote be taken whenever the situation changes—for example, when the employer responds to the union's demand or when he makes a counterproposal after a strike has begun.

Japanese unions seem to respect the majority vote rule mainly because the law requires it, or because they believe that it does. Most unions do not conduct another vote after they receive majority support for strike action in the beginning, even if the situation changes drastically. This is one of the reasons that, in many cases, those who are dissatisfied with the union leadership for continuing a strike for which there no longer is majority support secede and organize a breakaway union. Ohta Kaoru, former president of Sōhyō, wrote:

> Quite often attempts are made to alienate members from their leaders by propagating rumors that the union is being taken advantage of by power-hungry persons, or that it is taken over by outsiders. In such cases the leaders should always boldly ask for the support of their members by means of a general secret ballot. If the majority does not support them, or if only a slight majority does so, they should stop the strike. . . . In [the] case of the dispute at the Muroran Plant of the Nihon Steel Company, the split in the union was probably caused by the decision of the union's Central Committee to reject the company's proposal without seeking rank and file approval in a general vote. This provided a good excuse for a breakaway.[6]

Although Japanese unions obediently follow the legal regulations concerning a democratic strike vote, they do not really understand its meaning within the trade union movement, unlike unions in the West that have learned the bitter truth, from long experience, that a strike that is not supported by the majority of the union members will be lost sooner or later. These legalistic attitudes are not confined to the union movement in Japan, but are also found in other organizations, especially those that claim to defend human rights against the "conservative" or even "reactionary" government. From the beginning of the modernization of Japan in the Meiji period, those organizations whose aim was to defend people's rights have often been eager to claim legal rights against the government and to neglect them with respect to their internal democratic rules, ignoring or rejecting minority opinions within their own organizations, so that unions are rent by factionalism in the same way that extremist political organizations often are. The frequent splitting of union organizations that is found even today, especially after a period of autocratic rule by militant leaders, is only one example of a common feature of Japanese organizations.

The Right to Bargain as Enforced by the Courts

According to Article 7, Section 2, of the Trade Union Law, an employer's refusal to bargain with the union is an unfair labor practice, and the Labor Relations Commission shall order the employer to bargain in good faith. However, since the Constitution guarantees the workers' right to bargain, unions also may seek relief from a court when the employer refuses to negotiate. Legally speaking, the only remedy for an employer's infringement of this workers' right might be at most reparation of damages caused by the refusal. But practically, this does not mean very much, since the amount of damage caused by the refusal to bargain is almost impossible to determine or verify, and thus is not a very suitable remedy. In spite of this legal difficulty, unions continue to seek court remedies. They usually appeal for a provisional order to bargain, and in many cases a court will issue such an order. Provisional orders in civil procedures are measures to preserve the legal duty to deliver certain goods and other property or to affirm a temporary legal status in order to avoid a change in an existing situation until civil procedures are completed and a final decision issued. Thus, provisional orders are to be invoked only as supplemental to formal civil procedures. However, in most of the cases the unions never proceed to the formal procedures and are satisfied with only the temporary orders. Legally speaking, provisional orders to bargain do not make much sense since they are not enforceable. But the unions are not concerned about their legal effect. For them, a legal order without legal effect does make sense insofar as they can use it to increase their bargaining power. It is undeniable that unions find the court procedures useful in the following two ways: First, they use them as one stage in their disputes with employers. Second, when they do get a provisional order from a court, even if the order has no legal effect, they are able to use it to force a management to bargain.

One of the reasons for the unions' reliance on the courts for provisional orders is the delay in the procedures at the Labor Relations Commissions.[7] On the average in 1976, unfair labor practice cases before the Central Labor Relations Commission took 624 days from the date complaints were filed until orders or decisions were issued.[8] Such a long delay makes the function of the Labor Relations Commission almost meaningless in the sense of giving effective administrative remedies to the unions. The reasons for the delay are multiple. The long-established practice is to conduct hearings in a way that is very similar to court procedures, with lawers participating, formal cross-examination of witnesses, etc. However, the important fact is that the unions are not very eager to settle a case since they regard the appeal to the commission as another stage on which to challenge the managements. In fact, when the unions seek legal or administrative remedies either in the courts or at the commissions, they often actually are not seeking to bargain on a specific subject. What they really want is to get certification of their legitimacy by governmental institutions.

Thus, they seek union legitimacy not through the support of the workers, but as a legal concept. This tendency is very well exemplified by the strike vote, as it was described above. The Trade Union Law says only that a union must provide in its constitution for a majority vote for strike action if it is to be qualified and eligible for the protections provided by that particular law. Unions could ignore such a requirement if they chose not to have the privileges accorded to qualified unions. As the Constitution guarantees the workers' right to organize, the unions could enjoy the right to bargain and to act collectively, and they would have no difficulty functioning as trade unions without being qualified under the Trade Union Law. The differences between qualified and unqualified unions are that only the former are able to seek remedies before the Labor Relations Commissions, to be recognized as legal entities, and to extend the effect of collective agreements to cover unorganized workers. Both are allowed to perform the fundamental union functions of bargaining, striking, and concluding agreements with employers. But most union leaders and the rank and file still do not consider the possibility of remaining outside the legal system.

Legitimacy under the law is very important for Japanese unions; this is why they seek legal remedies even if quite often the order to bargain is issued by the courts[9] or the commissions after prolonged procedures. It is not unusual for an order to be issued to bargain on the year-end bonuses or wage increases for some year quite long in the past.

The reliance on legal remedies for bargaining purposes sometimes reaches such an extreme that a union will try to win certain wage increases without bargaining. Several Labor Relations Commission orders have been issued in cases where employers have tried to get a productivity clause in the agreement as a condition for the awarding of bonuses or wage increases. A productivity agreement normally is very simple, such as "the union will cooperate to improve productivity." Most unions affiliated with Sōhyō or other unions with a more or less radical ideology categorically refuse to accept such clauses.

In a typical case, the employer had granted wage increases or bonuses to the members of unions that had accepted the conditions, and he had paid them in accordance with the agreements concluded with those unions. The unions that did not agree with the conditions and whose members thus did not receive their bonuses or wage increases—mostly minority unions—appealed to the commission. They claimed that the employer had discriminated by refusing to pay the bonuses or to grant the wage increases which were given to the other unions and had at the same time interfered with and attempted to dominate the unions by insisting upon conditions that were unacceptable to them and by discriminating against their members as a result. In most of these cases, the commission has ordered the employers not only to stop their interference and to bargain with the unions in good faith without insisting upon the disputed conditions, but also to pay the same wages and bonuses to members of the appealing unions as were being paid to the members of other unions.[10] Thus the commission awarded these unions something that they had not gained by their own power in collective bargaining. Cases of this type have been growing in number, especially in the past few years. The trend seems to be that as some employers try to improve and rationalize their businesses in the face of problems caused by the recession following the oil crisis, they are becoming more and more hostile to unions that are not cooperative in such company efforts. However, some commission orders seem to be overprotective of unions and to be a denial of the principle of free collective bargaining. This overprotectiveness may well hamper the development of the unions' power through their own organizational efforts.

An Appraisal of the Overprotection of Unions
By Legal Theories and Cases

In the foregoing sections we have seen that the rights to organize, bargain, and act collectively are recognized only for workers, not for the employers. The legal theories and court decisions extend this one-sided protection, basing it in part on the constitutional guarantee of the rights of workers, but also partly on the ideological interpretation that labor law, substantively, is to protect workers. The protection of individual workers certainly is the basic idea of protective labor legislation. But the rationale for labor relations law is not necessarily to protect workers or unions. In most countries of the world, the idea underlying collective bargaining legislation is to assure the equality of bargaining power of the parties in a union-management relationship, the stability of industrial relations based on free bargaining, and the like.

In order to evaluate the real impact of both the trend toward overprotection of the union movement by legal theories and court decisions and the legalism which we find in union ideologies and in their apparent reliance upon legal arguments, we should take into consideration the fact that such legal arguments are not necessarily a reflection of all union activities and attitudes, but are only pathological phenomena of the trade union movement. Actually, the cases brought to the courts and the Labor Relations Commission represent exceptional situations in day-to-day industrial relations. The arguments concerning such cases might be regarded as rather extreme.

In comparison with some Western countries, the number of labor law cases in the courts or before the Labor Relations Commissions in Japan is surprisingly small.[11]

From this fact one can also argue that the impact of the legal theories or arguments on the Japanese union movement is not very great. If it were true, we should not take so seriously the charge that Japanese unions or employers are legalistic. However, as the attitude of the unions toward strike votes shows, the legalistic attitude reflects and at the same time regulates more or less the trend of the whole union movement. The small number of cases does not necessarily refute the charge of legalism among managements and unions in Japan. On the contrary, there are some symptoms of a strong influence of a legalistic way of thinking in Japanese industrial relations. Most Westerners will be surprised to find that there are more than ten journals specializing in labor law published in Japan, some of them monthly and some even biweekly. Quite a few organizations specialize in labor law as well as in labor economics or management science, doing business mainly by providing advice and information on labor law problems. These organizations hold lectures and discussion meetings that attract large audiences from the companies and unions. Newspapers quite frequently report court decisions concerning labor. The number of labor law scholars is surprisingly large. Most universities, even those without departments of law, have at least one full-time professor of labor law. The Japan Labor Law Association has more than 500 members. Thus, the small number of court and commission cases does not mean that legal arguments are not very influential in Japanese industrial relations; other evidence suggests the contrary.

Furthermore, the most essential character of an industrial relations system is often to be found in its crises—that is, when disputes occur. The most extreme cases of conflict in Japan become legal battles between management and labor. Chapter 8 is concerned with industrial conflict and conflict resolution and will show the extent and meaning of the trend of the union movement in the area of industrial conflict.

Notes

1 For a systematic explanation of the Japanese labor law system, see Hanami 1979a.

2 Japan v. Hirata, Supreme Court, III Petty Bench, December 11, 1956, *Saikō Saibansho Keiji Hanreishū* [Supreme Court, criminal cases] 10, pp. 1605–9. Emphasis added.

3 Ibid., p. 1609.

4 Kido et al. v. Japan, Fukuoka High Court, April 11, 1964, *Bessatsu Rōdō Hōritsu Jumpō* [Biweekly journal of labor law, appendix] No. 466, p. 2; Supreme Court, III Petty Bench, March 10, 1964, *Bessatsu Rōdō Hōritsu Jumpō* No. 525, p. 26.

5 In most societies, the custom of blood feud existed in their primitive period, and out of it the legal system of *talio, compensatio,* and self-defense developed into the modern legal notions of equity, compensation, or justifiable self-defense. The author's point in this chapter is that excessive and almost violent actions by union members could be justifiable under such modern legal notions, but regarding these actions as proper acts of dispute will result in the acceptance of these rather exceptionally justifiable acts as normal ones, and thus the development of a sound and rational union movement through the strengthening of their bargaining power will be hampered.

6 Ohta 1961, p. 67. The Nihon Steel strike of 1954 is one of the typical cases where union organizations split because of worker dissatisfaction over the long-continuing strike led by militant leaders.

7 Local Labor Relations Commissions are set up in each prefecture, while the Central Labor Relations Commission is located in Tokyo. The jurisdiction of the local commission applies when the parties live in the prefecture, or their headquarters are located in it, or if the labor dispute occurred there. The Central Labor Relations Commission reviews the orders and decisions taken by the local commissions in the field of unfair labor practices and adjudicates those cases which cover more than one prefecture or which are clearly of national importance. Equal numbers of representatives on the commissions are drawn from workers, company management, and the general public to make up the membership of the commissions.

The commissions have two main functions and a few minor ones. The main ones are adjudication of unfair labor practice cases and dispute settlement by conciliation, mediation, or arbitration. Other functions include screening the qualifications of unions to participate in adjudicative procedures or to be registered as legal entities, and extending the effect of collective agreements.

8 Chūo Rōdō Iinkai, Jimukyoku 1977, p. 9. In the United States, the procedure of the National Labor Relations Board, the counterpart of the Japanese Labor Relations Commission, took 334 days, on average, from the date of filing of charges to the issuance of orders during the first half of 1975. See Murphy 1975, pp. 551–53.

9 Legal theories are divided as to whether the court may issue an order to bargain, since it is doubtful, according to the orthodox theory of the law of civil procedure, whether it is possible to admit a temporary order which will in effect materialize the actual situation to be sought by the final decision. However, in about two-thirds of such cases, the courts do admit such an order. The leading cases are: Ashiwara Unsō [Branch of the National Trade Union of Automobile Transport Workers] v. Ashiwara Unyu Kikō Co., Osaka District Court, August 1, 1974, and November 14, 1974, *Rōdō Hanrei* [Labor law cases] No. 249, p. 63; *Zensompō* (All Japan Property Insurance Labor Union), Sumitomo Kaijō Kasai Branch v. Sumitomo Kaijō Kasai Insurance Co., Tokyo District Court, August 29, 1968, *Rōdō Kankei Minji Saiban Reishū* [Labor Law Civil Cases] 19:4, p. 1082.

10 Hōchi Newspaper Co. Case, Central Labor Relations Commission, March 19, 1973, *Bessatsu Chūo Rōdō Jihō* [Central labor journal] Appendix No. 850, p. 66; RKB Mainichi Broadcasting Co. Case, Fukuoka Labor Relations Commission, May 1, 1973, *Bessatsu Chūo Rōdō Jihō* No. 850, p. 44; Japan Mail Order Co. Case, Tokyo Labor Relations Commission, May 8, 1973, *Bessatsu Chūo Rōdō Jihō* No. 851, p. 69.

11 The following table shows the number of labor cases pending before the respective institutions in Japan and the United States in 1976 and West Germany in 1974. The number for West Germany is surprisingly high, and even that of the U.S. National Labor Relations Board (NLRB) is 15 times higher than the figure for the Japan Labor Relations Commission.

	No. of Cases	Civilian Labor Force Employed (1975)	Cases per Thousand in Labor Force
United States (NLRB)	34,569 (1976)	84,783,000	0.407
Japan		52,230,000	
Labor Relations Comm.	1,417 (1976)		0.027
Legal Court	2,719 (1976)		0.052
West Germany			
(Labor Court)	376,186 (1974)	24,828,000	1.515

Sources: Civilian labor force: ILO Yearbook 1976; NLRB: *Annual Report of the NLRB*, 1976; Japan, Labor Relations Commission: Chūō Rōdō Iinkai Jimukyoku, 1977; Japan Legal Court: *Hōsō Jihō* [Lawyers Association Journal] 29:7 (1977) German Labor Court: Bundes Ministerium für Arbeit u. Sozial Ordnung, *Arbeits- und Sozialstatistik*, 1975.

8 *Yasuhiko Matsuda*

Conflict Resolution in Japanese Industrial Relations

A labor law, or any law for that matter, can be examined in terms of how it affects the resolution of conflict. After all, a function of law is to prevent disputes between individuals as well as between an individual or a group of individuals and the society at large. It should also assist in resolving disputes when they occur by providing a set of substantive norms and standards, a set of procedures for conflict resolution, or both.

Under the Japanese Labor Standards Law, a controversy over wages, hours, or working conditions can be dealt with in either of two ways—as a dispute between the employer and the employee concerned or as one between the employer and the government, representing the people. Although the law prescribes certain standards, such as the eight-hour workday, that can be used in resolving employee–employer disputes, it also specifies some procedures, such as a labor inspection, correction orders, and criminal penalties, that the government may use in enforcing the standards.

The Trade Union Law, on the other hand, has very little to say about substantive rights or standards for settling collective labor disputes, and instead emphasizes a procedure—collective bargaining—for their voluntary resolution. The law is designed to help the parties in union–management relationships to develop their own substantive and procedural rules for the resolution of both individual and collective disputes by mutual agreement. To be successful in promoting the voluntary resolution of labor conflicts, the law must (1) assure that the parties deal with each other fairly in their relations, and (2) prevent an outcome of any labor dispute that would be detrimental to society. To achieve the former objective, the Trade Union Law specifies certain labor practices of the employer as unfair; to meet the latter, a system for settlement of labor disputes is set out in detail in the Labor Relations Adjustment Law. Labor Relations Commissions are charged with administering both functions. It should be noted, of course, that all of these substantive and procedural principles stem from articles in the Constitution that guarantee minimum standards of working conditions (Article 27, paragraph 2) and workers' rights to bargain and act collectively (Article 28).

However, no Japanese labor law provides any specific methods for applying either statutory or mutually agreed-upon standards in resolving labor disputes, except for a quasi-judicial procedure before a Labor Relations Commission in unfair labor practice cases. Thus, all disputes involving vested individual or collective rights come under the jurisdiction of ordinary courts and are governed by civil procedure law if the dispute is between private parties and by administrative litigation procedure law if it is between a private party and the government; examples of cases of the latter type would be a complaint against a Labor Relations Commission order or a dispute between the government and its employees.

There are two reasons that no specific procedure for labor litigation exists. According to legal theory, all individual conflicts over rights arise out of the employment contract, because the standards at issue are those concerning working conditions and the fair treatment of workers that have been incorporated in collective agreements or designated in the Labor Standards Law.[1] A dispute over the application and interpretation of a collective agreement is considered to be one that arose out of a contract between an employer and a union and thus it, too, is treated under ordinary contract law. In the absence of any specific statutory procedure, it might have been, or still might be, practical for employers and unions to negotiate voluntary grievance procedures for the resolution of disputes over rights and to include them in collective agreements.

The legal framework for conflict resolution thus outlined no doubt has had a considerable influence on the development of both the patterns of labor conflict—frequent but brief acts of dispute and the various forms they take—and the way they are resolved—the almost total reliance on the courts to play the role of arbitrator rather than developing a private system of grievance arbitration. The constitutional guarantee of the right of workers to organize seems to have had a formidable impact upon how labor disputes have come to be resolved in Japan. Under this constitutional guarantee, as broadly defined, many a labor dispute which would otherwise be regarded as involving interests may possibly be reduced to one over a constitutional right—that is, a constitutional provision is applied in the settlement. For example, a court, relying on the constitutional guarantee of the workers' right to organize, may resolve a conflict between an employer and a union over the scope of union activities on company premises during working hours by determining to what extent the employer should tolerate union activities, rather than leaving the matter to be settled in the prolonged collective bargaining process.

In this chapter an attempt will be made to answer such questions as: Why has not grievance arbitration been adopted in Japan? Why do Japan's courts sometimes act like arbitrators? Why are acts of dispute so brief and why do they occur so often and take on such a variety of forms? My purpose here, therefore, is to examine the possible relationship between the legal framework for conflict resolution in Japan and contemporary practices in both labor disputes and how they are settled.

Needless to say, there are a number of informal ways for resolving conflict that have very little, if anything, to do with the legal framework, and it is probably true that many problems in employer–employee relations in Japan are settled informally in conversation over drinks. Although this method of conflict resolution is an important one, it will not be dealt with in this chapter.

Conflict Resolution before the Labor Relations Commission: The Unfair Labor Practice Procedure

Two contradictory phenomena have been observed in the way the Labor Relations Commission handles unfair labor practice cases. On the one hand, the hearing procedure is becoming more and more like a court procedure in a civil suit, with less emphasis on prehearing investigation and more on strict adherence to the rules of evidence. Yet, on the other hand, the Commission's remedial orders are more diverse than they once were and now seem to resemble the results of mediation or even arbitration awards. The former trend may be attributed to a number of factors. An adversary system is employed and lawyers for each party are involved at every level. Also, a civil suit over the same unfair labor practice may be pending simultaneously in a court, and, above all, there is always the possibility of judicial review of the commission order. Unlike the practice in the United States, the reviewing court is not bound by a commission's findings even when these findings are supported by substantial evidence.

The complexity of employer unfair labor practice cases in recent years and the mixture of issues of rights and interests in labor disputes brought to the commission may be contributing to the trend for commission orders to read like mediated settlements. For example, a conditional order requiring the employer to post a notice in return for the union's apology to the employer was issued in the Nobeoka Post Office case. In this case it was found that the union's activities, which were never declared illegal, had provoked or led to the employer's committing an unfair labor practice.

In the Nobeoka Post Office case, the postmaster's prohibition of and interference with union members' access to the post office premises was found to have been provoked by the union officers' repeated entry into the post office building in spite of the postmaster's warnings. In this case, the Public Corporation and National Enterprise Labor Relations Commission ordered the postmaster to deliver a letter of apology to the union, along with a sworn statement that he would not repeat the unfair labor practice, on condition that the union should officially apologize to the postmaster for its repeated violations of office rules.[2] This order was sustained by the Tokyo High Court. Decisions of this type resemble settlements that might be reached in mediation, in that the employer does not have to comply unless the union meets the conditions specified in the commission order.

Another special type of remedy is the so-called "make-whole" order under which an employer who has not responded to union demands or who has refused to bargain is directed to provide members of the complaining union with the same working conditions as those already given to other employees.[3] In a way, such a remedy is not unlike an arbitration award in which disputed provisions of a new contract are decided by an arbitrator when the parties are unable to reach an agreement in negotiations and mediation has failed.

Orders of both types in unfair labor practice cases have been regarded as appropriate and useful to restore or maintain the smooth and stable operation of industrial relations systems.

It has happened that the public member in charge of a commission case, before reaching his decision, has informally sought the advice and assistance of his union and employer colleagues in an effort to explore every possible way to reach a conciliated settlement.[4] This arrangement has proved to be highly successful because of the influence the labor and management representatives may have on the parties to the conflict; it is particularly useful when an unfair labor practice case arises out of a labor dispute that has also been submitted to the commission for adjustment.

With commission procedures becoming more like court procedures, delay has become a serious problem. As pointed out in chapter 7, the average unfair labor practice case today takes well over 600 days to go through the procedure of the Labor Relations Commission just at the local level. Thus, at this point a brief description of the unfair labor practice procedure is in order.

When an aggrieved person or persons, including a union, files a complaint charging an employer with committing an unfair labor practice, the local Labor Relations Commission first notifies the charged employer and asks for his response to the complaint; then it engages in a prehearing investigation. Unlike the procedure before the U.S. National Labor Relations Board in unfair labor practice cases, in Japan the aggrieved becomes the charging party (like a plaintiff in a civil procedure). At both the prehearing investigation and at the hearing itself, the parties usually are represented by lawyers and the adversary principle applies. Thus, the commission, as represented by the public member in charge, is unable to take the initiative in collecting evidence or promoting a speedy procedure.

A public member conducts a hearing and other commission members who represent labor and management may participate, questioning witnesses or consulting with the public member. (As will be explained in more detail below, the role of these participating members is more significant than it may first appear.)

At the conclusion of a hearing or a series of hearings, the commission chairman calls a meeting at which all of the public members consider the findings and decide on an order, either granting in full or in part the relief sought by the complainant or dismissing the complaint.

Within a designated period, either or both parties may request a review of the local commission's order by the Central Labor Relations Commission, or they may bring an administrative suit against the commission in the district court. If the parties choose the former route and are still dissatisfied with the result, they or another party may seek judicial review of the central commission's order. If the parties select the latter route and bring a suit in the district court, the commission itself may find it necessary to seek an emergency court order to enforce its own order, in full or in part, from the court where the administrative suit is pending. Although the employer is not allowed to challenge the enforcement order, he may seek a suspension of execution, or *cesset executio,* of the original commission order in advance and thus be able to prevent the court from issuing an emergency order.

Of course all parties concerned, including the commission, may appeal the court decision to a higher court and eventually to the Supreme Court. While a commission's order is under challenge, it is not enforceable unless a court grants a commission's petition for an emergency order.

A commission's order becomes final either when it is sustained by a court and no appeal is filed or when the time period allowed for challenge has lapsed. If a final order is not obeyed, the court may levy penalties of fines or imprisonment, or both, on the recalcitrant employer. However, an employer may file a complaint in a higher court, contesting any fine or imprisonment imposed upon him for violation either of the commission's or of an emergency order, and it is possible for him to appeal all the way up to the Supreme Court.

Taking into consideration the fact that litigants are allowed to make new contentions and to introduce new evidence at almost every step of judicial review, one could easily assume that it might take decades for a dispute involving an employer's unfair labor practice to be resolved once and for all. In fact, many employers as well as employees and unions, for a variety of reasons, have attempted to use every device and exhaust every available procedure in these cases (Matsuda 1980, p. 178, n.10).

For employers, or at least those who can afford it, this sort of demonstration of an indomitable resolve to litigate a case, regardless of whether they expect to win or lose, may well be for the purpose of discouraging other employees from making unfair labor practice complaints. Desperate but determined employees or unions, particularly when they are sure that they will win, pursue cases to higher courts not only to publicize an employer's unfairness, but also to get a governmental institution such as the commission or the court to certify that they are legitimate unions or that they have been pursuing legitimate causes (see chapter 7). Thus, the lengthy procedure serves both parties well. They are using litigation not to resolve a conflict but to demonstrate their devotion to a cause or a principle.

Differences between decisions at the commission level and court rulings as well as inconsistency and unpredictability among the court decisions themselves are to some extent inevitable, because the cases more or less involve elements of conflict of interests. This factor has no doubt further encouraged the parties to insist upon litigating every dispute all the way to the end.

Conflict Resolution in the Courts

The Emergence and Predominance of Provisional Disposition Orders

Of more than 1,000 civil suits on labor that are brought to district courts every year, about half seek a provisional disposition order (see table 8.1). This procedure has become the primary method for resolving both individual and collective labor disputes in postwar Japan where no special procedure or special court for labor cases has ever been established, although most of the statutory labor law is based upon principles that are very different from those of the civil law system, and most of the litigation arises out of labor conflicts that are different from civil disputes.

As explained in chapter 7, provisional orders in civil disputes are used primarily to secure temporarily the conditions that are necessary for enforcement of a final judgment to be rendered in a civil suit, presently in progress,

Table 8.1
Number of Civil Cases Received by District Courts, 1974–80

Year	Total	Provisional Disposition Order Sought				Merit Determination Sought			
		Total	By Labor	By Employer	By Others	Total	By Labor	By Employer	By Others
1974	1,191 (100)	724 (60.8)	648	48	28	467 (39.2)	433	10	24
1975	1,482 (100)	892 (60.2)	812	61	19	590 (39.8)	543	25	22
1976	1,559 (100)	885 (56.8)	826	40	19	674 (43.2)	620	27	27
1977	1,630 (100)	743 (45.6)	711	22	10	887 (54.4)	626	237	24
1978	1,393 (100)	714 (51.3)	668	30	16	679 (48.7)	655	12	12
1979	1,294 (100)	667 (51.5)	663	27	7	627 (48.5)	589	26	12
1980	1,182 (100)	577 (48.8)	536	34	7	605 (51.2)	567	19	19

Source: *Hōsō Jihō* [Lawyers Association journal] 33:7, pp. 158–59.
Note: Percentages in parentheses.

between the same parties. Therefore, a petition for a provisional order is granted only when the danger to the petitioner or to his rights is so imminent that the plaintiff in litigation cannot wait for the final decision—and also when he is likely to win the case on merit.

It is interesting to note that among the earliest uses of provisional orders were cases where employers sought court orders to remove sit-down strikers from company premises or to stop workers from engaging in "production control" tactics, on the grounds that company property was in imminent danger and that the employer would otherwise suffer irreparable damages. Then employees who allegedly had been discharged illegally began to file petitions seeking provisional orders for the payment of compensatory wages. The courts granted these petitions, finding that, in light of the rapid postwar inflation, it was urgent that all discharged employees be paid because they had no other sources of earnings.

From this sketch of the historic experience under the provisional order procedure in labor cases, it is clear that this kind of rapid interim relief by a court was supposed to be primarily a temporary device, intended to deal with extraordinary situations in the immediate postwar years and not to be permanently adopted for the resolution of conflict. However, the provisional order turned out to be the decisive weapon used to resolve labor disputes, or at least to end them, as illustrated by the temporary restraining orders issued against the sit-down strikers and the workers engaged in "production control" (Yoshikawa 1968).

The trend toward using provisional orders as the last resort in cases of industrial conflict was further spurred when the courts began issuing "the provisional order with expectation of voluntary compliance," such as the one ordering the employer to treat the petitioner (a discharged employee) as his employee until a final decision could be made on the merits of the case (Hagisawa 1968, p.5). Although it is impossible to enforce this type of order, because of the belief that an employer ought not to be forced to make employees work and because of the difficulty in checking whether the employer in fact complies, the courts were willing to issue provisional orders in the belief that they would encourage the parties to resolve the dispute by themselves.

As the pace of inflation moderated and people's living conditions improved, a few courts began to reject that part of a petition for a temporary order seeking pay for a discharged employee; they would issue only one temporarily affirming employment status. But the general trend among the courts was to continue to grant both types of relief simply on the ground that loss of employment status and wages is a matter of life and death for workers.

Over the years, court procedures in suits seeking provisional orders have become markedly slower and more and more like hearings in cases to be decided on merit, with cross-examination of witnesses, etc. The court enjoys relatively broad discretion in the way it chooses to handle such cases. It can render a decision either on an *ex parte* basis or after hearing from both parties, or, if it wishes, after cross-examination of witnesses presented by both parties. Furthermore, judges may grant a provisional order whenever they have drawn an inference, not necessarily based upon a preponderance of evidence (as required in an ordinary civil procedure) but based upon the evidence submitted by either or both parties with regard to two things: (1) the urgency of the petitioner's need to obtain a remedy, and (2) the likelihood of the petitioner's claim being eventually affirmed in a prospective case on merit. In practice, judges may render an award when they are reasonably assured that the petitioner's claim is supported by *either one* of these two conditions. Therefore, in cases such as those in which a provisional order is sought to restrain illegal acts of dispute or to pay workers who are suffering hardship because of an allegedly illegal discharge, the court tends to issue orders quickly since it is evident that the petitioner's need for an immediate remedy is urgent. On the other hand, in cases where a provisional order is sought to secure a worker's employment status, the court has to consider carefully whether or not a petitioner should be provided with a cause for action (that is, a judgment that he would be the winning party in a suit on merit), because the need for a provisional order is not as urgent in this situation as when illegal actions or hardship are at issue.

Despite the fact that a provisional order procedure now takes an average of two to three years to run its course, it continues to be the one most used for resolving industrial conflict because even two to three years is still considerably less than the time required for a suit on merit, and the procedure is simpler and cheaper (i.e., the filing fee is about one-hundredth that of a civil suit on merit). Above all, through this procedure it is possible for a petitioner to obtain an unorthodox remedy, such as an order to bargain in good faith or an order to refrain from interference, to say nothing of an order with the expectation of voluntary compliance. As far as litigation on labor matters is concerned, therefore, it would not be inaccurate to describe the present situation as "government by provisional order."

Many people are critical of the way that labor conflict is presently being handled in Japan. They point out that court monopoly of this area contradicts the idea that various types of labor disputes should be resolved by the most suitable means and that the courts, by assuming jurisdiction over all dispute cases, have promoted both parties' reliance on the law as well as their legalistic attitudes. Thus, they have discouraged efforts toward the voluntary settlement of disputes through collective bargaining. At the same time, the critics agree that the responsibility for this situation should not be placed entirely on the courts because, as long as the parties persist in reducing their disputes to conflicts over rights and in bringing them to the courts, the courts, in turn, cannot avoid assuming jurisdiction.

At the least we can say that, no matter how far removed the provisional order procedure is from civil procedure and no matter how specially trained the judges are in handling labor cases, the provisional order procedure is not necessarily the most appropriate method for resolving all types of labor conflict brought before the court in the form of a dispute over vested rights. The chances are great that the court will fail to quickly and appropriately reach and resolve the real issue in the case, which is more often than not a case of interests, not vested rights.

Resolution of Conflicts over the Interpretation and Application of Collective Agreements

A remarkably small number of cases concerning the interpretation and application of collective agreements reach the courts. For instance, the author found that, out of more than 250 civil and administrative cases at all court levels reported in various law journals in 1976, only 12 involved a question arising out of a collective agreement. In 5 of these 12, the issue was the interpretation and application of a clause providing for union–management "consultation on personnel matters," in 3 a union-shop clause was the subject of dispute, and in the rest the court was being asked to clarify wage provisions, a reemployment agreement, or a memorandum on promotion.

Perhaps one of the most significant aspects of Japanese collective agreements is that they include a relatively large number of so-called "institutional" or "organizational" provisions, such as a consultation or a meet-and-confer clause, as opposed to "normative" provisions that set out certain standards that each party must observe. For example, only 44 percent of the unions having collective agreements reported to the Ministry of Labor in 1979 that their agreements specified the conditions under which a discharge would be for just cause; 52 percent of them said that just cause for discharge was covered in the rules of employment. On the other hand, 89 percent of all unions surveyed responded that they had participated in discharge cases, in one way or another, when the employees involved were members of the union, most often in accordance with a consultation clause in a collective agreement. Likewise, nearly 90 percent of the unions meet and confer with the managements on workforce reduction problems, either under a collective agreement or another arrangement, and 75 percent do the same on safety, health, and welfare matters under consultation clauses. Even in a case where an employee is discharged under a union-shop provision, 15 percent of the agreements require consultation between the union and the management (Rōdōshō, Rōseikyoku 1979, p.165).

It is safe to conclude, therefore, that, with the exception of the provisions on wages and hours, Japanese collective agreements provide procedural rules rather than substantive norms to be used in conflict resolution, reflecting the unwillingness of unions and managements to define in too much detail the standards to be applied to the working conditions of individual employees. In the absence of any statutory provisions specifying certain subjects as mandatory, permitted, or prohibited in bargaining, a collective agreement of this nature presumably makes it mandatory for the employer to bargain with the union over an issue such as employee discharge.

Under these conditions, employees find it difficult to raise questions concerning the interpretation and application of a collective agreement unless an employer completely ignores the consultation provision. Moreover, even when a conflict arises over the interpretation and application of that provision, the court will probably not be able to reach and deal with the underlying issue that prompted the dispute in the first place and that should have been the subject for union–management consultation. Suppose an employer changes a work schedule or modifies a safety device without first conferring with the union—that is, in violation of a consultation clause. Because the consultation provision has nothing to do with the way in which the work schedule or the safety device should be changed, all the court could do would be either to order the employer to pay damages for his breach of the contract or to order him to bargain with the union on the matter. In personnel matters, the majority of the courts have interpreted the consultation clause to mean that the union has a procedural right to be consulted and that an individual employee's right of employment is guaranteed, at least to the extent that an employer cannot discharge, discipline, or transfer him without prior consultation with, and sometimes the consent of, the union. Thus, the courts may declare that an employer's discharge, discipline, or transfer of an employee in violation of the consultation clause shall be null and void, on the ground that such a consultation provision has a normative effect on employer–employee relations. It appears that a conflict over an employee's right to his job would be resolved before it really begins.

There are reasons for the popularity of the consultation clause, specifically as it concerns personnel changes involving union members. One reason is the unwillingness of both parties to set up any clear standards or rules that would automatically be applied in the day-to-day affairs of the employer–employee relationship. A provision requiring consultation over personnel matters typically reads: "[After enumerating just causes for the discharge of employees] whenever the employer finds that a member of the union (employee) comes under one [of the just causes] prescribed above and deserves to be discharged, the employer may discharge him or her after having consulted on the matter (or sought the consent of) the union." An employer may insist that a discharge for just cause of the nature prescribed in the collective agreement should be effective even if he fails to consult with or obtain the consent of the union. The union, in contrast, may interpret this clause as a kind of review or reopener provision, under which it could either veto the employer's decision or resort to a strike in support of its claim that there had been no prior consultation as required in the contract and that the discharge was therefore illegal. The ambiguity of consultation clauses and the possibility for strikes over their interpretation are both good reasons for their popularity as well as for the frequent disputes over their interpretation and application. Unions and managements have concluded collective agreements and reduced provisions of this type to writing without ever agreeing on their meaning; each may well have a different interpretation in mind.[5] As with almost any contract interpretation in Japanese industrial relations, when there is disagreement over the meaning of a consultation clause, the court's interpretation seems to come out somewhere between each party's contention. Accordingly, almost all courts seem to seek a solution that would not disturb the union–management relationship; thus they may declare that a union's insistence upon opposing the employer in consultation justifies the employer's unilateral action, the requirement in the agreement for the union's consent notwithstanding.

Another reason for the popularity of consultation clauses of this type, as well as for the frequent conflict over them, may possibly be found in the way they function—that is, in an order that is the reverse of a Western-type grievance procedure. Grievance procedures are not popular in Japan; they are seldom used because employees are extremely reluctant to confront their foremen or supervisors individually even with union representatives present. A consultation clause, by making prior consultation before every personnel change an employer's contractual duty, may prevent the employee concerned from ever having to confront the employer, at least on his or her own initiative. From the employer's standpoint, too, preventing grievances by making use of the consultation system is desirable. Under the procedure, it is expected that when the employer proposes any personnel change, the union will find out from the individual concerned whether he or she has any complaint about the change and will try to persuade the member to obey the order in the future, if and when the union determines that the personnel change is reasonable. A prior consultation system, therefore, is a device with the same goal as a grievance procedure, and yet it enables a foreman to maintain good personal relations with his subordinate workers.

Another area of conflict over interpretation of a collective agreement—this one concerning the legal effect of a discharge made in compliance with a union-shop agreement—is not dealt with here, for its underlying problems have been described in chapter 7.

It should be noted that these two types of union-management conflicts arise not from substantive provisions in a collective agreement, but from "institutional" or procedural provisions that have introduced new systems into Japanese industrial relations, and thus have created new problems. On the other hand, almost no legal conflict stems from substantive provisions specifying standards for working conditions, despite the fact that Japan has never developed a system for grievance arbitration or any other form of industrial jurisprudence like that which has been developed in the United States to resolve disputes over application and interpretation of substantive provisions in a collective agreement. Furthermore, on issues of working conditions, the rules of employment have priority over the collective agreement, as will be mentioned below.

Resolution of Conflict Arising out of an Employment Contract

As table 8.2 indicates, 1,300 or more civil cases on labor have been brought at district courts of first instance every year since 1975. The vast majority of them, or more than 95 percent, are suits against employers, of which slightly less than half (45 percent) are filed by discharged employees or by employees who have quit their jobs. Among the cases that the district courts decide, employee discharge is the issue in more than 60 percent of the suits against employers. It can be assumed, therefore, that the rate of compromise or withdrawal is much lower in discharge cases than when the dispute is over any other issue.

Table 8.2
Nature of Civil Cases Brought by Labor in District Courts, 1974-80

Year	Total		Reinstatement, etc.		Wages, etc.		Others	
	N	%	N	%	N	%	N	%
1974	1,081	100	482	44.6	419	38.8	180	16.7
1975	1,355	100	579	42.7	566	41.8	210	15.5
1976	1,446	100	592	40.9	667	46.1	187	12.9
1977	1,337	100	582	43.5	640	47.9	115	8.6
1978	1,323	100	586	44.3	607	45.9	130	9.8
1979	1,222	100	516	41.4	584	47.8	132	10.8
1980	1,103	100	448	40.6	572	51.9	83	7.5

Source: *Hōsō Jihō* [Lawyers Association journal] 33:7, pp. 158–59.

The percentage of discharge cases as a proportion of all cases filed against employers, however, has been declining recently. Such cases comprised more than 80 percent in 1960 and almost 80 percent in 1966. It is claimed also that the number of cases has been increasing where wages or other payments due, such as pay for overtime, are the issue. Another significant phenomenon in recent years is the steady increase in cases where an employer's order of transfer or discipline, short of disciplinary discharge, is challenged. The number of damage suits against employers, brought by employees or unions on the ground of either breach of contract or tort, though still not high, is remarkable, particularly considering the traditional unpopularity of this kind of litigation in Japanese industrial relations.

These changing patterns of labor litigation most likely relate to a change in the parties who are bringing suits against employers. In the ten years after 1968, more and more cases were brought by minority unions or their members alleging discriminatory treatment and charging employers with breach of contract or violation of the rules of employment. When one specifically examines cases that ended with a court decision, this trend is all the more significant. Roughly one-third of all cases decided were filed by minority unions (or their members), composing only 3–4 percent of all labor unions. Multiple unions in a single establishment are still a rare phenomenon in Japan; only about 4 percent of organized plants have more than one union.

In summary, we may be able to conclude that the majority of employees would still be reluctant to pursue a suit against their employer unless they were discharged; for a minority, however, the courts have become familiar as a substitute for grievance machinery.[6]

As mentioned earlier, court remedies under the Japanese provisional order procedure have not been confined to the conventional ones available in a civil procedure, but have been expanded to include such orders as reinstatement of discharged employees, return of transferred employees to their previous positions, resumption of negotiations on a particular subject, and revocation of almost every kind of employer decision including employee discipline. Moreover, the way that Japanese courts take individual factors in each union-management relationship into consideration in deciding labor cases differs very little from the way an arbitrator reaches a decision. In every case of discipline or discharge, a court tends to give weight to extenuating circumstances in determining the legality of an action, maintaining that the idea of "natural justice," or factors to be considered in a criminal procedure, should be applicable to an even greater extent in discipline or discharge procedures in a firm. Thus, a court has often set aside a discharge or a harsh discipline of an employee because, in its opinion, the punishment was too severe or the penalty inappropriate for the alleged offense. Likewise, in the court's opinion, such factors as an employee's family situation should also be taken into consideration when an employer decides on a personnel change such as a job transfer. In one celebrated case, a transfer order that would have forced an employee to separate from his wife was found to be null and void because it was deemed detrimental to the employee.[7]

It is not too much to say, therefore, that as far as a court's interpretations are concerned, employees are better off under individual employment contracts or the rules of employment, even without a collective agreement, than they would be without contracts or rules. Indeed, in cases of job transfer as well as overtime assignments, many courts have indicated that, regardless of what the rules of employment might say, an employer may not order his employee to work for other companies or to work overtime without obtaining his consent on every occasion, unless the employee's duty to follow such an order is specified in a collective agreement. In other words, in the process of translating a rule of employment into a provision of an individual employment contract, the court tends to interpret that rule so that an employer's action under it is reasonable and acceptable to an employee, because the court considers it a duty to interpret specific rules of employment in accordance with labor law principles or "the spirit of the law"—even in the absence of any specific provision in labor law or the collective agreement that would supersede the rule of employment in question.

It should be remembered, however, that a court interpretation of an individual employment contract or the way in which a court resolves a labor conflict will not be far removed from the practices that prevail in Japanese industrial relations. For instance, a court's interpretation of a contract, as modified in the light of the Labor Standards Law, that an employee's consent is necessary on each occasion that an employer orders overtime work is supported by the fact that the overwhelming majority of employers have been asking for an employee's consent before ordering overtime. The same is true for a job transfer, regardless of whether prior consent is explicitly required by a rule of employment.

When the real issue in conflict is as simple as the example just given, court interpretations of contracts along such lines run into few difficulties. However, more often than not a labor case involves other issues. Suppose that, for business reasons, an employer cannot afford to comply with the common practice of seeking an employee's consent before ordering overtime work or a transfer, or that an employee refuses an overtime assignment or a job transfer for family reasons or reasons of union or political activities. In these cases, a court must seek to determine whether the overtime work or the transfer is necessary for the employer and whether the employee's reason for refusal is legitimate, before deciding which of the two conflicting positions should prevail. Many argue that a court is ill equipped for this kind of job. Why should it be possible for one court to conclude that a retirement age of 55 is reasonable in one transportation company, but for another to find that 55 years old is too early for compulsory retirement in another transportation company?[8] That is exactly what an arbitrator ought to decide, but not a court, the decisions of which should have a far-reaching effect. Still others argue that whether or not a court is qualified to make these kinds of judgments is beside the point, because a plaintiff who brings a case to a court is not seeking a decision by an expert, but simply an affirmation of his position by the government.

If a court plays the role of arbitrator, then labor litigation is no different from compulsory arbitration, which nobody likes to see in a free collective bargaining system. That may possibly be a reason that the number of labor cases is so small in Japan in comparison with other countries, despite the allegation that employees and unions in Japan are very aware of their endowed rights, if not suffering from excessive legalism. In other words, we may assume that the court's overcommitment to its role in resolving labor conflicts has an accelerating rather than a restraining effect upon the voluntary resolution of labor conflicts.

The Voluntary Resolution of Labor Conflict

Labor Disputes and Their Settlement

The statistics on labor disputes in table 8.3 indicate that brief strikes and other acts of dispute occur rather frequently. This number would be even greater if such tactics as work-to-rule and refusal to work overtime were included in the totals (it has been suggested that these be identified as acts of dispute, but the matter is still in question). For instance, 34 percent of all

Table 8.3
Labor Disputes, Workdays Lost, and Workers Involved,
by Type of Act of Dispute, 1970–80

Year	Total Labor Disputes	Total Labor Disputes Involving Act of Dispute		Strike 4 Hours and More		Lockout		Strike Less Than 4 Hours		Slowdown		Others	
		Cases	Workdays Lost	Cases	Workdays Lost	Cases	Workdays Lost	Cases	Workers Involved (in thousands)	Cases	Workers Involved (in thousands)	Cases	Workers Involved (in thousands)
1970	4,551	3,783	3,914,805	2,256	3,769,956	32	162,979	2,356	1,294.4	101	33.9	1	0.0
1971	6,861	6,082	6,028,746	2,515	5,977,608	36	56,063	4,653	2,616.4	64	33.1	3	0.1
1972	5,808	4,996	5,146,668	2,489	5,074,438	20	72,765	3,531	1,553.4	91	80.6	2	0.2
1973	9,459	8,720	4,603,821	3,320	4,542,986	29	64,802	6,667	3,226.5	117	252.6	NA	NA
1974	10,462	9,581	9,662,945	5,197	9,606,452	34	57,659	6,378	2,723.8	77	36.9	2	0.1
1975	8,435	7,574	8,015,772	3,385	7,974,133	25	62,210	5,475	2,449.1	55	11.3	1	0.1
1976	7,974	7,240	3,253,715	2,715	3,223,568	22	51,817	5,717	2,459.5	70	8.7	12	2.3
1977	6,060	5,533	1,518,476	1,707	1,498,295	12	20,181	4,522	1,924.5	35	5.0	5	0.1
1978	5,416	4,852	1,357,502	1,512	1,353,123	14	6,293	3,887	1,480.0	50	96.5	3	0.2
1979	4,026	3,492	930,204	1,151	918,500	11	12,364	2,743	1,022.5	58	103.5	1	0.1
1980	4,376	3,737	1,001,224	1,128	998,165	10	3,123	3,038	1,355.7	37	11.6	5	0.2

Source: Rōdōshō 1981, Appendix, pp. 88–89.
Note: Number of total labor disputes does not necessarily correspond to the sum of acts of dispute because one act of dispute often involves more than one kind of dispute.
NA: Data not available.

unions surveyed in 1977, or 584 out of 1,700 unions, reported that they had engaged in an act of dispute of one form or another during the preceding two years (Rōdōshō, Rōseikyoku. 1979, p.271).

However, the fact that unions do frequently engage in acts of dispute does not necessarily mean that the parties are failing to resolve their labor conflicts voluntarily or that they are finding it difficult to do so. Unions usually resort to acts of dispute at a very early stage in the bargaining process, long before negotiations become deadlocked. In other words, unions undertake a strike or another act of dispute simply to demonstrate that they disagree with the employer rather than to push their demands.

Indeed, as table 8.4 indicates, the rate of voluntary settlement of labor disputes is high, which might imply that the parties are generally unwilling to seek outside help in settling their differences. However, this statement needs to be qualified, for various reasons.

First it should be noted that Japan's labor dispute adjustment system is based strictly on the principle of voluntarism—that is, the Labor Relations Commission's adjustment service is invoked only with the parties' consent. Except for disputes in public utilities and similar essential industries, including those covered by the Public Corporation and National Enterprise Labor Relations (PCNELR) Law, conciliation is the only procedure that can be invoked ex parte or on the commission's own initiative. When the commission does appoint a conciliator or conciliators, they must limit themselves to

Table 8.4
Distribution of Labor Disputes, by Manner of Settlement, 1970–80

Year	Total	Collective Bargaining		By the Labor Relations Commission			By Others	Unresolvable[a]
				Concil.	Med.	Arb.		
1970	4,365	2,992	(222)[b]	401	28	15	31	898
1971	6,783	3,461	(334)	380	16	20	28	2,878
1972	5,684	3,361	(319)	329	9	21	34	1,930
1973	9,357	4,037	(290)	419	19	19	23	4,840
1974	10,319	5,614	(296)	554	4	36	28	4,083
1975	8,326	4,431	(316)	438	11	15	19	3,412
1976	7,895	3,969	(347)	405	11	21	28	3,461
1977	5,945	2,816	(202)	341	1	8	16	2,763
1978	5,324	2,421	(173)	268	3	12	50	2,570
1979	3,912	1,889	(185)	246	5	15	18	1,739
1980	4,253	1,958	(224)	277	5	17	19	1,977

Source: Rōdōshō 1981, *Appendix*, pp. 94–95.
[a]Unresolvable by parties themselves, such as political or sympathy strikes, etc.
[b]Cases in parentheses are those where a third party assisted in the bargaining process.

helping the parties reach a settlement; they are not supposed to propose any plan or make any suggestions for settlement.

Mediation, on the other hand, is undertaken by a tripartite committee and is used only upon the agreement of both parties, unless the labor dispute is in a public institution such as a utility or a medical facility where the consent of the parties is not required. When both parties accept a mediated plan, it becomes binding as a collective agreement. Arbitration is invoked only with the consent of both parties except for the cases under the regulations of the PCNELR Law. There, it is handled by a committee consisting of arbitrators who are selected from among the public members of the commission, and their award, too, has the same effect as a collective agreement (see chapter 10).

Thus, the infrequent use of mediation and arbitration may also be an indication of the parties' failure to agree upon using the services of a third party. For reasons to be explained later, unions and employers, particularly the latter, are reluctant to turn over their problems to a third party, who most likely will try to resolve a conflict of interests by establishing substantive norms rather than merely providing a procedure for voluntary settlement (as in conciliation).

Second, various forms of litigation often derive from labor disputes, especially the intractable ones. As noted earlier, Japan's courts and commissions frequently play the role of arbitrator on an ex parte basis. Regardless of any distinction between the nature of the conflicts involved in a labor dispute (interests) and in litigation (rights), in some cases an issue in a labor dispute is basically the same as the one being litigated in a court or in an unfair labor practice procedure. In addition, a court or commission decision often is more favorable to workers and unions than any they might achieve by using the collective bargaining process.

For example, on a number of occasions a court has upheld a union's claim that it has a right to be provided with office space by an employer under the same conditions as its rival unions enjoy, unless otherwise provided in a collective agreement. Also, union activities within a company's premises during working hours, such as posting and distributing handbills, have been regarded by the courts as an exercise of the workers' right to organize as guaranteed by the Constitution, insofar as these activities do not interfere with the normal operation of the business and insofar as they are not specifically limited by a collective agreement. In reaching such decisions, a court tends to take such factors as the inherent weakness or vulnerability of the Japanese union movement into consideration, declaring that since union organization is confined to an enterprise, it is indispensable that it be allowed, at least to a reasonable extent, to engage in its activities within the company premises and during working hours.

When the same considerations are taken into account in deciding cases concerning collective bargaining and acts of dispute, the impact on labor conflict may be even more significant. The union's vulnerability as an enterprise-wide organization has been a determining factor in decisions on the appropriateness or legitimacy of picketing, for example. Accordingly, a certain degree of physical force involved in picketing was in one case found to be permissible if it were exercised against members of a breakaway union or ex-members of the union.[9]

By and large, unions, particularly minority unions in multiunion situations, seem to fare better under court and commission decisions than under a collective bargaining agreement. No wonder, then, that these minority unions are parties to a third of the commission decisions in unfair labor practice cases and maybe even more of the court judgments on labor relations matters.

Therefore, it can be assumed that among the labor disputes that are recorded as being settled by collective bargaining, there are many that have in fact been resolved through court or unfair labor practice procedures, either by decisions, orders, or compromise. On the last point, it should be noted that every year more than 60 percent of the civil cases on labor and more than 80 percent of the unfair labor practice cases are settled by compromise or are withdrawn.

Finally, we should recall our previous assertion that, although the parties do make specific agreements on wages and hours, collective bargaining in Japan tends to conclude with the unions and employers reaching an agreement to establish procedural rules, such as for joint consultation and other meet-and-confer clauses, rather than substantive norms. The Ministry of Labor (Rōdōshō, Rōseikyoku 1979, p. 237) reports that the number of unions with joint consultation clauses in their collective agreements has been increasing at an annual rate of 10 percent, and there is reason to believe that a considerable number of labor disputes, with the exception of those over wages and hours, are settled by the parties' agreeing on procedures—that is, agreeing to extend collective bargaining by means of various forms of consultation.[10] This supposition finds support in two facts; in firms where joint consultation machinery has been established, the number of labor disputes over nonwage issues is considerably smaller than where there is no such system, and in quite a few union–management relationships there is no collective bargaining at all, because the parties have chosen to rely entirely on joint consultation.[11]

Compromise or Emerging Joint Consultation

Compromise, as defined here, means that the parties in conflict voluntarily resolve their differences not by applying any substantive rules or standards, but primarily on a give-and-take basis. Conflict resolution of this kind is basically ad hoc and thus provides no precedent for the resolution of future disputes of the same kind. However, in a continuing relationship, if one party agrees to make a relatively greater concession in one conflict, it should be easier for the compromise in the next case to be at the expense of the other party—just like a balance of payments being carried over to the account of the following settlement. In other words, a compromise is a means of settling disputes by appealing to the sentiment of each party as well as to reason, with an emphasis on the former. Thus it would be the best possible way of resolving conflicts that arise in a continuing relationship, without damaging its psychological foundation.

Parties in conflict usually reach a compromise in response to various pressures, from both outside and within, on each party or on both. Therefore, the greater the pressures on the parties, the easier it is for them to compromise. Also, in relationships where the parties are of a common mind, where they share both interests and goals, and where they understand each other, they should be able to compromise.

Such being the case, it is no wonder that in Japan a compromise has been the most popular means for resolving a labor conflict, regardless of whether it involves an interest or a vested right. A compromise over rights has often been condemned as undesirable, if not illegal, particularly when it is a worker's constitutional right that is at stake, as in an unfair labor practice case; notwithstanding, the rate of compromise in both courts and unfair labor practice procedures has been increasing.

As can be seen in table 8.5, 50–60 percent of all cases handled by district courts are concluded by compromise or withdrawal, the latter most likely to have resulted from a compromise outside the court. Also, as table 8.6 indicates, every year more than 75 percent of all unfair labor practice cases submitted to the local Labor Relations Commissions are settled by conciliation (compromise) or by withdrawal. The reasons or motives for compromise appear to be the same in both procedures—that is, pressure or suggestion from a court or commission, a judgment by each party as to whether it will win or lose if it carries a case further through the process, a desire to improve the union–management relationship, and a preference for a monetary settlement.[12] The difference between the courts and the commission in the rate of compromise may, therefore, reflect a court's relative unwillingness to suggest that the litigants compromise or to give any indication of which side is likely to win the case.

There can be little doubt that a joint consultation or any meet-and-confer system that stresses compromise in the resolution of conflict is more suitable than any other for Japanese industrial relations. Collective bargaining, insofar as the law defines a set of rules for resolving disputes, seems to be less favored by both unions and employers in Japan. Putting it another way, the

Table 8.5

Civil Cases Completed at District Courts, by Manner of Settlement, 1974–80

Year	Total	Provisional Disposition Order Sought				Determination Sought			
		Total	By Court Decision	By Compromise	By Withdrawal or Dismissal	Total	By Court Decision	By Compromise	By Withdrawal or Dismissal
1974	1,272	789 (100)	471 (59.7)	113 (14.3)	205 (26.0)	483 (100)	171 (35.4)	159 (32.9)	153 (31.7)
1975	1,406	854 (100)	468 (54.8)	149 (17.4)	237 (27.8)	552 (100)	200 (36.2)	184 (33.3)	168 (30.4)
1976	1,511	875 (100)	467 (53.4)	178 (20.3)	230 (26.3)	636 (100)	228 (35.8)	207 (32.5)	201 (31.6)
1977	1,410	738 (100)	363 (49.2)	169 (22.9)	206 (27.9)	672 (100)	225 (33.5)	233 (34.7)	214 (31.8)
1978	1,472	759 (100)	340 (44.8)	210 (27.9)	209 (27.5)	713 (100)	231 (32.4)	293 (41.1)	189 (26.5)
1979	1,326	701 (100)	294 (41.9)	196 (28.0)	211 (30.1)	625 (100)	191 (30.6)	275 (44.0)	159 (25.4)
1980	1,272	646 (100)	271 (41.9)	167 (25.9)	208 (32.2)	626 (100)	221 (35.3)	247 (39.5)	158 (25.2)

Source: Hōsō Jihō [Lawyers Association Journal] 33:7, pp. 158–59.

Note: Percentages in parentheses.

Table 8.6
Unfair Labor Practice Cases Completed,
by Manner of Settlement, 1974–80

		Withdrawal and Compromise			Orders and Decisions			
Year	Total	Withdrawal	Compromise	Total	Remedial Order	Dismissal	Total	Remitted
1974	574	89	366	455	108	11	119	0
	(100)	(15.5)	(63.8)	(79.3)	(18.8)	(1.4)	(20.7)	
1975	685	78	441	519	156	8	164	2
	(100)	(11.4)	(64.4)	(75.8)	(22.8)	(1.2)	(23.9)	(0.3)
1976	678	83	432	515	141	21	162	1
	(100)	(12.3)	(63.7)	(76.0)	(20.8)	(3.1)	(23.9)	(0.1)
1977	896	288	482	770	117	9	126	0
	(100)	(32.1)	(53.8)	(85.9)	(13.1)	(1.0)	(14.1)	
1978	629	75	432	507	111	10	121	1
	(100)	(11.9)	(68.7)	(80.6)	(17.6)	(1.6)	(19.2)	(0.2)
1979	564	79	344	423	128	13	141	0
	(100)	(14.0)	(61.0)	(75.0)	(22.7)	(2.3)	(25.0)	
1980	516	93	298	391	104	21	125	0
	(100)	(18.0)	(57.8)	(75.8)	(20.2)	(4.0)	(24.2)	

Source: Chūō Rōdō Iinkai, Jimukyoku 1974b, 1975–78.
Note: Percentages in parentheses.

unstructured and multifunctional nature of joint consultation better promotes compromise than do the rigidities of collective bargaining.[13] For example, under a consultation clause, if an employer believes a proposed plan is a reserved management prerogative, he may carry it out even if it meets with union opposition in joint consultation, while the union takes the position that employees may resort to an act of dispute if they fail to prevail in consultation. In practice, however, an employer seldom insists upon taking a unilateral action and a union seldom strikes over matters subject to consultation.[14] Such an interpretation of a consultation clause—or the fact that each side knows what the other believes—should make it a lot easier for them to compromise.

Under the constitutional guarantees that provide for collective bargaining, on the one hand, and the parties' propensity to resolve their conflicts by compromise, on the other, collective bargaining has been used to set up frameworks for compromise. As mentioned before, the Japanese place greater emphasis in their collective agreements on so-called "institutional provisions" than on normative ones. Today, more than 50 percent of the unions engage in joint consultation on nearly all matters, including management of the workforce and production. In addition to general consultation, there is extensive use of prior consultation on specific issues: 80–90 percent of the unions take part, in one way or another, in decisions on personnel changes; 83 percent participate in the administration of welfare facilities; 88 percent discuss safety and health matters; and 90 percent consult on workforce adjustment (Rōdōshō, Rōseikyoku 1979, pp. 216, 228, 231).

The final question then is: Has the legal framework for the resolution of labor conflict in Japan contributed to the development of the voluntary resolution of disputes by means of compromise? Yes, but not in the same manner as, for instance, a system of grievance arbitration has developed under the legal framework in the United States. In Japanese industrial relations, every right that an employer and a union has under the law, such as the right to bring a suit against the other party with the expectation of getting a favorable decision, the right to resort to various acts of dispute without being legally liable, or the right to discharge employees at will, is useful in pressuring the parties to compromise. Even an employer's willful violation of a labor law—the Labor Standards Law, for example—and a union's silence on such a violation works to promote compromise. But the parties may find it impossible to use this mechanism. This often happens in the public sector, where an employer's ability to compromise is circumscribed, or in a multiunion situation, where a compromise between an employer and a minority union is practically impossible. At such a time, all potential problems with the system become very real, and all the defects that were previously overlooked are exposed. In these situations, it is to be expected that employees will respond with a wave of acts of dispute, a series of unfair labor practice charges and litigation, and a mass of employee complaints charging an employer with violation of the Labor Standards Law, and the employer's reaction will be to take all kinds of unilateral actions. Of course, even here there would be pressures to compromise from a court, the commission, and society at large. This rather unusual method of resolving confict and achieving industrial peace through compromise is not exactly what the legal framework for dispute settlement was designed to promote, but Japanese labor law can nevertheless be credited with making a great contribution to industrial peace when the parties take advantage of it—and even when they willfully violate it.

Notes

1 Section 16 of the Trade Union Law provides that any part of an individual employment contract that contravenes standards in a collective agreement concerning working conditions or other treatment of workers shall be replaced by the standards provided in the agreement. Also, Section 13 of the Labor Standards Law provides that working conditions defined by a labor contract, if inferior to the standards set forth in the law, shall be replaced by the conditions specified in the law.

2 Nobeoka Post Office Case, PCNELR Commission, March 8, 1965, *Kōkitai Kankei Meireishū* [Cases concerning public enterprises], p. 206.

3 Typically, Japan Mail Order Co. Case, Tokyo Labor Relations Commission, May 8, 1973, *Bessatsu Chūō Rōdō Jihō* [Central labor journal] *Appendix,* No. 851, p. 69. This type of case was treated in chapter 7.

4 See chapter 7, fn. 7, for details of the commission organization.

5 Thus, one impatient court found, in such a situation, that there was no collective agreement at all because there had been no meeting of the minds in any real sense. Kure Kōtsu Rōdō Kumiai (Kure Transportation Workers' Union) v. Kure City, Hiroshima High Court, December 21, 1965, *Rōdō Kankei Minji Saiban Reishū* [Labor law (civil) cases] 10, p. 1141.

6 Issues in conflict in civil and administrative cases are strikingly similar to issues submitted to grievance arbitration in the United States, where 45 percent of arbitration awards deal with discharge and seniority, 13 percent with wages and other payments, and 12 percent with job allocation and other personnel matters (Federal Mediation and Conciliation Service, *Annual Reports,* 1963–1976). In Japan, 45 percent of the court decisions deal with discharge, 16 percent with wages and other payments, and 13 percent with personnel changes.

7 Teruo Hagiwara, et al. v. Akita Mutual Bank, Akita District Court, July 30, 1968, *Rōdō Kankei Minji Saiban Reishū* [Labor law (civil) cases] 19, p. 859.

8 The Supreme Court approved one employer's unilateral change of a rule of employment to establish 55 years old as the compulsory retirement age (Shūhoku Bus Co. Case, S. Ct. GB, December 25, 1968, *Minshū* [Supreme Court civil cases] 22, p. 3459); the Saga district court, however, found a compulsory retirement age of 55 to be unreasonable (Nishi Kyūshū Transportation Case, November 10, 1972, *Rōdō Keizai Hanrei Sokuhō* [Newsletter of labor and economy cases] No. 23, p. 3).

9 Picketing of on-coming streetcars conducted by members of a breakaway union was found to be within the scope of "peaceful persuasion." People v. Masasue Suguira, et al., Supreme Court, Third Small Bench, June 23, 1970, *Saikō Saibansho Keiji Saiban Reishū* [Supreme Court criminal cases] 24, p. 311.

10 A trend toward replacement of collective bargaining with joint consultation was found in a survey conducted recently by a group of researchers at Tokyo University's Social Science Institute (Ujihara 1979, p. 2).

11 Of the unions with no collective bargaining experience in the year preceding the survey, 23 percent responded that they had found it unnecessary, because they had joint consultation (Rōdōshō, Rōseikyoku 1979, p. 261).

12 A survey conducted by the Central Labor Relations Commission for 1952–55 revealed that one-fourth of all compromises were reached with the advice of the Labor Relations Commission or of the members thereof representing labor or management. More than 15 percent of the conciliated settlements were made because labor felt that it had attained its aim by making an employer sorry for what he had done or by forcing him to reflect upon it. Also, nearly a quarter of the employers and some 8 percent of the employees agreed on a compromise because they preferred a monetary settlement. Finally, 13 percent of the employers and unions responded that they had compromised for the purpose of main-

taining or restoring better industrial relations, and 15 percent of the employers and employees answered that their relationships had actually improved as a consequence of a compromise. *Bessatsu Chūō Rōdō Jihō* [Central labor journal] Supplement, February 1957.

13 Sometimes even a collective bargaining procedure has had ambiguous results. Some 42 percent of the unions that have concluded collective bargaining reported that they had failed to reduce their agreement to a formal collective agreement as prescribed by the Trade Union Law. (Rōdōshō, Rōseikyoku 1979, p. 267.)

14 In 52 percent of all cases of joint consultation on management and production matters, it is understood between the parties that an employer may alter the plan, taking the union's opinion into consideration even if they have failed to agree. In 14 percent, an employer is supposed to postpone the execution of a plan until the union agrees, and in only 10 percent may an employer carry out a plan unilaterally (ibid, p. 243).

9 *Kazutoshi Kōshiro*

Development of Collective Bargaining in Postwar Japan

Major Characteristics of the Japanese Collective Bargaining System

An American industrial relations scholar, Milton Derber, has written (1979) that "in the United States collective bargaining is viewed by the labor movement as the main route to industrial democracy" (p. 1). The same statement can be made about the labor movement in postwar Japan, in spite of the fact that bargaining is almost totally confined to the arena of the enterprise.

Collective bargaining has been practiced in Japan since the early 1920s, but it became the main route to industrial democracy only after World War II. By the early 1950s it was well established in the major industries, although the labor movement itself continued to be strongly flavored by revolutionary unionism until the mid-1960s. At the present time more than 12 million workers, or over 32 percent of all employees in the country, are union members.

Three features characterize the Japanese collective bargaining system: (1) it is practiced within the boundaries of each individual enterprise; (2) labor unions are concentrated in the large enterprises; and (3) both white- and blue-collar workers are members of and are represented by the same union.

However, there are marked differences between trade unionism in the public and private sectors. The public employee labor organizations have

205

been the stronghold of revolutionary unionism since World War II. Particularly in the late 1940s and early 1950s, unions of postal workers and electric power workers (the latter industry was under national control between 1939 and 1950) were the centers of this Marxist–Leninist movement. But after the Korean War, the leftist orientation of the leadership of the Japanese union movement began to abate somewhat and was superseded by the more business-oriented trade unionism that had developed in the private sector. By the latter half of the 1960s, after ten years of high economic growth, it was obvious to all observers that the economic trade unionism of the private sector had come to dominate the thinking of the movement's leaders. Then, the economic stress brought on by the oil crisis of 1973 stimulated a new impetus toward an even closer coalition among the several factions of trade unionists in the private sector. However, vestiges of the ideological rivalry between the two sectors of the labor movement remain to this day.

For the convenience of Western readers, it might be desirable to take the eight principles of industrial democracy that Derber (1979, pp. 1–2) identifies as established in the United States and to describe very briefly how they apply in Japan (see also Hanami 1979a):

1. *The legal right of non-supervisory employees, if they so desire, to form and join labor organizations of their own choice for purposes of collective bargaining with their employers, without unfair interference or domination by the employers.* This right is firmly established in Japan by Article 28 of the Constitution (see chapter 7) and is further and more precisely protected by the Trade Union Law, which defines employer unfair labor practices and permits the establishment of a union shop. A private-sector employee cannot refuse to join the union and remain an employee unless he is a member of a rival labor organization. This principle has been established by court decisions and is supported as well by academic theories.[1]

2. *The right to collective bargaining through representatives with exclusive bargaining rights.* The system of exclusive representation has not been adopted in Japan, although the employees' right to collective negotiations is protected by the same articles in the law that sustain their right to organize. Therefore, if any group of two or more workers chooses to organize its own union and wishes to negotiate with its employer on behalf of its members, the employer is obliged to bargain with them; thus, many employers may be forced to negotiate with several unions within a single enterprise. In this sense, majority rule is substantially circumscribed.

3. *The right to a grievance procedure.* This right is not explicitly stipulated in the Trade Union Law, but grievance procedures have been used to some extent since shortly after the war. In February 1948, the Supreme Commander of the Allied Powers (SCAP) advised the labor unions and employer associations to introduce grievance procedures in disputes in the

coal mining industry, where the parties were then at impasse over a number of issues. Since then, provisions for grievance procedures for the purpose of assuring industrial peace during the life of collective bargaining agreements have become prevalent, and the grievance procedure idea was incorporated in the Public Corporation and National Enterprise Labor Relations Law of December 1948 and in the Local Public Enterprise Labor Relations Law of July 1952.

In spite of these developments, grievance procedures have not functioned effectively in either the private or public sectors (Kubo 1963, pp. 97–99), primarily because the parties have preferred and adopted other methods of resolving the conflicts that occur within the workplaces.

4. *The right of employers to form organizations of their own choosing for purposes of collective bargaining with labor organizations.* Article 21 of the Constitution protects the freedom of association of any person, which means that employers also are guaranteed the freedom to organize, and Article 6 of the Trade Union Law states that employers' organizations may engage in collective bargaining with labor unions. Moreover, Japan has ratified International Labor Organization Convention 87, which requires that the right of employers to form organizations of their own choosing be protected (Rōshi Kankeihō Kenkyūkai 1967, 1:25–26). Several employer organizations have, in fact, been formed, but they have not played any great role in dealing directly with labor unions, except on a few occasions in several basic industries shortly after World War II. Their major functions are confined for the most part to research, public relations, communication among member companies, education and information services, and other matters related to labor policies.

5. *Protection against discriminatory practices.* Discriminatory practices based on race, nationality, religion, sex, or social status are prohibited by Article 14 of the Constitution, Article 5 of the Trade Union Law, and Articles 3 and 4 of the Labor Standards Law. However, no specific law to promote equal employment opportunity has yet been enacted.

6. *The protection of union democracy.* In order to be able to use the services of the Labor Relations Commissions, labor organizations must demonstrate that they adhere to several basic principles of union democracy: the equal rights of each member; nondiscrimination; direct election of officers by secret ballot; full disclosure of the organization's finances at least once a year; evidence that there is majority support for a strike before it is begun, either directly through a secret ballot of all union members or indirectly through a secret ballot of union delegates who have been elected by the members by a secret ballot; and so on (Article 5 of the Trade Union Law).

7. *Establishment by the government of socially acceptable minimum standards of employment.* The Labor Standards Law of 1947 and subsequent

legislation concerning minimum wages and work safety and hygiene require employers to maintain certain minimum standards.

8. *The right of labor organizations to engage in strikes and of employers to engage in lockouts if they reach an impasse in contract negotiations.* Labor's right to strike is protected by Article 28 of the Constitution as well as by more detailed provisions of the Trade Union Law and the Labor Relations Adjustment Law. However, there are several public-interest limitations on these rights: (a) public employees are not allowed to engage in any industrial actions (see chapters 10 and 11); (b) as a result of the great strike of 1952, special restrictions are imposed on acts of dispute of workers in the electric power generating and coal mining industries; and (c) when an act of dispute in a basic industry is determined to constitute a national emergency, the Prime Minister may order a 50-day cooling-off period. The only time a Prime Minister has used the national emergency procedure was in the 1952 coal mining dispute.

The employer's right to lock out is not clearly authorized by the labor laws. However, this controversial question was finally resolved by the Supreme Court in 1975, when it ruled that an employer's act of dispute was protected as long as it was defensive in nature and taken in an effort to restore the balance of power between the parties (Ishikawa 1978, pp. 267–74).

At a glance, these eight principles of the Japanese collective bargaining system appear to be basically identical with those in the United States, if we use a very broad definition of industrial democracy. Yet there are noticeable differences vis-à-vis American ideas. How these variations are affected by legal doctrines is not the subject of this chapter. Rather, in the following sections I shall demonstrate that collective bargaining has become the major means for achieving industrial democracy in Japan, in spite of the dominance of enterprise-wide bargaining and that it has been used frequently to improve and standardize other conditions of employment. Furthermore, I shall emphasize my conviction that a collective bargaining system based on enterprise unionism has proved to be an innovation in an advanced industrial country, in that it is compatible with the policies of both Keynesian economics and a welfare state. Not only the flexibility but also the viability of collective bargaining by enterprise unions will be reexamined from this perspective.

The Origin of Enterprise-Wide Collective Bargaining

One of the most salient features of the collective bargaining system in Japan is that the arena for the negotiations is confined to each enterprise. Could such a system be independent from an employer's intervention? Why doesn't the collective bargaining arena have regional or national boundaries?

In the West, the general tendency was for collective bargaining to expand from the initial single-shop or local stage to wider areas, and several classical labor studies have attempted to identify what caused a development of this kind. Sidney and Beatrice Webb stressed the importance of trade union policies that restricted the supply of labor or enforced common rules in order to prevent excessive competition among workers (1920, pp. 559–61, 704–39). John R. Commons (1913) developed the theory of the extension of the market, theorizing that labor was obliged to respond to the growing pressure from employers to reduce wages and other working conditions as product markets expanded. Thus, workers sought "the practical remedy, . . . the elimination of the competitive menace through a protective organization or protective legislation" (p. 261). This implies that the wider the area of competition among producers, the greater the competitive menace and the greater the necessity to reduce labor costs, so that the area of union control as well as of collective bargaining should be extended to keep pace with market competition.

These classical theories may explain the origin of trade unions but are too general to identify why a particular form of collective bargaining might have been adopted in certain industries in certain countries. David A. McCabe (1952) offers a more detailed theory to explain how areas of collective bargaining were determined in the United States. He postulates that there are two reasons that company-wide rather than industry-wide bargaining prevailed in the iron and steel and automobile industries: (1) The existence of a price leader in the product market encourages "follow-the-leader" practices in the labor market as well. Therefore, the unions' existence does not depend upon industry-wide bargaining. (2) There is a "lack of homogeneity between the small number of large integrated producers . . . and the smaller producers who are competitors of and at times purchasers of materials from the large integrated companies. Many of the smaller producers apparently are not in favor of industry-wide bargaining" (pp. 123–25). The smaller producers have to maintain some wage differentials in order to survive.

In addition to these two economic factors, McCabe stresses the importance of the policies of large companies, unions, and the government in influencing the form of collective bargaining adopted. If a company such as AT&T is strong enough to resist even granting company-wide bargaining, or if there are multiple unions representing workers in the company (for example, there were many independent local unions in the Bell System which the Communications Workers of America was unable to defeat in representation elections), or if the government does not have a public-interest reason compelling it to intervene in the parties' power relations, economic factors alone will not necessarily dictate any single form of collective bargaining.

Thus, McCabe proceeds to the conclusion that

there is no one area of bargaining that is a matter of union principle. The area of bargaining is but an instrument for the attainment of the particular objectives of the particular union. That area is likely to be accepted as a matter of union policy that promises the best results, given the position of the employers and, perhaps, the policy of the government. (p. 129)

The problem for us, then, is to seek out the major objectives of Japanese labor unions and see how they could pursue the best results in their embryonic stages, given the particular socioeconomic and historic conditions that existed at the time. Thus, we take into consideration the factors suggested by the classical theorists in proposing a new set to explain the origin of the *enterprise-wide* collective bargaining that distinguishes the Japanese from the American system of *company-wide* bargaining.

1. By the end of World War II, Japan's industrial structure had already matured to the stage where oligopolistic price leaders dominated the major industries.

2. Competition among the large companies in the major industries had become increasingly fierce following the dissolution of the zaibatsu financial and industrial complexes. This was true in spite of the existence of oligopolistic price leaders.

3. At the same time, an industrial dual structure persisted, so that many small companies not only were competing with, but sometimes were subordinates of, large parent firms. These small companies had to maintain wage differentials with the large firms.

4. There is one more economic and industrial factor that should be added to those that McCabe used to explain American collective bargaining patterns: that is, that internal labor markets were more extensively developed in Japan than in other countries. Long-term employment with incremental individual wage increases and intensive on-the-job training has been developing in Japan since the 1910s.[2] This factor made it very difficult for craft unions to organize labor markets on horizontal lines.

5. When the workers' right to organize was restored after World War II, their movements had two major objectives: First, they wanted to eliminate the class distinctions between white- and blue-collar workers, in both remuneration and status. It had long been the practice to differentiate between the classes by using such managerial devices as uniforms, housing, bonuses, and paid vacations. Second, they hoped to restore production as rapidly as possible and to achieve at least subsistence living conditions for workers. The most effective way of pursuing these objectives was through enterprise-wide organizations of all eligible employees that would combine the managerial and technological expertise of the white-collar workers and the will to work of the blue-collar workers. Equality of all workers was the irresistible social ideal of the day, and, in fact, many able managerial staff people took over

the leadership of the labor movements at the enterprise level (Tokyo Daigaku Shakai Kagaku Kenkyūjo 1950, pp. 143–86). These conditions prevailed until about 1949–50.

6. The labor policy of the government was strongly influenced by SCAP, which at first intentionally promoted the organization of labor unions. There was some evidence that SCAP questioned the legitimacy of "enterprise unions," but it did not have enough time to implement the additional reforms that would make the labor law similar to what was seen in the United States in the years between the National Industrial Recovery Act and the Wagner Act.[3] Rather, the labor policies of SCAP itself reflected the changing ideas in the United States that culminated in the enactment of the Taft-Hartley Act and the intensification of the Cold War (Sumiya 1966b, pp.198–99). Between February 1, 1947, when it prohibited the general strike, and July 1948, SCAP moved sharply away from its policy stance of encouraging militant unionism that might be influenced by Communists. This was part of a radical change not only in labor policy but also in general Occupation policies toward Japan, and under it employers were able to resist effectively the demands of militant unions to widen the area of collective bargaining beyond the boundaries of each enterprise. Thus, there was little room for the militant forces in the labor movement to press the government to prohibit or regulate enterprise unions, as the Roosevelt administration had done when it banned employee-representation plans in the latter half of the 1930s.

7. Another curiosity in the labor history of postwar Japan was the fact that the militant forces themselves tended to prefer enterprise-wide, all-inclusive unions because they intended to use their revolutionary strategies to transform them into "factory-Soviets." The Communist-dominated Sanbetsu Kaigi (All Japan Congress of Industrial Unions) hastily organized workers on an enterprise basis, while Sōdōmei, forerunner of Dōmei (Japanese Confederation of Labor), at first tried to organize horizontally by industry or occupation. That was one of the reasons that Sōdōmei fell behind Sanbetsu Kaigi in total membership.[4]

8. Many employers, including those in the nationalized industries, wished to, and made efforts to, retain their influence among the labor unions. For them, enterprise unions were certainly preferable to any outside organization. In addition, there had been five years of experience with Sampō, the wartime patriotic labor organization. Local branches of this organization embraced all employees of each enterprise. Although these enterprise-wide organizations could by no means be classified as voluntary associations of workers, they did provide some experience with organizing white- and blue-collar workers in a single group (Sumiya 1966b, p. 190).

These are the factors that explain the origin of enterprise unions in Japan. The next question, then, is why these unions persisted and became an integral part of the enterprise-wide collective bargaining system in the following years. In fact, as we shall see in the next section, many industrial associations of enterprise unions have been organized and have tried to develop federated industrial activities. Competition in the product markets among the giant oligopolistic corporations had become so intense that there should have been a strong impetus on the part of enterprise unions to increase their activities to standardize wages and other working conditions among the competing companies. If, in spite of this, we have not noticed any broadening of the area of collective bargaining, some functional alternatives to bona fide industry-wide collective bargaining should have appeared—and that did happen, as we shall see later. There are now two methods of standardizing wages and other working conditions under enterprise-wide collective bargaining: (1) by gradual and sometimes ad hoc transition to industry-wide or regional bargaining, and (2) by the innovative arrangements of the Spring Offensive (shuntō) that allow the enterprise unions to unite without depriving them of their autonomy.

The Operation of Enterprise-Wide Collective Bargaining

How enterprise-wide collective bargaining works is the question that needs to be answered before we proceed to a detailed analysis of the functional alternatives to industry-wide bargaining. The most noteworthy feature of Japanese enterprise-wide bargaining is the fact that union officials from outside an enterprise usually cannot take part in the bargaining at that enterprise. Only a small number of unions allow officials from higher union organizations to participate.

According to Ministry of Labor surveys of collective bargaining agreements, only 10 percent of those surveyed in 1967 and 13 percent in 1977 allowed the participation of outside union officials; of these, 3 and 4 percent, respectively, permitted only union officials of the federation of enterprise unions at multiplant corporations (kigyōren) to participate. Thus, it is very unusual for union officials of higher industrial or regional organizations to take part in bargaining at the enterprise level. Similarly, it is also very rare for representatives of employers' organizations to negotiate directly with unions. According to the same surveys, only 3 percent of the 1967 agreements permitted representatives of outside employers' organizations to participate in negotiations; in 1977, the figure was 2 percent (Rōdōshō, Rōseikyoku, 1969, pp. 204–24; 1979, pp. 160–63, 263).

Of course, the Trade Union Law stipulates that "representatives of a trade union or those to whom the powers thereto are delegated by the trade union shall have power to negotiate with the employer or the employers' organization on behalf of the members of the trade union for conclusion of a trade agreement or other matters" (Article 6). Moreover, it is prohibited, as an unfair labor practice, to "refuse to bargain collectively with the representative of the workers employed by the employer without fair and appropriate reasons" (Article 7, Section 2). Therefore, no employer may refuse to negotiate with outside union organizations if the workers employed by that employer affiliate with outside or regional union organizations and delegate authority to them. However, the percentages cited above show that very few unions entrust their bargaining authority to outside representatives.

An authoritative report on industrial relations in Japan was issued in 1967 by the Ministry of Labor's Study Group on Industrial Relations Law. It states that Japanese employers tend to persist in negotiating directly with their own employees and to refuse to deal with representatives of higher union organizations because they believe firmly that the law endorses direct bargaining. The unions, on their part, are unwilling to risk disputing this employer position (Rōshi Kankeihō Kenkyūkai 1967, 1:40; 2:83–104).

Cases of Industry-Wide Negotiations

In spite of the dominance of enterprise-wide negotiations, other forms of collective bargaining are practiced—industry-wide or regional, *taikakusen* (diagonal), *shūdan* (group), and *rengō* (associational).[5] Tanrō (Japan Coal Miners' Union) and Nihon Sekitan Kōgyō Renmei (Japan Coal Mining Association) negotiated wage increases for the industry as early as 1949, but the most representative examples of long-established and continuing industry-wide negotiations are those between Kaiin (the seamen's union) and Gaikō Rōmu Kyōkai (Association of Ocean-Going Maritime Companies for Labor Affairs) and between Zensendōmei (Japanese Federation of Textile Industry Workers' Unions) and Nihon Men Sufu Orimono Kōgyō Kumiai Rengōkai (Association of Cotton and Staple Fiber Textile Industries).

Diagonal negotiations take place between an industrial union and most of the major companies in the industry. In this case, the industrial union has the authority to negotiate directly with the major companies and to conclude agreements with each of them "diagonally." In a sense, this form of bargaining is quite similar to pattern bargaining in the United States. In shūdan or rengō negotiations, the industrial union does *not* have the authority to conclude agreements with the relevant employers' association or with each individual employer. Here, the major function of the industrial union is to coordinate negotiations by demanding the same wage-rate increase, by presenting demands to each employer on the same day, by scheduling strike actions for the same period, and by seeking mediation or conciliation services of the Labor Relations Commissions in cases of impasse. In these cases, the actual negotiations are between each enterprise union and its employer, but all of the union and employer representatives sit at the same table and the union negotiators are accompanied by industrial union officials. Then, if and when the parties are able to reach a broad agreement, the negotiations may be shifted to the enterprise level where minor adjustments or additions may be made.

Tanrō undertook taikakusen (diagonal) negotiations over wages with eight major coal mining companies in 1951, and Shitetsusōren (the private railway workers' unions) and the major private railway companies resorted to shūdan (group) bargaining between 1967 and 1971. Similar forms of negotiations were observed in the beer-brewing, glass manufacturing, superphosphate, and docking industries in the mid-1960s.

Regional Negotiations

Outside unions sometimes will undertake a regional negotiation. For example, Dōmei's metal workers' union in Kanagawa prefecture has a long tradition of regional negotiations in Yokohama that dates from before the war. The union directly organizes all metal workers in the region and tries to standardize their wages and working conditions as much as possible (Shirai and Kōshiro 1960, pp. 223–61). The practices of Sōhyō's metal workers' union are similar.

A notable development since the 1960s has been the emergence of the *gōdō rōso* (amalgamated general union).[6] Enterprise unions, of course, are firmly established at most of the large companies, but the increase in employment in miscellaneous industries that accompanied the rapid economic growth of the 1960s opened the way for this new type of union. The most representative example is Zenkokuippan (National Union of General Workers) whose members are taxi drivers, salesmen, clerks in small bookstores and supermarkets, and the like—all workers whom enterprise unions have been unable to organize. The nature of the membership of this union, which includes not only Communists but various factions of the New Left, tends to make it radical in its activities.

Zenkokuippan extended its organizing activities further into the Postal Service, where many young temporary workers (mostly students) are employed seasonally during the summer and at the year's end. Regular Postal Service employees are members of Sōhyō's Zentei (Japan Postal Workers' Union) or Dōmei's Zenyūsei (All-Japan Post Office Workers' Union), but both unions exclude temporary workers. In the late 1970s, Zentei was having repeated, serious disputes with the Postal Service; it devised a new tactic to encourage Zenkokuippan to organize temporary postal workers. Zenkokuippan did demand direct negotiations of wages and miscellaneous working conditions with each local postmaster. The Postal Service responded to this demand by offering to bargain regionally rather than locally, with the regional headquarters of the Postal Service doing the negotiating on the employer side.[7]

Tendencies toward
Centralization

In addition to the industry-wide negotiations discussed above, there have also been some signs of centralization in many industrial unions. This tendency began to become evident with the development of the Spring Offensive (shuntō).

For example, Tekkōrōren (Japanese Federation of Iron and Steel Workers' Unions) has no authority to negotiate directly with employers or to order its affiliates to strike, but it established an extended struggle committee to which enterprise unions transferred, on an ad hoc basis, the authority to order strikes. This was a device to coordinate acts of dispute among the five major enterprise unions. The union of Yawata Iron Works, however, refused to transfer its authority to the extended struggle committee in 1953 and 1954. In 1957, the left-wing-dominated Tekkōrōren decided that strike actions should be ordered by the vote of the general assembly, but after strikes called under this new procedure failed in both 1957 and 1959, the left-wing leaders lost their positions in Tekkōrōren. However, the slow trend toward centralization continued, and in 1961 the enterprise unions of the five major steel corporations established a pooled strike fund (Takanashi 1965, pp. 129–30).

On the employers' side, the five major steel corporations first used the technique of making a "one-shot offer" of a wage increase in 1959 and continued the practice throughout the 1960s and 1970s. In all except a few years, the federation has accepted the employers' offer without taking a strike vote. Because of the paramount importance of the iron and steel industry in Japan, for many years its wage settlement, with some modifications, established the pattern for other industries.[8] The pattern-setting effect of the steel settlements became even more important after the oil crisis in 1973, and in recent years, as all of the export industries have become increasingly cost-conscious, the iron and steel industry has taken the lead in holding down wage increases.

Similar concerted negotiations among enterprise unions have developed in the shipbuilding, electric appliance, and automobile industries, among others. Furthermore, the coalition of unions in the four metal industries mentioned above has been strengthened following the formation of the International Metalworkers Federation–Japan Council (IMF–JC). The macro- and socioeconomic aspects of these wage negotiations will be analyzed and assessed later, but first we turn to a description of the scope of collective bargaining in Japan.

The Scope of Bargaining

Because there is no provision in the Trade Union Law that defines the scope of collective bargaining, there have been a number of labor disputes over such issues. However, matters affecting the management and operation of public corporations and national enterprises are specifically excluded from collective bargaining by Article 8 of the Public Corporation and National Enterprise Labor Relations Law, and the same is true for local public enterprises under the law that governs their activities. Needless to say, of course, provisions of that kind in a law do not necessarily eliminate disputes over such matters.

The Central Labor Relations Commission surveyed the scope of collective bargaining in 193 major enterprise-wide agreements that covered 1,000 or more employees and reported the following provisions and the number of agreements in which they appeared (Chūō Rōdō Iinkai, Jimukyoku 1970, p. 113): conclusion of the collective bargaining agreement, 7;[9] revision and abolition of the collective bargaining agreement, 110; new working conditions, 53; wages and other working conditions, 61; grievances, 14; personnel affairs, 10; fringe benefits and welfare, 10; interpretation of the collective bargaining agreement, 23; subjects for joint consultation, 50; subjects not settled by joint consultation, 94;[10] management, 11;[11] subjects not settled by other agencies, 11; any subject recognized as necessary by the employer or the union, 61.

The survey reflects practices in large firms, and the results seem to indicate that the distinction between management prerogatives and negotiable issues is rather vague. In addition, there is no real distinction between disputes over interests and disputes over rights. The usual practice is for any conflict arising from the labor–management relationship at the plant or enterprise level to be submitted first to joint consultation and, if not resolved there, to collective bargaining. Thus, there is a procedural continuity between joint consultation and collective bargaining. In fact, collective bargaining is understood to differ from joint consultation only in that the union does not strike to back up its demands as long as the matter is in joint consultation, but it may resort to a strike action during collective bargaining.

A case study conducted in 1958 in a steel plant in Kawasaki (Kōshiro 1959, pp. 75–76) provides an illustration of the scope of collective bargaining as well as the levels within the company hierarchy where the various issues are discussed:

a. Between the company headquarters and the headquarters of the federation of enterprise unions of this company—the *average level* of standard monthly wages; the *average level* of payment by results, of the annual periodic increment of basic wages for individual workers, and of year-end and summer bonuses; and the major fringe benefits.

b. Between the plant management and the enterprise unions at the plant level—the distribution among union members of the negotiated wage increase (base-up), the annual individual increment, and bonuses; details of the payment by results (standard amount of production, yield rate, and piece rate); standard manning, production plans, hours of work (work schedules, shifts, overtime, factory hours, rest periods, paid time off or leaves for local union officials and organizers, etc.), transfers, changes in the company organization, appointment of foremen and subforemen, work safety and sanitary conditions, training, welfare facilities, and paid holidays and vacations.

It should be noted that the scope of bargaining was quite extensive within this plant, and the enterprise union was very active at the time of the study. However, it is unlikely that this was an exceptional case. Of course there are, in general, a great many gray areas as to which matters are negotiable and which are management prerogatives. The scope of collective bargaining appeared to widen perceptibly in the late 1950s as a result of *shokuba tōsō* (shop-floor struggles) in some coal mines, private railways, and steel plants. The scene of the most active struggles was the Miike Coal Mines until the collapse of militant unionism there in 1959–60.

Although industrial relations in the major industries have been generally peaceful during the past decade, a number of labor disputes have occurred. A classification of the issues in these disputes is presented in table 9.1. More than seven out of ten disputes concerned wages, bonuses, and allowances, and of those, 60–70 percent were over the general wage increase (base-up). The parties only rarely resort to arbitration, but often utilize conciliation and mediation when collective bargaining in the private sector reaches an impasse. Of 53,926 cases adjusted by the Central and Local Labor Relations Commissions between March 1946 and 1975, wage increases were at issue in 30.7 percent; bonuses in 19.1 percent; retirement allowances and pensions 4.1 percent; discharges, 4.0 percent; dismissal allowances, 3.6 percent; dismissals, 2.6 percent; and hours of work and vacations, 3.6 percent.[12]

Wage Negotiations

As is apparent from the discussion in the previous section, the most important subject of collective bargaining throughout the past three decades has been wages. Five stages can be identified in the development of wage negotiations.

First, from 1945 until 1947, the dominating idea was the living wage, and the objective that the labor movement pursued with revolutionary enthusiasm

Table 9.1
Content of Labor Disputes: Strikes and Lockouts
Classified by Major Issues, 1970, 1975

Issue	1970	1975
Total labor disputes	4,441	8,330
Total demands	4,533	10,050
	(100.0%)	(100.0%)
Union security and union activities	168	132
Conclusion and overall revision of the		
collective bargaining agreement	37	75
Effectiveness of the labor contracts	7	18
Wages and allowances	3,495	7,412
	(77.1%)	(73.7%)
Wage increases	2,110	5,294
Summer and year-end bonuses	1,240	1,923
Retirement allowances	81	40
Others	63	155
Other working conditions	50	375
	(1.1%)	(3.7%)
Hours of work	14	46
Holidays and vacations	9	150
Others	27	179
Management and personnel problems	267	316
	(5.9%)	(3.1%)
Dismissals and reinstatement	100	120
Plant shutdowns or curtailment of production	25	31
Others	142	165
Others	509	1,722
	(11.2%)	(17.1%)

Source: Rōdōshō, 1976, p. 323.

was to eliminate the traditional differentials between blue-collar wages and white-collar salaries. Radical changes were promoted by the *Densangata chingin* (the wage system modelled after the system of the electric power workers' union) in the fall of 1946.[13] In addition, the lagging production brought on by the war's devastation, aggravated by inflation, also worked to compel the managements to reduce the previous wage differentials by skill, education, responsibility, and status.

During the second period, from 1948 to 1952, managements regained power, primarily because of the economic recovery and the labor policy initiated by the Occupation Forces. In an attempt to restore the skill and responsibility differentials in remuneration, employers introduced a job classification plan. The highlight of the change during this period was the collapse of the leftist Densan, the electric power workers' union, in the fall of 1952.

Between 1952 and 1955, the third period when average real wages reached their prewar level, the employers insisted, with considerable success, that the general wage increase base-up should be replaced with an annual increment (*teiki shōkyū*). What they were advocating was that wage levels should remain the same, but that each individual worker should receive some wage increase every year. In general, this meant that the range of individual merit ratings would be broadened.

The fourth period, from 1955 through 1974, was one of rapid economic growth during which the trade unions were able to introduce and establish the Spring Offensive. This movement began merely as a tactic to challenge the employers' wage-restraint policy of the third period, but it turned out to be highly successful and evolved into an interindustry concerted movement for an annual wage increase. Unions in both the private and public sectors joined in the movement.

The era of rapid economic growth came to an end during the fifth period, the years since 1975, owing to the oil crisis of 1973. The rate of wage increases has moderated considerably, helping to dampen inflation. The unions in the four metal industries (iron and steel, automobile, electric appliances, and shipbuilding) took the lead within the labor movement in realizing the critical significance of the oil crisis for the total economy and in reacting to it in their wage negotiations.

Development of the Spring Offensive

In December 1954, Ohta Kaoru, then president of Gōkarōren (Japanese National Federation of Synthetic Chemical Industry Workers' Unions) proposed that a joint struggle be organized by five Sōhyō unions: the synthetic chemical workers, the coal miners, the private railway workers, the then still-surviving electric power workers, and the paper and pulp workers. A month later, two other Sōhyō unions (the metal workers and the chemical workers) and the electric machinery workers, an affiliate of another national center, Chūritsurōren (Federation of Independent Unions of Japan), joined the group, and together they undertook a concerted demand for wage increases.

Over the following years, the Spring Offensive increased in both size and scope. The public-sector unions became part of the movement in 1956; the unions of the iron and steel and shipbuilding industries participated for the first time in 1959, and in the same year Chūritsurōren unions joined with Sōhyō to establish the Shuntō Kyōtō Kaigi (Joint Struggle Council for the Spring Offensive).

The number of workers participating in the joint Spring Offensive has increased from only 730,000 in 1955 to 4,390,000 in 1961, 5,570,000 in 1965, 6,030,000 in 1971, 9,190,000 in 1973, 9,680,000 in 1975, and 9,810,000 in 1977; in 1979 the total decreased to 9,672,000 (Rōdōshō, Tokei

Jōhōbu 1980a, p. 516). This remarkable development is attributable not only to the increased influence of the Joint Struggle Council, but also to the participation of the unions of the two other national centers, Dōmei and Shinsanbetsu (National Federation of Industrial Organizations) as well as other independent labor organizations.

Changes among the Pattern-Setters

Over the years various unions have taken the lead in establishing the pattern for wage increases. In the first decade after the war, the electric power workers, the coal miners, and the public enterprise employees were the most influential, and during the second decade, from 1955 to 1965, the private railway workers and the steel workers were the ones who played important roles, in cooperation with other Sōhyō unions. But there was a noticeable change, beginning in the third decade, when a coalition of the four metal industries unions emerged to assume the pattern-setting role. The coalition's influence has increased gradually, interrupted only occasionally when the private railway and public employee unions led the way in setting the pattern for wage increases. Since 1975, however, the metal workers' coalition has been dominant.

The logic of the changes in wage pattern-setting can be explained by five factors: (1) the maturity (or immaturity) of labor–management relations, (2) business fluctuations, (3) organizational strength (cohesion) of unions, (4) social tensions, and (5) the ups and downs of a particular industry (Kōshiro 1973, pp. 90–99).

The Maturity of Labor–Management Relations.—Labor unions were unfamiliar with collective bargaining practices right after the war, and in order to avoid the social and economic confusion that would be created by large-scale strikes in essential industries such as electric power, the national railways, and coal mining, the Central Labor Relations Commission very often was obliged to intervene in labor disputes and mediate the key wage decisions. As labor–management relationships matured, reliance upon the commission's conciliation and mediation services declined.

Business Fluctuations.—Public utilities tend to be less subject than other industries to business fluctuations, so when economic recessions adversely affected private industries, the unions of the private railways or the public enterprises took over leadership in organizing the concerted actions for wage increases—including various activities less detrimental than strikes to the economy. For example, the private railway workers set the pattern for wage increases in 1958, 1963, and 1965, when the economy was in a recession at the time of the Spring Offensive.

Organizational Cohesiveness of Labor Unions.—In order to be a leader of the labor movement, a union must be organizationally cohesive. The electric power workers' union, Densan, lost its position of leadership when it split in the great intraunion dispute of 1952. Tanrō, the coal miners' union, also lost influence when its strongest affiliate, the Miike Coal Mine Union, was defeated in the 1959–60 strike. And despite repeated strikes in 1957 and 1959, the leftist leadership of Tekkōrōren, the iron and steel workers' unions, failed to win wage increases when faced by management's determination to establish the "one-shot offer" policy. Because of these defeats, the steel workers' unions retreated for a while and did not reemerge as leaders until the late 1960s.

A more gradual weakening of cohesion has been observed in the private railway workers' unions. The Shitetsusōren very often has been the center of private-sector unionism within the ranks of Sōhyō. However, since 1958 these unions have been reluctant to join in group negotiations. The unions of the major railway companies—Tōkyū, Kintetsu, Nishitetsu, and Odakyū, each of which was prosperous—organized a right-wing intraunion coalition in July 1961. At the same time, Dōmei's rival federation of private railway unions, Kōtsūrōren (Japan Federation of Transport Workers' Unions), increased its membership. Because of this decline in organizational strength, Shitetsusōren became less willing to take on the leadership of the Spring Offensives in the 1960s.

Social Conditions.—At times unions took advantage of social conditions to seek and win greater than usual wage increases. For example, Kōrōkyō (Joint Council of the Public Enterprise Unions) took the lead in setting the pattern for a 10 percent wage increase in the spring of 1961 because, during the previous summer, the National Personnel Authority (NPA) had recommended a 12.5 percent pay hike for the national civil service. The NPA recommendation had been made to compensate the civil servants for wage differentials with the private sector that had been accumulating since 1957. Furthermore, the Income Doubling Five-Year Plan had just begun under the Ikeda administration that had come to power in July 1960, shortly after the settlement of the bitter Miike Coal Mine strike and the disorders that followed the renewal of the Japan–U.S. Security Treaty. The economy had been prospering since 1958 and, therefore, the public enterprise employees were in a strategic position to take advantage of all these economic, political, and social circumstances.

A similar combination of events occurred in the spring of 1974. Consumer prices had risen by 24.5 percent in 1974 as a result of the oil crisis, and excessive expenditures by the Tanaka administration only aggravated the inflation. In addition, some of the large companies were being strongly criticized for land speculation and profiteering activities. At the same time the unions of the public enterprises, taking advantage of the political and social unrest, were intensifying their struggle to recover their right to strike, and the government was worrying about the recurrence of commuters' riots if illegal strikes by National Railways workers were to coincide with the Spring Offensive and affect adversely the Upper House election, due in July 1974. All of these social and economic developments combined to help the unions win a historically high wage increase of 32.9 percent in the spring of 1974.

Ups and Downs of Particular Industries.—Until the energy revolution of the late 1950s, the coal miners' union was one of the most militant and influential in Japan. In 1957 it obtained a large wage increase in the midst of business prosperity, but that was the last time that the coal miners were able to take the lead in establishing the pattern for the general wage increase. With the transition from coal to oil as an energy resource during the following few years, the bargaining strength of the coal miners declined.

The energy revolution has also had an impact on the labor movement in the chemical industry. Huge petrochemical complexes were built in the late 1950s through the early 1960s, and the enormous capital investment involved intensified the competition among the major chemical companies. The enterprise unions of the major petrochemical companies seceded from Ohta's Gōkarōren, which had been one of the most influential unions in the Sōhyō ranks, and even the Sumitomo Chemical company's union, the largest among those remaining in Gōkarōren, has been only lukewarm toward what it considers Ohta's strike-prone policies.

On the other hand, unions of the iron and steel, automobile, electrical machinery, and shipbuilding industries have strengthened their coalition in the ranks of IMF–JC. The ever-increasing pressure of international competition in these key industries in the late 1960s through the 1970s has stimulated their crisis consciousness and their realization that good employment opportunities are becoming increasingly scarce, so that they have turned to outright criticism of the traditional strike tactics of Sōhyō, which are urged primarily by the public-sector unions. In pace with the growing importance of these export industries in the Japanese economy, IMF–JC's business-minded philosophy has gained increasing influence in the labor movement. It was under such changed circumstances that the major steel corporations' "one-shot offer" of a wage increase could become the pattern over the past decade.

Standardization of the Rate of Wage Increases

With the development of the Spring Offensive, both the amount of the wage increase and the percentage have tended to become standardized. Table 9.2 shows the changes in the coefficient of variation of the amount of wage increases since 1956. The lowest variation was 0.05 in 1973, and although it

Table 9.2
Spring Offensive Wage Increases, 1956–79

Year	No. Companies Surveyed	Existing Average Monthly Wages (¥)	Average Amount of Increase (¥)	Average Rate of Increase (%)	Coefficient of Variation
1956	72–84	16,873	1,063	6.3	0.29
1957	72–84	17,651	1,518	8.6	0.20
1958	72–84	18,750	1,050	5.6	0.29
1959	72–84	19,708	1,281	6.5	0.20
1960	156	20,598	1,792	8.7	0.17
1961	163	21,522	2,970	13.7	0.14
1962	163	23,597	2,515	10.7	0.13
1963	162	24,718	2,237	9.1	0.16
1964	161	26,622	3,305	12.4	0.10
1965	257	29,635	3,150	10.6	0.16
1966	257	32,095	3,403	10.6	0.12
1967	257	35,037	4,371	12.5	0.07
1968	258	38,800	5,296	13.6	0.07
1969	258	43,339	6,865	15.8	0.07
1970	257	49,503	9,166	18.5	0.06
1971	257	57,459	9,727	16.9	0.07
1972	254	66,243	10,138	15.3	0.08
1973	244	75,446	15,159	20.1	0.05
1974	261	88,209	28,981	32.9	0.07
1975	265	116,783	15,279	13.1	0.16
1976	260	131,349	11,596	8.8	0.10
1977	268	143,109	12,536	8.8	0.10
1978	281	156,615	9,218	5.9	0.20
1979	287	166,026	9,959	6.0	0.10

Source: Rōdōshō 1979b.
Note: The coefficient of variation used here is defined as: (wage increase of a firm at the third quartile) − (wage increase of a firm at the first quartile) ÷ 2 × (median of wage increases):

$$\frac{W_3 - W_1}{2 \times W_m}$$

increased a bit during the recession following the oil crisis, it has remained at generally low levels.

The factors generating such standardized wage increases should be explained. First, the increasing pressure of a labor shortage in the 1960s and early 1970s contributed to a decrease in the wage differentials among companies and industries. The starting wage rates for new school graduates increased rapidly and then leveled off.

Second, the follow-the-leader practice among major companies has been reinforced by two other factors: (1) competing companies preferred to accept the same actual amount (or the same percentage rate) of wage increases, and (2) the desire to maintain industrial peace tended to compel the less profitable companies to pay the same (or similar) wages as the more prosperous companies.

The trend toward standardization of wage increases and of average wage levels among the major firms can best be illustrated by the experience in the iron and steel industry. Table 9.3 shows wage increases in the five largest steel companies since 1959 under the continuing "one-shot offer" policy; how standardized these average wage levels have become among the steel companies can be seen in table 9.4. The data are evidence of the strong desire of these competing firms to equalize their labor costs, and since this pattern satisfies the workers' demands for equitable wages, they too find it acceptable. Wage levels of the top two auto makers also are similar (table 9.5), as are those in other major industries.

Another aspect of the standardization of wages as a result of collective bargaining is illustrated by the leveling-off of the wage increase rate among firms of different size. Table 9.6 shows that the average percentage increase of wages in the unionized small and medium-sized firms has been even higher than that in the large firms since 1962, although the average absolute amount of the increase continues to be lower. Of course, the development has not been as simple and continuous as the average figures imply. For example, if we look at the differentials of wage increases in the iron and steel industry by size of firm, we note that they decreased by 10 percent between 1969 and 1974, but increased again by 15 percent between 1975 and 1978 (Tekkōrōren 1978, p. 8).

Nevertheless, one of the most important outcomes of collective bargaining seems to be the decreasing wage differentials by size of firm. The average wage differentials between firms with 1,000 or more employees and those employing less than 100 workers in manufacturing industries decreased between 1960 and 1970. For example, in 1960 male production workers who had completed only compulsory schooling (nine years) in firms employing 10–99 workers were earning 57 percent of the wages of similar workers in large firms, but by 1970 the percentage had increased to 78 and remained approximately the same in 1975. Over the same period, the salary differential among male white-collar workers (managerial, clerical, technical) who had graduated from senior high school (12 years of education) and were employed by firms of different sizes also declined, as did that of college and university graduates. In 1960, high school graduates in white-collar jobs in small firms were being paid 72 percent as much as the earnings of similar workers employed by large firms, but by 1975 their salaries were 91 percent of those paid in the large firms. Over the same period, the percentage figures for college and university graduates were 68 and 85 (see table 9.7).

Table 9.3
Average Spring Offensive Wage Increases in the Five Largest Firms
in the Iron and Steel Industry, 1959–78

Year	Amount of Base-up (¥ per month)	Including Annual Increment (¥ per month)	Estimated Increase (base-up %)	Including Annual Increment (%)	Notes
1959[a]	800	1,500	NA	NA	Tekkōrōren joined shuntō.
1960	1,100	1,850	NA	NA	Sumitomo: ¥600
1961	2,500	3,300	NA	NA	
1962	1,800	2,650	NA	NA	Pattern setting
1963	700	1,570	2.3	5.1	Some strikes
1964	2,300	3,250	6.8	9.7	Pattern setting
1965	1,500	2,500	4.1	6.8	
1966	1,500	2,550	3.9	6.7	Decreased strike propensity
1967	3,200	4,300	7.8	10.5	
1968	3,200	4,350	6.9	9.4	Failed to vote for strikes
1969	4,000	5,200	7.9	10.2	
1970[b]	6,000	7,500	10.3	12.9	Demanded "model" formula
1971	6,000	7,600	9.0	11.4	
1972	6,000	7,700	8.0	10.2	
1973[c]	8,700+α[d]	11,650+α[d]	10.3+α[d]	13.8	"Model formula" adopted: 35 yrs. old, 12 yrs. service
1974	23,000	25,500	23.5	26.0	
1975	15,500	18,300	12.6	14.9	
1976	9,000	12,000	6.4	8.5	Kawasaki union returns to Tekkōrōren
1977	9,800	13,000	6.4	8.5	
1978	3,700	7,000	2.2	4.2	

Source: Tekkōrōren 1978.
NA: Data not available.

[a] Before 1959 Tekkōrōren had negotiated wages in the autumn, outside the Spring Offensive. They received ¥1,000 (Yawata), ¥1,700 (Fuji), ¥1,550 (NKK), and ¥825 (Sumitomo) in 1955; ¥700 for each in 1956; and zero in 1957. Tekkōrōren was not able to organize wage negotiations in 1958.

[b] Shinnittetsu Corp. was organized by merger of Yawata and Fuji. Kawasaki unions' wage increase is included among the five-firm average after 1970.

[c] Figures since 1973 have been published by the companies. Prior to 1973, they were collected by Tekkōrōren.

[d] + α indicates an amount negotiated outside the formal agreement, to be used to make partial adjustments in the wage structure (e.g., shift allowances, regional allowances). It was unpublicized so as to prevent its use by unions in negotiations with other industries or companies.

Table 9.4
Average Monthly Straight-Time Earnings
at the Five Largest Steel Corporations, 1976–77

Corporation	After the Spring 1976 Wage Increase		After the Spring 1977 Wage Increases	
	¥	%	¥	%
Shinnittetsu	166,265	102.8	180,190	102.1
Nippon Kōkan	163,260	100.9	177,350	100.5
Sumitomo Kinzoku	160,472	99.2	175,735	99.6
Kōbe Seikō	156,301	96.6	171,051	97.0
Kawasaki Seitetsu	162,473	100.4	177,733	100.7
Average of the five corporations	161,754	100.0	176,412	100.0

Source: Tekkōrōren, Chōsa Jihō (Survey Review), No. 118 (Nov. 1977), pp. 58–63, which is based on its unpublished Tsukibetsu Chingin Rōdōjikan Chōsa (Monthly Survey of Wages and Work Hours).

Table 9.5
Average Wage Levels at the Two Top
Automobile Manufacturing Companies, March 1978
(in yen)

Companies	Average Monthly Straight-Time Earnings	Overtime and Other Additionals	Total Monthly Payments	Average Yearly Bonus Payments
Toyota	142,900	39,700	182,600	890,844[a]
	(100.0)	(100.0)	(100.0)	(100.0)
Nissan	140,190	41,664	181,854	860,944[b]
	(98.1)	(104.9)	(99.6)	(96.6)

Source: Supplied to the author by Jidōshasōren (Confederation of Japan Automobile Workers' Unions).

Note: Percentages in parentheses.

[a] Equivalent to 6.1 months pay.

[b] Equivalent to 5.8 months pay plus unpublicized amounts negotiated outside of the formal agreement.

Factors That Explain Wage Changes

In the mid-1960s, the experts were beginning to discuss the necessity and feasibility of introducing an incomes policy, and a committee of five prominent economists, headed by Kumagaya Hisao, was established by the Economic Planning Agency to study the problem. The committee, in its report published in 1968, stated that a wage increase exceeding the rate of increase of national productivity (the real amount of GNP per employed person) tended to stimulate inflation. The committee also used the concept of the Phillips curve to analyze wage changes in Japan and tried, in its report, to

Table 9.6
Average Negotiated Wage Increases in Unionized
Small- and Medium-Sized Firms, 1962-79

Year	Average Wages before Increase (¥)	Average Amount of Increase (¥)	Increase (%)
1962	16,533	2,338	14.1
1963	17,645	2,091	11.9
1964	19,992	3,159	15.8
1965	22,325	2,704	12.1
1966	24,407	2,704	11.1
1967	26,009	3,362	12.9
1968	28,835	4,162	14.4
1969	32,533	5,389	16.6
1970	37,170	7,390	19.9
1971	43,770	8,003	18.3
1972	50,417	8,329	16.5
1973	58,445	12,333	21.1
1974	69,816	23,508	33.7
1975	91,494	12,886	14.1
1976	103,271	10,045	9.7
1977	112,298	10,609	9.4
1978	121,367	7,825	6.4
1979	128,521	8,321	6.5

Source: Rōdōshō Tōkei Jōhōbu 1980b, p.470.
Note: The figures are for approximately 8,000 firms that have fewer than 300 employees each, surveyed by the Ministry of Labor.

persuade the public to avoid inflationary wage increases. However, it did not strongly recommend that Japan adopt an incomes policy. More negative positions on this question were taken by two other governmental committees in the following years, even after the oil crisis. (Keizai Kikakuchō 1968, pp. 1-91, esp. pp. 60-91; 1972; 1975.)

When we review the figures on wage increases in table 9.2, we note that the rate of increase was more than 15 percent between 1969 and 1974, the final stage of Japan's historically rapid economic growth and the period when, for the first time in its history, it was not subject to the strong constraints of foreign currency reserves. The excess demand for labor had continued for more than a decade, and symptoms of accelerating inflation were apparent, particularly after 1971. However, most economists, to say nothing of politicians and trade unionists, had been very reluctant to recommend any outright wage restraints, although employer organizations had been strongly advocating them since around 1970.

Behind such reluctance was the following rationale: (1) the real reason that wages had been increasing was the excess demand for labor, and a wage-

Table 9.7

Average Wage Differentials for Different Categories of
Male Workers, by Size of Manufacturing Firm, 1960–75

Worker Characteristics, by Size of Firm	Average Monthly Earnings, June					
	1960		1970		1975	
	¥	%	¥	%	¥	%
Production workers						
Compulsory schooling graduate						
1,000 and over	26,738	100.0	74,500	100.0	155,500	100.0
100–999	18,987	71.0	61,200	82.1	133,800	86.0
10–99	15,303	57.2	58,000	77.9	120,900	77.7
Senior high school[a] graduate						
1,000 and over	20,325	(100.0)	63,400	(100.0)	137,700	(100.0)
100–999	16,948	(83.4)	57,000	(89.9)	127,200	(92.4)
10–99	16,092	(79.2)	59,800	(94.3)	125,000	(90.8)
Administrative, clerical, and technical workers						
Senior high school graduate						
1,000 and over	28,803	100.0	78,400	100.0	166,400	100.0
100–999	23,098	80.2	71,000	90.6	154,600	92.9
10–99	20,780	72.1	71,600	91.3	152,000	91.3
College or university graduate						
1,000 and over	35,950	100.0	95,700	100.0	195,400	100.0
100–999	26,801	74.6	78,900	82.4	166,500	85.2
10–99	24,559	68.3	81,300	85.0	167,200	85.6

Source: CKKT, conducted every year for June 30.

[a] Wages for senior high school graduates (12 years of education) are lower than those for compulsory schooling graduates (9 years of education) because the former group is on the average younger than the latter.

restraint policy would not be workable without tight fiscal and monetary policies; (2) Japan's economy was not constrained by a deficit in its international balance of payments, and there was no urgent need for a strict anti-inflationary policy; and (3) enterprise unions had a pattern of being quite sensitive to the economic conditions of their own firms, and they would not go so far as to "kill the goose that laid the golden eggs."

The following regression analysis of negotiated wage changes indicates that the percentage increases during the period of high economic growth can be explained in large part by the tightening demand for labor (Koshiro 1978a, p. 173; t-values in parentheses):

$$\dot{WS} = 4.713 + 9.035\ UY \qquad\qquad (1)$$
$$(3.85) \quad (8.04)$$

$\bar{R}^2$ (adjusted coefficient of determination) = .841
SEE (standard error of estimate) = 1.328
D.W. (Durbin–Watson ratio) = 1.34

where $\dot{WS}$ is the percentage change in average wages negotiated at major companies between 1961 and 1973, and the explanatory variable, UY, is the ratio of job vacancies to the number of persons seeking jobs through the public labor exchange offices. However, following the oil crisis in the fall of 1973, the situation changed dramatically. Prices moved up sharply and the demand for labor suddenly slackened. Yet wages increased by 32.9 percent in the spring of 1974. Therefore, the explanatory value ($\bar{R}^2$) in a wage equation like that above dropped to .327 with the 1974 data and to .325 when the 1975 data were used. At this point it seemed as if an incomes policy was the only measure that would save the economy from the aggravating inflation, and in fact, right after the Spring Offensive of 1974, the Economic Planning Agency did set up a new committee to consider measures to deal with wage–price spirals. This committee, too, refrained from recommending adoption of an incomes policy (Keizai Kikakuchō 1975).

This hesitation on the part of the government as well as most economists stemmed from the belief that the Japanese economy and industrial relations systems were flexible enough to adapt to the new pressures. The government chose instead to rely upon independent market forces to dampen the inflation, although it did strengthen the tight money policy. However, it should be noted that government officials, labor experts, and trade union leaders in the private export industries all preached moderation in their attempts to persuade the public as well as rank-and-file union members that wage increases should be held down.

Succeeding developments in Japan's economy proved that the experts were right in their belief that Japan's economy would adapt. Large companies in manufacturing industries reduced their workforces dramatically for the first time since the Korean War; the number of regular employees in manufacturing decreased by more than 1.3 million during the five years following the 1973 oil crisis. Those workers who had exercised self-restraint and had forgone wage increases now feared that they would be unemployed. Workers who are members of enterprise unions have easy access to information on their own company's financial condition through the elaborate communication networks established by joint consultation schemes, and if they find that their company is continuing to lose money, they usually tend to work harder in efforts to save both the company and their jobs—unless, of course, the employer is deemed to be a ruthless exploiter.

Wage increases in Spring Offensives of the years after the oil crisis are usually explained by three factors: the ratio of job vacancies to job seekers

(*UY*) in January through March of every year, the rate of increase in consumer prices (*PC*) in the same period compared to the previous year, and the ratio of current corporate profits to the amount of sales of major companies surveyed by the Bank of Japan in the second half of the previous year (π). Using these factors, the percentage rate of wage increase of major unionized companies can then be largely explained by the following regression equation (Economic Planning Agency 1979, p. 293; t-values in parentheses):

$$\dot{WS} = -5.148 + 11.672\ UY + 0.6184\ PC + 1.4586\ \pi \qquad (2)$$
$$\quad\ \ (2.70)\qquad (7.48)\qquad (6.14)\qquad (2.84)$$
$$\bar{R} = .904 \qquad SEE = 1.864 \qquad D.W. = 2.56$$

Government economists and labor experts have often used this type of wage equation as an educational weapon to persuade labor unions to moderate their wage demands within a limit that would be compatible with macroeconomic anti-inflationary policies.

The present author formulated a new wage equation that uses the average wage increase (*DWS*) as a dependent variable and a different index of corporate profits—in this case, the average current profit per employee of 826 major companies surveyed by the Japan Economic Newspaper Company, Nihon Keizai Shimbunsha, in the previous fiscal year, here denoted as $(\pi/L)_{-1}$. The other two independent variables are *UY*, as used in equation (2), and the rate of increase in consumer prices excluding perishable goods (*PCX*) in January through March compared with the previous year. π denotes current profit, *L* is the number of employees, and -1 indicates a lag of one fiscal year. The observation period is 1966–79 (Kōshiro 1980a, p.7; t-values in parentheses):

$$DWS = -5637.3 + 4312.2\ UY + 816.0\ PCX + 7.896\ (\pi/L)_{-1} \qquad (3)$$
$$\qquad\ (-2.58)\quad\ (2.83)\qquad\ (7.38)\qquad\ (3.92)$$
$$\bar{R}^2 = .924 \qquad SEE = 1.992 \qquad D.W. = 2.02$$

From these results it can be concluded that changes in negotiated wage increases over the period can be explained very well by changes in these other economic factors, although the extrapolated values are different. These results are usually interpreted as verifying the hypotheses that enterprise unions exercise very little bargaining power and that wage levels are determined primarily by the economic forces of the market, without serious distortions.

Is Union Militancy Really Minimal?

Whether union militancy in Japan is really minimal is a difficult question. As has already been described, the labor movement plays an important role not only in wage negotiations, but also in a wider area of society. If we assume that we can measure the influence of trade union militancy upon wage increases by regression analysis, then it is not necessarily difficult to demonstrate the magnitude of that influence, as Watanabe Tsunehiko, Ono Akira, and I once attempted to do.

Watanabe (1966) used a dummy variable to represent the influence of institutional changes in the labor market in postwar Japan and found that before the war a 4.8 percent unemployment rate was necessary for a change in monetary wages to be zero, but after the war the unemployment rate had to be 6.7 percent to get a zero change in monetary wages.

Ono (1972, p. 27) proceeded further to estimate the influence of labor disputes on wage increases between 1953 and 1968 simply by adding, as an explanatory variable in a regression equation, the average annual percentage of all manufacturing employees who actually participated in acts of labor dispute each year. According to his analysis, about 43 percent of the wage increases (measured on the basis of monthly average earnings in establishments employing more than 30 workers) was attributable to the impact of work stoppages in the latter half of the observation period.

I applied Ono's idea in an attempt to explain changes in wages negotiated in the Spring Offensive, but in so doing I doubted the rationality of using the average participation rate in work stoppages in manufacturing as a proxy for union influence, for two reasons: (1) Strike propensity varies markedly among manufacturing industries. In the iron and steel, shipbuilding, automobile, chemical, pulp and paper, and electric power industries, for example, strike participation rates have been declining since the early 1960s (table 9.8A), but in such industries as electrical machinery, rubber, printing, and metal working the rate has been increasing (table 9.8B). But it would be difficult to conclude that union militancy in the latter group of industries had the effect of pushing up the general wage level, since we have noticed that the influence of the less strike-prone unions has been increasing since around 1965. (2) If union militancy is of any importance in wage determination, labor disputes in such public enterprises as the National Railways and the Postal Service must have had a great impact in the course of the unions' concerted industrial actions in the Spring Offensives. This view would seem to be all the more feasible in the early 1970s when these public employees increased the number of their illegal dispute actions tremendously as they intensified their campaign for restoration of their right to strike. Table 9.9 shows the trend in the strike participation rate for the National Railways in terms of absences due to industrial actions in the spring and throughout the year. Either of the indices can be a proxy for union militancy in the public sector.

Now let us illustrate the hypothesis of wage determination under collective bargaining in Japan, taking into account the previously mentioned union strength, as measured by the strike participation rate. In figure 9.1, ΔW_p is

Table 9.8
Work-Stoppage Rates in Industry, 1955–74
A. Declining Rates

Year	Iron and Steel	Transportation Equipment	Chemical	Paper and Pulp	Electric Power	Manufacturing
1955	44.6	15.4	16.4	6.4	6.0	15.2
1956	34.1	37.2	17.8	9.5	1.9	13.7
1957	42.0	29.2	21.1	25.4	4.0	15.6
1958	5.2	11.9	29.4	20.1	10.7	11.3
1959	31.9	27.9	15.0	13.2	4.4	12.0
1960	2.7	14.1	18.7	12.8	15.2	8.2
1961	34.0	21.2	27.7	20.7	9.1	17.3
1962	4.1	26.9	5.6	19.5	71.0	10.5
1963	20.6	33.0	13.4	17.3	21.0	10.7
1964	2.6	23.6	15.7	15.8	21.0	10.7
1965	27.2	20.9	18.8	17.3	16.6	16.1
1966	3.9	18.6	8.8	9.0	12.1	10.3
1967	2.4	7.8	6.6	6.4	7.8	6.7
1968	1.9	13.2	11.2	5.5	4.6	9.6
1969	3.4	4.5	9.7	6.1	5.1	10.8
1970	2.0	8.2	13.0	2.3	1.0	14.7
1971	2.6	6.4	14.2	5.7	11.3	15.2
1972	3.8	5.8	10.6	12.1	3.0	11.5
1973	1.7	6.0	11.4	2.6	7.5	14.7
1974	4.5	6.6	25.3	9.6	17.3	23.9

the rate of wage increases in the private sector which, in principle, is supposed to be determined only by collective bargaining. But the structure of bargaining in that sector is not clearly defined; thus (X————F_P) is in the "black box" at the lower left of the figure, since the functions of X (negotiating process) and F_P (union militancy in the private sector) are unknown. A popular view of wage determination in Japan, as illustrated by wage equations (1), (2), and (3), is that union influence is almost minimal and, therefore, (X————F_P) has no effect. Rather, according to this popular view, such economic factors as UY (ratio of job vacancies to job seekers), PC (rate of increase in consumer prices), and π (rate of current corporate profits) operating in the market can satisfactorily explain wage changes.

However, if we take account of another factor, union militancy in the public sector, F_G, in determining W_P, as illustrated by figure 9.1, a different type of wage equation, based on the collective bargaining hypothesis, can be formulated. There is good support for this hypothesis. As is explained fully in chapter 11, public employees do not have the right to strike and their employers do not have enough autonomy to negotiate wages with their unions. Therefore, they have developed a function equivalent to direct nego-

Table 9.8 (continued)
Work-Stoppage Rates in Industry, 1955-74
B. Increasing Rates

	Electrical Machinery	Metal Works	Rubber	Printing	All Industries
1955	12.1	1.9	2.1	5.1	20.7
1956	29.6	1.8	1.0	1.4	17.5
1957	27.6	3.5	3.3	10.3	25.1
1958	30.0	0.9	6.0	2.3	18.8
1959	16.2	1.7	8.6	3.8	15.6
1960	23.5	1.8	8.5	4.5	9.2
1961	25.5	3.6	16.5	5.1	17.1
1962	25.3	9.4	18.5	4.0	13.9
1963	13.6	4.2	11.1	1.5	10.2
1964	32.4	1.8	10.6	2.0	8.3
1965	47.4	9.6	24.4	4.0	13.0
1966	33.3	5.4	8.8	0.7	8.6
1967	14.6	7.8	24.9	1.7	5.6
1968	32.7	6.7	21.7	2.1	7.9
1969	39.0	6.4	39.2	1.9	9.4
1970	59.0	5.2	30.7	3.6	10.9
1971	49.3	9.3	30.7	4.7	11.7
1972	32.2	5.5	31.0	4.3	9.5
1973	54.8	11.7	10.9	7.3	12.5
1974	67.0	16.9	39.7	11.1	20.8

Source: Kōshiro et al. 1975, pp. 32-33; Kōshiro 1978b, p. 86.
Note: The work-stoppage participation rate is (number of workers involved in strikes and lockouts) ÷ (number of employees in each industry at the end of previous year).

tiations. Instead of bargaining the public sector wage increase rate (ΔW_G) directly—$F_G \rightarrow \Delta W_G$—public employee unions have preferred to use two other methods of exerting pressure for wage increases. One is the "arbitration award inducing effect" ($F_G \rightarrow \Delta W_P$). Since the parties are unable to reach a wage settlement through direct negotiations, they appeal to the Public Corporation and National Enterprise Labor Relations Commission for an arbitration award. The commission has established the practice of basing its award on the estimated average wage increase in the private sector reached during the course of the appropriate Spring Offensive. Therefore if, by their concerted industrial actions, the public employee unions can create a social and political atmosphere that is favorable to them, then the commission may move toward adjusting their wage disputes with a strong concern for maintaining social peace. Of course such tactics can be and, in fact, have been condemned by the government and by conservative political forces as unduly distorting the legitimate democratic process. Nevertheless, interactions of this kind have been observed many times.

Table 9.9
Trends in Absentee Rates Caused by Industrial Actions
in the National Railways, 1955–74

Year	Annual Average No.			Average No. Each Spring		
	Absentees	Employees	Ratio of Absentee/Employee	Absentees	Employees	Ratio of Absentee/Employee
1955	10,000	445,637	2.24%	NA	NA	NA
1956	110,000	447,196	24.60	15,500	445,637	3.48%
1957	262,000	449,634	58.27	159,000	447,715	35.51
1958	35,600	450,387	7.90	23,700	450,273	5.26
1959	30,470	449,353	6.78	29,900	450,425	6.64
1960	3,600	448,542	0.80	200	448,996	0.05
1961	3,942	450,615	0.88	(1,142)[a]	448,390	0.26
1962	5,322	452,688	1.18	3,096	452,688	0.68
1963	2,436	455,020	0.54	1,458	452,688	0.32
1964	2,060	461,931	0.45	(1,030)[a]	461,931	0.22
1965	7,256	462,120	1.57	4,200	462,436	0.91
1966	13,102	469,693	2.79	12,284	459,693	2.62
1967	4,136	468,267	0.88	1,658	458,742	0.35
1968	35,656	466,711	7.64	20,178	467,071	4.32
1969	25,074	466,743	5.37	14,098	466,699	3.02
1970	30,694	459,677	6.68	8,384	459,677	1.82
1971	48,808	450,388	10.84	48,808	450,388	10.84
1972	73,954	441,054	16.77	73,954	441,054	16.77
1973	88,700	434,934	20.39	149,600	438,334	34.13
1974	383,900	431,958	88.87	299,200	432,270	69.22

Source: Kōshiro et al. 1975, pp. 42–43; Kōshiro 1978b, p. 81.
Note: The absentee rate due to industrial actions is (number of employees recognized as absent due to industrial actions) ÷ (number of employees at the end of each fiscal year).
NA: Data not available.
[a] Estimates (insufficient information).

Another method used by public employee unions to exert pressure for wage increases is the "threat effect" $[F_G \rightarrow (F_P\text{———}X)]$. Since militant unionism in the public sector is viewed in the private sector as an undesirable element in the industrial relations system, private employers are motivated to prevent such an element from invading their sacred precincts. Thus they may choose to pay for industrial harmony in their own sector with generous wage increases for their employees.

Assuming the existence of such interactions, the author has constructed an alternative wage equation as follows:

$$\Delta W = f(UY, MLS, GLS) \tag{4}$$

Here, ΔW denotes the average negotiated wage increase in all the industries surveyed each year by the Ministry of Labor. UY represents demand

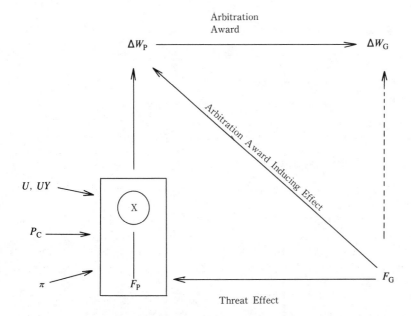

The average wage increase (¥8,239) is the sum of the following increases due to each variable:

Constant −3,401
UY (0.9187) × 6,869 = 6,311
MLS (0.3051) × 7,344 = 2,241
GLS (13.1613) × 234.6 = 3,088

These are the parameters of UY, MLS, and GLS respectively as shown in Table 9.10. The absolute value of the constant term is added to the contribution of UY because of a theoretical interpretation.

Figure 9.1. A Collective Bargaining Model of Wage Determination. *Source*: Kōshiro et al. 1975, p. 70; Kōshiro 1978b, p. 70.

and supply conditions in the labor market as in the previous equations, and *MLS*, the ratio of man-days lost owing to work stoppages in manufacturing industries from February through May of each year during the Spring Offensive, represents a combined effect in the private sector of union militancy and employer efforts to avoid work stoppages through, for example, raising wage offers. *GLS* in figure 9.2 is a proxy for a theoretical F_G; it represents the ratio of strike participants among employees of the National Railways

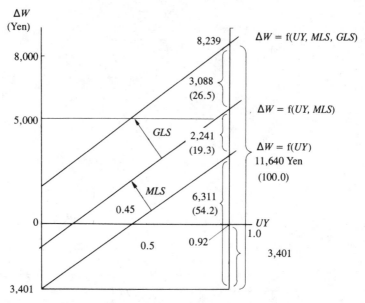

Figure 9.2. Contribution of Explanatory Variables to the Average Wage Increase between 1961 and 1975. The average wage increase (¥ 8,239) is the sum of the following increases accounted for by each variable: Constant = −3,401; UY (0.9187) × 6,869 = 6,311; MLS (0.3051) × 7,344 = 2,241; GLS (13.1613) × 234.6 = 3,088. (These parameters are shown in Table 9.1.) The absolute value of the constant term is added to the contribution of UY because of a theoretical interpretation. Source: Kōshiro 1978b, p. 126.

during the Spring Offensive. This statistical series is my own innovation, in cooperation with the personnel bureau of the National Railways.

Both the input data and results of equation (4) are presented in table 9.10. From these results, as illustrated in figure 9.2, we can conclude that about 27 percent of the average wage increase during the observation period 1961–75 can be attributed to GLS, about 19 percent to MLS, and about 54 percent to UY (Koshiro 1978b, pp. 126–28). Thus, it would be fair to say that the impact of work stoppages by public employees was large enough for us to question the validity of the popular view that labor unions in Japan have little influence on wage determination. We must have some reservations whether quantitative measurement of the impact of union militancy on wage determination by regression analysis is methodologically appropriate, but for the time being we cannot suggest a better way of analyzing this problem.[14] Despite the recognized limitations, it should at least be obvious that reconsideration of the prevailing view of the bargaining strength (or weakness) of enterprise unions is in order.

Table 9.10
Input Data and the Observed Parameters,
Wage Equation (4), 1961-75
(Input Values for Each Variable)

Year	ΔW (¥)	MLS (%)	GLS	UY
1961	2,970	0.4585	0.26	0.64
1962	2,515	0.2670	0.68	0.63
1963	2,237	0.1517	0.32	0.54
1964	3,305	0.2644	0.22	0.67
1965	3,150	0.4066	0.91	0.63
1966	3,403	0.2014	2.62	0.55
1967	4,371	0.1303	0.35	0.78
1968	5,296	0.1912	4.32	0.97
1969	6,865	0.2605	3.02	1.06
1970	9,166	0.2807	1.82	1.30
1971	9,727	0.4340	10.84	1.10
1972	10,138	0.3182	16.77	1.02
1973	15,159	0.2236	34.13	1.63
1974	28,981	0.6726	69.22	1.54
1975	15,279	0.3160	51.94	0.72

	Constant	UY	MLS	GLS
Observed parameter	$\Delta W_s = -3,401$	6,869	7,344	234.6
(t-values in parentheses)	(−2.83)	(6.05)	(2.57)	(11.10)

$\bar{R}^2 = 0.972$	SEE = 1.236	D.W. = 2.47

Source: Kōshiro 1978b, p.127.
Note: ΔW is the average wage increase of major companies surveyed by the Ministry of Labor. MLS = (working days lost due to work stoppages in the manufacturing industry between February and May each year) ÷ (number of regularly employed workers in manufacturing establishments with 30 or more employees × average number of days worked). GLS = (number of employees recognized as absent due to industrial actions during the Spring Offensive each year) ÷ (number of employees at the end of each fiscal year). UY = ratio of job vacancies to job seekers (seasonally adjusted) through the labor exchange offices, January through March of each year.
The average value of each variable between 1961 and 1975 is as follows:
$\overline{\Delta W}$ = ¥8,710   UY = 0.9187   MLS = 0.3051   GLS = 13.1613

A New Economic Interpretation of Wage Determination by Enterprise Unions

Despite the analytical limitations inherent in attempting to measure union impact upon wage determination, the findings in the previous section prompt us to try to reconcile an economic interpretation with the bargaining power approach. For this purpose we introduce a new wage equation based on a simple economic theory of demand for labor—namely, a regression model deduced from the profit-maximizing behavior of firms, where P_i = the price of products, P_m = the price of materials, Q = the amount of products produced, a = a unit amount of materials input to produce Q, w = the average wage rate, L = the number of employees, and rK = the capital cost. Then the amount of profit, V, can be defined as

$$V = P_i \cdot Q - a \cdot P_m \cdot Q - w \cdot L - rK$$

Therefore, the condition of profit maximization is deduced by taking the partial derivative of V with respect to L:

$$\partial V / \partial L = (P_i - a \cdot P_m)(\partial Q / \partial L) - w = 0$$

Therefore,

$$w = (P_i - a \cdot P_m)(\partial Q / \partial L) \tag{5}$$

To simplify, let us assume that a logarithmic linear equation can be fitted to quantify (5). Thus,

$$\ln W = \alpha + \beta \ln P_i - \gamma \ln P_m + \delta \ln(Q/L) \tag{6}$$

Here, W is the average wage level of major companies surveyed by the Ministry of Labor after the wage increase each spring, P_i is the wholesale price index of manufactured goods, P_m is the wholesale price index of materials surveyed by the Bank of Japan, and Q/L is the rate of national productivity (real GNP per employed person), a substitute for $\partial Q / \partial L$ for statistical convenience. The observation period is 1961–78. The input data are shown in table 9.11 and the observed parameters in table 9.12.

From this analysis we can safely conclude that the changes in the average wage level following the Spring Offensive have been almost totally in response to price changes in the product and materials markets, and hence to the profitability of firms and to the improvement of national productivity.

These analyses suggest strongly that wage determination under collective bargaining in Japan has been surprisingly consistent with macroeconomic anti-inflationary administration under the post-Keynesian welfare state. This is not to say that the bargaining power of enterprise unions has been necessarily weak, but rather that the remarkable ability of labor–management relations to respond to economic changes and the flexibility of the price mechanism have worked to produce very desirable consequences. Behind this responsiveness lies the consciousness of Japanese workers that well-paid job opportunities are scarce. This concept will be developed in more detail in the last section of this chapter.

Other Sources of Pay Flexibility

So far we have focused on basic wages or straight-time earnings, but they constitute only about 70 or 80 percent of the total annual earnings of Japanese workers. Two other earnings sources, overtime payments and summer and

Table 9.11
Input Data, Wage Equation (6), 1961-78

Year	Average Wages of Major Firms after Spring Offensive (W)	Wholesale Price Index		National Productivity Rate (Q/L) (¥ in thousands)
		Manufactured Products (P_i)	Materials (P_m)	
1961	24,492	61.6	55.2	659.0
1962	26,112	60.4	53.3	693.9
1963	26,955	61.1	54.4	770.2
1964	29,927	61.0	54.7	842.1
1965	32,785	61.0	54.5	883.2
1966	35,498	62.1	56.0	967.4
1967	39,408	62.9	56.9	1,071.6
1968	44,096	63.0	56.5	1,201.7
1969	50,204	64.2	57.7	1,338.1
1970	58,669	67.0	60.2	1,459.4
1971	67,186	66.2	58.5	1,538.1
1972	76,381	66.8	58.5	1,685.9
1973	90,605	76.9	70.7	1,773.9
1974	117,190	98.5	97.4	1,772.6
1975	132,062	100.0	100.0	1,823.6
1976	142,945	104.4	106.5	1,915.8[a]
1977	155,645	106.2	107.2	1,995.2[a]
1978	165,833	104.5	100.8	2,057.6[a]

Source: Kōshiro 1980a, pp. 2-13.
Note: P_i, P_m, 1975 = 100, the Bank of Japan.
(Q/L) at the 1970 price; quoted from Nihon Seisansei Hombu 1979, p. 31.
[a] Figures revised by Keizai Kikakuchō (Economic Planning Agency).

Table 9.12.
Observed Parameters of Wage Equation (6), 1961-78

Parameter of Independent Variable				R^2	SEE	D.W.
α	β	γ	δ			
−11.234965	4.206923	−2.282412	0.961898	0.9976	0.033	1.94
(−18.05)**	(5.31)*	(−3.67)*	(22.98)**			

Source: Kōshiro 1980a, p. 11.
The correlation matrix of variables is as follows:

	W	P_i	P_m	(Q/L)
W	1.000	0.998	0.803	0.930
P_i	0.998	1.000	0.782	0.915
P_m	0.803	0.782	1.000	0.963
(Q/L)	0.930	0.915	0.963	1.000

Note: t-values in parentheses.
* Significant at 5% level.
** Significant at 1% level.

year-end bonuses, are even more responsive than basic wages to changes in business conditions. The flexibility of all three contributes in large part to the ability to adjust wages to economic trends, although it should be added that wages are fairly inflexible on the downward side.

According to a 1978 wage survey by the Ministry of Labor, the average worker received ¥2,572,600 in 1978, of which 71.8 percent was basic earnings (straight-time monthly earnings including family and other stipulated allowances, but excluding overtime), 6.6 percent was overtime payments (including Sunday premiums, night-shift premiums, etc.), and 21.6 percent was summer and year-end bonuses. The bonus percentage is higher in large firms than in medium-sized and small firms (table 9.13).

Overtime Payments.—Article 37 of the Labor Standards Law requires employers to pay "at least a 25 percent" premium for overtime work, rest-day work, or midnight work, provided that the majority of workers or the union in a workplace agree (Article 36). In fact, trade unions have been negotiating to increase the premium rate, but only a few have succeeded in

Table 9.13
Component of Annual Earnings of an Average Worker
in All Industries Surveyed in 1978
(¥ in thousands)

Firms by Size	Basic Earnings	Overtime Pay, Etc.	Bonuses	Annual Earnings
All firms	1,848.8	169.2	556.6	2,572.6
	(71.8)	(6.6)	(21.6)	(100.0)
1,000 and over	2,119.2	243.6	819.6	3,182.4 (100.0)
	(66.6)	(7.6)	(25.8)	(100.0)
100–999	1,804.8	160.8	546.9	2,512.5 (78.9)
	(71.8)	(6.4)	(21.8)	(100.0)
10–99	1,662.0	114.0	349.2	2,125 (66.8)
	(78.2)	(5.4)	(16.4)	(100.0)

Source: Rōdōshō 1980a, pp. 108–9, quoting CKKT for 1978.
Note: Percentages are in parentheses.

doing so. In 1975, 8.8 percent of all employers paid more than a 25 percent premium, and the majority of those (90 percent in 1975) paid a 50 percent premium only for midnight overtime. Only 9.4 percent of the latter were paying more than a 50 percent premium (Rōdōshō, Tokei Jōhōbu 1976, pp. 31–33).

In spite of such progress and the strict regulations in the law regarding overtime work by female workers and minors, male adult workers tend to accept somewhat excessive overtime because, once an employer succeeds in getting the consent of the majority of his employees (if they are organized, the majority of the union members), then he can ask as many of them to work overtime as he wishes (Article 36 of the Labor Standards Law). Therefore, a number of unions have endeavored to set some maximum on the number of overtime hours available to each worker each month. For example, 191 unions surveyed by Dōmei in July 1973 had set 32.9 hours as the average monthly maximum of overtime per worker (Dōmei 1974, p. 29).

Bonus Payments.—Almost all the unions also negotiate for bonus payments. About a fourth of the enterprises surveyed by the Ministry of Labor negotiate the annual amount of the bonus payment once a year; some negotiate in the summer and a few in the winter (Nihon Seisansei Hombu 1980, p. 78).

In negotiating bonuses, both the employer and the union can be flexible and may use the financial achievement of the company during the preceding year as well as a forecast of future prospects as the basis for their negotiations. Here again, however, unions are becoming increasingly adamant about demanding more than they received the previous year. Table 9.14 shows the changes in bonus payments in recent years, in equivalents of straight-time monthly earnings. According to a 1973 survey by the Central Labor Relations Commission, Chūō Rōdō Iinkai, the bonus payment in that year was 5.9 months' pay in large companies that employ more than 1,000 workers,

Table 9.14
Bonus Payment Amounts in Terms of the Monthly Basic
Earnings' Equivalent, in All Surveyed Industries, 1973–78

| Year | 30 + Employees[a] | | | 100 + Employees[b] | 1,000 + Employees[c] |
	Summer	Winter	Total	Total	Total
1973	1.50	2.06	3.56	5.28	5.9
1974	1.60	1.99	3.59	5.28	5.8
1975	1.54	1.84	3.38	4.95	5.2
1976	1.58	1.92	3.50	4.99	5.0
1977	1.56	1.87	3.43	4.90	5.2
1978	1.55	1.88	3.43	4.90	5.1

Sources:

[a]Rōdōshō, Tōkei Jōhōbu 1980a, p. 100; 1977, p. 90.

[b]Jinjiin, *Shokushubetsu Minkan Kyūyo Jittai Chōsa* [Survey of occupational pay in the private sector], quoted in Nihon Seisansei Hombu 1980, p. 78; 1977, p. 70.

[c]Chūō Rodo Iinkai, Jimukyoku, *Chingin Jijō Chōsa* [Survey of wage situations], quoted in Nihon Seisansei Hombu 1979, p. 79, with supplemental information on 1978 data by Rōdōshō, Chūō Rōdō Iinkai Jimukyoku.

but decreased to 5.0 months' pay in 1976, a reaction to the recession that followed the oil crisis. Similar fluctuations can be observed in other surveys of firms of different sizes. It sometimes can happen that a company suffering economic reverses will ask its enterprise union to accept a substandard bonus or, possibly, a zero payment until the company recovers. The case of the once bankrupt Sasebo Heavy Industry Company is a good illustration: as part of its renovation efforts, the company offered the union a package of rationalization programs which included a temporary halt in bonus payments for three years. The union of Sasebo, affiliated with Dōmei's Zōsenjūkirōren (National Federation of Shipbuilding and Heavy Machinery Workers' Unions), at first accepted the proposal, but after the workers' standard of living deteriorated markedly, the union demanded that the rationalization programs be modified. After a 208-day strike in 1979–80, the union was victorious, winning a lump-sum payment of bonuses that averaged ¥150,000.[15]

It should also be noted that the wage differentials between large and small companies are even greater if we take account of bonus payments. In 1978 the basic earnings differential between large enterprises with 1,000 or more employees and small ones employing 10–99 persons was 100:78, whereas the bonus payment differential was 100:43, bringing the annual earnings differential that year down to 100:61 (table 9.13).

Hours of Work, Employment Security, and Participation

Thus far we have indicated that (1) the enterprise-wide collective bargaining system has not necessarily prevented unions from standardizing wages to a considerable extent, not only among major firms but also among the small firms where the supposedly disadvantaged workers have been able to improve their wage levels faster than have employees of the larger firms, and that (2) pay-determination under this procedure has proved to be highly responsive to changes in business conditions, which has made the collective bargaining systems in Japan nearly compatible with the post-Keynesian system of the welfare state. Under Japan's industrial relations system, workers are, in principle, guaranteed the basic right to engage in collective actions, and yet they dare not take full advantage of these rights if, in doing so, economic efficiency will be crippled. Unfortunately, space limitations preclude our developing a detailed analysis of this point with regard to other aspects of working conditions. However, we must add a brief sketch of three other subjects—hours of work, employment security, and participation.

Hours of Work

In the area of reducing the number of hours of work per week, collective bargaining and enforcement of the law have proceeded side by side since World War II. Before the Labor Standards Law of 1947 established an 8-hour day and a 48-hour week, many unions succeeded in reducing the workday from nine or more hours to eight hours. In spite of these reforms, the total number of actual hours worked tended to increase from 180 hours a month in 1950 to 207 hours in 1960 as the economy recovered during that decade and employers asked workers to extend their overtime so as to increase production.

In the latter half of the 1950s, labor unions began to respond to such employer offensives by organizing united actions for a shorter workweek. Sōhyō's first organized movement for a 40-hour week began in August 1956, and Zensendōmei, the textile workers' union, succeeded in establishing a workday of 7 hours and 45 minutes, with a provision for no night work after 10 P.M. in their labor contract.

The average number of monthly hours of work including overtime in manufacturing decreased from a peak of 192 in 1965 to 187 hours in 1970 and to 168 hours in 1975, when many employers responded to the need to reduce production by cutting down on or eliminating overtime. During the years of recovery following the oil crisis, we have again observed an increase in the number of hours worked; the average was 178 in 1979 in manufacturing industries (Rōdōshō, Tōkei Jōhōbu 1980a, p. 169).

In the early 1960s management initiated further moves toward a shorter workweek in several leading companies in the electrical machinery and camera industries. Also, the Dōmei textile workers' campaign for a five-day, 40-hour week in 1967 resulted in gradual improvements in that industry. In the spring of 1970 the five major companies in the iron and steel industry introduced a modified form of a five-day workweek by employing a system of four crews on three shifts, and a few years later most of the major shipbuilding companies began scheduling a five-day workweek every two weeks.

According to a recent Ministry of Labor survey (Rōdōshō, Tōkei Jōhōbu 1980a, pp. 178–79), 42 percent of all manufacturing companies employing more than 30 workers have reduced their standard workday to between seven and eight hours. By 1978 almost nine out of ten large companies had already introduced a five-day week in some form, but only a third of them, and less than 5 percent of all companies surveyed by the Ministry of Labor, had completely acceded to a standard five-day week.

Total annual hours of work in manufacturing industries employing more than 30 workers still stood at 2,108 hours in 1978, according to the Ministry of Labor; this number is 202 more hours annually than British workers worked in 1973 and 303 more hours than were recorded by West German workers in 1972 (Rōdōshō, Tōkei Jōhōbu 1979, p. 167).

An econometric cross-sectional analysis of the income–leisure preferences of Japanese manufacturing workers in 1970 (Koga 1974, pp. 2, 7) revealed that they tended to reduce the number of hours of work by 0.2 percent in response to a 1 percent increase in real wages, or about two-thirds of the leisure preference of American workers that Finegan (1962, pp. 459–60) found in his survey using 1950 data. In other words, Japanese workers are not necessarily "workaholics," as Westerners often claim; rather, they are exhibiting behavior patterns similar to those of Americans but under more difficult living conditions characterized by higher costs for housing, sport facilities, and most agricultural products. These higher costs are directly attributable to the fact that the amount of inhabitable land per person in Japan is very limited. Japan supports 1,867 persons per square kilometer of culti-vable land, whereas in Western Europe the number is 310, in North America 110, and in Australia only 28 (Kōshiro 1978a, p. 9).

In other words, the present greater number of hours of work per day or per year of Japanese workers does not necessarily reflect the weakness of their enterprise unions, but instead results from difficult environmental factors that affect their living conditions. Japanese unions will have ample opportunities to reduce the number of their members' hours of work in the future if the nation is able to overcome the energy shortage and continue its economic growth at a stable rate.

Employment Security

Japanese workers have long been conscious that job opportunities are scarce, but the reality of the situation was magnified when nearly five million people returned from abroad during the demobilization and decolonization in the five years following the end of World War II (Umemura 1964, p. 64). Even after the Korean War, when the economy had recovered, the persist-ence of dual labor markets had the effect of keeping workers aware of this scarcity. A mass dismissal of redundant workers in the late 1940s and early 1950s (at Toshiba in 1949, Hitachi in 1950, Nissan Automobile in 1953, and Nihon Seiko in 1954) further impressed upon them the unpleasant fact that there were few opportunities for well-paying jobs, especially if they were dismissed following bitter experiences in prolonged labor disputes. Even in the late 1950s there were several well-known labor disputes of this sort—at Oju Pulp and Paper in 1959 and the great Miike Coal Mine strikes of 1959–60.

During those days the trade unions concentrated their energies on dispute actions against employer policies—usually in vain in terms of any direct, positive outcome. But these disputes seemed to have rather profound indirect impacts upon employers' policies as well as on court decisions. Articles 627 and 628 of the Civil Code grant employers the freedom to dismiss employees. Also, Articles 19 and 20 of the Labor Standards Law require employers to give a 30-day notice prior to dismissal or 30 days' pay in cases of dismissal without notice, and to refrain from dismissing workers who are ill, those who have been injured on the job, and female employees at the time of child-birth and for 30 days thereafter. Except for these limitations, the statutes preserve in principle the freedom of employers to dismiss employees.

However, the courts have developed a series of highly sophisticated restrictions on this employer right, based on the doctrine of "abuse of the right to dismiss." Employers must inform the worker(s) of the reason in a case of dismissal without notice, and the reason or reasons must be able to withstand a court challenge.[16]

With the increase in technological change beginning in the late 1950s, many unions worked out elaborate employment security schemes to regulate not only mass dismissals but also transfers within and outside particular companies. For example, while Nippon Telegraph and Telephone (a public corporation) was automating the telephone system between 1953 and 1970, it transferred 88,000 workers, including telephone operators. In November 1957, in the midst of this technological change process, Zendentsū (Telecommunications Workers' Union of Japan) concluded an agreement with Nippon Telegraph and Telephone that required consultation prior to the introduction of any further rationalization involving worker transfer. This agreement stipulated that (1) working conditions must be improved, (2) no one should be laid off, (3) the union would be consulted in advance of any investment programs that affected working conditions and future manning, (4) any changes in work standards should be explained to the top union leadership, and (5) the corporation should endeavor to eliminate differentials among welfare facilities at Nippon Telegraph and Telephone establishments (Kōshiro 1977a, pp. 204–5).

The Japan National Railways worked out similar arrangements with its unions, although they experienced a series of difficulties in dealing with Dōryokusha National Railway Locomotive Engineers' Union between 1967 and 1969 on the issue of eliminating firemen as crew members (Dōryokusha Undōshi Hensan Iinkai 1973, 2:247–352).

Rationalization in the maritime industry, with the introduction of large tankers and automated vessels, had a drastic effect on Kaiin (the seamen's union), and it was able to reach an accord on manning only after a 36-day strike in 1961. On the docks, too, the introduction of container ships and lighters aboard ships between 1969 and 1971 caused repeated disputes, and the dockers' unions were able to save some jobs by negotiating featherbedding agreements (Kōshiro 1977a, p.206).

Large-scale employment reductions occurred in the manufacturing industries following the oil crisis. In the four years between December 1973 and February 1978, more than one million workers lost their jobs (table 9.15). Other workers were temporarily suspended, receiving 60 or 80 percent of their regular pay, as the effects of the recession spread over the textile, metal working, machinery, electrical machinery, shipbuilding, iron and steel, chemicals, and various other industries between 1974 and 1975. Hitachi, Toshiba, and other electrical machinery companies together suspended more than 100,000 workers; Mitsubishi Heavy Industry alone had 10,000 workers on temporary suspension. At the bottom of the recession in April–June 1975, 71 percent of the manufacturing establishments had in operation some form of employment reductions, of which 23 percent were "transfers or dispatches to related companies" and 20 percent were "temporary suspensions with pay" (Rōdōshō, Tōkei Jōhōbu 1976, pp. 7–9). Among the other employment adjustment measures used were reduction in overtime, a reduction or cessation of recruitment of "half-way" or "mid-career" workers,[17] a halt in the recruiting of temporary, seasonal, and part-time workers, and the encourage-

Table 9.15
Trends in Regular Employment in Major Industries
Following the Oil Crisis, 1973–78

| Industry | Number of Regular Employees (in thousands) | | Increase or Decrease | |
	Dec. 1973	Feb. 1978	No. (in thousands)	%
All industries	19,246	17,551	−1,695	− 8.8
Manufacturing	8,129	7,093	−1,036	−12.7
Textiles	653	439	− 214	−32.8
Chemicals	548	474	− 74	−13.5
Iron and steel	462	412	− 50	−10.8
Electrical machinery	1,202	1,037	− 165	−13.7
Transport equipment[a]	943	878	− 65	− 6.9
Wholesale and retail trades	2,529	2,413	− 116	− 4.6
Service industries	2,992	3,307	+ 315	+10.5

Source: Compiled from MKTC, both months.

Note: Statistics are for firms with 30 or more employees, and continuously for more than one month.

[a]Both the depressed shipbuilding industry and the booming automobile industry are included in this category.

ment of voluntary retirements by offering retirement allowance premiums (Rōdōshō, Tōkei Jōhōbu 1976, p. 9). In other words, all sorts of attrition policies were utilized to reduce the size of the workforces.

During these years, the employers complained that the "overemployment" was due to the practice of "lifetime commitment." However, a careful study of the problem revealed that the magnitude of the manpower reductions in the manufacturing industries in Japan was about the same as that in the United States if measured in terms of total manhour inputs, but if the measure was the number of employees involved, Japan's reduction was only a third of that in the United States (Shinozuka 1978, p. 25).

Thus, it is apparent that labor–management relations based upon enterprise unionism have been able to protect the jobs of regular workers to the greatest extent possible and that various methods have been worked out to enable the parties to respond to slack labor market conditions. One that has been used most effectively to reduce redundancy is large-scale interplant and intraplant transfers. Many steel and shipbuilding workers, for example, were moved temporarily to automobile companies; during these periods the transferred workers retained their employment status at their original companies, but they were paid by the automobile companies to which they were dispatched. If a particular worker's earnings were less at the company to which he was sent, then his original employer made up the difference with a subsidy. However, if all other means of reducing the labor surplus proved to be insufficient, the only alternative—and a last resort—was a modified form of layoff. For example, an employer might induce "voluntary separations" with severance-pay premiums.

All of these means of adjusting employment are of primary importance to both parties to collective bargaining, and thus the enterprise unions concentrated most of their energies on protecting the interests of affected members.

At the present time most enterprise unions are also deeply concerned with the problems of an aging population in the coming decades. It is estimated that about 45 percent of the total labor force will be aged 45 and over by 1995, and that the proportion of the population aged 65 and over to the population under age 15, now at 37 percent, will increase to 71 percent by the year 2000 (Kōreika Mondai Kondankai 1980, p. 19; Kōseishō 1978, p. 452). With the life-spans of the people becoming longer, one problem is how to support them from the age of 55 to 60, the present retirement age, until age 77 or 78. Therefore, most unions have been working on ways to cope with this and other problems related to aging. Raising the mandatory retirement age from the traditional 55 or 60 is the major target of many unions. The success of the Tekkōrōren (iron and steel workers' unions) in negotiating the gradual increase in the mandatory retirement age to 60 between 1981 and 1989 in its October 1979 agreement has provided an impetus for other companies and unions to move in the same direction. In order to win this concession, Tekkōrōren had to agree to a reduction in the wage rates of workers after they reached the age of 50 and to a similar downgrading of supervisory workers after the age of 55.[18]

Participation and Joint Consultation

In dealing with the problems of technological change and rationalization, Japanese enterprise unions have cautiously developed a mixture of collective bargaining and joint consultation at the enterprise or plant level. Usually they are willing and ready to back their bargaining demands with strikes and other kinds of industrial actions, if necessary, but they do not strike over issues that are in joint consultation. Therefore, many employers prefer to resolve as many issues as possible by the joint consultation process.

According to a survey by the Japan Productivity Center (Nihon Seisansei Hombu 1973, p. 43), 80 percent of the 1,600 major companies whose stocks were listed on the Stock Exchange in 1972 had established a permanent system of joint consultation at the enterprise level. It is noteworthy that 9.1 percent of these companies were not unionized; those that were unionized had both collective bargaining and joint consultation systems. Identified in this survey were three types of relationships between joint consultation and collective bargaining: (1) in 48 percent of the labor–management relationships, the two systems were clearly distinguished; (2) in 47 percent the same subjects were dealt with under both systems, but certain additional topics were discussed in joint consultation; (3) in the remaining 5 percent, joint consultation was a preliminary step before collective bargaining (Nihon Seisansei Hombu 1973, p. 13). A Ministry of Labor survey of 1,168 unions in the summer of 1972 revealed that 52 percent of them transferred issues unresolved in joint consultation to collective bargaining. Larger companies tended to prefer this mixing of the two procedures. Very few of the unions and companies chose to settle their differences by resorting to outside arbitration (Rōdōshō, Rōseikyoku 1974, pp. 147–48).

There seems to be a general tendency in Japanese industrial relations, especially as labor–management relationships mature, for the parties to seek solutions to most of their problems, particularly those involving the day-to-day operation of a plant, through joint consultation rather than collective bargaining. This tendency has also been observed at the industry level. The textile industry was the first to introduce a joint consultation scheme at the industry level—in September 1956, when Zensendōmei (textile workers' unions) and four employers' federations in the industry established a consultation plan to deal with trade conflicts with the United States. By the early 1970s joint consultation arrangements had been set up in 11 industries: textile, shipbuilding, automobile, electric power, maritime, metal mining, coal mining, iron and steel, electrical machinery, cement, and electric and wire cable. Most of them were established during the 1960s to handle the reorganization of industrial structures after the liberalization of international trade and capital investment (Dōmei 1975, pp. 18–20). It is noteworthy that most of the unions who are parties to consultation schemes are affiliated with Dōmei, and a few with Chūritsurōren. The only Sōhyō union among them is Tekkōrōren (iron and steel workers) which has, in fact, shared Dōmei's philosophy of economic-based unionism since 1960, when Miyata Yoshiju took over the leadership.

The parties have been finding joint consultation increasingly useful in dealing with the problems caused by industrial reorganization, technological change, and international trade conflicts, although at times they discuss ways of preventing industrial pollution, a serious problem in Japan as elsewhere. Most joint consultation committees meet every three or four months.

The unions of the automobile, iron and steel, and electrical machinery industries have been the ones most actively concerned with the trade conflicts with the United States that followed the oil crisis. The electric power unions, on their part, have been deeply apprehensive about the future of Japan's energy supplies, including the problem of increasing atomic-energy power-generating plants. The shipbuilding and maritime unions have long been affected by the recessions in their industries and by the resulting large-scale rationalization problems. Without continuing communication between labor and management in those key industries, there would have been far more labor disputes.

Direct labor participation in the management of the enterprise has been discussed from time to time over the past decade, but so far there have been only a few experiments with the idea. A newspaper, Sankei, appointed the president of the enterprise union to the company's board of directors in June 1974, and the Hitachi shipbuilding company revised its collective bargaining agreement in October 1975 so as to permit union representatives to take part in the deliberations of the managerial board (Kōshiro 1977a, p. 219). Mitsubishi electric machinery company has also been active in encouraging more participation by union representatives in the company management. The Japan National Railways proposed in 1979 that two union representatives join the supervisory (auditing) board, and the Nippon Telegraph and Telephone Public Corporation also has been actively considering the introduction of a new form of labor participation in management. But these are pioneering experiments and it is unlikely that arrangements of this type will become prevalent elsewhere in the near future.

The Basic Determinants of Japan's Industrial Relations

The last question that is addressed in this chapter is how and why Japanese collective bargaining manages to be so highly responsive to changes in the economy. In other words, we need to explore why Japanese workers have such strong live-and-let-live attitudes toward the enterprise that employs them. Observers from both outside and within Japan have offered interpretations of this phenomenon.

The Company-Dominated Union Hypothesis

This explanation finds the root cause of the responsiveness and flexibility toward company policies in the weakness of unions formed on an enterprise-by-enterprise basis. This rationale is widely supported not only by classical Marxists, but also by Japan's New Left critics and such foreign commentators as Walter Galenson (1976, pp.642–55, 667–71). They argue that unions at the plant or enterprise level do not make much of an effort to determine or to enforce effectively any regulations of work pace and content and that, because they are so weak and dispersed, they are ineffective in rallying political and social power in support of improvements in social security measures and environmental conditions. Thus, these critics say, it is difficult to distinguish a union organized on an enterprise basis from a company-dominated union, and such a union may at times become so organizationally weak that it is easily exploited by a company.

However, it would be a mistake to conclude that a Japanese enterprise union is the same as the so-called "company union" in the United States, as we have explained in earlier sections (see pp. 208–12). Nor should we attribute Japanese workers' propensity for diligence and their high regard for harmony and group interests to their position as an oppressed and exploited underclass, subject to the kinds of heinous injustice described in *Das Kapital*.

The Cultural Uniqueness Hypothesis

Japanese society's egalitarian traditions, its singular recourse to human relations in the handling of disputes, and the value perceptions that stem from the vertical structure of its society have had a profound influence on labor–management relationships within industry. Accordingly, a great number of interpretations stress the tendencies of the Japanese people toward group activity and the patterns of action that give priority to group interests. These run from the lucid, but extreme, interpretations of Nakane (1967) and the works of Kawashima (1964, 1967) to the highly praised conclusions in the recent book by Vogel (1979). Furthermore, most of the classical studies by scholars in the labor field, such as Ōkōchi (1952, pp. 1–18), originally emphasized the cultural and traditional influence as well as certain economic factors.

However, there are many obscurities when one comes to identify elements of cultural uniqueness, and it would not be accurate to overemphasize qualities peculiar to Japan while making little of the technological and market forces that tend to bring about a convergence of national systems of industrial relations.

The Capital-Intensive Hypothesis

This hypothesis was offered by Dore (1973, p. 414) in his discussion of what he called the "late development effect." He argued that because the importation of technology requires huge capital expenditures, there are strong pressures to make the fullest use of that technology and to improve the rate at which it operates. The cooperative attitudes of enterprise unions toward company efforts to increase productivity and toward the flexible deployment of labor within firms as well as the low absentee and high commitment rates of Japanese workers also can be explained fairly well by this hypothesis. Kobayashi (1966, pp. 188–89) reaches a similar conclusion in his book assessing the humanization of work procedures that he introduced at Sony.

Thus the hypothesis provides a plausible explanation of the characteristics of labor–management relationships in Japan, where various measures are devised to promote the will to work hard at the work site. It depends rather too much on clarifying the motives of management, however, and neglects the question of why workers often respond "voluntarily" to these measures and, moreover, feel satisfied when they do so.

The Competitiveness of the Market Hypothesis

The fierce competition for market shares among postwar Japan's oligopolistic giant industries heightened the desire of each worker to defend his company-as-a-family organization. This factor contributed to the preservation and cultivation of the will to work and worker discipline as well as the flexible attitudes of enterprise unions. Many economists, explicitly or implicitly, prefer to rely upon this hypothesis. However, in any advanced, free, national economy, oligopolistic competition exists to a greater or lesser degree. Thus it would be impossible to explain why only Japan has been able to retain these characteristics in its industrial relations system, unless we make a detailed comparison of the scale and intensity of competition.

The Developed Internal Labor Market Hypothesis

As many academicians in labor studies have pointed out, Japan has developed highly internalized labor markets. Koike (1977, pp. 213–40) stresses this point in his comparative study of American and Japanese manufacturing industry. There is no doubt that this point is important in an economic explanation of the modern origin of such major characteristics of Japanese industrial relations as the "lifetime commitment" system of employment, the "seniority wage," and the enterprise-oriented value system. The strength of this hypothesis lies in the fact that it is quite consistent with human capital theory.

However, here again the development of internalized labor markets is more or less common to any advanced society; therefore we have to explain how and to what degree Japan's internal labor markets contribute to generating the unique features of its industrial relations system. Is there any critical point or pressure that evokes harmonious and flexible attitudes on the part of labor unions during the course of the development of internal labor markets?

The Hypothesis of the Scarcity of Well-Paid Job Opportunities

The present author would like to suggest and argue the logic of yet another hypothesis—the scarcity of good job opportunities.[19]

Japan's huge population is crowded into a very limited land area, and the nation lacks many natural resources. Yet the aim of the Japanese people always has been to maintain and improve their standard of living, and they often have had to struggle to do so. The total land area of Japan is 370,000 square kilometers, with a population density in 1975 of 298 people per square kilometer—not very different from Britain's 229 or West Germany's 249. However, because most of the land in Japan is mountainous and forested, only about one-fourth of it is habitable. When the measure is population density of the habitable land, Japan is 26 times more dense than the United States, 6.6 times more than France, 3.4 times more than Britain, and 2.4 times more than West Germany. The population density per square kilometer of tillable land is much higher again, as I pointed out earlier in this chapter.

Such adverse ratios of population to land lowered the marginal productivity of agricultural labor and applied downward pressure on the living standards of the farm population in the early stages of industrialization. Moreover, as these people began to migrate from the depressed rural areas to take jobs as laborers in the new industries, factory wages were driven down to a level that was a bare minimum for survival.

These factors operate today to push up to relatively extreme levels the prices of farm products, residential and other land, and both leisure and sport activities in comparison with the value of manufactured goods. (Of course, in each case one cannot overlook the defects and insufficiencies of policies providing inordinate protection of agriculture and private land rights.) The result is major distortions in the workers' income–leisure patterns, inevitably strengthening their preference for income.

What is more, Japan must raise the productivity of labor in her export-oriented industries to provide the foreign exchange to support a population of more than 115 million people.

For these reasons, since the Meiji Era, over a century ago, Japan has invested the best of her capital and labor in undertakings that would strengthen the competitive position of her export industries. The competitive education system that Vogel praises for its egalitarianism, the information-gathering power of her major industries, and the policy-making power of government all grew out of these demographic and geographic factors. The industrial structure of Japan has become a production system centered upon and giving priority to key export industries. This structure has been reinforced through an "indirect finance policy" involving capital and through fairly large wage differentials, according to industry size, for the workers. At the same time scarce resources have been distributed in a way that gives priority to those government and financial divisions that support the export sector of the economy. The development of highly internalized labor markets in Japan is the product of this priority-resource–allocation system. And for the worker, this sector naturally is the place where he can find optimum working conditions and the most secure employment opportunities. The competition among workers for this limited number of "good employment opportunities" has become particularly fierce and today has expanded into competition within the education system where the rivalry to get into good schools now even affects two- and three-year-olds.

What this means in numerical terms is that about ten million workers in a labor force of 55 million in Japan have what might be called opportunities for "good jobs" broadly defined as having (1) high pay, (2) employment security, (3) fringe benefits, and (4) occupational prestige (see table 9.16). This general idea is, of course, a relative one based upon the income level and prestige of the company. But because Japan is a nation in which there are few fixed social classes and in which there is a competitive social structure with a high degree of mobility, the competition for the relatively few good employment opportunities is open to one and all and, therefore, is quite furious.

Thus we can find the basis for the extraordinary diligence of the Japanese worker and his strong sense of identification as a member of his company's "family" in this prevailing consciousness of the scarcity of good employment opportunities. Among the various interpretations of the psychology of the Japanese worker, Cole (1971a) has made observations that, somewhat updated, are extremely appropriate:

Japan's economy is still basically a production-oriented economy of scarcity, and the corresponding psychology is deeply imprinted on the minds of the Japanese. This psychology is reflected in worker–employer relations and serves as a major support for traditional values and structures. Management uses these values to justify holding down wages. Although the signs of an emerging mass-consumption society are becoming more evident, these values and practices which emphasize scarcity persist.

Table 9.16
The Scale of Japan's Opportunities for "Good Jobs"[a]
(in millions)

Employment Opportunities	A	B
1. Employees of major industries as listed with the bank of Japan	3.0	2.2
2. Employees of companies registered in first and second sections of Tokyo Stock Exchange	4.41	
3. National and local civil servants	4.23	0.85
4. Employees of the three major public corporations	0.79	0.79
Total { 1 + 3 + 4	8.02	4.64
{ 2 + 3 + 4	9.43	

Sources:
1. From Bank of Japan's *Major Industries' Short Term Economic Survey,* August 1978, p. 21.
2. Tōyō Keizai Shinpōsha, *Statistical Monthly Reports,* facts for 1,602 companies in November 1978.
3. Jinjiin, *Annual Report,* 1976.
4. Prime Minister's Office, *Japan Statistical Yearbook,* 1975.
[a]See p. 253 for definition of "good jobs."

Japan's dearth of natural resources has forced the people to raise themselves from poverty by their own collective will and little else. (pp. 3–4)[20]

Of course some problems with this hypothesis remain to be explained. Among them, the following three questions seem to be paramount: (1) Why, in spite of the deeply rooted consciousness of scarcity, do the Japanese people have a strong sense of being middle class? (2) Why do those who are excluded from the well-paying job opportunities share the work ethic of diligence? (3) Why is this hypothesis not necessarily applicable to most of the less well-developed countries where there is a similar scarcity of well-paying job opportunities?

It will suffice here to answer these questions only briefly. To respond to the first question: A major explanatory element may be the democratization of the nation after the war, particularly the disappearance of class differences between factory and office workers and the dramatic reduction in wage differentials between them, as illustrated earlier by *Densangata chingin* (the wage system of the electric power workers' union). Indeed, when we look at the Gini coefficient of income distribution, we find that in 1970 the figure was 0.317 in Japan, indicating that the income of the two groups was more equal than it was in the United States (0.368) or in Sweden (0.356) at that time, and also even more equal than in Britain (0.332) or West Germany (0.331) (Keizai Kikakuchō 1975, p. 118). In addition, as we explained earlier, factory and office workers are all together as members of the same enterprise union, and the wage differential between professional and technical workers, on the one hand, and blue-collar workers, on the other, is considerably smaller than it is in either Europe or North America. There are almost no differences in their living styles. Such feelings of equality tend to overcome any sense of inequality stemming from differences between employment in large industries and the small and medium-sized companies and promote a middle-class consciousness among all the people because, in Japan, the possibility is great that, through the competitive educational system, the child of a manual laborer can move up into the upper classes.

More empirical research will be required to answer the second question. At this time we do not have empirical evidence that those workers who do not have well-paying jobs are equally diligent and loyal to their employers as are the well-paid employees, but it is generally felt that labor-management relations in small and medium-sized companies are neither as harmonious nor as modern as they are in the large companies. If these less fortunate workers are equally diligent, then it must be for two reasons—one being the spillover effect from the large companies (there are many good small companies or subsidiaries of large firms where worker morale is high), and another being the influence of less fortunate fathers who leave their unfulfilled hopes to their children. These fathers tend to work hard to realize their dreams of giving their children a better education than they themselves had.

The last question is the most difficult because it requires more intensive as well as extensive study of comparative economic development. Here the historical heritage of each country, cultural and religious elements, and the preconditions for industrialization are mixed together so that there is no simple answer. The development of agriculture and small handicraft industries prior to industrialization was the prerequisite for the emergence of the modern work ethic in both the European countries and Japan. Without similar historical developments as well as the availability of capital resources, the mere existence of poverty or scarcity of opportunities would not suffice as a motivating factor for efficiency. It should be noted that our argument was to explain how the responsiveness of Japanese industrial relations to economic factors differs from that in other advanced Western nations that share common historical preconditions but are now facing very different industrial relations situations. The general theory of industrial relations which embraces developing countries should be left for future studies.

Notes

1   Ishikawa 1978, pp. 67–72. When a union-shop agreement is concluded and is in effect, the employer is required to discharge those employees who refuse to join the union. This practice prevails widely in Japan. As noted in chapter 7, the

situation becomes rather complicated when a union splits into two or more rival organizations. Employers usually refuse to discharge any employees who have seceded from the union if the seceded workers have organized their own rival union organization, even though it may be a minority union.

2 Sumiya 1976, pp. 49–87; Hyōdō 1971, pp. 404–79, describes these changes as a process of transition from loose, indirect, manpower control through subcontractors or foremen to direct control by the personnel divisions of large companies.

3 Takemae (1970) describes the events as follows: GHQ of SCAP was eager to prevent "company unions" during the process of legislating the Trade Union Law in December 1945. Also, *The Final Report of the Advisory Committee on Labor in Japan: Labor Policies and Programs in Japan,* July 29, 1946, recommended that managerial personnel should not be allowed to join labor unions and that financial assistance by employers should be prohibited in order to prevent labor unions from deteriorating into company unions (pp. 151, 160). Takemae's assessment is endorsed by the full text of the final report which is translated into Japanese and available in Rōdōshō, Rōseikyoku 1951, pp. 820–21.

4 Sumiya 1966b, pp. 189–92. Nihon Rōdō Kumiai Sōdōmei decided to organize labor unions on the basis of prefectural associations on January 17, 1946 (Rōdōshō, Rōseikyoku 1951, pp 446–47). It modified its organizing policy toward preferring industrial unions in May 1946 (ibid., p. 523). On the other hand, Sanbetsu Kaigi decided at its inaugural convention in August 1946 to organize local enterprise unions into industrial unions and also to encourage the organization of professional, technical, and managerial personnel into the same organizations (ibid., pp. 571–74).

5 Rōdō Sōgi Chōsakai (Research Group on Labor Disputes) 1956–58 reported the major cases of industry-wide bargaining in the 1950s. The report of the Ministry of Labor's Study Group on Industrial Relations Law (Rōshi Kankeihō Kenkyūkai 1967) refers to several cases in the 1960s. The volumes of the Ministry of Labor's *Shiryō Rōdō Undō Shi* (Rōdōshō, Rōseikyoku 1951–79) are the most comprehensive sources of original information, but it requires a lot of work to select appropriate cases from them.

6 This idea was forged as early as the fall of 1950. Sōhyō appointed 100 organizers in 1955 and increased the number to 300 in 1959 (Nomura and Ujihara 1961, pp. 66–67). For later developments, see Numata 1963.

7 The present author was chief conciliator in the dispute between Zenkokuippan and the Postal Service at the Conciliation Service of the Kantō District, Public Corporation and National Enterprise Labor Relations Commission, between 1978 and 1981 (the details of the dispute are not published).

8 Patterns in the iron and steel industry are discussed in Sano et al. 1969, pp. 93–149; Sano 1970, pp. 121–60; Kōshiro 1973, pp. 80–104, and 1978b, p. 260; Nihon Seisansei Hombu 1972.

9 "Conclusion of the collective bargaining agreement" means that the employer recognizes the union as representing the employees. But in Japan, the "collective bargaining agreement" (*rōdō kyōyaku*) very often is a statement of the union's basic rights and does not include details of wage rates and fringe

benefits. These important subjects usually are stipulated in separate documents such as a "wage agreement," a "retirement pay agreement," a "pension agreement," an "hours of work agreement," etc.

10   These would be issues not resolved in joint consultation prior to collective bargaining.

11   Provisions in this category would be managerial policies related to company operation, rationalization of work processes or office procedures, the desired financial achievement of the company, any organizational restructuring, and job analysis.

12   Chūō Rōdō Iinkai, Jimukyoku 1976, pp. 85–86. A "discharge" most often is a disciplinary sanction; a "dismissal" may be because of redundancy or business fluctuations.

13   The basic idea of the *Densangata chingin* (wage system of the electric power workers' union) was (1) to distinguish basic wages for standard hours of work from overtime and other allowances specific to extraordinarily dirty or hazardous work. (2) The essential part of the basic wage was determined strictly on the basis of age and number of dependent family members irrespective of job and performance, so that (3) skill differentials and payment by merit were compressed to a minimum. Within a few years the engineers and skilled workers became very dissatisfied with this excessively egalitarian system, and the discrepancy of interests among the different grades and occupations within the union brought on an organizational split in 1952. Rōdō Sōgi Chōsakai 1957, 2:149–241.

14   See Hines 1964 and Laidler and Purdy 1974. Kōshiro 1980b delves more deeply into the details of the methodological problems involved in measuring the impact of public employees' labor disputes.

15   *Asahi Shimbun,* February 13, 1980, evening and February 14 morning editions; *Nihon Keizai Shimbun,* January 21, 1980, morning edition.

16   For discussions of this issue see Ariizumi 1963, pp. 132–73, esp. pp. 142 ff.; Hanami 1979a, pp. 81–84.

17   The usual practice in large Japanese firms is to hire new employees in April when they graduate from high school. However, in periods of rapid business expansion, the companies prefer to seek and hire new employees from among persons who have been working for smaller companies or who have been self-employed. These employees are called "half-way workers" or "mid-career workers." In Japan, unlike in most Western countries, previous work experience with other companies is not fully valued, and thus these "half-way workers" are handicapped in their working careers by their limited employment duration and amount of on-the-job training. At their time of employment their wage rates are lower than those of "regular" workers who were employed by the company at the time they left school, and the differential may continue until the time of retirement, although the differential may narrow if "half-way workers" display a continuously good performance on the job.

18   *Asahi Shimbun,* evening edition, October 17, 1979.

19   Kōshiro (1978a, 1980c, 1980d) has developed this idea. The following explanations are reproduced for the most part from (1980c), pp. 51–55.

20   Cole develops this idea further in his 1979 book, pp. 224–50.

10 *Kazutoshi Kōshiro*

Labor Relations in Public Enterprises

The public sector in Japan has been an arena for labor–management conflict since World War II.* Before the war, the public-sector labor movement tended to be right-wing, but in the postwar period public employees who were primarily leftist in orientation—particularly postal workers, teachers, and some National Railways employees—took over the leadership, although there were, and still are, discernible cleavages among them. Three factors can be identified as contributing to the change: (1) with the collapse of the imperial regime, the old nationalistic value system was rejected; (2) the reforms right after the war deprived public employees of privileges they formerly enjoyed; and (3) the mass of dissatisfied workers in the lower-grade public service tended to be attracted by Marxist ideology.

Even during and following periods of high economic growth after 1955, public employees have constituted a focus of conflict in Japan's industrial relations, as they continue their struggle for restoration of their right to strike. On the other hand, more pragmatic attitudes ("bread-and-butter unionism") have developed among the private-sector unions, especially since 1965 under the pressures of liberalized foreign trade and direct foreign investment in Japan. These workers have become very much concerned about competitive

*The original draft of this chapter was prepared for presentation at the Asian Regional Office of the International Labor Organization, Bangkok, May 1977. Additions and revisions were made to update the information. The author is grateful to Ivan M. C. S. Elsmark, Chief, ILO Publications Services, to Dr. Johannes Schregle, Chief, Industrial Relations and Labor Administration Department, ILO, and to K. F. Yoshimura, Assistant Director-General, Regional Office for Asia, ILO, for permission to reproduce the paper here.

threats and the increasing scarcity of good job opportunities (see chapter 9). The result is that the cleavage between private- and public-sector unions in the Japanese labor movement has tended to widen year after year.

Nevertheless, public- and private-sector unions both share the characteristics of "enterprise unionism." Some foreign observers have believed that enterprise unions are always economic-minded, that they are weak and are reluctant to challenge employers, and that they do not become involved in political struggles. On the contrary, enterprise unions in the public sector are both politically active and militant, and they play an influential role in Japanese industrial relations. Thus, without an understanding of the characteristics and problems of labor–management relations in the public sector, one cannot understand Japan's total industrial relations system.

In the first section of this chapter is an examination of the diversities of the concept of public enterprises, followed by a summary of their development and scope since the Meiji Era. One of the most important characteristics of public-sector industrial relations is the strict and complex legal constraints under which the system operates. Therefore, the institutional and procedural framework for labor–management relations in the public sector is analyzed in the second section. At the same time, the origins of industrial conflict in Japan's public sector are examined.

The procedures for the settlement of labor disputes and grievances in the public sector are unusual and are described in the third section. Because of the strike prohibition, conciliation and arbitration processes are highly developed; nevertheless, there have been repeated illegal strikes that have caused tremendous conflicts among labor, management, and the government. The causes of industrial unrest also are analyzed in this section.

Finally, in the fourth section is a discussion of the problems that have been and still are the focus of heated disputes not only between the parties but in public exchanges, namely, (1) how to refine the principle of wage and salary comparability with the private sector; (2) whether the limited autonomy of public-enterprise authorities should be enlarged; (3) how to reconcile the labor–labor conflicts between rival unions; and (4), last but not least, how to resolve controversies over judicial opinions concerning the right of public employees to strike. Some approaches that might be used to improve labor–management relations in public enterprises also are suggested.

Evolution, Development, and Scope of Public Enterprises

Concept of Public Enterprises

There is no single definition for the concept of public enterprises in Japan. Article 2 of the Public Corporation and National Enterprise Labor Relations

(PCNELR) Law stipulates that three public corporations (Japan National Railways, Nippon Telegraph and Telephone, and the Tobacco Monopoly) and five national enterprises (the Postal Service, the National Forestry, the Government Printing Office, the Mint, and the Alcohol Monopoly) shall be defined as "Public Enterprises et alii," but there is no specific definition of what a "public enterprise" is. In fact, various other institutions might be included if one were to view public enterprises from the standpoint of economics, business administration, or administrative law instead of labor law.

In 1949 Urabe Kuniyoshi (see Urabe 1949) set forth a now widely accepted definition, characterizing public enterprises by three factors: (1) public ownership, (2) public control, and (3) managerial autonomy. He said that a "public corporation is an enterprise run under public control because of its public ownership. At the same time, it is allowed managerial autonomy for the purpose of integrating both social aspects and economic rationality into its operations" (p. 33). Similarly, some administrative law scholars define the concept as "a judicial establishment that has an orientation as a business enterprise controlled by the government because of its nature as public property,"[1] or as "an enterprise that is run by the national or local government for the purpose of directly enhancing the public interest of the society" (Yamada 1957, p. 49).

In contrast, there are those who emphasize the functional aspects of the concept. Takahashi Tatsuo (1956), for example, says that "there is no particular type of enterprise that has special and common features characterizing it as such. . . . That is a flexible concept which should be specified from time to time in terms of policy orientations set forth by a particular economic policy" (p.15). Similarly, Katō Kan's (1966) definition is that "public enterprises are a means for the government in a mixed economy to achieve particular economic purposes or objectives"(p. 11). Many other economists take a functional approach.

Whatever the definition, it is difficult to encompass all types of public enterprises in a single concept, since their existence depends upon both historical background and the economic necessities of the time. However, it is possible to construct a practical classification of public enterprises, combining the essential aspects of the several definitions stated above. This classification would include five groups of public enterprises in Japan:

1. Those enterprises whose total assets (or capital) are exclusively owned by the national (or local) government and that are run directly by the government—the five enterprises mentioned in the law and such local (prefectural, municipal) public enterprises as water, transportation, electricity (only in some localities), and gas (mostly outside of major metropolitan areas).[2]

2. Those enterprises whose capital is owned by the government (but whose assets are not exclusively government-owned), but which are run by autonomous management. In principle, they are required to be self-supporting. Examples are the three public corporations listed in the law.

3. Those public enterprises whose capital is owned by the government, but which are run by autonomous management with a lesser degree of governmental control than the second group—*kōdan* (Japan Housing Corporation, Japan Road Corporation, New Tokyo International Airport Corporation, etc.). These corporations are established to engage in governmental construction projects that require organization on a smaller scale than do the three public corporations and five national enterprises.

4. Public financial corporations, of which there are three categories, (a) *ginkō*, (b) *kōko*, and (c) *kinko*:[3]

a. *Ginkō* literally means "bank," but here it means the government banks that are established by special laws and are fully capitalized by the government. The top executives are appointed by the prime minister and their budgets and financial reports must be approved by the Diet. Two special banks of this type are the Japan Development Bank and the Export–Import Bank of Japan, which make loans to specified enterprises at politically determined rates. In addition to these two, there is another special government bank, the Bank of Japan; it is, however, the central bank and therefore must be regarded as an essential part of the governmental framework. However, in terms of industrial relations, the personnel of all three banks are covered by the same laws that apply to private corporations.

b. The basic characteristics of the *kōko* are almost the same as those of the special banks, but they are managed under comparatively stricter control of the government and the Diet than are the ginkō. There are eight of them, including the Housing Finance Kōko.

c. Two financial corporations for cooperative financing are classified separately under the name of *kinko*. The Central Bank for Commercial and Industrial Cooperatives is partially capitalized by the government, and it finances cooperative organizations of small and medium-sized trading and manufacturing enterprises. The Central Cooperative Bank for Agriculture and Forestry has had no new government capital since 1959, but its investments are confined by law to cooperatives involving agriculture, forestry, and fisheries.

5. Semi-independent agencies. There are at least three categories in this group, (a) *jigyōdan*, (b) *kikin*, and (c) others (Gyōsei Kanrichō 1978, pp. 313–18):

a. A *jigyōdan* is a small-scale public corporation established to carry out particular administrative services other than construction. There were 20 in

1976, organized for such purposes as the rationalization of coal mining, development of new technology, employment promotion, metal ore exploration, and the construction of atomic-powered ships.

b. A *kikin* is a small-scale, public financial corporation whose major function is to make loans to or guarantee debts of specific segments of industry. There were 8 kikin in 1976, organized for such purposes as making payments to medical doctors under the social insurance plans, furthering international economic cooperation and cultural exchanges, and providing credit for forestry operations.

c. There are various other kinds of institutions with some government funding that have been established by special legislation for a specific purpose: Japan Broadcasting Corporation, Japan External Trade Organization, Japan Airlines, International Telegraph and Telephone Company, Power Resources Development Corporation, and 11 others. Also in this group are the Japan Atomic Energy Institute, the Japan Institute of Labour, the Institute of Developing Economies, and the Institute of Social Security. Such institutions are termed "special juridical persons," and some would not necessarily be appropriately classified as public enterprises because their function is purely scientific or artistic.

In spite of the complexity surrounding the concept of public enterprises, three types are clearly distinguishable as far as labor-management relations are concerned. First, the five national enterprises (such as the Postal Service) and the three public corporations (such as the National Railways) are covered by the Public Corporation and National Enterprise Labor Relations (PCNELR) Law. Second, local public enterprises owned and run by local governments are inclusively covered by the Local Public Enterprises Labor Relations (LPELR) Law. Third, all of the other institutions and agencies noted above are covered by the Trade Union Law, which also governs labor relations in the private sector.

Evolution and Growth of Public Enterprises[4]

From the Meiji Restoration in 1868 until World War II, public enterprises in Japan had three goals: (1) to foster industrialization, (2) to aid military expansion, and (3) to facilitate colonial expansion.

In the beginning, the Meiji government was compelled to industrialize rapidly and over a short period of time to protect the nation's independence. It established such key industries as shipbuilding, cotton spinning, weapons manufacturing, cement and firebrick manufacturing, iron and steel processing, as well as railways, telegraph and telephone, postal services, and public utilities. A few decades later some manufacturing plants were sold to private entrepreneurs, and these became the core of the pre–World War II zaibatsu (industrial and financial complexes). The government, however, retained most of the key industries as state enterprises. The public telegraph system was started in 1869, the postal service was inaugurated in 1871, and the uniform postal system was introduced in 1873. In 1877 the telephone was imported and major cities were connected by the late 1880s. The railways were first built by the government in 1873, but after 1881 many private railroads were also constructed; the major trunk lines were nationalized in 1906. At the same time the government faced the need for increased revenue and it set up the tobacco and camphor monopolies in 1904 and the salt monopoly in 1905. It had already established the Yahata Iron Works in 1901.

The government organized state banks in 1872 to facilitate the financing of industry, and in the next few years other banks were established—the Bank of Japan in 1882, the Yokohama Specie Bank in 1880, and the Japan Hypothec Bank in 1897.

Overseas expansion was accomplished with the cooperation and assistance of some special, partly nationalized companies such as the South Manchuria Railroad Company (1906) and the International Electric Communication Company (1925), and several colonial banks were founded. During the late 1920s and through the 1930s, a number of special, "mixed" companies, including steel, were organized in preparation for a state-controlled economy.

Another feature of public enterprises before World War II that should be noted is the development of public utilities by prefectural and local governments. In Yokohama a public gas works was first established in 1875, followed by a public waterworks in 1888. Municipal electric power was supplied in Kyoto in 1893. The year 1911 saw the introduction of a public gas works, a public waterworks, and municipal electric power in Tokyo. A municipal tramway appeared in Osaka in 1904; Tokyo had its first municipally owned bus service in 1924.

The role of public enterprises underwent a great change after World War II. Economic restoration and the strengthening of social "overhead capital" became the new underlying philosophy. The dominance of state enterprises in pioneering industrialization disappeared and was replaced by the growing role of public enterprises as an essential part of the infrastructure of the total economy. Thus, new types of enterprises were set up to meet the needs of the changing philosophy. The Housing Loan Corporation (1950), the Japan Housing Corporation (1955), the Aichi Water Resource Corporation (1955), the Japan Road Corporation (1956), the Metropolitan Highway Corporation (1959), and several local development companies are examples. Also, to aid the basic as well as the export-oriented industries, the Japan Export Bank (later reorganized as the Export–Import Bank of Japan) was established in 1950 and the Japan Development Bank in 1951.

Table 10.1

National Public Enterprises, January 1976

	N	Institutions
National enterprises	5	Postal Service, National Forestry, etc.
Public corporations	3	National Railways, Nippon Telegraph and Telephone, Tobacco Monopoly
Kōdan	16	Water Resources Development, Housing, Roads, Petroleum Development, New Tokyo International Airport, etc.
Jigyōdan	20	New Technology Development, Atomic-Powered Ship Development, Space Development, Prevention of Industrial Pollution, Coal Mining Rationalization, Employment Promotion, etc.
Kōko	10	Hokkaido and Tohoku Regional Development, Housing Loans, Medical Loans, Medium and Small Enterprise Financing, etc.
Special banks (ginkō) and kinko	5	Bank of Japan, Development Bank, Export–Import Bank, etc.
Special companies	12	Japan Airlines, International Telephone and Telegraph, Electric Power Resources Development, Export of Ammonium Sulphate, etc.
Others	47	Japan Broadcasting Corporation, Overseas Economic Cooperation, Atomic Energy Institute, National Theater, Japan External Trade Corporation, Institute of Developing Economies, etc.

Source: Ichinose et al. 1977, pp. 18–19; also see Gyōsei Kanrichō 1976.

In January 1976, there were 118 national institutions that could be broadly defined as public enterprises (Gyōsei Kanrichō 1978, pp. 313–18), although, as noted earlier, the total includes a number of scientific and artistic institutions. There were also 9,635 local public enterprises at the end of 1973.

The Institutional and Procedural Framework for Labor–Management Relations in Public Enterprises

As mentioned in the previous section, three different laws govern labor–management relations in public enterprises, coverage depending upon the status of the personnel. Employees of the three public corporations (National Railways, Telegraph and Telephone, and Tobacco Monopoly) and the five national enterprises (Postal Service, the National Forestry, the Government Printing Office, the Mint, and the Alcohol Monopoly) are covered by the PCNELR Law rather than the Trade Union Law and the Labor Relations Adjustment Law that apply in the private sector. However, those provisions

Table 10.2
Local Public Enterprises, 1973

	N	%
Directly managed by local governments		
Local public enterprises	6,929	71.9
Indirectly managed by local governments		
Foundations	1,249	13.0
Corporate juridical persons	251	2.6
Joint-stock corporations	317	3.3
Limited companies	8	0.1
Special local public corporations	863	9.0
Local development jigyōdan	18	0.2

Source: Sakata 1976, p. 387.

of the Trade Union Law that are not specifically modified by the PCNELR Law (Article 3) also apply to employees of the public enterprises.[5] Thus, the law recognizes that these people have the right to organize and to join unions of their own choosing (Article 4), but they are not permitted to engage in concerted actions (Article 17), and they are required to resolve disputes through *assen* (conciliation), *chōtei* (mediation with formal recommendation), or *chūsai* (compulsory arbitration) (Articles 26–35). Article 8 formally gives them the right to bargain collectively, subject to substantial modifications when financing arrangements beyond those already budgeted are required to implement collective bargaining agreements (Articles 16 and 35). These limitations have become the major cause of conflict in the public sector, as will be elaborated later.

The PCNELR Law was enacted in December 1948, following the Order of the Supreme Commander for the Allied Powers in July 1948 which deprived all public employees of the rights to bargain collectively and to strike. Before the Order, both civil servants and public-enterprise employees had come under the Trade Union Law of 1945 and the Labor Relations Adjustment Law of 1946. After the Order, however, the national civil service was covered by the National Civil Service Amendment Law of 1948, which also applied to the personnel of the five national enterprises. Accordingly, these employees had no rights to bargain collectively or to strike until coverage of employees of one or another of the public enterprises was shifted to the PCNELR Law at various times between June 1949 and January 1953. The rationale for this change was said to be the necessity to segregate the then highly militant postal workers from other segments of public employees. During the transition period, pay and other working conditions for the five national enterprises were determined by the same system that applied to the national civil service, under which the recommendations of the National Personnel Authority played a strategic role. It should be remembered that, even after 1953, employees of these national enterprises have retained the status of national civil servants insofar as their appointments, tenure, retirement allowances, and pensions are concerned (Minemura 1969, pp. 31–32).

Employees of the National Railways and the Tobacco Monopoly have come under the regulations of the PCNELR Law since it became effective in June 1949. In August 1952, the Department of Telecommunications, which was separated from the Department of Postal Services in September 1950, was reorganized into a public corporation, the Nippon Telegraph and Telephone, and it was determined that these employees also would be governed by provisions of the PCNELR Law. Thus, it was not until January 1953 that the three public corporations and the five national enterprises were consolidated under a uniform institutional framework.

Employees of prefectural and municipal enterprises have been covered by a separate law, the Local Public Enterprises Labor Relations Law (hereafter the LPELR Law), since July 1952 when they were separated from the local civil service. Local civil servants were brought under the regulations of the Local Civil Service Law in December 1950 and thereby lost their rights to bargain collectively and to strike.[6] Pay and other working conditions were determined on the basis of recommendations by the Local Civil Service Commissions (or equity commissions in small municipalities). Following the 1952 reorganization, employees of local public enterprises regained the right to bargain collectively, but not the right to strike. Procedures similar to those for national public enterprises apply to this group.

Finally, as already mentioned, employees in the other public enterprises described in the previous section, together with private-sector employees, come under the provisions of the Trade Union Law and the Labor Relations Adjustment Law. However, it is appropriate to make a distinction between two groups in this category. At the end of 1973, there were 112 special juridical "persons," of which three were public corporations (described above) and the remaining 109 were kōdan, kōko, kinko, ginkō, jigyōdan, special mixed corporations, or other institutions. Of these 109, 18 (Japan Broadcasting Corporation, the Bank of Japan, 12 special mixed corporations, and others) were almost completely free from government control of their labor–management relations, including pay determination. However, the Ministry of Finance maintained substantial control over wages and salaries in the others (Kōshiro 1977d, pp. 173, 177). By 1976, the number of juridical "persons" had increased to 114, and by 1981, to 137.

The Right to Organize

As already pointed out, there are noticeable differences in the legal framework surrounding the public corporations and national enterprises (PCNE) and private-sector establishments. A few points with regard to the right to organize are worthy of further discussion.

Eligibility for Union Membership.—One of the most problematic features of the PCNELR Law prior to its amendment in 1965 was the provision that limited eligibility for union membership to employees of PCNE (Article 4, Section 3). This provision proved to be in violation of the principle of freedom of association, as was clarified in the prolonged disputes over ratification of the International Labor Organization (ILO) Convention No. 87. However, prior to ratification of the Convention, those who were dismissed or discharged by PCNE authorities were automatically deprived of their right to membership in unions of PCNE employees. Therefore, once union officials were dismissed because of their responsibility for instigating illegal industrial actions (Articles 17 and 18), they lost their union offices, or else the authorities took advantage of the presence of "illegal officials" as a "just cause" for refusing to bargain with the unions.

Labor disputes of this sort occurred after 1953, first at the Japan National Railways and then at the Postal Service and other agencies. The public employee unions of these enterprises determined to try to resolve this issue by appealing to the ILO, beginning in 1958. The confrontation between the government, the ruling Liberal-Democratic political party, and PCNE authorities on the one hand, and the unions and opposition parties on the other, eventually culminated in the ratification of ILO Convention No. 87 in 1965, when the controversial provisions of Article 4, Section 3 (together with similar provisions in Article 5, Section 3, of the LPELR Law) were finally repealed.[7]

Another feature of the PCNELR Law concerning eligibility for union membership is the provision that prohibits "managerial and supervisory" personnel from joining unions (Article 4, Section 2). The details of the rule are stipulated in the administrative rules issued by the PCNELR Commission.[8]

Prohibition of the Union Shop.—Whereas the Trade Union Law acknowledges the principle of the union shop if the majority of workers employed at a plant or establishment are organized into a single union, the PCNELR Law (Article 3) excludes application of this provision to the PCNE. Article 4 of the PCNELR Law recognizes not only the right of employees to organize and to join unions of their own choosing, but also their right not to do so.

Unfair Labor Practices.—The provisions concerning "unequal treatment" by employers, paralleling similar provisions of the original Trade Union Law (Article 11), were applicable to the PCNE until the amendment of the PCNELR Law in 1952. After the 1952 amendment, and despite the extension of unfair labor practice provisions to cover the PCNE, differences between the two systems remain. Penalties against employers who commit unfair labor practices are not applicable to PCNE authorities because they are supposed to be "good employers" by definition (Minemura 1969, p. 97). Moreover, the "proper acts" of trade unions protected by law are more narrowly defined in the PCNELR Law than in the Trade Union Law because of the prohibition of strikes and industrial actions as well as the limited scope of collective bargaining (Minemura 1969, pp. 101–2).

Collective Bargaining and Terms and Conditions of Employment

The collective bargaining system in Japanese public enterprises can best be illustrated by the practices and experiences of the PCNE. The system is regulated by the provisions in Articles 8, 16, and 35 of the PCNELR Law. Article 8 stipulates that personnel are allowed to bargain collectively and to reach written agreements on the following subjects: (1) wages and other pay, hours of work, rest time, holidays, and vacations; (2) promotion, demotion, transfer, discharge, suspension, seniority, and principles for disciplinary actions; (3) work-related safety and sanitation procedures and the terms of work-accident compensation; and (4) other conditions of employment. This means that employees cannot negotiate on administrative and managerial topics if these are not related to conditions of employment. Unions in the PCNE have succeeded in making agreements with management on negotiation procedures in order to avoid conflicts over issues of this type; they have also reached agreements on conditions for introducing rationalization and new machinery and equipment, particularly since 1955.

However, on wage issues, management in the PCNE is constrained by strict government and Diet control. Article 16 says that any agreement that requires additional financial expenditures beyond the predetermined budget shall not be binding on the government and that the government shall not spend any amount of money before the Diet authorizes the expenditure. Similarly, Article 35 stipulates that an arbitration award by the PCNELR Commission shall be final and binding on both parties concerned, but if that award needs additional financing for implementation, the government shall not be bound by the award, subject to the provisions of Article 16. It was understood at the time the legislation was passed that the purpose of financial control by the Diet was only to preserve financial democracy (Matsuzaki 1952, pp. 200–203; Minemura 1971, p. 119). If the government had been realistic in its efforts to maintain industrial peace, it would have asked the Diet for additional financing to implement such awards. But it did not. Instead, the conservative government adhered to a narrow interpretation of the legal principle and repeatedly cut the recommended wage increases until about 1957. These actions led to severe confrontations between the government and the public-employee unions (Kōshiro 1973; 1975d, pp. 43–61).

The political climate had changed by 1956 when the government amended the PCNELR Law, revising Article 35 to the extent that the government was now obliged to exert as much effort as possible to implement arbitration awards. Under new practices developed since then, arbitration awards have been respected. However, another obstacle for collective bargaining on wages had been introduced in 1950 in the form of the "payroll budget." Although the original PCNELR Law contained the restrictive provisions of Articles 16 and 35, it did not include the payroll budget system. Thus under the old regulations PCNE authorities could divert money for increased wages within the limits of the approved total budget. Introduction of the payroll budget system, however, made it impossible for the authorities themselves to divert money for the wage increases, although they still retained the autonomy to reallocate money for purposes other than wage increases. The authorities were now obliged to seek the prior permission of the government even within the approved budget or to ask the Diet to legislate supplemental appropriations for wage increases, if mere reallocation of funds within the budgetary limits did not release a sufficient amount to cover the increases. That is to say, the employers were virtually prohibited from negotiating any wage increase beyond the predetermined payroll budget, and thus their latitude for bargaining on wages was severely reduced.

Reflecting the limited discretion the PCNE authorities were allowed, they repeatedly answered "zero" to union wage demands until 1960, and they continued to answer "almost zero" from 1961 until 1969. It was only after 1970 that PCNE authorities were able to offer some explicit amount of money at the bargaining table. The payroll budget system has been gradually relaxed since 1971 to the extent that an additional 5 percent of the previous year's payroll has been budgeted in advance.[9] Moreover, the authorities responded with a wage increase of more than 7 percent in the 1977 negotiations. However, these modifications are not yet enough to satisfy the unions' wage demands, and final solution of the disputes has continued to be dependent upon arbitration awards by the PCNELR Commission.

Comparability of Pay between Public Enterprise Employees and Civil Servants

It is not surprising, considering the historical background, that terms and conditions of employment in public enterprises are strongly affected by those of the civil service. The principles of pay determination for employees of the PCNE are: (1) wages shall correspond to the content and responsibilities of the job and shall consider the degree of realized efficiency; (2) wages shall be determined by taking into account the pay levels of both the national civil service and employees in the private sector, together with other conditions such as the cost of living and supply and demand in the labor market.[10]

In fact, a highly sophisticated system of comparing wage levels among national civil servants, public-enterprise employees, and private-sector employees has been developed since 1948, and especially since 1955 when the Spring Offensive was inaugurated by unions in the private sector. The unions of civil servants and of public-enterprise employees joined in these actions in 1956 and have played a substantial role in increasing the influence of organized labor (Kōshiro 1973, 1978b; Ono 1973). As a result of the Spring Offensive, the market wage level (the average rate of wage increases in major private enterprises) has become recognized as an important yardstick used both by the PCNELR Commission to adjust pay levels of the PCNE employees through arbitration awards and by the National Personnel Authority in its pay recommendations for the national civil service.

Through such interaction of collective bargaining in the private and public sectors, rules and practices for comparing wage levels among the groups have been elaborated. Similar interaction can also be observed between employees of local public enterprises, local civil servants, and local private labor markets. These developments do not necessarily mean uniformity of wage levels among the different sectors. It is widely believed that pay levels of employees of large prefectures and municipalities are higher than those in the national civil service; therefore, wages of employees of local public enterprises in such localities may also be higher than those of national civil servants, although a number of these local public enterprises have experienced financial problems.[11]

The Institutional Framework for the Settlement of Labor Disputes and Grievances

Mechanisms for Dispute Settlement in Public Enterprises

The three different methods established for the settlement of labor disputes correspond to the three types of public enterprises in Japan, outlined previously: (1) Kōrōi, the Public Corporation and National Enterprise Labor Relations Commission (PCNELR Commission) for the three public corporations and five national enterprises; (2) Chirōi, Local Labor Relations Commissions for local public enterprises in each prefecture; and (3) Chūrōi and Chiroi, the Central Labor Relations Commissions for other public enterprises covered by the Trade Union Law. If a particular case involves "two or more prefectures" or "issues of national importance," the Central Labor Relations Commission "may assume original jurisdiction" (Trade Union Law, Article 25). Because of limited space, I shall concentrate on the PCNELR Commission to illustrate how these dispute-settlement mechanisms work.

The PCNELR Commission consists of 17 commissioners, with seven of them representing the public interest (public commissioners), five representing the public corporations or national enterprises (employer commissioners), and five representing the employees (labor commissioners); the ratio was five to three to three until the 1975 amendment. The chairman is elected from among the public commissioners. To deal with its business, the commission also has an "executive office," the personnel for which are supplied by the Ministry of Labor.

Commissioners are appointed by the prime minister from a list of candidates prepared by the minister of labor, who is required to hear and consider the opinions of the employer and labor commissioners before preparing the list of proposed public commissioners. Employer commissioners are recommended by the PCNE authorities, and the labor commissioners by the unions concerned (Article 20, Section 2). The law requires that "two or more of the public commissioners shall not belong to the same political party" (Article 20, Section 5).

Methods of Dispute Settlement

The PCNELR Law provides for three types of dispute settlement: assen, chōtei, and chūsai.

Assen may be undertaken by the commission on application by either or both parties concerned, or through a resolution of the commission. Conciliation is to be undertaken by individuals nominated by the commission chairman from among the commissioners or by other conciliators as stipulated in the law (Article 26, Section 2). Needless to say, conciliators' recommendations are not binding on either of the parties, but they are presented in order to facilitate the settlement of disputes. Conciliators usually are nominated from among the public commissioners, and commissioners representing the parties involved are expected to assist.

Chōtei (mediation or nonbinding arbitration)[12] is to be undertaken by a committee established for cases covering the jurisdictional area of two or more Regional Mediation Commissions.[13] The PCNELR Commission undertakes mediation in the following cases (Article 27): (1) when both of the parties concerned have applied to the commission for mediation; (2) when either party concerned has applied to the commission for mediation under provisions of a collective bargaining agreement; (3) when the commission, on application of either party, has decided that mediation is necessary; (4) when the commission, on its own initiative, has decided that mediation is necessary; or (5) when the relevant minister has requested the commission to undertake mediation.

A mediation committee is tripartite, with each side having three or fewer mediators and the unions and employers having an equal number of representatives. The commission may ask a mediation committee (or a Local Mediation Commission) to submit a report on its activities, or it may give the committee necessary instructions (Article 31). A mediation committee is expected to resolve disputes by submitting a report with recommendations (*chōteian*). Many cases are settled by mediation, but for disputes over major wage adjustments, a new practice has been developed since 1967 whereby the chairmen of the mediation committees publicly announce their personal opinion of the desirable wage rate (or amount) at the final stage of the committees' deliberations; then the parties concerned "reject" it so that the commission will begin arbitration (Yamashita 1973, p. 231).This curious procedure has become necessary in order to escape the rigidities of Articles 16 and 35 of the PCNELR Law and the payroll budget system mentioned earlier. In actuality, both parties agree to accept the chairmen's recommendation for settlement, but without an arbitration award from the commission it has been difficult to get the necessary concurrence of the finance ministry, the Diet, and the public.

The circumstances under which chūsai is undertaken by the commission reflect the same conditions that hold for chōtei (circumstances 1, 2, and 5, above) and two other sets of circumstances: (1) when either party has applied to the commission for arbitration, in cases where the commission has failed to settle a dispute within two months after the start of conciliation or mediation, or (2) when the commission itself has decided that arbitration is necessary in cases where it has undertaken conciliation or mediation.

An arbitration committee is composed of all of the public members of the commission or of three arbitrators nominated by the chairman from among the public commissioners (Article 33, Section 2). An arbitration award from the commission is final and binding on both parties, and the government shall "exert all possible effort for its implementation" (Article 35). The latter words were added to the article in 1956 when liberal elements in the government persuaded the ruling party to respect arbitration awards and thereby improve labor–management relations in public enterprises. In accordance with this provision, the payroll budget system was relaxed to the extent that the predetermined wage fund could be increased if the commission submitted an arbitration award that required the additional funds, although the government is still required to ask the Diet to legislate an additional appropriation if the wage increases cannot be implemented by a reallocation of budget monies. Unfortunately, as noted, such revisions were not sufficient to persuade the unions to refrain from conducting illegal industrial actions.

Grievance Procedures

Disputes of rights and disputes of interests are not clearly differentiated in Japanese labor law. However, grievance procedures as such are provided for in the PCNELR Law (Article 12), independent of the collective bargaining regulations. For example, the Postal Service reached an agreement with the unions concerning grievance settlement and a three-stage format was established: (1) a local grievance committee composed of representatives of the local post office and local branches of the unions; (2) a regional grievance committee composed of persons from the parties' regional head offices; and (3) a central conference between the ministry and the unions' national headquarters. Individual grievances concerning pay and other conditions of employment are dealt with through these procedures. In the Postal Service, 77 cases were decided by the central conference from the time it was established through April 1976; most of them concerned individual pay problems (Yūseishō 1976a, p. 341). If two or more individuals have similar grievances, they are settled through collective bargaining or joint consultation.

Joint Consultation

Article 8 of the PCNELR Law spells out the scope of collective bargaining and specifically excludes certain matters affecting the management and operation of the public corporations or national enterprises. However, this does not mean that these subjects are completely outside negotiations or conferences between the parties. Mechanisms of various types have been set up in public enterprises for informal negotiations and formal conferences separate from and supplementary to the collective bargaining process. Especially since the late 1950s, there has been joint consultation in most public enterprises over the introduction of new technology and rationalization.

In the late 1950s, the Nippon Telegraph and Telephone Public Corporation succeeded in concluding an agreement with its union (Zendentsū) concerning the corporation's second five-year modernization plan. The agreement stipulated that the authorities should consult with the union about the details of rationalization programs prior to their introduction ("prior consultation") and has since been copied by other public enterprises (Okamoto 1975, p. 50). The Postal Service concluded a similar agreement with its unions (Zentei and Zenyūsei) in 1961–62 and 1964, respectively, to establish joint consultation systems in each of its major service divisions (postal service, savings, and insurance) (Yūseishō 1976a, pp. 359–60). The Japan National Railways also established prior consultation mechanisms with its unions in 1958, covering manning programs, transfer and retraining, and abolishment and/or retrenchment of worksites. The parties proceeded further to conclude an agreement dealing with employment stabilization and rationalization in 1962 (Kōshiro 1975a, pp. 28–32). These examples indicate that joint consultation is distinguished from, but supplementary to, collective bargaining and that it functions in the gray area between subjects for collective bargaining and "matters affecting management and operation." Impasses resulting from joint consultation have usually been settled through collective bargaining or through conciliation, mediation, or arbitration by the PCNELR Commission.

Unfair Labor Practices

Article 25, Section 5 stipulates that "the Commission may carry out investigations, hold hearings, find facts, and issue necessary orders, in cases where a complaint that the public corporation and national enterprise has violated the provisions of Article 7 of the Trade Union Law has been filed therewith." Under unfair labor practices, Article 7 includes discharging or in any way discriminating against workers for union membership or union organizing activities; refusing to bargain collectively without "fair and appropriate" reasons; interfering with (or for that matter, financially supporting) the formation or management of a union; and discharging or discriminating against workers who file complaints with or in other ways appear before the Labor Relations Commission. Most of the cases concerning discriminatory treatment have been related to disciplinary discharges by the authorities, unequal treatment as between members of rival unions, or transfer to different jobs or different worksites (Yūseishō 1976a, pp. 313–18).

Refusal to bargain without fair and appropriate reasons often has prompted an unfair labor practice complaint. Most charges of this type have been related to the scope of collective bargaining, the time and place of bargaining, or improper behavior on the part of negotiators. Although the employer is permitted to refuse to bargain on matters of management and operation (Article 8, proviso), this issue has sometimes arisen when the distinction between negotiable issues was unclear or the employer persisted in resolving a particular issue through the grievance procedure, joint consultation, or informal conferences with union representatives rather than bargaining over them. The Miyakonojō Post Office Case of 1961, which was finally settled by the Supreme Court on June 3, 1976, in a ruling against the employer, is an example of the latter. One of the issues disputed in this case was whether the time schedules at a local post office should be negotiated at the post office level. The postmaster had refused to negotiate the matter with the local branch of the Zentei union because the fixing of time schedules for a post office had been considered a management prerogative under the discretion of the postmaster, and had proposed instead that he meet and confer with the union on the issue. His position was supported by the commission, but the union appealed to the Tokyo District Court, which reversed the commission's decision. The commission then appealed to the High Court and finally to the Supreme Court, in vain. The courts ruled that time schedules were an aspect of working conditions and should be subject to collective bargaining at the local level, in spite of the national agreement.[14]

Table 10.3

Cases of Adjustment and Adjudication by the PCNELR Commission, 1970–76

Year	Conciliation	Mediation	Arbitration	Adjudication over Unfair Labor Practices
1970	3	49	20	13
1971	2	51	25	25
1972	5	42	18	23
1973	1	56	24	13
1974	11	61	50	8
1975	1	35	17	1
1976	2	36	17	2

Source: The PCNELR Commission's Executive Office *Year Book* for each year.
Note: The figures refer to cases dealt with by the commission during the year, irrespective of whether final solution was made within the year. Cases of complaints made to Local Mediation Commissions were omitted from this table. Other types of cases dealt with by the commission concerned authorization of trade union status, and the scope of management and supervisory personnel.

Unfair labor practice charges also arise in instances where unions claim employer interference in trade union administration and activities. In the case cited above, the commission had supported the union's complaint that the postmaster had refused to permit local union officials to take paid vacations in order to attend the annual meeting of the district union. The employer insisted that the applications were made so that the officials could attend a meeting to plan "work-to-rule" struggles against the authorities, in violation of the prohibition on industrial actions. In other words, the employer's reasons for refusing permission arose because of his judgment about the possible outcome of the union meeting. The commission considered this an illegitimate interference in union activities.[15]

Frequency of Intervention by the Labor Relations Commission

The PCNELR Commission has intervened in labor disputes in public corporations and national enterprises on a number of occasions, as shown in table 10.3. The commission's interventions are classified by the causes of the disputes in table 10.4; most cases involved wage problems.

Limitations on Industrial Actions

It has already been noted that industrial actions by both employees and employers are banned by the PCNELR Law. Article 17 states, "Employees and unions shall not engage in a strike, slowdown or any other acts of dispute hampering the normal course of operation of a public corporation and national enterprise, nor shall any employees or union members and union officers

Table 10.4
Cases Adjusted by the PCNELR Commission,
Classified by Causes of Disputes, 1972–1974

Causes of Disputes	Conciliation	Mediation	Arbitration	Total
Wages				
Wage increases	1	48	49	98
Temporary lump-sum				
allowance	0	29	15	44
Overtime pay	0	30	0	30
Housing allowance	0	14	14	28
Fuel and coal allowance	0	4	8	12
Annual periodic increment	7	1	4	12
Subtotal	8	126	90	224
Hours of work and paid days off	5	15	0	20
Personnel issues	5	12	0	17
Others	2	1	0	3
Total	20	154	90	264

Source: Office of the Ministers Concerned with the PCNE, Document No. 86 (April 10, 1975), pp. 54–55; compiled by the PCNELR Commission's Executive Office.

conspire to effect, instigate or incite such prohibited conduct," and "2. The public corporation and national enterprise shall not engage in a lockout." Article 18 imposes dismissal as a possible penalty for violations. Similar provisions are found in Articles 11 and 12 of the LPELR Law.

More than 1,000 union officials in public corporations and national enterprises have been dismissed or discharged since 1953 for violation of the strike prohibition, according to Akita (1977). The public-enterprise unions have been openly hostile toward the strike prohibition since October 1960 when Sōhyō and the unions of the public enterprises and the civil service set up the "Committee to Recover the Right to Strike." In spite of active conciliation by the ILO's Dreyer Commission, disputes over the issue were not settled by Japan's ratification of ILO Convention No. 87 in 1965.

The Deliberating Council on the Civil Service System was created in October 1965 and published its final report on September 3, 1973. The Council was not able to present a unanimous conclusion, but it reported three opinions concerning the right to strike of public-enterprise employees: (1) the right should not be recognized for any employees of the three public corporations and five national enterprises; (2) the right to strike should be recognized only in those sectors where work stoppages would impinge little on the daily lives of citizens; and (3) the right to strike should be recognized in all sectors, on condition that dispute-resolution procedures were established prior to the implementation of any dispute action. In particular, compulsory mediation, prior notification of a strike, injunctions by order of the prime minister, compulsory arbitration, and penalties for violation of pre-strike procedures were proposed (Kōmuin Seidō Shingikai 1973, p. 1).

Following the council's indecisive report and recommendations, the government set up a Conference of Ministers Concerned with Public Enterprises in April 1974, and in August of that year an Expert Committee was appointed to assist and advise the conference. The committee reported back on November 26, 1975, recommending that the problem of the right to strike of employees of public corporations and national enterprises should be considered in close association with the forms of management prevailing in each enterprise; that some of the public enterprises should be transformed into private enterprises; and that the operation of other enterprises should be improved before considering any reform of labor–management relations (Senmoniin Kondankai 1975). In summary, it expressed a highly cautious and primarily negative view on the question of permitting public-enterprise employees to have the right to strike. In protest of the report and the government's policies, the public-enterprise unions struck from November 26 through December 3, 1975.

In another effort to solve the problem while "respecting the essence of the opinions of the Expert Committee," the government established another 97-member Council on Basic Problems of Public Enterprises, headed by Dr. Nakayama Ichirō, president of the Japan Institute of Labor. This council reported its recommendations in July 1978; its details will be elaborated later in this chapter (p. 288).

Another aspect of the problem of the right to strike has been manifested by the courts, particularly since the Supreme Court decision of October 26, 1966, in the Tokyo Central Post Office dispute. These judicial interpretations and controversies involving them will be discussed in the following section.

Labor–Management Relations in Practice—
Problems and Suggested Approaches

Union Organizations

Workers in Japan's public enterprises are highly organized; in 1975, about 89 percent of the employees of the three public corporations and five national enterprises, and 72 percent of the employees of local public enterprises, were union members (table 10.5). In fact, they constitute a stronghold of organized labor in the country. These unions are organized on an enterprise basis, and there usually are rival unions within each enterprise. Membership figures are listed in table 10.6.

Table 10.5
The Unionization Rate in Private and Public Enterprises
and in the Civil Service, 1975

Applicable Labor Laws	Total (in thousands)	Organized Labor		Unorganized and Ineligible Employees (in thousands)
		No. Employees (in thousands)	Organization Rate (%)	
Trade Union Law	31,379	9,180	29.3	22,199
Public sector	5,081	3,410	67.1	1,671
PCNELR Law	1,153	1,020	88.5	133
LPELR Law	328	230	70.1	98
National Civil Service	827	290	35.1	537
Ordinary	500	290	58.0	210
Special	327	0	0	327
Local Civil Service	2,773	1,870	67.4	903
All employees	36,460	12,590	34.5	23,870

Sources: Prime Minister's Office 1975; Jichishō 1976; RKKC 1976; all cited in Kōshiro 1973, p. 172.

Pay Comparability with the Private Sector

As already described earlier, collective bargaining is extensively developed in the public enterprises. Although financial limitations restrict autonomous bargaining, wage levels and working conditions of public-enterprise employees covered by the PCNELR Law and the LPELR Law have been generally well protected, owing to the prevailing principle of comparability with the private sector. The pay comparability principle was reconfirmed in 1964 when then Prime Minister Ikeda Hayato met with Ohta Kaoru, then secretary-general of Sōhyō.

At the same time, wage levels and working conditions in the public enterprises are also closely related to those of the National Civil Service. The National Personnel Authority (NPA) is charged with determining the pay and other employment conditions for national civil servants, and every spring it surveys the wage levels and working conditions in private enterprises with 100 or more employees. The survey results are compiled and analyzed by August, and the NPA then sends its report and recommendations to the Cabinet and the Diet. Since 1970, the government has implemented these recommendations completely; prior to that year, however, there were major confrontations with the unions because implementation was delayed or (until 1959) pay increases were below those recommended by the NPA (Kōshiro 1973, ch. 6).

In any event, the laws for employees in public enterprises stipulate that comparability of terms of pay with both the National Civil Service and the average levels in private enterprises should be maintained. For example, in

Table 10.6
Union Membership in Public Enterprises, 1975, 1981

	1975	1981
Public Corporations		
Japan National Railways		
Kokurō (Sōhyō)	237,000	245,405
Tetsurō (Dōmei)	70,000	46,247
Dōrō (Sōhyō)	47,000	44,434
Others	9,000	NA
Nippon Telegraph and Telephone		
Zendentsū (Sōhyō)	276,000	290,972
Others	NA	NA
Tobacco Monopoly		
Zensenbai (Sōhyō)	36,000	32,070
National Enterprises		
Postal Service		
Zentei (Sōhyō)	193,000	186,107
Zenyūsei (Dōmei)	56,000	60,962
Others	NA	NA
National Forestry		
Zenrinya (Sōhyō)	55,000	45,903
Nichirinrō (Dōmei)	10,000	8,889
Government Printing Office		
Zeninsatsu (Sōhyō)	6,700	6,208
Mint		
Zenzōhei (Sōhyō)	1,700	1,474
Alcohol Monopoly		
Arukōru Sembai (Sōhyō)	900	742

Source: Sankōsha Gogengyō no Gaikyō, RKKC, 1975, pp. 61–71, and 1982, p. 73.
Note: In the local public enterprises, the largest unions are Toshikōtsu (Municipal Traffic Workers Union) with 56,000 members, Jichirō (Prefectural and Municipal Workers Union) with 41,000 members, and Zensuidō (Water Supply Workers Union) with 38,000 members, all Sōhyō unions. Memberships are drawn mostly from local and prefectural civil servants.
NA: Data not available.

the spring of 1977, wage increases in the major sectors of the economy were determined in the following order: on April 13, five major companies in the iron and steel industry, which had been playing the pattern-setting role in the Spring Offensive during the previous decade, made a "one-shot offer" averaging ¥13,000 a month, or an 8.5 percent increase. In close alignment with this proposal, on the same day eight major shipbuilding companies offered ¥13,000 or an 8.7 percent increase; the Big Two in the auto industry, Toyota and Nissan, made an offer of a ¥13,000 increase, or 9.9 percent; and 14 major electric appliance companies offered an increase of between ¥12,000 and ¥13,000, or 9.5–10 percent. Unions in most of these companies accepted these pay increases without going on strike. This pattern meant that the wage increase for 1977 was about ¥1,000 higher than that of the previous year, or about the same percentage as the 1976 increase. Then, on April 16, after a one-day strike, nine major private railway companies offered a ¥13,300 increase (9.12 percent) which with an attached lump-sum payment of ¥30,000 was said to exceed a 10 percent increase, which the unions considered quite satisfactory. The unions of Kōrōkyō (Joint Council of the Unions of the Public Enterprise Unions) then scheduled a 72-hour strike, beginning April 20, to demand a wage increase of more than 10 percent. They did, in fact, strike. On the evening of April 20, the mediation committee of the PCNELR Commission recommended an increase of ¥13,606, or 9.12 percent, which was considered equivalent to the increase in the private railway industry. Kōrōkyō finally accepted this recommendation by agreeing to settle the dispute through arbitration, the award of which was the same as the mediation committee's recommendation.[16] These processes have evolved through the experiences gained in over 20 years of conducting the Spring Offensive.

Autonomy of the Public Enterprise Authorities

As described earlier, the autonomy of authorities of the public corporations and national enterprises has always been substantially restricted by law. These limitations adversely affected the development of healthy collective bargaining in the public sector in spite of the fact that pay and other employment conditions for public-enterprise workers were eventually adjusted to maintain comparability with those prevailing in the private sector. A sense of dissatisfaction has emerged among both workers and management personnel in the public enterprises. It stems from the feeling that they have been humiliated by the excessive intervention of the conservative political forces that have controlled the government for more than a quarter of a century.

Quite a few recommendations of special councils on the public corporations and national enterprises have recommended greater autonomy for the authorities, in order to improve the efficiency of those enterprises.[17] The recommended revisions include: (1) relaxation of budgetary control by the Diet; (2) repeal of the "payroll budget" system; and (3) changes in the system by which the Diet sets charges and fees.

Relaxation of Budgetary Control by the Diet.—The present budget system requires that all accounts of a public corporation be approved by the Diet. It has been repeatedly recommended that legislative control should be confined to the construction account (investment) and that the profit and loss account should be freed from Diet control because public corporations are also charged with being financially self-supporting as business enterprises.

Repeal of the Payroll Budget System.—Present laws governing each public corporation and national enterprise provide a legal maximum for payrolls beyond which no money can be spent without prior approval by the appropriate minister or the Diet. Although this budgetary control has been moderated over the past decade, it still limits the authorities' autonomy in negotiating wage increases to the extent that top executives in public corporations cannot give the unions a definite answer until the PCNELR Commission's arbitration award is announced. A result of this imposed impotency is a substantial deterioration of morale among management personnel and of labor–management relations generally. Moreover, excessive control by the Diet has contributed to reducing any incentive for both management and workers in public corporations to improve efficiency because any cost-savings would only result in a reduction of future "payroll budgets." One way to break out of this vicious circle of excessive control and lowered efficiency would be to relax control over the wage fund so that improved efficiency could be reflected in improved remuneration. To be sure, some kind of public control over budget and pay levels in public corporations is indispensable to prevent undue exploitation of their monopolistic position. However, the principle of comparability of pay between the public and private sectors has become so firmly established that decontrol of the payroll budget would not lead to excessive wage increases in the public sector.

Changes in the System by Which the Diet Sets Charges and Fees.— Modifications in the Diet's control over public charges and fees would also be necessary so that price-setting could become more flexible and able to reflect changing economic conditions. It has taken the Diet too long to effect price changes to meet the economic necessities of the public corporations; this delay, in turn, has aggravated their financial conditions and eventually has made necessary huge subsidies to enable them to avoid bankruptcy. If the public really wants to keep public enterprises self-supporting, they should allow price-setting to become as free as possible within the constraint that the enterprises will not take advantage of their monopolistic positions.[18]

In addition to these reforms, political intervention in personnel matters and labor–management relations in public enterprises also should be restrained. Such intervention has become inevitable because of repeated illegal strikes and industrial actions by the unions. However, management in the public corporations and national enterprises has become more and more reluctant to undertake disciplinary actions against illegal labor disputes, now that almost all of the officials of Sōhyō unions in the three public corporations and five national enterprises have been dismissed, pursuant to Article 18 of the PCNELR Law.[19] This means that disciplinary actions of this type no longer function to restrain illegal industrial actions, although the unions have suffered substantial burdens by being forced to compensate their disciplined members for lost earnings.

Change in Court Judgments Concerning the Right to Strike of Public Employees

One of the most notable developments in the field of labor–management relations in the public sector is the change in court judgments since 1966 when the Supreme Court handed down an important decision in the Tokyo Central Post Office case. The opinion states that employees in public corporations and national enterprises are "workers" as defined in Article 28 of the Constitution of Japan and therefore, in principle, they deserve to be protected by the provisions concerning the basic rights of workers; in other words, they are also guaranteed "the right of workers to organize and to bargain and act collectively" (Article 28). The decision further says that "it is not permitted to deny the basic rights of workers in the public service on the grounds that they are servants of the whole community and not of any group thereof, as stipulated in Article 15 of the Constitution."[20]

However, although the decision made it clear that the rights of public employees should be subject to restrictions with regard to the interests of the general public, there were four qualifications: (1) that the restrictions should be minimal in the sense that they are deemed rational; (2) that they should involve only occasions where they are unavoidable to prevent stoppages of activities which would be harmful to the public interest and which may create serious obstacles in the daily life of the citizens; (3) that taking criminal sanctions against acts of dispute should be confined to minimal levels, and that mere strikes or slowdowns should generally not be penalized by criminal sanctions; and (4) that compensatory measures should be set up for cases where the basic rights of workers are by necessity to be restricted. In short, the decision interpreted the PCNELR Law to mean that "the Law itself is intended not to take criminal sanctions against violations of the prohibition of acts of dispute."[21] The law requires only the discharge of workers who commit illegal industrial actions and permits suits for damages against them. The Sōhyō public-enterprise unions welcomed this decision, saying that it emancipated them from criminal sanctions.

The Full Bench of the Supreme Court went further on April 2, 1969, in another decision—this one concerning the Teachers' Union of Tokyo and the Judicial Employees' Union of the Sendai District [22]—when it extended the rationale of the Post Office case to the nonindustrial civil service. While the Post Office case was an interpretation of the PCNELR Law, which simply stipulates, "Any employee found to have engaged in conduct in violation of the provisions of the preceding Article shall subjected to dismissal" (Article

18), without any mention of criminal sanctions per se, the new decision of April 2 applied the principle of freeing public employees from criminal sanctions to the National Civil Service Law and the Local Civil Service Law, both of which do specify such sanctions for violations of the strike prohibition.[23]

In its 1969 decision, the court interpreted the prohibition of acts of dispute to mean that the instigation or incitation of only those acts of dispute that would be greatly in violation of the law should be subject to criminal sanctions. This decision stressed the high priority given to Article 28 of the Constitution. Although the court, in its ruling, did not go so far as to free civil servants from all disciplinary sanctions or civil prosecution for illegal industrial actions, the unions regarded the decision as a big step toward "emancipation from administrative disciplinary sanctions"; and, in fact, it was only after the April 2, 1969, decision that several local courts followed the Supreme Court's interpretation with regard to applying the strike prohibition provisions to both civil servants (teachers) and workers in public enterprises (Japan National Railways and Postal Service). The local courts' decisions relaxed the strike prohibition to the extent that even administrative discipline would be confined to cases where the public interest would be seriously compromised (Hanami 1972, pp. 2–7).

However, this movement in the direction of liberalization in judicial decisions was brought to a halt by the Full Bench decision of the Supreme Court on April 25, 1973, in three cases, one of which involved national civil servants in the Ministry of Agriculture and Forestry.[24] In that case the court overruled its April 2, 1969, decision because, in its judgment, "such decisions . . . might eventually lead to releasing civil servants from the prohibition of acts of dispute."[25]

The Sōhyō public-sector unions denounced this decision and prepared once again to fight for restoration of the right to strike. Table 10.7 illustrates the trend toward an increasing number of labor disputes on the National Railways in the 1970s.

In 1975 the public-employee unions staged a strike in support of their demand for the right to strike, but it failed, primarily because it occurred in the midst of an economic depression brought on by the oil crisis. It also had the result of turning public opinion against strike actions by public-employee unions.

The controversy over the right of public employees to strike again reached the Supreme Court in the Zentei Nagoya Central Post Office case, decided by the court on May 4, 1977. That case involved post office workers who had conducted a two-hour "shop-floor meeting"[26] during working hours in March 1958 in order to participate in the joint actions for the Spring Offensive of that year. As a result, four of the full-time Zentei union officials were

Table 10.7
Employees Involved in Acts of Dispute
in the National Railways, 1955-75

Year	Employees Total No.	No. Involved in Acts of Dispute	Strike Participation Ratio[a](%)
1955	445,637	10,000	2.24
1956	447,196	110,000	24.60
1957	449,634	262,000	58.27
1958	450,387	35,600	7.90
1959	449,353	30,470	6.78
1960	448,542	3,600	0.80
1961	450,615	3,942	0.88
1962	452,688	5,322	1.18
1963	455,020	2,436	0.54
1964	461,931	2,060	0.45
1965	462,120	7,256	1.57
1966	469,693	13,102	2.79
1967	468,267	4,136	0.88
1968	466,711	35,656	7.64
1969	466,743	25,074	5.37
1970	459,677	30,694	6.68
1971	450,388	48,808	10.84
1972	441,054	73,954	16.77
1973	434,934	88,700	20.39
1974	431,958	383,900	88.87
1975	430,296	420,660	97.76

Source: The figures were supplied to the author by the Bureau of Personnel Affairs, Japan National Railways. The table is from Kōshiro 1975c, p. 42.

[a]Obtained by dividing total number of employees into number of employees involved in disputes.

dismissed for violating Article 17 of the PCNELR Law and were prosecuted for inciting a violation of Article 79 of the Postal Service Law, the latter violation being the crime of not undertaking postal business, which carries penalties of imprisonment not exceeding one year or a fine not exceeding ¥20,000. The Nagoya High Court declared the defendants not guilty in October 1969 on the grounds that the acts committed should be considered proper acts of dispute protected by Article 1, Section 2, of the Trade Union Law (criminal immunity). Thus the workers should not be prosecuted under Article 79 of the Postal Service Law, although they could be dismissed for violating Article 17 of the PCNELR Law. It was quite evident that this decision reflected the liberal attitude toward industrial actions by public employees that had prevailed since 1966.

The new decision of May 4, 1977, which overruled the High Court finding, also meant overruling the Supreme Court decision in the Tokyo Central Post Office case of 1966. The new opinion said that (1) Article 17, Section 1 (prohibition of strikes) of the PCNELR Law is constitutional; (2) therefore, the criminal immunity of proper acts of dispute (Article 1, Section 2, of the Trade Union Law) should not be applied to employees of public corporations and national enterprises; and (3) the acts of dispute in violation of Article 79 of the Postal Service Law should be penalized as crimes, but only those who played a leading role during the acts of dispute should be penalized and the mere participants should not.[27]

Two of the 15 judges dissented, essentially arguing the rationale of the 1966 decision. One of the ex-judges of the Supreme Court, Iwata Makoto (1977, pp. 3–5), also severely criticized the new decision, saying that acts of dispute by employees of public corporations and national enterprises are illegal in terms of the PCNELR Law and Civil Codes, but that they should not be construed as illegal in terms of criminal law. Therefore, it would be a sufficient penalty to discharge those workers who were responsible for conspiring, instigating, or inciting illegal acts of dispute and/or to sue them for damages.

Conflict between Rival Unions

One aspect that cannot be overlooked in examining the expanding conflict over the right of public employees to strike is union rivalries in the public enterprises. These rivalries began in 1957 at the National Railway in Niigata Prefecture where a splinter union was organized in opposition to the leftist drift of the Sōhyō-affiliated Kokurō. Comparable movements occurred in many localities in the early 1960s, and these rival unions were finally integrated into the Dōmei-affiliated Tetsurō (Japan Railway Workers' Union) in October 1968.

Similarly, in the Postal Service, forces critical of Sōhyō-affiliated Zentei emerged in 1958 and a new Dōmei-affiliated union, Zenyūsei, was organized in October 1965. In the National Forestry, criticism of the Sōhyō-affiliated Zenrinya (National Forest Workers' Union of Japan) began in 1959 and the opponents finally combined into a new Dōmei-affiliated union, Nichirinrō (Japan National Forest Workers' Union). Similar developments were observed in other public enterprises, although to a lesser extent.[28]

These rival Dōmei-affiliated unions merged into Zenkankō (All Japan Council of Public Employee Unions) as early as 1959 and have developed since by absorbing latecomers into their ranks. Conflicts between Sōhyō's Kōrōkyo and Dōmei's Zenkankō have intensified year by year over the past decade as Kōrōkyo's illegal industrial actions have increased.

Illustrative of the rivalry are the unfair labor practice cases involving the National Railways in 1971. National Railways authorities, in cooperation with Tetsurō, had endeavored to revitalize the railways through increased productivity. During these productivity movements, it was widely believed that Tetsurō members were favored by management in promotions and wage increments. Dissatisfied members of two Sōhyō-affiliated unions, Kokurō and Dōryokusha, appealed these cases to the PCNELR Commission as unfair labor practices and also asked the minister of labor to advise the authorities to refrain from these activities. The commission supported the complaints and ordered the Japan National Railways to cease the practices and to apologize to the unions for them. The parties concluded agreements to improve labor–management relations. The Japan National Railways authorities halted the productivity movements and disciplined the supervisory personnel who had been responsible for promoting them. This was a hard blow for Tetsurō, and, in contrast, an encouraging victory for Kokurō and Dōryokusha.[29]

Similar conflicts occurred in the Postal Service, but under somewhat different circumstances. In 1969 authorities in the Postal Service launched productivity reforms by reducing union-inspired "restrictive labor practices" or "overcontract practices" at some post offices. Paricularly in Tokyo, they were determined to dismiss local union officials for illegal industrial actions in protest of management's rigid policies. Zentei decided to undertake "leave of absence" tactics and finally succeeded in inviting the intervention of the minister of the Postal Service. However, militant forces within the union rejected the compromise worked out by the minister and Zentei's president, Takaragi Fumihiko. The intraunion rivalry culminated in the resignation of President Takaragi at the Zentei convention in February 1971, and conflict between labor and management in the Postal Service continued not only over the right-to-strike issue but also concerning day-to-day operations and related conditions of employment until 1980.[30]

It must be remembered that Dōmei forces within the public enterprises have been strongly opposed to the leftist policies of the Sōhyō–Kōrōkyō forces, particularly the latter's use of illegal acts of dispute in efforts to restore the right to strike. Dōmei unions do, of course, support restoration of the right of public employees to strike, but with some conditions consistent with preserving the public interest. The differences of opinion between the two groups have been closely interwoven with their ideological and emotional rivalries and have contributed to a great extent toward making the issue highly political and complicated.

Some Suggested Approaches for Improving Labor–Management Relations in Public Enterprises

The author has already described some proposals for improving labor–management relations in public enterprises. Therefore, it will suffice here to add only a few points that have not been explicitly mentioned previously.

One practical solution for the disputes concerning public employees' right to strike would be to give them conditional permission to conduct industrial actions; this idea, together with two other options, had already been suggested by the Deliberating Council on the Civil Service System in 1973. One public member of the council, Ishikawa Kichiemon (1974, pp. 105–23), elaborated the idea of conditional permission a few years ago. It would consist of the following procedures: (1) Mediation prior to the inauguration of acts of dispute is obligatory. If the parties cannot accept the recommendations of the mediation committee, they are free to undertake industrial actions after a five–day cooling–off period. (2) If the public interest is seriously endangered, the prime minister may order the acts of dispute be halted for 15 days. After that, the parties are again free to conduct acts of dispute. (3) If the public interest is threatened by resumption of the acts of dispute, the prime minister must apply for arbitration by the PCNELR Commission. Acts of dispute are prohibited once arbitration has been implemented, and the commission must agree on an arbitration award within one week. The arbitration award is final and binding on both parties, and the government shall respect it. (4) Acts of dispute conducted during the period of strike prohibition are illegitimate, but they are not to be subject to criminal sanctions.

At least three other plans to implement conditional permission of the right to strike have been published, and plans also have been suggested that would permit acts of dispute only in nonessential parts of public enterprises. However, the difficulty with the latter lies in how to distinguish nonessential from essential activities (Yamaguchi 1977, pp. 10–15). The most conservative plan—to maintain the present legal system of total prohibition of strikes in public enterprises—is still supported by many, including most of the ruling Liberal-Democratic Party and the Ministry of Finance, to say nothing of the public security forces.

On July 19, 1978, the Council on Basic Problems of Public Enterprises published its report. The report actually was ten separate reports on particular subjects, but the major portion summarized the Council's recommendations as follows: (1) Some parts of the Japan National Railways, Tobacco Monopoly, and Alcohol Monopoly should be transformed into private businesses. (2) It is not appropriate to acknowledge the right to strike of employees of public corporations and national enterprises "at the present moment" because of (a) essentiality of those services, (b) lack of competition in the product market and therefore little room for economic restraints against strikes, (c) immaturity of labor–management relations in these enterprises, and (d) necessity of the present system of financial control over the management of these enterprises.[31]

The government accepted this report and established another council in November 1978, the Deliberating Council on the Labor Problems of Public

Enterprises, to implement the above recommendations. This council is tripartite, and several prominent scholars such as Nakayama Ichirō, Ōkōchi Kazuo, and Sumiya Mikio have been members. However, it is not expected that there will be much progress in the very near future unless circumstances change dramatically.

It is noteworthy that in recent years there has been criticism that public employees receive more favorable treatment than private employees in terms of old-age pensions and retirement age. Public opinion thus is aroused against the "misuse" of public money by various public enterprises at a time when most citizens are experiencing financial difficulties.

Of course there is no excuse for corruption and financial manipulation of the kind disclosed at the International Telephone and Telegraph Company. But there are some basic problems concerning the collective bargaining rights of public employees. For example, the National Railways Construction Public Corporation and Nippon Telegraph and Telephone Public Corporation are criticized because they have made overtime payments or extra year-end bonuses by means of *karashutchō* and *karachōkin* (financial manipulation to falsify travel expenses or overtime allowances). These arrangements are devised in order to meet the requirements of "hidden agreements" with the unions.

Under provisions of financial laws, these deceptive practices are absolutely illegal. But the problem is that both the National Railways Construction Corporation and Nippon Telegraph and Telephone Corporation are allowed to bargain collectively with their unions on wages and other working conditions, which often is incompatible with financial control. Too, the managements of these public enterprises have long suffered from deteriorating relations with their unions. If they are facing the need to rationalize their industries and they want to have the unions' cooperation in these efforts, it is quite understandable that they would feel compelled to find some loopholes in the financial control regulations. And this is what they had actually done—to improve efficiency.

Considering the multiple aspects of the problem, I tend to be rather pessimistic about the possibility of better industrial relations in the public sector because the parties (managements and unions) are frustrated in their attempts to develop cooperative relationships by excessive legal restrictions on management's autonomy. The "enterprise consciousness" of public-enterprise workers used to be as strong as that of workers in the private enterprises, but the financial control by both the Diet and the Ministry of Finance did not allow this element to be vitalized through labor–management cooperation. There certainly is the danger of collusion between labor and management in public enterprises where the monopolistic position of the enterprises makes it possible for the parties to exploit their advantages. Fears of traces of Marxism–Leninism among the public-employee unions are also still antagonizing the ruling Liberal-Democratic political party, which in recent years has faced the loss of its long-standing majority in the Diet.

However, the political situation changed unexpectedly and dramatically with the landslide victory of the Liberal-Democratic Party in the general elections of June 1980. The Liberal-Democratic Party won stable majorities in both Houses.[32] Therefore, the prospect of a new coalition government that would adopt moderate labor policies toward public enterprises has faded away. But it is quite interesting to note that these political changes—negative from the point of view of the public enterprise unions—seem to have forced the unions to choose more realistic approaches toward improving labor–management relations in the various public enterprises, especially the National Railways and the Postal Service. It is very difficult at this time to predict precisely in which directions the labor–management relations in the public enterprises will move, but it seems very unlikely that they will be improved to a considerable extent under the existing legal framework. In the summer of 1982, the Second Temporary Research Council for Administrative Reorganization, chaired by Dokō Toshio, recommended the reorganization of public corporations. At least some parts of the Japan National Railways, Nippon Telegraph and Telephone, and the Tobacco Monopoly will be reorganized into private companies, which will fundamentally change the focus of discussion.

Notes

1 Sugimura Shōzaburō, "Kōkyō Kigyōtai no Seikaku" [The nature of public enterprises], in Yanagawa 1956, p. 20.

2 Article 2 of the Local Public Enterprise Labor Relations Law of 1952 stipulates the areas where it applies. In addition to those industries mentioned in the text, some provisions of the law also apply to hospitals owned and managed by local governments.

3 See the analysis in Katō 1968, ch. 4 and appendix; Yoshitake 1973, pp. 12–19; and Katō 1976, pp. 35–38.

4 For more details, see Katō 1976, pp. 39–55; Yoshitake 1973, pp. 38–69; and Katō 1968, pp. 41–46.

5 Major differences between the PCNELR Law and the Trade Union Law are in the following areas: (1) eligibility for union membership, (2) procedures for unfair labor practices, (3) the scope of collective bargaining, (4) regional compulsory extension of collective bargaining agreements, (5) methods for dispute settlement, and (6) prohibition of strikes and other industrial actions. These subjects will be discussed in more detail in the following subsections. For further discussion, see Minemura 1969, pp. 15–16, 28–30.

6 A brief statement about police and firefighters would be appropriate here. The Trade Union Law of 1945 did not recognize the right to organize of police,

firefighters, and prison officers. Further, the Labor Relations Adjustment Law of September 1946 prohibited them from going on strike. Pay and working conditions for these groups come under both the National Civil Service Law and the Local Civil Service Law.

7 For more details about the disputes over freedom of association and ratification of ILO Convention No. 87, see Harari 1973 and International Labor Office 1966.

8 Prior to the amendment of the PCNELR Law in 1965, the notifications were issued by the minister of labor with the consent of the commission (Article 4, Section 1 proviso and Section 2).

9 Kōshiro 1975b, pp. 13–14. However, the Ministry of Finance exerted pressure to reduce this amount to 2.5 percent in fiscal 1979, to 2 percent in fiscal 1980, and to 1 percent in fiscal 1981.

10 The Special Treatment of Pay for Employees in National Enterprises Law, Article 3. Similar provisions are found in the Japan National Railways Law (Article 28), the Japan Tobacco Monopoly Law (Article 21), the Japan Telegraph and Telephone Law (Article 30), and the Local Public Enterprise Labor Relations Law (Article 38).

11 For example, the average pay level of prefectural civil servants was 10.8 percent higher that that of national civil servants in April 1976, according to the wage survey by the Local Autonomy Ministry, reported in *Nihon Keizai Shimbun*, November 19, 1976.

12 Chōtei is officially called "mediation," but this seems to be an erroneous translation in terms of the actual procedures, which have been drawn from traditional Japanese patterns of dealing with disputes of any kind; in other words, the practice of "chōtei" existed in Japan long before the term "mediation" was introduced by the Occupation Forces in the original English draft of the Law, and in substance it is very close to nonbinding arbitration in Great Britain or factfinding with recommendation in the United States. For more details on the traditional system of conflict resolution in Japan, see Kawashima 1964.

13 Regional Mediation Commissions were established to undertake PCNELR Commission activities relating to mediation in regional areas. They also are tripartite in composition and may perform conciliation activities as well as mediation. There are now ten LMCs; the Kantō Regional Mediation Commission, for example, has jurisdiction over the region that includes the Tokyo Metropolitan area.

14 PCNELR Commission Order No. 28, March 8, 1965 (K. Nagano v. S. Hidaka case), FY 1965 *Annual Report* of the PCNELR Commission 36; City of Miyakonojō Kita Morogata-gun Branch of Zentei v. PCNELR Commission, Tokyo District Court, May 26, 1969, *Rōdō Kankei Minji Saiban Reishu* [Labor law civil cases] 20:3, p. 399; PCNELR Commission v. City of Miyakonojō Kita Morogata-gun Branch of Zentei, Tokyo High Court, December 28, 1974, *Hanrei Jiho* [Law case journal] No. 769, p. 92; PCNELR Commission v. City of Miyakonojō Kita Morogata-gun Branch of Zentei, Supreme Court, First Petty Branch, June 3, 1976, *Rōdō Hanrei* [Labor law cases] No. 254, p. 20.

15 PCNELR Commission Order No. 28, p. 37.

16 This information comes from the following newspaper reports: *Asahi Shimbun*, April 4, 17, and 21, 1977; *Nihon Keizai Shimbun*, April 13 (evening) and 14, 1977; *Asahi Shimbun*, May 18, 1977.

17 Rinji Kōkyō Kigyōtai Gōrika Shingikai 1954; Kōkyō Kigyōtai Shingikai 1957; Rinji Gyōsei Chōsakai 1964.

18 Kōshiro 1975b, pp. 9–16. In fact, laws to enable some public enterprises to change prices without specific legislation were enacted in December 1980. A law to promote the reconstruction of Japan National Railways was enacted and enforced on December 27, 1980; a law to amend the Postal Service Law was enacted on December 11, 1980, and enforced on January 20, 1981.

19 The former president of the National Railways, Fujii Matsutarō, expressed support for conditional restoration of the right to strike for public-enterprise workers in the fall of 1975 (*Asahi Shimbun*, October 16 and 20, 1975).

20 Japan v. Sotoyama et al. (Zentei Tokyo Central Post Office case), Supreme Court, Full Bench, October 26, 1966, *Rōdō Kankei Keiji Saiban Reishū* [Labor law criminal cases] 20:8, p. 901.

21 Ibid.

22 Japan v. Hasegawa et al. (Tokyo Teachers' Union case), Supreme Court Full Bench, April 2, 1969, *Rōdō Kankei Keiji Saiban Reishū* [Labor law criminal cases] 23:5, p. 305; Japan v. Sakane et al. (Zenshihō case), Supreme Court, Full Bench, April 2, 1969, *Rōdō Kankei Keiji Saiban Reishū* 23:5, p. 685.

23 Article 98 of the National Civil Service Law prohibits strikes and other acts of dispute against the government. "Any person who conspires to effect, instigate, or incite such prohibited conduct shall be sentenced to penal servitude of not more than three years or shall be fined not more than ¥100,000" (Article 110). The local Civil Service Law has similar provisions (Articles 37 and 61).

24 Japan v. Tsuruzono et al. (Zennōrin case), Supreme Court, Full Bench, April 25, 1973, *Rōdō Kankei Keiji Saiban Reishū* [Labor law criminal cases] 27:4, p. 547.

25 Supplementary opinions by the majority judges, ibid.

26 The meeting was held outside the Central Post Office of Nagoya, at an assembly hall near the office. The union members left the post office to attend the meeting.

27 Japan v. Kikuchi et al. (Zentei Nagoya Central Post Office case), Supreme Court, Full Bench, May 4, 1977, *Rōdō Kankei Keiji Saiban Reishū* [Labor law criminal cases] 31:3, p. 182.

28 Nihon Rōdō Kyōkai 1969, pp. 660–65. Additional information was supplied to the author by the Executive Office of the PCNELR Commission.

29 Kōshiro 1977c, pp. 211–14. For details, see Rōdōshō, Rōseikyoku 1971. In recent years in the National Railways, some Communist forces in Hokkaido and a New-Left radical faction in Chiba have revolted against the leadership of Dōryokusha. Both seceded from Dōryokusha to form an independent union.

30 Kōshiro 1977c and Rōdōshō, Rōseikyoku 1971. In the summer of 1980 Zentei changed its policy from one of continual opposition to management on every issue to one of closer communication with the postal authorities. The years of

vehement conflict had become increasingly costly to the unions as it had to provide financial support for members who had been disciplined.

31 Official reports of the council were not published in a form available to the public, but they are reproduced in *Jūristo*, No. 671, August 15, 1978, pp. 100–115. Comments and criticisms by experts are contained in the same issue.

32 See *Japan Labor Bulletin*, 20:1 (January 1981): 5–8.

The Public Sector: Civil Servants

The nature of labor relations in Japan's public sector requires that it receive special attention. First of all, there is a civil service system with its unique features—financing by taxes, the lack of a profit motive in a government operation, and the employer's sovereign status. In addition, it should be noted that in Japan the public-sector labor unions are more politically and ideologically oriented than are the unions in the private sector and that their membership is extensive. According to the 1976 Ministry of Labor survey, union membership in the public sector was 3.4 million, or 27.5 percent of the 12.5 million union members in the country.[1] These unions also are powerful, and their representatives hold the important leadership positions in Sōhyō. Sōhyō's chairman, Makieda Motofumi, is from Nikkyōso (Japan Teachers' Union), and the general secretary, Tomizuka Mitsuo, is from Kokurō (National Railway Workers' Union).

The discussion in this chapter will focus upon labor relations in the civil service, which herein refers to those central or local government employees who work in the administration of government. The law and regulations that apply to national and local public employees are similar; I shall focus upon the national civil service, with an occasional reference to the situation of elementary and high school teachers, who are employees of local governments.

The labor relations of the national and local public enterprises and corporations, the subject of Chapter 10, are treated here only insofar as provisions of the National Civil Service Law and the Local Civil Service Law apply to them as well as to civil service employees. Most provisions do apply to both, the exceptions being those concerning the National Personnel Authority and the prohibitions on acts of dispute.

From "Royal Servant" to "Public Servant": A Brief History

The prototypical civil service was established in France during the regime of an absolute monarch; in Japan it was introduced with the Meiji Restoration of 1868. Under the Meiji Constitution, in effect until 1946, it was the emperor's prerogative to appoint civil servants, and each was required "to uphold his office with profound loyalty toward the emperor and his government" (Decree on the Civil Service, Article 1). A civil servant, then, was a "royal servant," which meant that he was the emperor's instrument. His legal status was not contractual, but was considered to be a "special power relation" with its basis in the power of the emperor and his government. Theoretically, civil servants were not employed by the emperor's government, but were appointed by the emperor as his agents. Discipline was prescribed by the emperor's order, not by the law.

On the other hand, civil servants had a number of privileges. A good example was a pension scheme that was fully financed from the national treasury; by contrast, pensions did not exist for employees of private enterprises at that time. Another example was their exemption from liability while performing duties in the course of their work. The principle, "The king can do no wrong," was extended to his agents, and as the courts interpreted the exercise of public power in a very broad sense, even an accident of a fire engine on a trial run was considered to be a protected exercise of public power.[2]

However, the new Constitution of 1946 proclaimed that "All public officials are servants of the whole community and not of any group thereof" (Article 15). The civil service was transformed from "royal servants" to "public servants." In other words, civil servants became simply government employees. In order to regulate their conditions of employment, the National Civil Service Law was enacted in 1947, and, based on this law, the National Personnel Authority was established to deal specifically with problems concerning personnel in the national civil service.[3]

Conditions of Employment

The Legal Nature of Labor Relations

Labor relations in the civil service, though now on a contractual basis, have some special features since the public interest is directly involved. According to the National Civil Service Law, any employee in the civil service shall attend to his duties in the interest of the public and shall exert his utmost effort in the performance of those duties (Article 96).

Before the war, when traditional German legal doctrine was strongly influential in Japan, labor relations in the civil service were considered to constitute a special power relationship which meant, as stated above, that once a person entered the civil service, he was subject to the emperor's authority and had to carry out whatever orders he was given. He was not permitted to resist an order, nor could he resort to a court suit to avoid carrying it out. Under the present system, every condition of employment is to be determined by law. Any civil servant is allowed to process a grievance or to challenge an unreasonable administrative order in court. So far as the present system is concerned, the former doctrine of a special power relation is neither valid nor appropriate.

Appointment and Promotion

The head of each Ministry has the right to hire civil service employees in his division; however, when a minister wants to hire someone for a particular position, he must choose from a list of available candidates. The National Personnel Authority compiles these lists from among those who were successful in the annual civil service entrance examinations. There are examinations for three categories of recruits—senior, junior, and primary (table 11.1).

Originally, the National Civil Service Law (Article 37) also mandated that examinations should be used to determine who would be eligible for promotion, and many such examinations were held for positions as directors or managers. This competitive system turned out to be very unpopular among civil service employees; they found it very strange when they compared it

Table 11.1
Applicants and Candidates for the Senior Category Civil Service Examination
and the Number of Appointees, 1973–77

Year	Applicants	Candidates	Appointees
1973	30,129	1,410	648
1974	30,688	1,375	678
1975	37,828	1,206	662
1976	44,518	1,136	627
1977	48,514	1,206	674[a]

Source: Jinjiin Placement Office.

[a]Out of 674 appointees, the Ministry of Finance appointed 26, the Ministry of Trade and Industry 43, the Ministry of Agriculture 146, the Ministry of Labor 28, and the Ministry of Social Welfare 29.

with the seniority wage system in private enterprises where promotion was decided mainly by length of service. Thus, promotion based on examinaton was discontinued within a few years, and a system based on performance was instituted. It is now extremely rare to find competitive examinations used for promotions, although a few exceptions can be found in the school system for teachers who want to become principals or headmasters.

Salary

Wage rates in private enterprises are determined through collective bargaining. In the civil service, however, conditions of employment as well as wages are determined by law. We call this the "legal determinism principle." As far as the national civil service is concerned, its salary scale is set by special acts approved by the Diet. The procedure is as follows: when the National Personnel Authority wishes to apply for pay increases for the civil service, it first conducts its own wage survey and, on the basis of the findings, prepares a bill, called the "National Personnel Authority Recommendation." This recommendation is presented to the Cabinet and the Diet, and they are required to treat it with the respect due an established custom. Since wages in the private sector have risen every year as a result of the Spring Offensive, the National Personnel Authority has issued a recommendation annually for the past 18 years in an attempt to redress the balance between the two sectors. Table 11.2 shows the basic pay of national civil servants in 1978, and the pay distribution is displayed in table 11.3.

It should be noted that the salary of a civil servant increases even if he is not promoted. An employee who is promoted to a position in a higher grade, of course, receives a higher salary, but one who is not promoted also receives a pay increase within his salary grade. This "periodic pay increase" allows us to say that the seniority wage system is strong in the civil service and that the linkage between the job and the salary is weak. The salaries listed in table 11.2 are only the basic rates, to which both a regional allowance and a family allowance are added.

In addition, there are annual bonuses, known as the seasonal allowance and the good-result allowance.[4] The former is paid in June, December, and March; the latter in June and December. Together, these annual bonuses amount to 4.8 times the basic monthly pay. Civil servants' salaries are said to be a little lower than private enterprise salaries; local public employees, on the other hand, receive higher pay than do national civil servants.[5]

Among fringe benefits, the pension and the retirement allowance are the most important. Both are more favorable than those in the private sector. The average retirement allowance in the private sector is about ¥10 million; yet a managing director who retired from the Tokyo municipal government a few years ago was reported to have received a retirement allowance of ¥50

Table 11.2
Monthly Pay in the National Civil Service, 1978
(yen in thousands)

| No. | Grade | | | | | | | |
---	1	2	3	4	5	6	7	8
1	251.4	193.9				100.4	88.0	
2	262.5	202.0	172.1	145.6	122.0	105.4	91.9	72.8
3	273.6	210.3	178.9	151.8	127.4	110.5	95.9	74.9
4	284.8	218.9	185.8	158.1	132.9	115.7	100.4	77.1
5	296.0	227.5	192.7	164.4	138.7	120.8	104.8	79.3
6	307.1	236.2	199.7	170.7	144.5	125.9	108.8	82.1
7	318.2	244.9	206.9	177.2	150.3	131.0	112.8	85.0
8	329.4	253.6	214.1	183.9	156.0	136.0	116.6	88.0
9	340.6	262.3	221.3	190.7	161.7	140.5	120.2	90.5
10	351.8	271.0	228.6	197.6	167.4	144.9	123.7	92.9
11	360.0	279.3	235.9	204.5	173.2	149.3	126.9	95.3
12	366.1	287.5	243.1	211.3	178.9	153.6	130.1	97.5
13	372.2	295.3	250.3	218.1	184.6	157.9	133.2	99.7
14	377.8	301.4	257.4	224.9	190.2	161.8	135.9	101.9
15	382.6	307.5	264.5	231.4	195.6	165.6	138.6	104.1
16		311.8	270.1	237.9	200.6	169.3	141.2	106.2
17			275.6	242.9	205.5	172.9	143.7	107.8
18			279.5	247.9	209.0	176.0	146.1	
19			283.3	251.5	212.3	179.0	148.1	
20			287.1	255.1	215.4	181.3		
21				258.7	217.9	183.6		
22				262.3	220.3	185.8		
23					222.7	188.0		
24					225.1			

Source: Jinjiin Placement Office.
Note: This table applies mainly to clerical employees. Starting pay for university graduates is Grade 7, No. 2.

million. Similarly, pensions in the public sector are better than those in the private sector by a factor of 1.5 to 1.9. Table 11.4 cites examples of these differentials.

Hours of Work and Vacations

National Personnel Authority regulations have shortened the length of the workweek for civil servants to 44 hours. Furthermore, since October 1977 the National Personnel Authority has been pressing for a five-day workweek. Twenty days of annual paid vacation are also provided by National Personnel Authority regulations.

Short absences for union activity are often permitted under civil service work rules. Although the rules also state that the prior approval of a supervi-

Table 11.3
Distribution of Salaries in the National Civil Service, 1978
(no. of employees)

No.	Grade							
	1	2	3	4	5	6	7	8
1	62	33				462	3,982	
2	102	81	179	293	537	1,508	4,945	53
3	137	148	190	361	914	2,821	4,962	1,449
4	172	200	254	407	1,473	4,662	5,402	3,921
5	190	299	278	461	1,678	5,388	5,794	4,161
6	102	243	295	504	2,161	6,381	4,227	7,115
7	135	275	347	664	2,585	6,082	2,545	4,037
8	83	363	425	954	2,857	5,319	674	1,563
9	66	294	555	1,235	3,029	4,475	104	414
10	46	352	684	1,713	3,055	3,718	49	52
11	14	399	920	2,518	3,646	2,672	39	4
12	6	491	1,228	3,299	4,472	1,789	14	1
13	2	551	1,356	4,816	5,576	1,211	7	
14	3	320	1,446	5,855	7,074	1,098	2	
15	3	189	1,462	4,945	7,724	1,111	2	
16		98	1,158	3,098	7,636	1,048	2	
17			725	2,019	6,409	1,049	4	
18			385	1,167	4,655	1,089	3	
19			129	668	5,260	1,264	1	
20				212	4,853	960		
21					2,833	833		
22					1,273			
23					449			

sor is required, in a case where a supervisor failed to grant approval for the absence, the Supreme Court held that, since the application had been properly submitted, the refusal was illegal and therefore the union members were not subject to disciplinary sanctions even though they were absent from their jobs without permission.[6]

For female civil servants, including nurses and teachers, a special leave of absence for child care is available until the child is one year old.

Discipline

Civil service employees are subject to discipline and sanctions for violations of the law or of work rules. Since the most important duty of a civil servant is to put forth his greatest efforts on his job, holding more than one position is forbidden (National Civil Service Law, Articles 96 and 101). This ban applies not only in cases where an individual may be holding two civil service positions concurrently, but also where the individual has a position

Table 11.3 (continued)
Distribution of Salaries in the National Civil Service, 1978
(no. of employees)

	Grade							
	3	28	21	10	40	94	1	
	(362.6)	(295.8)	(268.3)	(245.3)	(210.4)	(175.9)	(140.6)	
		14	2	3	3	18		
		(299.9)	(271.9)	(248.7)	(212.7)	(178.0)		
		5			1	11		
		(304.0)			(215.0)	(180.1)		
					2	5		
					(217.3)	(182.2)		
						5		
Exception[a]						(184.3)		
						1		
						(186.4)		
						1		
						(188.5)		
						3		
						(190.6)		
						3		
						(192.7)		
						1		
						(194.8)		
Total	1,126	4,383	12,139	35,672	80,195	55,389	32,769	22,770

Source: Jinjiin 1978, p. 19.

[a] Salaries for this group (¥ in thousands) given in parentheses.

Table 11.4
Difference in Amount of Paid Pensions, 1978

Person	Age	Sector	Job Held at Retirement	Period Covered	Annual Sum Paid by Pension (¥ in thousands)
A	63	public	director	28	1,493
B	63	public	managing director	36	2,146
C	62	private	managing director	28	1,189
D	63	private	vice-president	28	1,238

Source: *Sankei Shimbun*, May 8, 1978.

of director, consultant, or adviser in a private enterprise in addition to his civil service employment. Senior civil servants are not allowed to accept positions in private enterprises which have a close relationship to their position in the civil service for two years after resignation from the civil service (National Civil Service Law, Article 103).[7]

In cases of violations, disciplinary penalties range from reprimand to suspension without pay or discharge. In some national enterprises, the work rules also provide for a warning. Any civil servant may complain to the National Personnel Authority about the discipline and/or the penalty imposed. After the grievance procedures have been exhausted, the complaint can be brought before a court for litigation.

Political Neutrality

The National Civil Service Law states that civil servants shall not take part in any policial activities except for voting in elections (Article 102). The regulation (National Personnel Authority Regulation 14–7) implementing this provision is very restrictive, and it has also been strictly interpreted by the Supreme Court. An example is an election campaign case several years ago that involved a post office clerk in a rural area of Hokkaido. After working hours, he had put up six copies of a poster for a Socialist candidate on the municipal bulletin board. As the clerk was a union official of the district, his action had been fully authorized by his union. Although the clerk did not use the facilities of the post office itself, nor did he implicate the post office on the Socialist candidate's behalf, the Supreme Court decided that his acton was not politically impartial and fined him ¥5000.[8] This decision overruled the district and high courts which had held that the restriction on political action should be enforced only when such enforcement could not be avoided, and they had found that the clerk's action had not infringed upon political neutrality.

Job Security

Civil servants may not be dismissed or discharged except on grounds specified by the National Civil Service Law and National Personnel Authority regulations, which means that there are restrictions on the freedom of governmental units to dismiss or lay off employees. This has been cited as one of the most important privileges enjoyed by public employees as compared with workers in the private sector, and it is still true to an extent. However, since the courts in Japan hold that even in the private sector dismissal or layoff without appropriate grounds is null and void because it constitutes an abuse of employees' rights, the difference between the two sectors is more illusional than real.[9]

The really notable difference in employees' job security between the private and public sectors lies in the fact that there is no compulsory retirement in the latter. In the private sector, compulsory retirement is the principal reason for employment terminations and usually occurs when workers are between age 55 and 57 or 60—whatever the enterprise work rules say. By contrast, the civil service has no such rules. Theoretically, a civil servant can hold his job as long as he wishes, which causes some recruitment problems for the civil service system. Table 11.5 shows the number of employees over 55 years old in the national civil service, and table 11.6 presents the same data for the Tokyo Municipal Government. Reportedly, some employees in Tokyo Municipal Hall are more than 85 years old.[10]

Despite efforts of the National Personnel Authority and the government to introduce compulsory retirement at the age of 60 or 65,[11] labor unions and the employees strongly oppose the idea, so it is unlikely that such a rule could become effective in the near future. Instead, when a civil servant

Table 11.5
Civil Service Employees Over 55 Years Old, 1967-76

Year	Civil Service	National Enterprise	Total	As % all employees
1967	38,919	34,074	72,993	8.7
1968	39,077	34,273	73,350	8.7
1969	39,224	33,846	73,070	8.7
1970	40,485	32,065	72,550	8.6
1971	40,807	32,233	73,040	8.6
1972	42,810	29,458	72,268	8.5
1973	43,491	29,258	72,749	8.6
1974	46,305	29,398	75,703	8.9
1975	47,916	29,030	75,946	9.0
1976	48,406	28,542	76,948	9.0

Source: Jinjiin 1978, No. 329, p. 27.

Table 11.6
Aged Employees in the Tokyo Municipal Government, 1977

	Total No. Employees	Over 60	Over 70
Central administrative office	90,884	2,217	249
Local administrative office	74,926	4,619	1,059
Teacher	68,347	1,292	67
Policemen and firemen	61,122	100	3
Totals	295,279	8,228	1,378
	(100.0%)	(2.8%)	(0.5%)

Source: *Asahi Shimbun*, December 15, 1977.

reaches a certain age (usually 60 years old), he is "encouraged" to retire voluntarily. If he decides to accept this "encouragement," some "sweeteners" are added to his retirement allowance. However, recently there was a case where a local authority "encouraged" teachers over age 60 to retire, and when this action was challenged, the court ruled that the authority had resorted to improper means of exerting undue influence on the teachers. The remedy ordered by the court was "compensation for mental damages."[12]

Another approach a government authority may take is to make agreements with the union about retirement. In Osaka City, such an agreement had been reached covering the nonteaching staff of elementary and high schools. A retired janitor brought suit against the compulsory system provided for in the collective agreement, and the court ruled that his retirement was null and void because age cannot be a ground for dismissal.[13] This decision caused a great deal of controversy during the summer of 1978.

In addition to the fact that there can be no dismissal or discharge except as a disciplinary penalty for rule violations, the absence of compulsory retirement provides incomparable job security for civil service employees.

Employee Organizations

The rights of wage earners and salaried employees are enumerated in Article 28 of the Constitution—the right to organize unions, the right to bargain collectively, and the right to act collectively. The right to act collectively may sound rather strange, but what it refers to are strikes and other concerted activities of unions. The rights approved for civil service employees, listed in Table 11.7, are more limited under existing law and are elaborated below.

The Right to Organize and Union Recognition

The National Civil Service Law (Article 108–2) gives civil service employees the right to organize what are called employees' associations. There are some exceptions; policemen, firemen, prison employees, and

Table 11.7
The Legal Rights of Public-Sector Employees

	Organization	Collective Bargaining	Right to Strike
Policemen, firemen, etc.	No	No	No
National civil servants	Yes	No	No
Public corporations and national enterprises	Yes	Yes	No
Public employees in local government	Yes	No	No
Local public enterprises	Yes	Yes	No

members of the self-defense forces and the coast guard may not form employees' associations. The open shop is compulsory (National Civil Service Law, Article 108-2), and the union shop and the closed shop are banned.

The law also says that civil servants shall not be subject to any discriminatory treatment by reason of their membership in a union, for attempting to join or organize a union, or for having performed proper acts of a union (National Civil Service Law, Article 108-7). The National Personnel Authority may not reject a union's application for registration,[14] and a registered union becomes a legal entity with the right to bargain. With the permission of his supervisor, an employee who is elected to union office may engage exclusively in union activities; this is called a "union officer's leave," during which an employee taking such leave is not paid by his governmental employer nor is he promoted.[15]

There was a new development in union organization in August 1977 when firemen from every prefecture gathered, with the support of Jichirō (All Japan Prefectural and Municipal Workers' Unions) to organize the National Council of Firemen. The stated purpose of the council is to further mutual understanding and to investigate working conditions. As pointed out above, under existing law firemen are not allowed to organize a union. However, if the Council conducts investigations into wage rates, working hours, and other conditions of employment, for all practical purposes it will be functioning very much like a trade union.[16]

Collective Bargaining

Registered employees' associations have the right to negotiate, but they may not conclude agreements (National Civil Service Law, Article 108-5). However, this regulation has more form than substance. First, any matters connected with the management and operation of governmental affairs are outside its realm, and although wages and working conditions are within its scope, collective bargaining has little meaning, for only the Diet can approve the laws by which such working conditions are regulated (legal determinism). Second, the right to bargain is not backed up by any unfair labor practice restraints, as is the case in the private sector.[17] Of course a union that has been refused bargaining rights by the employer can sue for damages, but the threat of such a suit is not much of an incentive for collective bargaining. Third, the right to bargain does not include the right to conclude an agreement.[18] Any agreement between the government and a union is merely a gentlemen's agreement. Accordingly, the Dreyer Commission, in its report (International Labor Office 1966, paras. 2124 and 1241), concluded that this system is not true collective bargaining, but rather is a kind of petition.

Negotiating procedures imposed by the National Civil Service Law are intricate: (1) the party on the employer's side must be delegated proper authority; (2) negotiations have to be carried out between specially appointed bargaining agents; and (3) both sides must have previously agreed upon the subject, time, place, and other relevant matters. One can indeed question whether the National Civil Service Law provisions are designed to promote collective bargaining.

The Right to Strike

Strikes are expressly prohibited by existing law. The National Civil Service Law stipulates that employees shall not strike or resort to delaying tactics which reduce the efficiency of governmental operations (Article 98, paragraph 2), and that any employee who takes part in a strike or other unlawful action shall not contest the government about his discharge (paragraph 3). Beyond that, an employee who has attempted, conspired, or incited strikes is subject to up to three years' imprisonment or a fine not to exceed ¥10,000 (National Civil Service Law, Article 110).[19] Participants in a strike in the civil service are likely to be subject, not only to criminal liability, but also to civil liability and disciplinary sanctions.

It is against this background that the right to strike has been such a crucial issue between the government and the unions for the past 15 years or more. Immediately after World War II, civil service employees had the right to strike, and their repeated strikes often hampered the operation of the government and endangered the economic recovery of Japan. Finally the government, supported by a memorandum from the General Headquarters of the Allied Occupations, issued Decree 201 in July 1948. This decree, in addition to denying civil servants the right to back their collective bargaining demands with a strike or any form of collective action (Article 1), stated that if they did engage in such conduct, they would lose their rights under their employment contracts (Article 2). Following the decree, the National Civil Service Law was amended in December 1948 so as to expressly prohibit strikes, slowdowns, and other acts of labor dispute. As a result, any labor dispute that resulted in a work stoppage or slowdown became illegal and anyone participating was subject to legal sanctions. The number and kind of disciplinary penalties enforced against postal workers are shown in table 11.8. The union calls disciplined members "victims" and offers them financial assistance from a special union fund (Yamaguchi 1971, p. 102).

The most critical issue was that, under the amended law, union officials could be held criminally liable for any illegal labor dispute. Zentei, Nikkyōso, Jichirō, and Kokurō brought the problem before the ILO's Committee on Freedom of Association, attacking the government's use of criminal liability rather than disciplinary sanctions. The ILO responded by sending a

Table 11.8
Disciplinary Sanctions against Union Activities
among Civil Service Employees: Postal Workers, 1956–75

Year	Discharge	Suspension	Pay Cut	Reprimand	Warning	All Sanctions
1956	0	128	22	0	5,864	6,014
1957	0	16	13	28	94	151
1958	7	392	513	542	29,556	31,010
1959	0	311	631	172	6,800	7,914
1960	0	187	221	100	11,900	12,408
1961	0	373	1,586	8,024	609	10,592
1962	0	0	0	0	0	0
1963	0	255	291	5,452	136	6,134
1964	0	0	0	0	0	0
1965	11	166	2,781	1,449	1,723	6,130
1966	13	415	1,030	4,081	4,486	10,025
1967	0	143	138	2,253	183	2,717
1968	0	144	2,848	80	3	3,075
1969	2	243	2,662	6,445	36	9,388
1970	8	400	6,666	7,841	490	15,405
1971	0	20	8	140	2	170
1972	3	356	3,242	4,835	9	8,445
1973	20	368	462	5	20,665	21,520
1974	4	210	258	246	424	1,142
1975	9	164	1,722	24,591	142,000	168,486
Total	77	4,291	25,094	66,284	224,980	320,726

Source: Yūseishō 1976b.

subcommission (the Dreyer Commission) to Japan on a fact-finding mission in early 1965, and its report to the ILO was submitted at the end of August 1965. In it, the Dreyer Commission recommended, first, that the government of Japan should recognize its role as employer; second, it should distinguish essential from nonessential government services; and third, it should establish an impartial institution for the protection of the interests of public employees.[20]

Following these recommendations, the Supreme Court revised its position. Originally it had held that, since civil service employees were the servants of the whole community, it was quite appropriate that they should be treated differently from private-enterprise employees; therefore, Decree 201, which deprived them of the right to strike, was not unconstitutional.[21] This view had long prevailed in the courts.

Surprisingly, in the fall of 1966, the Supreme Court stated that the right to strike was to be approved as a rule not only for private-enterprise employees but also for public employees, as the fact that they were servants of the whole community did not deprive them of their right to strike. It added further that the right to strike is not an absolute right, but is subject to inherent restrictions consistent with the national welfare. In conclusion, the court ruled more concretely that in order for such restrictions to be judged constitutional: (1) they should be as limited as possible; (2) in instances where strikes were prohibited, an alternative dispute-settlement procedure should be available to the parties; and (3) the imposition of penal sanctions against those engaging in an ordinary walkout should be a measure of last resort.[22] This first Supreme Court case involved postal workers who were employees of a national enterprise. Similar cases followed in which the plaintiffs were teachers and the court clerks who were either civil servants or local public employees.[23] This series of decisions was called a "thawing" of the Supreme Court.

Only four years later, the court reconsidered these "thawing" decisions and ruled that, as strikes in the public sector are not consistent with the public interest, restrictions imposed on them are fully reasonable from the standpoint of the national welfare,[24] and, in addition, that the National Personnel Authority operates efficiently as a substitute for the right to strike. In effect, the court went almost all the way back to its previous position.

In the meantime, in the fall of 1965 the government entrusted the issue to the Deliberating Council on the Civil Service System, a tripartite committee composed of representatives of management, the unions, and the public. This council presented its report in the fall of 1973, even though it had failed to reach a unanimous recommendation. Instead, it offered three alternatives: (1) to maintain the status quo; (2) to approve the right to strike for civil service employees, except for those at the executive level and those involved in essential services; or (3) to approve the right to strike for all civil servants. Informal advisory committees, which succeeded the council, discussed the problem and again failed to find a solution. In 1976 the Council on Basic Problems of Public Enterprises was formed and assigned the task of finally resolving the issue of the right to strike against the public corporations and national enterprises. In its report, presented to the government in June 1978, it recommended that "in the present situation the right to strike is not to be approved for the time being." Even if this language seems ambiguous and open to different interpretations, it does not seem likely that civil servants will win the right to strike in the near future (Yamaguchi 1978, p. 5).

Other Concerted Activities

Employees of public corporations, especially the National Railways workers, have struck repeatedly during the Spring Offensive, regardless of the prohibition in the existing law. By contrast, there are very few strikes in the civil service proper. Nikkyōso, which formerly was very militant, now seldom calls strikes. Civil service employees do engage in various types of slowdowns—working-to-rule, for example, which has been declared illegal by the Supreme Court.[25] However, because the effort put forth by civil servants on the job is not as great as they claim it is, the effect of a prohibition on collective action would be less damaging than a similar ban in the private sector would be.

A favorite job action is the "ribbon-wearing" tactic—that is, during working hours the employees wear ribbons that usually carry slogans and union propaganda. This collective tactic is a union act, to be distinguished from an individual's wearing of ribbons. At first the courts held that this kind of union activity was not a strike, since it did not involve a work stoppage, but was a legitimate act in labor disputes. Hence, employers could not impose disciplinary penalties.[26] However, the High Court reversed it a few years ago and said that such acts as ribbon-wearing were illegal because they infringed upon the duty of civil servants to give full service (National Civil Service Law 101).[27]

Judging by this reasoning, the decision of the courts may seem very restrictive as far as union activities of civil servants are concerned. Certainly the unions claim that this is so. Yet, in any country the courts do not and cannot stand far from the conscience of the people. The unions in the public sector went on an eight-day strike in the late fall of 1975 to "restore" the right to strike (Yamaguchi 1976a, p. 6). This action was clearly illegal under existing law, and the author believes that it was this strike that went a long way toward destroying popular sympathy for the public employees.[28] At the present time, more than half of the new school employees are not joining Nikkyōso, and the public appears to be demanding the introduction of compulsory retirement in the civil service. The public employees and their unions seem to be at a crossroads.

Notes

1 RKKC 1976, p. 16. This figure was 36.4 percent in 1954, 30.5 percent in 1963, and 26.2 percent in 1972.

2 Murakami v. Japan (Fire Engine case), Supreme Court, Fourth Civil Section, August 31, 1935, *Hōritsu Shimbun* [Law journal], No. 3886, p. 7.

3 The Local Civil Service Law for local government employees was enacted in 1950, and Local Personnel Management Boards, based on this law, were established soon thereafter.

4 These payments are also made to those who did not get a "good performance" rating.

5 Starting pay for university graduates in private enterprises was ¥101,000 per month in May 1978.

6   Yasuda v. Fukunaga (Mukoumachi Post Office case), Supreme Court, I Petty Bench, October 13, 1977, *Bessatsu Rōdō Hōritsu Jumpō* [Biweekly journal of labor law] No. 940, p. 67.

7   The employment of ex-civil servants in private enterprises after their resignation from the civil service is called "stepping down" (*amakudari*). The NPA opens the list to the public every year.

8   Ōsawa v. Japan (Sarufutsu case), Supreme Court, Full Bench, November 6, 1974, *Rōdō Kankei Keiji Saiban Reishū* [Labor law criminal cases] 28:9, p. 393.

9   Decisions are numerous. The Supreme Court decision which approved this trend is Ichikawa v. Nihon Shokuen Co. (Nihon Shokuen case), Supreme Court, II Petty Bench, March 28, 1975, *Minshū*, 29:4, p. 456.

10   *Asahi Shimbun*, December 15, 1977.

11   *Kokkōrō Chōsa Jihō* [Research journal of the public sector unions] No. 182 contains a quantity of rich material on the movement for compulsory retirement.

12   Sakai & Kawano v. Shimonoseki City (Shimonoseki Shōgyōkōkō case), Yamaguchi District Court, Shimonoseki Branch, September 2, 1974, *Rōdō Hanrei* [Labor law cases] No. 213, p. 63.

13   Sakamine et al. v. Osaka City (Osakashi Gakkō Yōmuin case), Osaka District Court, May 24, 1978, *Rōdō Hanrei* [Labor law cases] No. 299, p. 20.

14   Among the requirements for registration, the most important one is to provide a copy of the union rules (National Civil Service Law, Art. 108-3).

15   During the time a union officer is on leave, he is paid by the union. This type of leave must not be confused with a short absence from the job for union activities, mentioned earlier.

16   *Sankei Shimbun*, August 23, 1977.

17   While the ban on unfair labor practices applies to public corporations and national enterprises, it is not applicable to the civil service. The rationale for this distinction is that the government is supposed to be too good an employer to engage in antiunion conduct.

18   On the other hand, local public employees are permitted to conclude an agreement, unless it violates the law or the regulations of the local government.

19   The provisions for local public employees are nearly the same. See Local Civil Service Law, Arts. 37 and 61.

20   International Labor Office 1966, paras. 2134-2156. The summary is found in para. 2248 et seq.

21   Japan v. Hasegawa et al. (National Railways Hirosaki Kikanku case), Supreme Court, Full Bench, April 8, 1953, *Rōdō Kankei Keiji Saiban Reishū* [Labor law criminal cases] 7:4, p. 775. This case was heard at a time when employees of the National Railways were considered to be civil servants.

22   Japan v. Sotoyama et al. (Zentei Tokyo Central Post Office case), Supreme Court, Full Bench, October 26, 1966, *Rōdō Kankei Keiji Saiban Reishū* 20:8, p. 901.

23   The teachers' case was Japan v. Hasegawa et al. (Tokyo Teachers' Union case), Supreme Court, Full Bench, April 2, 1969, *Rōdō Kankei Keiji Saiban Reishū* 23:5, p. 305; the clerks of the court case was Japan v. Sakane et al. (Zenshiho case), Supreme Court, Full Bench, April 2, 1969, *Rōdō Kankei Keiji Saiban Reishū* 23:5, p. 685.

24 Japan v. Tsuruzono et al. (Zennōrin case), Supreme Court, Full Bench, April 25, 1973, *Rōdō Kankei Keiji Saiban Reishū* 27:4, p. 547.

25 Katō et al. v. Japan National Railways (Dōrō Takaski Chihon case), Tokyo High Court, March 29, 1977, *Rōdō Hanrei* [Labor law cases] No. 276, p. 41.

26 Kurita et al. v. Japan (Nada Post Office case), Kobe District Court, April 6, 1968, *Rōdō Kankei Minji Saiban Reishū* [Labor civil law cases] 18:2, p. 302. The sanction given in this case was a warning.

27 Japan v. Kurita et al. (Nada Post Office case), Osaka High Court, January 30. 1976, *Rōdō Kankei Minji Saiban Reishū* 27:1, p. 18.

28 As for the claim for damages, see Yamaguchi 1976b, p. 6.

12 *Shigeyoshi Tokunaga*

A Marxist Interpretation of Japanese Industrial Relations, with Special Reference to Large Private Enterprises

The seniority wage system (nenkō), lifetime employment, and enterprise unionism are generally considered the three major characteristics of Japanese industrial relations. These terms certainly are convenient in attempting to explain Japan's system, but it should be noted that their meaning varies according to the writer who is using them, as does the explanation of the factors that led to their adoption. In addition, their meaning should not be thought of as having remained static, for the content and significance of the terms have changed as Japanese capitalism has evolved. In this chapter the author will discuss how the present industrial relations system developed and will describe its present structure and character. First, we shall review briefly the significance of the postwar reforms that shaped the framework of the present system.

The Postwar Crisis and Reforms

The most important of the postwar reforms initiated by the Allied Occupation—the democratization of the economic system, agricultural land reform, and promotion of trade union organization—created drastic changes in Japanese capitalism as it had existed in the prewar period.[1] These changes, of course, were made within a capitalist framework and did correct several defects of prewar Japanese capitalism, converting it into a more rational form.[2] For example, land reform, which enabled farmers to own their own small parcels of land, put an end to serious tenancy disputes and served to stabilize agricultural class relations in Japan (Tanaka 1976). It also contributed indirectly to economic growth since the increased number of independent farmers continued to be a rich source of labor for industry and the upgrading of the farm standard of living expanded the domestic market for industrial goods. The disbanding of the zaibatsu (the large industrial and financial complexes) fostered economic competition and produced one of the preconditions for the high rate of economic growth in the following decades.

The labor movement was much encouraged by the Supreme Commander for the Allied Powers (SCAP) in the early period of the Occupation, but as soon as symptoms were observed that the social order might be disrupted by Communist activities, promotion turned into restraint. The first clear case of this was SCAP's prohibition of the February 1 General Strike in 1947 (more fully described in chapter 13). In July 1948, the government denied government employees the right to strike, in accordance with SCAP's "directive," and the right to strike of employees of the public corporations (the National Railways, the Postal Service, Nippon Telegraph and Telephone, etc.) remains a crucial controversial issue today. The denial of this right doubtless weakens the bargaining power of trade unions and is evidence of the Japanese government's negative or conservative attitude toward the trade union movement. The change in American policy brought about by the Cold War further intensified this conservative tendency. The government's deflation policy of 1949 led to mass layoffs, during which the employers, supported implicitly and explicitly by SCAP, dismissed Communists and their sympathizers (Takemae 1970, pp. 240–45). In the same year the Trade Union Law was amended, the fundamental aims being to contain union activities within a narrowly defined framework and to restrain their political radicalization.

Many collective agreements concluded just after the war provided for far-reaching union rights. For example, the agreement concluded in 1946 at the Nihon Kōkan (Japan Steel Tube Company) had the following provisions: (1) decisions concerning the standards and principles of hiring and discipline of employees had to be negotiated with the union; (2) decisions on discharge, transfer, and the adoption and alteration of supervisory systems were matters for consultation with the union; and (3) the company approved in principle the right of union officers to engage in union activities during working hours (Orii 1973, pp. 164–65). In contrast, after enactment of the 1949 amendments to the Trade Union Act, which denied the validity of existing collective agreements that had no time limits, the employers joined in denouncing agreements that provided for broad union rights; there followed a "period of no collective agreements."

The contents of collective agreements concluded after this period were quite different. In them, the employers' "right to manage" was clearly prescribed, and there were few, if any, provisions requiring union approval of personnel matters. Furthermore, qualifications for union membership were narrowly defined, so that managerial personnel were excluded from the union.

Although many unions were organized on an enterprise basis prior to 1949, they also pursued objectives beyond the individual enterprises and at times were very militant. However, in 1950 the Occupation carried out a "red purge." With the outbreak of the Korean War, business had begun to recover and the postwar economic crisis was brought under control.

It was also around 1948–49 that Sanbetsu Kaigi, the All-Japan Congress of Industrial Unions, controlled by the Communist Party, began to lose union support. Hoping to restrain union militancy, SCAP backed the formation of Sōhyō, the new General Council of Trade Unions of Japan, to replace the tottering Congress as the leading confederation of the trade union movement. However, Sōhyō was not to remain compliant, as SCAP had hoped, for very long.

The Period of Transition

It was some time before the new framework created by the reforms began to work very well. The unions fiercely resisted the measures of the Occupation, the government, and managements, considering them to be reactionary and repressive. However, they were defeated in almost all the major strikes carried out in the leading companies in each industry—for example, at Hitachi Electrical Machine Company (1950), Toyota (1951), Nissan (1953), and Nihon Steel Muroran Works (1954). With each of these defeats, many active unionists as well as ordinary workers were discharged, and the managements succeeded in changing the character of the unions from militancy to cooperation. A reaction against union militancy arose as well from another direction. Four unions, but principally the seamen's and the textile workers unions, affiliated with Sōhyō, criticized Sōhyō's political unionism within Sōhyō's governing council in 1952, and in 1954 this group organized a new national center, Zenrō, that followed a more moderate line. Later, as the new national center developed, it changed its name to Dōmei, Japanese Confederation of Labor, in 1964.

In short, the present cooperative enterprise unions came into existence as a result of the defeats of unions that were bold enough to carry out long-term strikes against the discharge of their members. This fact implies that, contrary to common belief, enterprise unions originally were not cooperative in their attitude toward management, but were born in the course of bitter struggles. Moreover, the lifetime employment system was not prescribed in collective agreements, but existed only by custom (cf. Takahashi 1965); thus, if a management considered a situation serious, it could dismiss even regular employees (*honkō*).

The bitter industrial struggles carried on until about 1955 had a significant impact on both sides. For management, the stabilization of industrial relations was essential in the large companies that had already begun rationalization plans using foreign technology and were intending to invest in such facilities on a much greater scale. These technological changes precipitated a drastic reform of the management of the labor force. In the main, it consisted of the adoption of a new foreman system (*sagyōchō*), the enrichment and expansion of company education programs, the adoption of wage systems based on job evaluation, and utilization of joint prior consultation (*jizen kyōgisei*).

Among these, the sagyōchō system was the most important. The objective of this system was to exert greater control over the workers at the workshop level by giving the sagyōchō, or new foreman, the added responsibility of supervising the workgroup in addition to his production-management function. The new function included the primary assessment of workers for promotion and wage increases and recommending or selecting them for transfer or training courses. The new foremen themselves were selected from among employees who demonstrated, in an examination, a relatively high competence in English, mathematics, physics, and chemistry. This promotion plan, with its stress on written tests, was intended, on the one hand, to promote a new type of foreman who would be able to handle the more sophisticated production methods. At the same time, it was designed to foster competition among workers and to divert their interest from solidarity with their fellow employees to competition for promotion and success.

The objectives of the various company training courses were the same. In such courses, employees were, and are, given not only the technical information they need to carry out their jobs, but also a thorough indoctrination in enterprise consciousness—"loyalty to the company." They usually are asked to take tests or to write reports at the end of the course, and the results are considered in personnel assessment. Education within the enterprise has two aspects, technological and ideological, and one should not underestimate the importance of the latter. The adoption of job evaluation was intended to amend the extreme living-wage character of the seniority wage system by increasing the relative weight accorded to the nature of the job in determining a worker's wages.

On the trade union side, the leaders, after being defeated by the large companies in the prolonged major strikes, felt keenly that the defects of the enterprise unions had to be corrected. A principal problem was that the bargaining power of the individual enterprise unions was handicapped by the members' fear of damaging the competitive position of the firms employing them. One plan devised to counter this was the concerted Spring Offensive, which aimed at giving the enterprise unions bargaining power similar to that of industrial unions, by standardizing demands as far as possible at the industrial level and then presenting them simultaneously. The Spring Offensive was begun in 1955 by eight federations of private-sector unions, who later were joined by the public-sector unions as well as others in the private sector. It is well known that the Spring Offensive has become the dominant wage-determination mechanism in Japan.

Another fault of enterprise unions that needed to be rectified was their lack of power at the workshop level. A proposal to enhance that power was presented in Sōhyō's 1958 "Draft for Organization Programme" (see Rōdōshō, Rōseikyoku 1959, pp. 800–803). The draft was an ambitious plan to transfer the so-called three union rights—to bargain, to order strikes, and to conclude agreements—to the workshops in order to establish them firmly at that level and eventually to make the workers themselves "masters in the workshop" (Hyōdō 1977). However, the idea was not approved at the Sōhyō Congress. Soon after, the famous strike at the Mitsui-Miike coal mine began. The Miike Coal Miners' Union was regarded at that time as the strongest union in Japan and as a model of "workshop-struggle" activity. But the strike ended in 1960 with the miners' defeat. After this, a view which simply denied or avoided the "workshop-struggle" idea gained support among union leaders, and the attempt to strengthen enterprise unions by this means was, for all practical purposes, abandoned. At the Sōhyō Congress in 1961, "workshop-struggle" was still retained as a slogan, but stress was placed on the "struggle for conversion of government policy" and the "struggle for joint prior consultation" in the actual schedule of action (Rōdōshō, Rōseikyoku 1961, pp.994–98).

The consequences of these developments should be clear. At the workshop level, the workers were firmly under management's control as company men, whereas union activities at that level progressively lost their effectiveness. The result was a situation in which unions could hardly resist and regulate effectively management's introduction of new technology, a reorganization of working systems, or a drive to increase production. It is only a slight exaggeration to say that the main function of trade unions had become limited to using the Spring Offensive to regain a part of the returns from rapidly increasing production through wage increases and a shortening of the hours of labor. In the following sections we will examine this aspect in more detail.

Some Problems of the Spring Offensive

The level of wages in Japan has increased markedly since the beginning of her postwar economic boom. Nominal wages in manufacturing industries increased tenfold and real wages 3.05 times during the 20 years from 1955 to 1975 (Rōdōshō 1977, Appendix pp.8–9). The rate of increase per year was about 12 percent and 5.7 percent, respectively. Hours of work per week declined from an average of 48.1 in 1960 to 40.3 in 1976, but Japan is still behind other industrialized countries with regard to paid holidays and vacations. The 5-day workweek has begun to be adopted but is not yet the rule; the percentage of employees who enjoyed a 5-day workweek was only 23.6 percent in 1976. Annual paid vacations averaged 13.4 days in the same year, but employees in fact used only 8.2 days.[3]

Nevertheless, the difference in nominal money wages between Japan and Western European countries narrowed or partly reversed over this period, and it can be said that in this sense Sōhyō's slogan of 1963, "Wages as high as in Europe," has been nearly realized. However, when one considers the real purchasing power of Japanese wages, these nominal gains must be discounted to a large extent.

Does this mean that Japanese trade unions have functioned well? The author wishes to examine this question from two dimensions: the national level, centering on the Spring Offensive, and the workshop level.

In appraising the role of the Spring Offensive as a wage-determination mechanism, we must bear in mind the following problems. First, we cannot simply ascribe this remarkable increase in wage levels to union bargaining power. There are many differing opinions about what factors determine wages, and it is difficult to say how much influence each has, in fact, exerted. It is well known that the enterprises' enormous demand for young manpower resulted in an increase in the level of all wages. Because of this labor market factor, trade unions were more effective initially in spreading wage increases to other categories of workers, but their relative weakness is suggested by the fact that the rate of increase in wages has slowed since 1975 at the same time that the demand for labor was diminishing.[4]

Second, wage increases did not fundamentally damage the capital accumulation structure of the Japanese economy, which has made a high accumulation rate possible. Traditionally, labor's relative share in Japan has been much lower than that in other industrial countries (see table 12.1), and the long-term trend has been to keep it low (table 12.2). In fact, with the exception of 1965, labor's relative share declined constantly until 1970. In other words, the yields of enterprises and employers' incomes increased more than wages have increased.[5]

Table 12.1
Comparison of Labor's Relative Share, 1971

Country	%
Australia	52.6
Canada	52.3
Italy	43.8
Japan	34.6
Sweden	52.6
United Kingdom	53.4
United States	45.8

Source: Nihon Chingin Kenkyū Sentā 1976, p. 347. Original figures taken from the UN publication, "The Growth of World Industry," 1972 edition.
Note: Gross added value and wages of establishment were used. Australia and U.K. figures are for 1970.

Table 12.2
Labor's Relative Share, Wages, and Productivity, 1960, 1965-74

Year	Labor's Relative Share (net)	Money Wages	Real Wages	Productivity of Labor
1960	35.0	100.0	100.0	100.0
1965	38.6	161.7	119.5	144.3
1966	35.7	180.7	127.0	163.1
1967	34.0	204.5	138.3	190.0
1968	34.1	234.7	150.8	217.2
1969	33.9	273.3	166.7	249.6
1970	34.0	321.5	182.1	284.4
1971	37.2	365.6	195.3	303.5
1972	37.7	423.5	216.4	329.9
1973	35.5	523.5	239.3	396.2
1974	37.3	662.1	243.2	NA

Source: Tōkei Shiryō Kenkyūkai 1978, 2:57.
Note: Original figures on labor's net relative share are based on Japan Ministry of International Trade and Industry, *Census of Manufactures, Manufacturing Industries.* Money wages, real wages, and productivity are for manufacturing industries only.
NA: Data not available.

Third, labor productivity increased markedly during this period. Thus, wage costs in manufacturing tended to decline until 1968, after which they leveled off or increased slightly. The increase in productivity was, needless to say, brought about by the rationalization of production facilities. This process not only meant technical changes, but also implied the reorganization of the systems for managing the workforce, such as changes in workforce composition, in the organization of work, in the allocation of manpower, etc. The increased productivity was accompanied by an increase in labor intensity because trade union control over working conditions was very weak, as we shall see later. Since the late 1960s, management has placed priority on investment in facilities that would require less manpower and adopted a policy of making the fullest possible use of each worker (*nōryoku shugi kanri*). Wage increases and fewer hours of labor were realized in exchange for this rationalization and intensification of labor.

Fourth, although trade unions made a number of demands in the Spring Offensive, the principal one was for wage increases and the others were of secondary importance. In the process of rapid economic growth, many problems unrelated to wage increases arose: pollution, housing,[6] inflation, the rising education level (now most middle school students go on to high school), and so on. (Problems of the labor force itself, such as work intensification, have already been pointed out.) Hence, wage increases no longer resulted in a rise in the standard of living, and differences remained between Japan and European industrialized countries in the level of social security systems (see table 12.3). In 1973, Sōhyō extended Spring Offensive demands to encompass these wider aims (the "People's Spring Offensive"—*kokumin shuntō*), but little was attained in the way of results except for the introducton

Table 12.3

An International Comparison of Social Security Expenditures, 1970, 1971

(percentage)

Country	Year	Ratio of Expenditure on Social Security Benefits to		Contribution to Total Social Security Benefits by		
		Gross Domestic Consumption	Total Consumption	Insured	Employer	State
Holland	1971	20.2	27.4	38.5	43.0	9.2
Sweden	1971	20.1	26.2	10.5	26.5	28.8
Italy	1971	16.9	21.4	14.4	61.8	18.8
West Germany	1971	16.3	22.9	29.2	42.9	24.4
France	1970	13.9	19.5	13.8	70.2	6.8
United Kingdom	1970	13.2	16.5	19.9	24.9	45.2
United States	1970	9.8	11.8	22.9	32.4	25.9
Japan	1970	5.0	8.4	27.0	29.6	25.0
	1975	(8.2)	NA	NA	64.0	(27.8)
India	1970	2.0	2.4			2.9

Source: Kenkō Hoken Rengōkai 1978, pp. 356–57, 362, 468–69.
NA: Data not available.

of an indexation system for old-age pensions. Of course, these problems cannot be solved by trade unions alone, since their solutions are mainly the responsibility of government and the political parties. Therefore, although the government's procrastination on social welfare issues and its preferential policy toward industries and enterprises should be held largely responsible for the deplorable neglect of the issues of pollution, social security, etc., the trade unions must share the blame because of their weak stand on these matters.

Fifth, with the development and institutionalization of the Spring Offensive system, collective bargaining has become remote from the workshop level. Formerly there was much more discussion in the workshops about what the union demands should be, and the bargaining process was more or less positively backed by the rank and file. Now union leaders settle on the demands without consulting the rank and file, and the latter are informed only post facto in writing.[7] Communications between union leaders and the membership have diminished and become stereotyped, and bargaining often takes place "behind closed doors," without resort to supporting mass actions.

A good example is the case of large companies in the iron and steel industry. The *ippatsu kaitō* (literally, the first and final reply—a "take it or leave it" offer), like "Boulwarism" in the General Electric Company, has become the established wage-determination mechanism. In these situations, management has the final say on wages, but before management makes its decision, official and unofficial negotiations with the union take place (Ishida 1976, ch. 6). Since the establishment of this system in 1965, the five largest companies in the iron and steel industry have not experienced any strikes. Thus, wage negotiations in many monopolistic large enterprises seem to be an event far removed from the rank and file.

Industrial Relations in the Workshops

The union organization at the plant level characteristically is based on the enterprise's managerial units—the plant, section, division, and so on; in other words, there is considerable overlap in the two organizations. Moreover, it is common for low-ranking supervisors, such as a sagyōchō and kōchō (group leader), or a candidate recommended by management to be elected an officer of local union branches in large enterprises. In either case, most posts in local branches are occupied by people who are loyal to their enterprise.[8] It may be in a sense natural that low-ranking supervisors are elected, for they usually have served longer with the company and have more experience, but the problem remains nonetheless that they are supervisors and the executors of management's will within the workshop. Their principal function is to pursue management's interests, not those of the union. To their minds, union activities are subordinate to the interests of management. Thus, it is not unusual to find in some cases that a union has become an important element of the enterprise's management of the workforce and operates as a subsidiary to it.

Therefore, the unions' effectiveness in controlling management policy is minimal. For example, agreements between unions and managements on transfers, promotions, wage increases, the introduction of new technology, and methods of production are so general and vague that they are applied very elastically, and the union impact in these areas is usually weak. A manager of one large steel company said: "I have been in charge of labor management here since 1953, but I have the impression that unions nowadays [1970] can no longer say what they want to. I feel somewhat impatient. It would be better for the unions to be more straightforward in their demands" (Nihon Rōdō Kyōkai 1975, p.194).

There has been one exception to this trend: unions have resisted strongly the discharge of their members, all of whom are regular workers, and on occasion such discharges have led to major strikes. Therefore, a management will dismiss regular employees only after it has tried to adjust employment by other methods, for example, by cutting overtime, transfers, and/or discharge of nonregular workers. The "lifetime employment" system for regular workers depends upon the existence of a corps of part-time workers, workers on subcontract (shagaikō) or employed by subcontracting enterprises, and seasonal laborers from the country (dekasegi). However, the system exists only as traditional practice, and there is no rule, like the American seniority principle, written into collective agreements in Japan. Thus the possibility remains that active unionists might be discharged for various reasons, but large companies usually would not take such an imprudent step. Of the regular employees, those most susceptible to discharge are older workers receiving relatively high wages.

The emasculation of trade unions was one of the preconditions for the extremely rapid increases in productivity and labor intensity in Japanese industry that began in the late 1950s. In particular, since the late 1960s, this emasculation has facilitated the efforts of Nikkeiren (Japan Federation of Employers' Associations) to implement and expand management systems designed to produce the utmost efficiency of labor (nōryoku shugi kanri).

One aspect of this effort has been the spread of wage systems based on ability (nōryoku shikakukyū) at the expense of job-ranking plans (Nikkeiren 1969, pp. 2, 7–8; 1971, p.11). Ability-qualification plans are more effective than pure seniority systems in securing labor efficiency, since the former increases the part of wages that is determined by management's assessment and evokes more competition among workers.

Job-ranking and job-evaluation plans had been introduced to some extent previously. However, it became increasingly difficult to apply these wage systems beginning in the late 1960s when companies, in response to the labor shortage, began training regular employees as multiskilled workers (*tanōkō*) who could be used in several different skilled jobs. For example, at the Mitsubishi Nagasaki dockyard every regular worker was required to become qualified in welding, gas-cutting, and crane-operating, irrespective of his trade. Under this system the employer can reduce idle time and thereby increase the intensity of labor. The frequent transfer of workers from one job to another, regardless of their qualifications, also made it difficult to extend wage systems based on job-ranking or seniority.

Here the author would like to emphasize especially the importance of personnel assessment as an element of the new ability-based wage systems. This assessment is apt to include not only objective elements, but also such subjective or vague ones as "contribution to the enterprise," especially in firms where the unions are weak. It is not unusual for such factors as a "worker's attitude toward learning after working hours" or "good personal relations in the workshop" to be considered in the assessment.[9] Many workers do not even know on what standard their wages are calculated.[10] The earlier nenkō system extracted from workers their maximum service to the enterprise through discrimination in the assessments of ability. In this sense the nenkō system is far from irrational, since management finds it very useful. Therefore, the new system for workforce management (nōryoku shugi kanri), advocated by Nikkeiren, does not completely replace the nenkō system, but is intended to modify it by making the "seniority-ranking" aspects only one of the factors used in assessing ability (Nikkeiren 1969, pp. 48–49).

Since the latter half of the 1960s, management also has attached great importance to motivation management through small study groups such as Quality Control (QC) and Zero Defect (ZD) circles (see table 12.4). This was one of management's measures to counter the decline in enterprise consciousness among young employees under the conditions of full employment. Whether an employee participates in the circle or not is, in principle, based on his free will, but participation becomes in fact semicompulsory and often is a factor considered in personnel assessment.[11]

According to two union studies of workers' attitudes toward some of these management systems, one-third of the workers surveyed answered that they "become busier and feel mentally burdened." On the other hand, only 7–10 percent of them responded that they "feel a sense of active participation in the work" (see table 12.5). These studies seem to show that these new management techniques increased the intensity of labor but that the enterprise

Table 12.4
Adoption of Motivation Management Methods by Enterprises, 1968, 1974
(percentage)

	1968	1974	
		Total	Companies Employing over 5,000
Motivation management	36.8	40.1[a]	53.8
Small groups			
Quality Control (QC)	26.1	39.3	50.5
Zero Defect (ZD)	23.2	25.8	46.2
Group for suggesting improvements	23.2	41.3	61.3
Others	0	12.9	38.7

Source: Nikkeiren 1975, pp. 4, 28–29.

[a]Of all enterprises which introduced this management technique, 42.5 percent used it as a factor in personnel assessment.

Table 12.5
Union Members' Evaluation of Motivation Control, 1970
(QC Circles and ZD Circles)

	Steel Workers' Federation (%)	Chemical Workers' Federation (%)
Become busy and feel mentally burdened	32	36
Feel somewhat burdened, but can cope	39	30
Feel sense of active involvement in the work	10	7
Don't know	14	20
No answer	5	7

Source: Ishikawa 1975, p. 88.

did not necessarily succeed in enhancing the employees' willingness to work harder.

In short, trade unions are integrated into the organization of the enterprises from the bottom up and do very little in fulfilling their primary functions of acting as a check on management actions and exerting some control over working conditions, whereas the enterprises practice various systems of workforce management to intensify the workers' enterprise consciousness.

Moreover, the relatively favorable conditions of regular workers in large enterprises sustain a so-called "enterprise-egoism" and serve to contain their

Table 12.6
Worker Dissatisfactions and Anxieties with Workshop Life
in the Big Steel Companies, 1976

	Nippon (Kimitsu)		Nihon Kōkan (Fukuyama)		Sumitomo (Kashima)		Kawasaki (Mizushima)		Kōbe (Kakogawa)	
	Rank	%	Rank	%	Rank	%	Rank	%	Rank	%
A. Low wages	I	37.5	II	35.7	I	37.5	I	52.4	I	45.7
B. Poor working conditions	II	30.2	I	37.9	II	35.2	II	37.7	III	29.3
C. Overwork due to undermanning	III	29.1	IV	25.5	III	33.3	III	28.9	II	38.2
D. Unfairness in promotion and wage increases	IV	18.2		8.2		5.0		9.8		8.8
E. Strict time and cost management	V	16.8		9.2		9.3		14.1		10.3
F. Possibilities of accidents and occupational diseases		14.2	III	29.9	IV	24.3	IV	24.4	V	18.9
G. Monotonous jobs, little chance to improve knowledge and skill		16.3	V	15.2		11.8		8.9		8.8
H. Difficult to take holidays and vacation fully		11.4		14.1	V	16.7	V	15.0	IV	24.7

Source: Tekkōrōren 1977, p. 122. This research was done in January 1976 and covered about 5,000 workers.
Note: Each worker was allowed three choices.

interests within internal enterprise affairs. Such an atmosphere naturally makes it difficult for class consciousness to penetrate, much less spread, amongst the working class.

Of course this does not mean that workers are completely satisfied with their enterprises. Even workers in large companies have many complaints (see table 12.6), and it is noteworthy that the most common ones are the growing intensity of labor (items C, F, and H) as well as low wages. Their dissatisfactions, however, are not organized by the trade unions nor directed into a positive counterenterprise force.[12]

Workers also express dissatisfaction with the present state of their unions, some of it in the form of strong criticism of union activities that they consider weak-willed and indecisive. Leftist minority unions are one explicit source of this criticism. The so-called New Left groups came to the fore in the latter part of the 1960s mainly among students who carried on radical political struggles in universities and on the streets.[13] The movement soon declined, but a few workers influenced by the New Left ideology formed their own trade unions, usually as minority groups, in several enterprises. Apart from New Left groups, there are other minority unions which are still affiliated with Sōhyō. Workers who were unwilling to join a less militant union, generally affiliated with Dōmei, formed these unions when a union split occurred during a strike or when there was a company amalgamation. Left-wing minority unions of both types are very small, but they seem to have established themselves on the scene.[14] Although the minority unions also take the form of enterprise unions, they advocate class solidarity and engage in various kinds of actions such as protection of nonregular workers and control of and check on promotions, safety, and other enterprise activities.

However, despite the emergence of the New Left groups, the discontent felt by workers and their criticisms of the unions' present state are generally not yet strong enough to force significant changes in the policies of the main body of unions and to alter their course from docile cooperation to a more self-assertive line. In addition, management itself, as well as the unions, reacts sensitively to worker discontent and copes with problems before they become serious, which is one of the reasons that workers' discontent does not assume a more explicit form. Moreover, enterprise unions have a weak point in that they are organized only by regular employees whose relative security depends on the existence of the so-called fringe labor force—the shagaikō (workers employed by firms outside of the one in which they work), temporary and part-time laborers, and the external subcontracting firms. The position of regular employees is relatively favorable compared with that of the fringe labor force, and this situation makes it rather difficult for enterprise unions to alter drastically their course of action on their own initiative. Such a change would make it necessary for the enterprise unions to organize the fringe labor force and to accept these other workers as equal members, which would mean that the regular employees would have to give up voluntarily their own privileged position.

Conclusion

Relatively stable industrial relations have been achieved in Japan since the defeat of the trade unions in several crucial disputes in leading enterprises.[15] Since then, in the period of high economic growth, the unions have concentrated mainly on problems of wages and hours, as symbolized by the Spring Offensive.

The program to intensify the "struggle at the workshop level," which aimed at remedying some weaknesses of enterprise unions, was not generally implemented, although some unions did try it. Union political activities have been remarkably infrequent since the movement opposing the Japan–United States Security Treaty of 1960; the only exceptions have been during election campaigns for the National Diet and local councils.

The lack of union activity at the workship level made it possible for the managements to carry out their rationalization plans smoothly, thereby increasing productivity and labor intensity.

The level of wages did rise remarkably over this period, mainly because of the enormous demand for labor during the period of high economic growth. But we should not forget that these wage increases were realized at the cost of severe rationalization and an increase in labor intensity. An enterprise's management of the workforce has come to penetrate all corners of a factory and to neutralize union activity; in some cases a union has even collaborated with the enterprise and undertaken subordinate management functions. This tendency toward harmony has resulted in an increase in worker apathy toward unionism and, at times, even in their strong criticism of union leaders. In the late 1960s and early 1970s, a strong radical student movement mounted struggles for political and social as well as educational reforms. The movement faded rapidly, at least superficially, but small groups of workers influenced by it or other movements remain as leftist minority unions in a few enterprises.

Since the late 1960s, various major problems resulting from Japan's high economic growth have begun to become apparent—for example, the deterioration of living and environmental conditions through pollution, declines in housing standards, traffic problems, inflation, and the growing intensity as well as monotony of labor. This led Sōhyō to organize and advocate a "Standard of Living Struggle" (*seikatsu tōsō*) and then the People's Spring Offensive (*kokumin shuntō*), but neither could be called successful. Rather, with the present depression, "anxiety about employment" has increased and the rate of annual wage increases has declined every year since the Spring Offensive of 1975. Such poor results, deemed "defeats" by many unions, have intensified a sense of crisis among union leaders. A reorganization of unions seems to be inevitable in the near future.

If Japanese trade unions wish to emerge from their present blind alley, they will have to mount a struggle to effect a change in the basic accumulation structure of Japanese capitalism; they cannot continue to operate within a sphere that never threatens it. As a first step in this direction, it will be necessary for the unions to begin to check on workshop management's more or less arbitrary decisions on such matters as promotion, assessment, and overtime and to reconstruct a basis for worker solidarity.

Notes

1 These policies led the Japanese Communist Party (JCP) at first to define the Occupation Forces as "Emancipation Forces." However, this definition was criticized by the Cominform in 1950, and the party then changed the definition completely: Japan, they argued, was a subordinate country of the United States. A national emancipation movement like that in colonial countries then became the JCP's principal aim.

2 Marxists belonging to the *Kōzaha* (literally, Lectures School) defined prewar Japanese capitalism as Emperor-absolutism and emphasized its "militaristic and semifeudalistic" character. They saw as its fundamental problem the "semifeudalistic landownership" in agriculture. According to Yamada, the level of wages in Japanese industry was below that of India. Cf. Yamada 1934 and also Hirano 1934. This school's view was based fundamentally on the Comintern's 1932 definition of Japanese problems and tried to justify that analysis. The JCP accepted this thesis.

   Another Marxist school, *Rōnōha* (literally, Labor and Peasant School), criticized the Kōzaha view. It emphasized the capitalistic elements of Japanese society, viewing the economic and social system as fundamentally capitalistic. Cf. Sakisaka 1937, 1947. Many academics who belonged to this school became the "brain trust" of the Japan Socialist Party.

   The author assumes that both Kōzaha and Rōnōha were incorrect, or at least inadequate. For the author's methodological views on labor problems, see Tokunaga 1970, ch. 6.

3 Ministry of Labor, Bureau of Statistics and Information 1977. There is a tendency among employees not to take their full vacations. This is due partly to their lack of awareness of their rights and partly to their solicitude for their colleagues.

4 The rates of wage increase were 32.2 percent in 1974, 13.7 percent in 1975, 8.8 percent in 1976, 8.8 percent in 1977, and 5.9 percent in 1978.

5 After 1971 the relative share began to increase gradually. But this was due to the decrease in the added value of the firms owing to the recession rather than to wage increases.

6 For example, the price of a house with 3 rooms and a small amount of land (110 square meters) was about 2.6 times average annual earnings in 1960; it rose to about 4.5 times earnings in 1974. Housing is one of the most serious problems in Japan.

Relation between the Price of Housing and Annual Earnings
(¥ in thousands)

	1960	1965	1970	1974
A. Housing prices[a]	1,260	3,040	5,410	11,511
B. Annual earnings[b]	490	880	1,450	2,550
A/B	2.57	3.45	3.73	4.51

Source: Japan, Economic Planning Agency 1977, p. 153.

[a]The house is 55 square meters: 3 rooms and dining kitchen, with land (110 square meters) in Tokyo and surrounding district.

[b]Annual family earnings of employees in large cities.

7   "Once the executive members used to come to our shop and hold meetings, but recently no one comes any more. Instead of meetings, we only get notices of their decisions. Everything is run as if it was a business," said one steel worker (Tekkōrōren 1971, p. 34).

8   For big business in the steel industry, see Tekkōrōren 1971, p. 46; Saitō 1974, ch. 4. For Toyota Motor Co., see Kamata 1973, p. 211. For the case of a big electromachine company, see Kawanishi 1978, supplementary chapter.

9   For the case of one big motor company, see Yamamoto 1978.

10 See, for an example, Tekkōrōren 1971, pp. 10, 41.

11 For example, Saitō (1974, pp. 38 ff.) reported this policy in the case of Sumitomo Chemical Workers.

12 Although the collective bargaining agreements of enterprise unions stipulate precise grievance procedures, many workers do not file their grievances with their trade unions (see the table below). The grievances are often settled by the management through their supervisory channels. Sometimes the joint consultation committees deal with the problems. But in most cases workers do nothing, even if they feel dissatisfied.

Workers' Reactions to Dissatisfaction with Work and Working Conditions
(percentage)

Type of Problem	Enterprise Union	Prefer Doing Nothing	Consult			
			In the Workshop	With Supervisors	With the Trade Union	No Answer
Manning and allocation	Nippon Steel	42.7	21.3	21.6	3.7	10.7
	Nihon Kōkan	47.4	26.5	18.1	4.1	3.9
	Sumitomo Steel	43.7	23.9	21.9	2.0	8.5
Overtime	Nihon Steel	39.6	36.2	12.4	1.7	10.2
	Nihon Kōkan	41.8	33.9	17.2	1.7	5.4
	Sumitomo Steel	40.2	33.1	16.2	2.2	8.2
Quality of work	Nihon Steel	38.3	32.4	17.7	1.3	10.3
	Nihon Kōkan	36.7	41.2	15.8	1.1	5.2
	Sumitomo Steel	35.6	37.0	17.9	1.3	8.2

Source: Extracted from Tekkōrōren 1977, p. 127.

13 The most detailed work on the New Left's labor movement is Totsuka et al. 1976.

14 It is difficult to state figures on the present condition of all minority unions. Kawanishi (1978, pp. 27, 79) estimates that cases where plural unions exist within one enterprise constitute about 15 percent of the total number of unions affiliated with Sōhyō and that average membership per union is 113.

15 Some aspects of industrial relations in the public sector and in small and medium-sized enterprises are quite different. See chapters 4, 10, and 11.

13 *Taishiro Shirai*

Japanese Labor Unions and Politics

Introduction

A widespread impression among foreign observers is that Japanese unionism is a type of political unionism, placing more emphasis on political strategies than on such economic activities as collective bargaining and grievance handling to achieve better working and living conditions for union members. These foreign observers also seem to be impressed by the strong influence of Marxism or Marxism-Leninism on Japanese union ideology; some of them have concluded that at least a major part of the Japanese labor movement is Communist-dominated and far removed from democratic trade unionism as developed in Western industrialized societies. Such evaluations have hindered, until very recently, any mutual understanding or exchange between the AFL–CIO (American Federation of Labor–Congress of Industrial Organizations) and Sōhyō, the country's largest union center. The purpose of this chapter is to describe briefly what the actual relationships are between the unions and political parties in Japan and to explain how they have developed and evolved. Some conjectures on prospects for the future will be presented in the final section.

The foreign observers do have some grounds for their evaluation of Japanese unionism as politically oriented. Japanese labor organizations first displayed what appeared to be "Communist-dominated political unionism" in a general strike scheduled for February 1, 1947, and averted only by the order of the Supreme Commander for the Allied Powers (SCAP). This general strike, organized by the Communist-led Sanbetsu Kaigi (All Japan Congress of Industrial Unions), was joined by millions of unionists, including those in such basic industries as railways, the postal service, telecommunications, and coal mining, all indispensable at the time for people living in a war-devastated country. Although the general strike was organized as a struggle of the rank and file to improve their working conditions, the real aim was to overthrow the incumbent conservative government and to establish a "Democratic People's Government" composed of left-wing Socialist, Communist, and union leaders who were then advocating social revolution.

Following this abortive general strike, the policy of the Allied Occupation toward the radical, leftist-oriented labor movement stiffened, leading to the SCAP order of 1948 which deprived civil servants and employees of government-owned enterprises of the right to strike. This action was followed by the "red purge" in 1950, immediately after the outbreak of the Korean War, when more than ten thousand Communist and other leftist union activists were ousted from their positions.

In the meantime, anti-Communist leaders at various levels of the labor unions organized the "Union Democratization Alliance," and, with the support of rank-and-file members, succeeded in winning the power struggle over the Communists in the major industrial unions. It was these unions that founded Sōhyō in 1950. The vast majority of Japanese unionists at the time were affiliated with the new national union center.

Sōhyō was expected to embark on economic-based, democratic trade unionism, as the Allied Occupation desired. However, such was not to be the case. Instead, within a year of its formation, Sōhyō took a course that foreign observers viewed as too political in orientation and still strongly tinted with Marxist ideology.[1]

When the Peace Treaty and the United States–Japan Mutual Security Agreement were being concluded between 1950 and 1952, Sōhyō, under the leadership of Takano Minoru, a leftist socialist, opposed both agreements because Soviet Russia and the People's Republic of China were not participants. It advocated its own four principles for peace: an overall peace treaty with all of the Allied Powers, maintenance of Japan's neutrality, no military bases for American forces in Japan, and no rearmament for Japan. The principles were formulated under the assumption that the United States and her allies were "forces of war," while Soviet Russia, China, and other socialist countries were "forces of peace." As time went on, Sōhyō continued its militant leftist course and became increasingly involved in political activities, such as a series of general strikes opposing enactment of the Subversive Activity Prevention Law of 1952 and revision of the labor relations statutes in the same year. An internal struggle between rightist and leftist factions within Sōhyō developed over the Peace Treaty issue; as a result, the rightist group broke away to form another national center that eventually evolved into the present Dōmei in 1964.

A second occasion when foreign observers were particularly impressed with the political orientation of Japan's union movement was the mass rally, on an unprecedented scale, in opposition to the proposed Security Treaty between the United States and Japan in 1960. Although the rally did not succeed in impeding the conclusion of the treaty, it did force the government to cancel President Eisenhower's official visit to Japan and brought about the resignation of Premier Kishi Nobusuke's cabinet. Although Sōhyō did not condone the extremism, involving students' violence, in the mass demonstration, it certainly played the leading role in organizing the rally by mobilizing masses of union members and other workers. From this event some foreign observers, particularly those in the United States, concluded, perhaps too hastily, that Sōhyō was a Communist-dominated organization devoted to anti-American policies.

The following years were ones of political stability in Japan. Favored by the high economic growth of the 1960s, Japanese labor unions were, for the first time in their history, in an advantageous position to utilize their bargaining power to win improvements in the working conditions of their members through collective bargaining. Sōhyō organized the united Spring Offensive in 1955; it developed during the following decade into a successful mechanism for wage determination covering an ever-increasing number of union members. As might have been expected, the overwhelming majority of labor unions in Japan came to place more emphasis on economic than on political activities. However, this trend did not radically change the pattern of political activities of Japanese unions. Sōhyō and its affiliates, often joined by unions of other national centers, continued to organize political drives and campaigns directed against the incumbent conservative government. Examples are the united drives opposing the Korea–Japan Treaty in 1965 and the renewal of the United States–Japan Security Treaty in 1970, although in both cases there was a marked decline in the number of union members mobilized as compared with the mass rally of 1960. Nevertheless, Sōhyō-affiliated unions, particularly those in the public sector, have continued to wage political strikes from time to time, against both domestic and foreign policies of the government, in defiance of the law. On the occasions of such political activities, most unions, including a considerable number of non-Sōhyō affiliates, expressed their ideas and demands using words and phrases typical of Marxist-Leninist language.

Anyone interested in the Japanese industrial relations scene would, of course, raise some of the following questions:

How could the seemingly radical and leftist-oriented political activities of unions be congruent with the generally cooperative and peaceful labor–management relations at the enterprise level, based primarily on enterprise unionism? Why has the strong influence of classical Marxism or Marxism–Leninism persisted in the labor movement, despite Japan's affluence and relatively classless society with its highly developed democratic political institutions? What has been the effect of the political activities of Japanese unions on the power structure of the nation and the political decisions of the government? Will there be any changes in the political ideologies and behavior of Japanese labor unions in the foreseeable future and, if so, what factors would bring about changes?

These are the questions and focal points that this chapter addresses, as far as possible, in the following sections.

The Pattern of Political Activities of Japanese Labor Unions

An interpretation of the political activities of Japanese labor unions as "political unionism" requires some reservations. It does not seem to fit the model of political unionism as conceptualized by Adolf Sturmthal (1963; 1972, pp.1–10), in which a movement responds to a developing stage of industrialization and a labor market where a union's collective bargaining function is more or less circumscribed. Even in the prewar days, especially after the end of World War I when the union movement was launched on a substantial scale, the Japanese labor market was not one that could be characterized as an "unlimited supply of unskilled labor."[2] Japan is now a highly developed industrial society where collective bargaining functions as a full-fledged labor market institution, and the rights of workers to organize, bargain collectively, and engage in concerted actions such as strikes are guaranteed, as we have seen in earlier chapters. Japanese labor unions are far from being instruments of either the government or the political parties. Union leaders are elected by the membership through democratic procedures with no interference from either the government or the parties. What, then, are the major political activities of unions in Japan? In addition to the emphasis on political rallies and strikes against the government just noted, the unions display a number of other features.

Unions' Relations with Political Parties

Japanese unions have close links with the Socialist Party, the Democratic Socialist Party, and, in a few minor instances, the Communist Party. The pattern of such relationships seems peculiar to Japan, when compared with those in other industrialized countries as described by Windmuller (1974–75). Never in the history of the Japanese labor movement have unions taken a nonpartisan position, as have their counterparts in the United States. There is no Labor Party founded by the unions themselves, as in Britain. Most unions do not take a politically neutral stand, as the Deutscher Gewerkschaftsbund (DGB) in West Germany does toward all political parties, including the Social Democrats. It is very rare in postwar Japan for high-ranking incumbent officers of national centers or national industrial federations of unions to occupy an executive office of a political party, as often is the case in France and Italy. In an sense, the Japanese unions and political parties have developed a relationship of mutual independence in formal or official terms. However, this does not mean that either side would not dare to interfere with the other; just the opposite holds.

The close linkage between unions and political parties consists, first of all, in the heavy dependence of the Socialists and the Democratic Socialists on the unions for manpower and financing in election campaigns. Unions are very active in both national and local elections; often they directly nominate or sponsor candidates. Because of the unions' ability to influence the votes of workers and their families, both the Socialist Party and the Democratic Socialist Party usually are willing to accept the unions' nominees for elective office; most of these are ex-officers of industrial unions or national union federations.

Nominees of such large unions as Dentsūkyotō (Joint Council of Telecommunication Industry Trade Unions), Jichirō (prefectural and municipal workers), Nikkyōso (teachers), Kokurō (National Railway workers), Dōryokusha (National Railway locomotive engineers), and Zentei (Japan Postal Workers' Union), all of which are Sōhyō-affiliated and in the public sector, are in a favored position to win an election. The same is true for candidates nominated by such large private-sector unions as Jidōsharōren (Confederation of Japan Automobile Workers' Unions), Denkirōren (All Japan Federation of Electric Machine Workers' Unions), Zensendōmei (textile workers), Zōsenjūkirōren (shipbuilding and heavy machinery workers), and Tekkōrōren (iron and steel workers). Accordingly, the number of union-nominated candidates of each party as a proportion of those winning seats is substantial, particularly in the House of Councilors, where half of the total number of members are elected by a single, nationwide constituency (see table 13.1).

The nomination of union-sponsored candidates emanates from a highly complicated power struggle between and among political factions within the unions. It has long been an established practice of Japanese labor unions to decide at their annual conventions which political party or parties they will support. For Dōmei and its affiliates, there have been almost no internal struggles over this issue since these unions are strongly committed to support the Democratic Socialist Party; however, some minority factions favoring the Socialists or Communists exist within the affiliated organizations, partic-

Table 13.1
Ex-union Officers in Seats Held by the Socialist
and Democratic Socialist Parties in the Diet, July 1, 1978

Party	House	All Affiliated Congressmen[a]		Total		Ex-union Officers Public-Sector Unions		Private-Sector Unions	
		No.	%	No.	%	No.	%	No.	%
Socialist	Representatives	119	100.0	72	60.5	49	41.1	23	19.3
	Councilors	53	100.0	39	73.6	31	58.5	8	15.1
Democratic-	Representatives	28	100.0	9	32.1	2	7.1	7	25.0
Socialist	Councilors	11	(100.0)	8	(72.7)	0		8	(72.7)
Communist	Representatives	19	(100.0)	5	26.3	4	21.0	1	5.2
	Councilors	16	(100.0)	7	43.7	6	37.5	1	6.3
Kōmeitō	Representatives	56	(100.0)	1	1.8	0		1	1.8
	Councilors	28	(100.0)	0		0		0	
Shaminren[b]	Representatives	3	(100.0)	0		0		0	
	Councilors	3	(100.0)	1	33.3	0		1	33.3

Source: Rōdōshō, Trade Union Section, unpublished data.

[a]The total number of congressmen, on July 1, 1978, was 511 in the House of Representatives and 252 in the House of Councilors.

[b]Shaminren (Social Democratic Federation) is the party formed by a group that seceded from the Socialist Party in March 1978 during an internal struggle with the party's doctrinaire Marxist–Leninists.

ularly in Kaiin (seamen's union), Jidōsharōren (Federation of Japan Automobile Workers' Unions), and some unions at the enterprise level.

For Sōhyō and its affiliated national unions, the matter is more complicated. Sōhyō has been largely divided into two groups. The majority, or "Mainstream Faction," supports the Socialist Party, and, until quite recently, the minority, or "Anti-mainstream Faction," had supported the Communist Party. Lately, however, this group has revised its position, asserting the principle of "freedom of the membership to support or not to support any political party." The majority position of the Mainstream Faction has enabled Sōhyō to decide at its convention to support the Socialist Party, compromising to the extent that it will "cooperate with" other progressive parties on an ad hoc basis. By "progressive parties," Sōhyō means the Socialists, Kōmeitō (Clean Government Party, the political arm of a Buddhist organization, Sōkagakkai), the Communist Party, the Democratic Socialists, and even other minor parties that are in opposition to the ruling Liberal-Democratic Party.

In the cases of the national industrial federations within Sōhyō as well as the affiliates of the smaller national centers Chūritsurōren and Shinsanbetsu, and some other independent groups, political support varies depending upon the leadership and internal ideological factionalism within the respective organizations. Some unions support only the Socialists, some support the Socialists and the Democratic Socialists, some give their support to Kōmeitō as well, some support the Socialists and Communists, and some do not name any particular party or parties but just say that they will cooperate with "progressive parties." In most instances, this process of deciding which political parties to support or not to support involves more heated discussion on the floor of annual union conventions than do any of the day-to-day collective bargaining issues, thus tending to give the impression that the convention delegates are generally more concerned with political than with economic matters.

The convention decision on which political party to support has no binding effect on the actual votes of union members at the time of an election, although it may influence considerably their selection among the candidates. For example, a membership attitude survey conducted by some leading unions found that more than half of the surveyed members of some public-sector unions had been influenced in their actual voting by their union's decision.[3] However, among some private-sector unions, the proportion of members influenced by their union's decision was no more than about 30 percent. Irrespective of any effect on the actual votes of their members, most union leaders and members feel it is necessary for them to come to some decision on what party or parties to support. One reason is that only after a convention decision are union officials and activists authorized to raise and contribute money to the supported party or parties and to devote time and energy to election campaigns. A related reason, among others, is to discourage the activity of a minority faction that failed to win the union's support for the party of its choice. Through this practice, unions have made themselves the major suppliers of money and manpower, including candidates, for the Socialists and/or the Democratic Socialists in national and local elections. At the same time they have secured a considerable number of public offices for retired or retiring union officers. In actuality, membership in the national and local legislature is deemed to be one of the high-ranking positions on the promotion ladder of union leaders.

Not only has the union's procedure for determining its support of a particular party or parties been questioned, but the practice itself has come under increasingly severe criticism from both within and outside the union world. The practice necessarily creates disunity and intraunion splits; it also opens the way for union intervention in policy decisions and the internal affairs of the political parties as well as encouraging too much dependence by the parties on the unions for manpower and financing. This ultimately undermines their efforts to maintain and enlarge their strength on their own. In particular, the union–party relationship has been criticized as bringing about the most continuous decline of the Japanese Socialist Party in recent years. Leaders of both groups are well aware of the problem and have openly discussed the need to change the practice. However, it seems quite unlikely that they will succeed in effecting any of the desired changes and improvements.

Unions' Political Action as Pressure Groups

As in other countries, unions in Japan conduct their political activities by operating as major pressure groups. They exert pressure on the political parties they support as well as on those with which they have cooperative relationships in efforts to achieve their political goals. Since these parties are in the opposition in Japan, and since there has been virtually no prospect of the opposition parties becoming the ruling party or forming a coalition government by themselves in the foreseeable future, the unions have been forced into attempting to influence directly or to apply pressure on the government, or the ruling Liberal-Democrats. Their methods are varied, including political demonstrations, petitions to the Diet and the government, parliamentary lobbying, and formal and informal discussions with ministers, other high-ranking government officials, and leaders of the ruling parties.

Among these options, the political demonstration is the action the unions most favor, and they frequently organize mass rallies and marches over issues that include national defense, foreign affairs (territorial problems, international trade, and relations with specific neighboring countries), annual national and local budgets, environmental problems, and political scandals as well as industrial, social, and labor policies that are more directly related to the daily interests of workers. During these demonstrations, the unions carry flags, mostly red in color, so that foreign observers are often misled into believing that the rallies were organized and led by Communists.

Political Strikes

Although the Constitution of Japan and the Trade Union Law guarantee the workers' right to organize, bargain collectively, and engage in concerted actions, including strikes, political strikes have no legal protection. Nevertheless, Japanese unions often have conducted strikes that are essentially political. However, it is almost impossible to say that any such union action is purely political, for in most instances the union demands are both political and economic, the latter emphasizing issues to be handled by collective bargaining.

Most leading unions in the private sector, particularly those affiliated with Dōmei, the second largest national center, oppose political strikes in principle. Even for unions that do not disavow the political strike, it is quite difficult to conduct one not only because it is illegal, but because of the internal strife and factional ideological splits that are almost inevitable.

A majority of the political strikes in Japan have been conducted by public-sector unions affiliated with Sōhyō—unions in the National Railways, the Postal Service, and local governments. The Japanese public looks with disfavor on political strikes, particularly those waged by the public-sector unions. When the National Railways unions struck for eight days in the fall of 1975 in an attempt to restore their right to strike, they incurred a severe loss of popular sympathy. Japanese unions do not have enough strength to conduct frequent political strikes or to strike for a period long enough to force the government either to adopt a policy the unions advocate or to abandon one they oppose. Although the left-wing unions know this, they still embark on political strikes either because the leaders feel it is actually necessary or because of ideological imperatives.

The Ideology of Political Activity of Japanese Unions

As referred to above, classical Marxism or Marxism–Leninism has had a persistent and significant influence on the Japanese labor movement since shortly after World War I. It is true that Marxism has become increasingly less influential in recent years, but major segments of the labor movement, including some unions not affiliated with Sōhyō, continue to express their ideas, policies, and action programs in terms of Marxist concepts and doctrines. Why has Marxism or Marxism–Leninism retained its dominant position in the ideology of the labor movement in Japan?

Weakness of Alternative Ideologies

First and foremost, no ideology in the pre–World War II days was able to compete with Marxism. Christianity enjoyed only very minor popularity in Japanese society; thus, the Christian ethics and values that were the roots of many social reformist ideas in Western countries never were able to gain a foothold. It is true that some of the outstanding labor leaders of that era, such as Kagawa Toyohiko, Suzuki Bunji, and Matsuoka Komakichi, were Christians, but their thoughts had only a very limited influence on other union leaders and the rank-and-file members.[4]

What the union activists sought was a strong and convincing ideology as a rationale for devoting themselves to a union movement in defiance of the hostile attitudes and oppressive policies of employers and the government. At that time the labor movement had no legal protection; the laws and administrative ordinances either suppressed or severely restricted union organization and activities. Some socialist and/or social-reformist ideas, such as anarcho-syndicalism, Fabian socialism, and what might be called democratic socialism as it developed in the postwar period were introduced and adopted by some union leaders, but the Marxist doctrine of the historical necessity of a socialist revolution by exploited workers was the one that had the greatest appeal.

Prior to World War II, the organizational strength of unions led by right-wing leaders was far greater than that of either the left-wing group or the so-called middle-of-the-road unions, both of which were strongly imbued with Marxism or Marxism–Leninism, but this situation was destined to change. Ideologies other than Marxism were not as attractive or persuasive for intellectuals and union activists, and in the prewar period as well as in the early postwar years, many of the intellectuals who were strongly influenced by Marxism–Leninism took over the leadership of the union movement.

Prestige of the Marxists

Marxism has enjoyed a predominant position in the Japanese academic world since before World War II, particularly in the field of economics and related social sciences. Marxist theory seemed far superior to "bourgeois" economic theories in the scientific analysis of the Japanese economy, at least at that time. Later, the Marxists' appraisal of the course that Japanese imperialism could take and its inevitable outcome turned out to be accurate. Despite severe government oppression, they—both Communists and non-Communist left-wingers—were the groups in the Japanese labor movement who vigorously advocated democracy and persistently fought against the imperialistic war, and it was this prewar and wartime experience that greatly enhanced their prestige and popularity in Japan's postwar labor movement.

Leaders of the right wing and most officials of middle-of-the-road groups, with a few exceptions, took cooperative and even affirmative positions toward the policy of military expansionism. Some of them even cooperated with the government's measures restricting a free labor movement, which finally resulted in the forced dissolution of existing unions and the formation of Sampō, the patriotic labor organization the wartime government encouraged in order to secure workers' support for the war effort.

When the union movement revived after the war, as might have been expected it was the Communists and non-Communist left-wingers who were in a far better position than any of the anti-Communists or moderate liberal leaders to assume leadership in the revolutionary offensive developing in the war-devastated land. The main goals of the revived radical labor movement were the condemnation of the prewar ruling class for its responsibility for the destructive war and the establishment of a "Democratic People's Government."

Impact of the Communist-Led Revolutions in Russia and China

The successful social revolutions led by Marxist–Leninists in the two great neighboring countries, Russia and China, had a tremendous impact on the ideology of the Japanese union movement. First, the Russian Revolution of

1917 occurred during the so-called "Taishō Democracy" era in Japan, shortly after World War I, a period of upheaval for the labor movement.[5] Second, the Chinese Revolution, which resulted in the founding of the People's Republic of China in 1949, was in progress at the exact time of an even greater upheaval for the Japanese labor movement after World War II. These incidents also greatly enhanced the credibility of Marxism–Leninism among Japanese intellectuals as well as workers: they were considered examples of the historic inevitability of socialist revolution, as Marx had argued. The defeat of France and then the United States in Vietnam only reinforced these conclusions.

It is true, as noted earlier, that the prestige of Marxism–Leninism has been significantly diluted in Japan because of subsequent incidents in Czechoslovakia and in Hungary, the antagonism that developed between Russia and China, the aftermath of the Vietnam War, conflicts between and among Japanese socialists, Communists, and the New Left factions, and, notably, the evidence of less than successful achievements of socialist planned economies. These developments certainly gave rise to ideological confusion and dismay among the leftist unions in Japan, but it still seems unlikely that Marxism will totally lose its influence as their controlling doctrine.

Antagonism between Unions in the Public Sector and the Government

The core of support for the leftist union movement in Japan is in the Sōhyō-affiliated unions in the public sector—Kokurō, Dōryokusha, Zentei, and Nikkyōso—as well as in some private-sector unions, also Sōhyō-affiliated, that cater to workers in medium-sized and small industries. The former are among the largest and strongest unions in Japan and have generally been particularly antagonistic in their relations with the conservative government.

The conflict between these unions and the government revolved primarily around the issues of the basic rights of labor, such as freedom of association and the right to strike. In addition, Nikkyōso has often opposed the government's educational policies. In their confrontations with the conservative government, these unions utilize the Marxist theory of class struggle to justify their demands as well as to persuade, encourage, and mobilize rank-and-file members to join the struggles that might well lead to their having to submit to disciplinary sanctions by national and local authorities.

Weak Class-Consciousness among Workers

Union leaders in the private sector also have utilized Marxist theories of capitalist exploitation and class struggle to activate rank-and-file members and gain their militancy during disputes with employers. In general, however, class-consciousness among Japanese workers is weak, and this tendency is especially noticeable among employees of large enterprises, where the majority of union members are found.

The classical Marxist concept of the class consciousness of the exploited proletariat does not seem to have much appeal for employed workers in Japan. The higher social and occupational mobility they enjoy, their more open and free access to higher education, and their more equitable income distribution as compared with workers in other industrialized societies all contribute to their weak class consciousness, or their lack of it. Surprisingly, an overwhelming majority of the Japanese people consider their standard of living to be "middle class."[6]

Moreover, as referred to particularly in chapter 2, workers in the large enterprises tend to have a stronger identification as members of the enterprise community where they work than as members of the working class or of a workers' community. On the other hand, workers in small industries tend to be either submissive to paternalistic employers or apathetic toward the union movement. Accordingly, union leaders in this sector often feel it necessary to emphasize the Marxist theory of class struggle in order to activate workers as union members, and to obtain their support in a union's struggle against an employer as well as in united union activities on an industrial, regional, or national basis, particularly for political purposes.

Persistent Dissatisfaction among Workers

Despite the affluence brought about by high economic growth in postwar Japan, many workers—blue-collar and white-collar alike—still have a number of complaints about their working and living conditions.[7] Most of them feel that the so-called "social infrastructure"—housing, medical care, old-age pensions, unemployment benefits and other social security measures, and recreational facilities—is far below the level existing in advanced industrial countries, particularly what they presume has been achieved in socialist planned economies. They believe, with or without grounds, that the conservative government, representing capitalists' interests, should be blamed for "the backwardness of Japanese society" in terms of the welfare of workers and the common people. Marxism or Marxism–Leninism, which emphasizes the superiority of a socialist planned economy over a capitalist market economy in terms of workers' welfare, continues to be an attractive proposition, however illusory, to a substantial number of workers and can be utilized to motivate them in the unions' struggle against employers and the government.

Another aspect of the "affluent society" is responsible for the revival of Marxism as advocated by the New Left in Japan. As in other industrialized countries, young workers are becoming noticeably dissatisfied with the "administrative society," particularly its highly developed bureaucratization and its organizational control over individuals.

The Effectiveness of Political Activities of Japanese Unions

How effective, then, have been the political activities of Japanese unions? Have they had any meaningful impact on the political power structure of Japan or on the formulation of policy and enactment of legislation favoring organized labor and working people in general? Have they been effective in leading or orienting the political consciousness of union members in the direction the leaders desire? I believe the answer generally is "no," for the following reasons:

Constraints Resulting from Organizational Disunity

The effectiveness of the unions' political activity is fatally circumscribed, first and foremost, by their organizational disunity. There is no single national union center in Japan that is similar to Britain's TUC (Trades Union Congress), the AFL–CIO in the United States, the DGB in West Germany, and the LOs (*Landsorganisationen*) in the Scandinavian countries. Despite the numerical strength of organized labor, which is next to that of the United States and Britain in the non-Communist world, Japanese unions have failed to form a single pressure group with significant political power. Occasionally the four national centers have formed a joint body for political action on an ad hoc basis in order to exert pressure for favorable legislation or other governmental actions, but the united front has often been disrupted and frustrated by ideological conflict and mutual distrust among the centers. Union disunity is in evidence not only at the level of the national centers, but also in the industrial federations and some enterprise unions.

As noted earlier, there are two ideological factions within Sōhyō, and this factionalism is replicated within Sōhyō affiliates, especially in the powerful public-sector unions such as Nikkyōso and Kokurō. At the same time there is inherent conflict between the private-sector unions and those in the public sector. With such organizational splits based on ideological differences, unions in Japan can hardly be expected to be very powerful or effective as an integrated pressure group.

Little Change in the Political Power Structure

Within the pattern of their present relationships with political parties, unions have failed to bring about any meaningful changes in the political power structure of Japan. Their practice of supporting one or two political parties has been unsuccessful in helping to create any strong opposition group that has a realistic prospect of becoming a ruling party or parties in the near future. Except during a brief period of coalition rule in 1947–48, the government has been completely monopolized by the conservative Liberal-Democrats. It is true that throughout the 1970s their dominant position was weakened, primarily because of the Lockheed scandals, stagflation, industrial pollution, and other instances of maladministration; but the strength of the Socialist Party also declined, and the Democratic Socialists, despite their growth in recent years, continue to be only a small minority, as is shown in table 13.2. These two parties have enjoyed the direct support of unions through the usual convention resolutions, but they have failed to gain new members, in contrast to Kōmeitō and the Communist Party, both of which have attracted new members without any direct union support.

Little Impact on the Political Consciousness of Union Members

The unions' political activities thus far do not seem to have had any great impact on the political consciousness of rank-and-file members. The results of opinion surveys conducted recently by the government as well as by some leading unions are inconsistent, but they indicate in general that increasing numbers of workers and union members, particularly the younger ones, are losing sympathy with the Socialist and Communist Parties and their advocacy of social revolution and are tending to transfer their support to the Liberal-Democratic Party and other moderates that favor gradual social reform.[8]

Unions as a Weak Pressure Group

Despite their enormous numerical strength of more than 12 million members, Japanese unions have failed to put together a pressure group with as much influence on national and local governments as some smaller labor movements have in other industrialized countries. It is true that Japanese unions have supplied manpower and monetary resources to the Socialist and the Democratic Socialist Parties and through them have had an influence on governmental policies and actions that may be fairly estimated as nonnegligible. They also have been generally successful in gaining the support of other opposition parties, such as Kōmeitō and the Communists, in attempts to achieve their demands for certain legislation and budgetary arrangements, although these accomplishments have been of less overall value because of the weakness and disunity among the opposition parties. And the unions frequently have been successful in organizing citizen groups around such issues as peace, pollution, prices, taxes, education, and political scandals. In that sense they have been a meaningful countervailing power to the conservative government.

However, their strength is largely undermined by two basic factors. One is the internal ideological disunity of the labor movement, which makes it difficult to organize and maintain a united political front that could otherwise

Table 13.2

Seats Won by Political Parties in General Elections, 1969–79

A. House of Representatives

Party	December 1969		December 1972		December 1976		October 1979	
	No. Seats Won	Share in Total Votes (%)	No. Seats Won	Share in Total Votes (%)	No. Seats Won	Share in Total Votes (%)	No. Seats Won	Share in Total Votes (%)
Liberal-Democratic	288	47.6	271	46.9	249	41.8	248	44.6
Japan Socialist	90	21.4	118	21.9	123	20.7	107	19.7
Kōmeitō	47	10.9	29	8.5	55	10.9	57	9.8
Democratic-Socialist	31	7.7	19	7.0	29	6.3	35	6.8
Japan Communist	14	6.8	38	10.5	17	10.4	39	10.4
New Liberal Club	0	0	0	0	17	4.1	4	3.0
Social Democratic Federation	0	0	0	0	0	0	2	0.7
Others	16	5.6	16	5.2	21	5.8	19	5.0
Total	486	100.0	491	100.0	511	100.0	511	100.0

345

Table 13.2 (continued)
Seats Won by Political Parties in General Elections, 1969–79

B. House of Councilors

Party	June 1971			July 1974			July 1977		
	No. Seats Won	Share in (percent) Total Votes		No. Seats Won	Share in (percent) Total Votes		No. Seats Won	Share in (percent) Total Votes	
		National	Local		National	Local		National	Local
Liberal-Democratic	63	44.4	44.0	62	44.3	39.5	63	42.1	39.8
Japan Socialist	39	21.3	31.0	28	15.2	26.0	27	18.8	26.3
Kōmeito	10	14.1	3.4	14	12.1	12.6	14	12.5	6.0
Democratic-Socialist	6	6.1	4.7	5	5.9	4.4	6	6.5	4.4
Japan Communist	6	8.1	12.0	13	9.4	12.0	5	6.6	9.9
New Liberal Club	0	0	0	0	0	0	3	2.8	5.6
Social Democratic Federation	0	0	0	0	0	0	1	0.8	0
Others	2	6.0	4.9	8	13.0	4.9	7	10.0	4.9
Total	126	100.0	100.0	130	100.0	100.0	126	100.0	100.0

Source: Asahi Shimbun, 1969, 1971–72, 1974, 1976–77, 1979.

346

be a real threat to the governing conservative party. Their attempts at concerted political action thus far have not only failed to achieve the desired goals, but have aggravated the hatred and distrust among union groups, particularly between Sōhyō and Dōmei and between unions in the public sector and those in the private.

The second contributing factor is that Japanese unions are generally inept when they try to formulate creative but workable social, economic, and labor policies. They have been loud in their criticism of the government policies, but they usually have failed to propose realistic and acceptable alternatives. As a result, what they and their supporters in the opposition parties actually achieved at best was an occasional political compromise, by prodding the government into making some modifications in or temporarily giving up legislation that the unions opposed. Only on rare occasions have they been successful in forcing the government to adopt a policy that they have independently formulated and advocated.

In an attempt to overcome their weaknesses in policy formation and effective concerted action, more than ten leading unions in the private sector, irrespective of their affiliation with any of the national centers, came together on October 7, 1976, to found Seisaku Suishin Rōso Kaigi (Trade Union Council for Policy Formulation). By 1978 the council had developed into a large organization composed of more than 20 national industrial union federations having a total membership of five million workers. Since its establishment, the council, led by the major private-sector unions, has played a significant role as the core of a movement for union unification, but its final achievement is yet to be seen.

Prospects for the Future

What, then, are the prospects for effective political action on the part of Japanese unions? Some significant signs are already apparent; they seem to indicate a gradual but steady change in unions' political outlook and behavior. In general, they are becoming more pragmatic than before. Marxism or Marxism–Leninism is declining in influence and repute among union leaders and rank-and-file members. The traditional political relationships between the unions and political parties are becoming increasingly difficult to maintain, and the unions seem to have already begun to take a more flexible position in their relations with political parties, including conservative ones. There are a number of reasons for these trends.

Popularity of Marxism Eroding in the Egalitarian Society

The Marxist or Marxist–Leninist doctrine as well as the political movement inspired by the doctrine has been steadily losing repute and popularity among the Japanese people in general, especially in the past 20 years of unprecedented long-term prosperity. In the academic world, the prestige of Marxist economists eroded after they apparently failed to foresee and correctly analyze the remarkable postwar growth and viability of the Japanese capitalist market economy; they had taken the position that there was a fatal vulnerability intrinsic in its semifeudal structure and had predicted its collapse. The once widely cherished illusion that socialism would beget limitless growth in productivity, an ever-rising standard of living for the people, full-fledged freedom and democracy for the masses, and a foreign policy emphasizing peace was shattered for an increasing number of workers and intellectuals as the realities of the socialist regimes in Soviet Russia, China, and other countries were revealed. On the domestic scene, the inability of the Japanese Socialist and Communist Parties to represent workers' interests effectively led to ever-deepening disappointment among union leaders and members. The internal strife within both parties also has been repellant and disenchanting to an overwhelming majority of workers.

At the same time, unions in general became more economic-oriented than before as collective bargaining came to be practiced more widely and sustained high economic growth enabled it to function effectively. There were also improvements in the distribution of income among the people, so that differences in standards of living narrowed conspicuously. The opportunity for higher education became more open and accessible for workers' children, increasing social mobility, which had already been more fluid than in most other industrialized countries. The class structure of prewar Japan, which was characterized by uneven income distribution and status differentiation, largely disintegrated as a result of the far-reaching social reforms right after the war as well as the impact of the labor movement with its highly egalitarian orientation. The Marxist–Leninist doctrine, emphasizing class differentiation and class struggle between the bourgeoisie and the proletariat as well as a persistent deterioration of the working and living conditions of workers in a capitalist economy, could no longer be applied to the actual conditions of postwar Japanese society. Thus it was quite natural and inevitable that Marxism or Marxism–Leninism would lose its appeal for many union leaders and activists. Most of them continue to speak Marxist jargon, but the cleavage between language and action is becoming more apparent than ever.

New Type of Union Leadership Emerging

Union leadership in Japan is now entering a period of large-scale generational change. A younger generation of union leaders, who are free from ideological rigidity, have a more pragmatic and liberal outlook, and place more emphasis on collective bargaining than on political action, is now taking the place of the old-timers whose thinking is influenced by traditional Marxism. The younger union leaders, although deeply involved with general economic, social, and political problems, are primarily concerned with collective bargaining issues that directly affect the conditions of daily employment of the rank-and-file members. Even left-wing leaders who still use the time-honored slogans of political class struggle have had to adopt more realistic policies in order to meet the expectations of the membership, for if they maintain the traditional, fundamentalist leftist position, they are doomed to lose the support of a younger generation of workers. It was noted in chapter 11, for instance, that more than half of newly hired teachers are not joining Nikkyōso, one of the most politically oriented unions in Sōhyō, where traditional Marxist language is used in the continuing factional struggles between Socialists and Communists.

Recent Changes in Sōhyō

Leaders of Sōhyō and its affiliated unions in the public sector are well aware of the possibility of their being isolated as the rest of the unions move away from a Marxist orientation. One of the major changes within the Japanese labor movement in recent years is the remarkable development of a closer relationship of Sōhyō and its affiliates with unions in the non-Communist world through the International Confederation of Free Trade Unions (ICFTU) and International Trade Secretariats (ITSs) as well as the AFL–CIO.

Sōhyō officially takes a neutral stand toward both world federations—the ICFTU and the World Federation of Trade Unions (WFTU), but until quite recently it had been closer to unions in the socialist countries affiliated with the WFTU than to those in the non-Communist world. It became increasingly apparent, however, that its association with unions in the socialist countries was useless in solving the problems it and its affiliates faced. The cooperation and assistance extended by unions in the West to Sōhyō at the time of the International Labor Organization commission inquiry on the issues of "freedom of association" and the "right to strike" for employees of public corporations and civil servants, beginning in 1958, as well as the issue of Japan's international trade in recent years gradually forced Sōhyō to change its attitude and reevaluate and strengthen its relationship with unions in free market economies. It was a new departure for Sōhyō when its leaders, led by President Makieda Motofumi, visited and met with their counterparts in the AFL–CIO and the DGB in the fall of 1978. Following these visits, Sōhyō was officially admitted to the Trade Union Advisory Committee (TUAC) of the Organization for Economic Cooperation and Development (OECD) with the consent of Dōmei, which had long been affiliated with both the ICFTU and TUAC.

Sōhyō took a further and even more significant step when Tomizuka Mitsuo, the general secretary, visited the 12th World Congress of the ICFTU in November 1979 in Spain and officially announced Sōhyō's intention to examine affiliation with the world body when a new national union center was established as a result of the union unification movement in progress in Japan. These events clearly indicate that Sōhyō is possibly moving toward a stronger commitment to the union movement in the non-Communist world than it has had in the past.

Reshuffling of Relationships between Unions and Political Parties

The traditional pattern of relationships between unions and political parties will become increasingly pointless and difficult to maintain as the preferences of members for political parties become more diffused.[9] The very fact that a number of major unions and their federations have recently conducted opinion surveys of their memberships reflects the leaders' apprehension about the likelihood of their being able to maintain the traditional policy of party support. Although the results of these opinion surveys vary from union to union and fluctuate from time to time, a growing number of union members tend to express no specific party preference or to be indifferent to all of them. Apparently the proportion of those who support the Liberal-Democratic Party is increasing in the private-sector unions, and in the public-sector unions the Socialist Party is losing support except among middle-aged and older members.[10]

If the political power position of the Liberal-Democrats changes, necessitating the participation of other parties in the government, it will become not only difficult but useless for the unions to continue their traditional commitment to a particular party or parties through convention resolutions.[11] They and their members will find it advisable to assume a nonpartisan policy of "reward your friends and punish your enemies," leaving the members with a range of choices among the parties. Already, following the 1979 general election in which the Socialist Party suffered another defeat, the leaders of Sōhyō quickly moved to establish an alliance between Kōmeitō and the Socialists.

Undoubtedly it will take time to change a long-established union practice. In the meantime, confusion and setbacks will be unavoidable, particularly among unions supporting the Japanese Socialist Party and within the party itself. If a coalition government comes to pass in the near future, the most likely and workable alliance would involve the Liberal-Democratic Party, or at least the majority faction of it, and some of the present opposition parties that have a more or less moderate and realistic outlook toward cooperation with the conservative party. A coalition will force the Socialists to make a critical choice between joining the government or remaining an opposition party with ever-declining strength. Any choice the party makes will further aggravate the ideological conflict among and within unions that have close ties with it.

There has always been a hard-core leftist group, Communist as well as non-Communist, in Sōhyō unions that is bitterly critical of the "right-wing inclination" represented by major unions in the private sector. As a matter of fact, when Sōhyō's 1979 approach to the ICFTU was disclosed, the Communist Party, in its Central Committee Meeting held in mid-November 1979, denounced the action and proposed that another national center be founded to cope with the "right-wing inclined unification movement" in progress. Responding quickly to the party's urging, 29 leftist industrial federations, with a membership of about 620,000, which are under Communist influence and which had already organized Toitsurōsōkon (Conference of the Trade Unions for the Promotion of a United Front), decided to examine the "desirability of a national center." Accordingly, the ongoing movement for union unification in Japan may lead to another organizational split, with the minority forming a revived leftist-oriented union center.

The long-run trend, however, seems to be irreversible. It indicates that an overwhelming majority of Japanese unions are moving toward more realistic and flexible relationships with political parties than they have had in the past and holds out the promise that they thereby will become a stronger pressure group.

Notes

1 For detail on the formation of Sōhyō and its activities following the Peace Treaty, see Levine 1958, pp. 74–82.

2 See Shirai and Shimada 1978, pp. 272–71, and Taira 1970. It should be noted, however, that there have been serious discussions about the applicability of the Lewis Model to labor market conditions in prewar Japan. Minami (1971a) insists that the Japanese labor market was in the stage of an unlimited supply of labor until around 1960.

3 Report of the survey on the political consciousness of union members, Telecommunications Workers' Union of Japan, *Zendentsu*, vol. 18, no. 4, January 1979. The report includes a comparison between surveys conducted by three unions in the public sector and two in the private sector.

4 These leaders were Christians who led the right-wing labor movement in pre–World War II Japan. With the exception of Matsuoka, they were intellectuals. Kagawa was a famous evangelist educated in American universities; Suzuki was a graduate of Tokyo University. See Shirai and Shimada 1978, pp. 253–54, 312–13; see also Kōshiro 1977e, pp. 36–37.

5 *Taisho* refers to the years during the reign of Emperor Taisho from 1912 to 1926. It was the first time in modern Japan when new ideologies, such as democracy, liberalism, socialism, anarcho-syndicalism, and communism, were introduced and flourished. The government was forced to adopt more liberal policies than in the past toward labor and people in general. Examples are repeal of the notorious

Article 17 of the Public Peace Police Law, promulgation of universal suffrage, and several attempts to introduce trade union laws between 1924 and 1926.

6 A series of opinion surveys conducted by the Prime Minister's Office and the Economic Planning Agency over the past 15 years revealed that the proportion of people who consider themselves "middle class" increased from 72.4 percent in 1958 to 90.1 percent in 1976, and to 91 percent in 1979. On the equalization of income and living standards, see Economic Planning Agency 1977, pp. 69–81.

7 It is noteworthy that an increasing number of people are satisfied or fairly satisfied with their present living conditions. According to another survey conducted by the Economic Planning Agency (Keizai Kikakuchō 1976), the proportion of those "satisfied" or "fairly satisfied" increased from 55 percent in 1972 to 64 percent in 1975.

8 Sōrifu 1971, pp. 9–11. See also Telecommunications Workers' Union of Japan, *Denkirōren*, No. 41, November 1978, pp. 32–33.

9 In another survey conducted by the Prime Minister's Office (Sōrifu 1978, pp. 76–77), 61.7 percent of surveyed workers reported that they were negative toward a union's practice of supporting a particular political party.

10 In addition to the opinion surveys conducted by Zendentsu and Denkirōren, just cited, such industrial union federations as Kaiin, Dōryokusha, Kagaku Enerugī Rōkyō (Japan Council of Chemical and Energy Workers), Zensekiyu (All Japan Oil Workers' Union), Shuppanrōren (Japan Federation of Publishing Workers' Unions), and Unyuippan (All Japan Transport and General Workers' Union), conducted membership opinion surveys between 1970 and 1972.

11 The prospect of forming a coalition government was totally shattered when the ruling Liberal-Democratic Party (LDP) won a landslide victory in simultaneous elections for both houses of the Diet, held on June 22, 1980. LDP made a spectacular gain to win 286 seats in the 511-seat House of Representatives as well as winning a comfortable majority in the House of Councilors. In contrast, the major opposition parties, Kōmeitō, the Japan Communist Party, and the Democratic Socialist Party, lost many seats that they had controlled before the election, while the Japan Socialist Party barely managed to retain its preelection strength.

With the triumph of the LDP, leading labor unions, and particularly those of the private sector as represented by the Seisaku Shuishin Rōso Kaigi (Trade Union Council for Policy Formulation), have begun to hold meetings regularly with the LDP which, in turn, has shown greater interest in cooperation with labor unions.

14 *Haruo Shimada*

Summaries and Evaluation

We had three purposes in mind when we were organizing and writing the present volume.

First, we wanted to offer to the English-reading and presumably non-Japanese audience some candid and, we hoped, new ideas of our own and of other Japanese scholars on Japan's industrial relations. As was demonstrated in the review in chapter 1, a considerable amount of English-language literature has accumulated. Although most of the scholars contributing to this stock of knowledge are foreign, the Japanese themselves have made a sizable contribution. However, the English-language literature by Japanese authors, though quite informative, has tended to be primarily descriptive, typically employing the "descriptive institutional approach" and repeating and confirming the conventional stereotypes, but seldom provoking new and stimulating ideas. One of our intentions in writing this book was to avoid this rather sterile pattern that Japanese scholars seem to have adopted, particularly when they are writing for a non-Japanese audience.

A second goal we hoped to attain was to state frankly the heterogeneous views of Japanese scholars without concealing points of controversy. Foreigners commonly believe that the Japanese are "born consensual people" and that they refrain from disagreeing with each other and especially from expressing conflicting views in the presence of foreigners. Moreover, their writing often appears to be more in the style of authoritative pronouncements than of scientific persuasion, a characteristic that makes it seem superficial and uninteresting. However, and quite naturally, the Japanese do disagree among themselves and they do criticize each other, just as any other people do. We tried in this book to present this reality openly to our readers because we believe that non-Japanese will thereby receive a much better sense of the diversity of the Japanese academic literature on industrial relations as well as of the complex reality that it reflects.

Third, we have tried to provide information in areas that have been relatively ignored in the English-language literature on industrial relations. As we saw in chapter 1, foreign observers concentrated most of their attention on labor–management relations in large firms. Thus, relatively little has been revealed about such relationships in the public sector and in small firms as well as about the role of female workers. This book attempts to fill these gaps, with the hope that foreign readers will come away with a more balanced picture of the total operation of the Japanese industrial relations system.

Fourth, we decided to write this book in English from the beginning rather than having Japanese manuscripts translated into English, as had been done with most of the previous works of this kind. We do not mean to imply that existing translations are poor or erroneous, but it is our feeling that when a writer is writing in the language in which he is thinking, he can be more effective in communicating his ideas than when he is writing in a language that will be translated later. We are, of course, aware that our limited competence in English might constrain our expression more than if we were writing in our own language.

In the following section are synopses of the preceding 12 chapters (excluding only chapter 1, the literature survey). In each I summarize the author's principal arguments and stress his particular additions to the so far available total picture of Japanese industrial relations systems and how they operate. The final and closing section of this chapter is our evaluation of the contribution that our book makes to the stock of knowledge about Japanese industrial relations systems.

The Synopses

Chapter 2. Internal Labor Markets: Workers in Large Firms

Kazuo Koike describes and interprets for the Western audience the operation of the "internal labor markets" of large Japanese firms and offers his "white-collarization" hypothesis. Blue-collar workers in the large firms in Japan, he argues, resemble white-collar workers in West European countries and the United States in many respects, but particularly in the wages and fringe benefits they enjoy, their labor mobility and commitment, their prospects for promotion, and their occupational career patterns. He suggests that certain of these patterns, especially those of the occupational careers and the workforce management of blue-collar workers, have tended to become more like those of white-collar workers as industrialization proceeds, and that this "white-collarization" is an inevitable concomitant of the growth of large monopolistic firms during the industrialization process. According to Koike, Japan is where this phenomenon can be most readily observed since her industrialization was rapid and was accomplished in the absence of established and powerful craft unions.

The author presents a twofold analysis. In the first part he uses national statistical data for both Japan and Western nations to argue that blue-collar workers in large Japanese firms share some important attributes with white-collar workers in Western industrialized countries. As evidence for this point, he shows that (1) the relatively steep age–wage profile of Japanese blue-collar workers is most similar to those of white-collar workers in advanced Western nations; (2) the proportion of long-service workers in the total workforces of Japanese firms is not very much greater than the proportions in West European and U.S. companies; (3) enterprise unions in Japan are not necessarily a unique form of workers' organization in view of the prevalence of enterprise-level organizations performing similar functions in Western nations—local unions in the United States, works councils in Germany, and enterprise committees in France; and (4) the fringe benefits of Japanese workers are not exceptionally high when compared with those that workers in advanced Western nations receive. By supporting these observations with empirical data, he also rebuts what he describes as "the majority opinion," which presumably emphasizes that permanent employment carries with it an implication of paternalism.

In the second part of his analysis, Koike argues, largely on the basis of his field surveys of large industrial plants in Japan, the United States, and some European countries, that the career patterns of Japanese blue-collar workers are much more internalized than those of their counterparts in other countries. Although very young Japanese workers have high turnover rates, after they are in the mid-twenties and have become settled in jobs the degree of internalization of their working careers is reinforced by intensive and successive on-the-job training, by the considerable autonomy enjoyed by the teams of workers at the workshop level as far as allocating and assigning workers to jobs is concerned, and, above all, by the extensive opportunities available to workers to develop skills through frequent and flexible transfer within a broad cluster of jobs which are organized along extended promotion lines. It is within an internal labor market of this type that enterprise unions, whose configuration matches most closely the arena in which workers' careers develop, can protect and represent the economic interests of those workers most effectively.

Although there is still room to strengthen the empirical evidence, the idea proposed by Koike in this chapter is highly perceptive and worthy of further investigation. His argument may be broadly classified as a version of the "convergence thesis." In particular, it resembles Dore's hypothesis suggesting convergence toward Japanese practices. However, Koike's version is unique in that the logic of convergence toward the white-collar pattern is elaborated in economic terms within the framework of the operation of internal labor markets, centering upon the skill formation and career development of workers.

Chapter 3. The Quality of Working Life in Japanese Factories

Kazutoshi Kōshiro presents relevant information on aspects of the quality of working life of employees of large Japanese firms. It is widely known that Japanese workers perform much better than their counterparts in other industrialized countries today. For example, attendance rates of workers in large plants of major industries surveyed by the author ranged between 90 and 96 percent, and labor turnover was found to be very low as well. In other words, the managements can be said to have utilized their labor forces successfully and most efficiently.

The author's key question is whether such a remarkable achievement from management's standpoint is compatible with the quality of working life (QWL) of the employees. A common critical explanation is that Japanese workers appear to be diligent because they are exploited and are forced to sacrifice their freedom and human dignity on the job. Foreign observers have expressed skepticism, if not open criticism, along these lines. Marxists are even more critical, maintaining that the managements' relatively humane policies that allow for the workers' own choices and initiatives, such as QC (quality control) circle activities, are only new and more sophisticated methods of exploitation. However, Kōshiro, on the basis of his case studies of several major plants, arrives at a conclusion that counters these criticisms—namely, that the institutional and organizational arrangements in large Japanese firms not only keep the workers' motivation and productivity at high levels, but at the same time provide them with a high degree of satisfaction and sense of security. In support of this conclusion, he presents detailed descriptions of the innovative methods introduced into workshops in large plants in four manufacturing industries—automobiles, shipbuilding, steel, and textiles—together with evaluations of their outcomes; in addition, he supplies rich descriptive information on various organizational arrangements. The implication he draws from these observations is that the systems of labor and personnel management which have been developed and practiced within large Japanese firms during the postwar period of rapid growth are perhaps among the most humane and effective in the world when they are evaluated in the light of contemporary Western concepts of QWL. At the same time, however, the author admits that the stability of such systems in large firms depends to an important extent on the existence of the less privileged sectors. His concluding suggestion, therefore, is that it will be more meaningful to direct efforts toward improving the quality of life for all working people by seeking possible ways to diffuse the humane system of the large firms to the rest of the economy, rather than by relying on the false premise that workers in large firms suffer from institutionalized exploitation.

Chapter 4. Workers in Small Firms and Women in Industry

Kazuo Koike reexamines the nature of employment and the working conditions of workers in small firms and female workers in general largely by comparing descriptive official statistics of Japan and some of the Western countries, but partly by using results of his own questionnaire survey of small firms. There is a widely held perception, within the context of the dual labor market hypothesis, that workers in small firms suffer from low wages and poor working conditions, in sharp contrast to the privileges that workers employed by large firms enjoy. Also, the author claims that it is generally assumed that Japanese women workers lag far behind men in terms of their labor force participation and working conditions because of the backwardness of social and institutional arrangements for working women. This he calls the "lag-behind hypothesis." In spite of the prevalence of these presumptions, there is scant evidence to support them, as these two important aspects of the Japanese labor market certainly have not received the attention they deserve, at least in the literature written for the non-Japanese audience.

On the basis of statistical comparisons and his survey results, Koike makes a number of observations about male workers in small firms, including such points as (1) the wage profiles and patterns of career formation of white-collar workers in small firms are much the same as those of blue-collar workers in large firms; (2) the flatter age-wage profiles of the blue-collar workers compared to their white-collar counterparts can be explained by the fact that the process of their skill formation and the structure of their careers are less internalized; and (3) a sizable number of blue-collar workers in small firms do not finish their occupational careers as employees, but instead embark on new careers as owners of small workshops. Thus, when the career patterns of workers in small firms are examined carefully, any conclusion that would lump them all together and characterize them simply as low-wage and exploited workers, as the dual labor market hypothesis suggests, would be misleading.

As for female workers, Koike acknowledges that to some extent they are not as advanced as women workers in other industrialized countries: for example, as there are fewer Japanese women in administrative positions, and in the prime ages, the male–female wage differential is considerably greater than those in some other advanced countries. He maintains, however, that the major explanation of this phenomenon is the highly developed internalization of Japanese labor markets, particularly for large firms.

Chapter 5. A Theory of Enterprise Unionism

Taishiro Shirai presents evaluations of Japanese enterprise unions, their structure, goals, and functions, and, to place the evaluations in context, he describes the elements involved in their formation and offers a rationale for their existence.

The many critics of enterprise unionism, both abroad and within Japan, censure unions of this type for being dependent upon and dominated by management and for being weak and vulnerable to management's interference. Although acknowledging the validity of some of the criticisms and admitting that some inherent weaknesses exist, the author nevertheless presents convincing counterarguments. Through his systematic analysis and comprehensive discussion, he is successful in conveying a realistic picture of Japanese enterprise unions that demonstrates that they are, indeed, bona fide and viable unions and that they are the type that has been deliberately chosen and endorsed by the majority of Japanese workers under the particular economic, social, and historical circumstances of Japanese industrial society.

Shirai emphasizes at the outset of the chapter that Japanese enterprise unions, unlike so-called "company unions," do enjoy autonomy and independence from management. He stresses further that their achievements have been significant, especially in view of their very short history compared to their counterparts in Western industrialized countries, and he suggests that their viability should not be underestimated. Let me summarize some of the major points he makes in support of his position.

On the structure of enterprise unions, he points to some American local unions and German works councils as examples of enterprise organizations abroad that perform functions equivalent to those of Japan's enterprise unions. Discussing the factors that gave rise to enterprise unions, he examines and rejects a number of hypotheses that have been offered—that this form of union organization developed under the guidance of the Supreme Commander for Allied Powers, that it was influenced by the Communists, that it was an outgrowth of Sampō (the united labor front during World War II), and that it was the only form that employers would tolerate. In his view, enterprise unionism developed because of economic, historical, and cultural factors—the economic factor being the internalized labor markets of the enterprises in which all aspects of the economic life of workers, such as wages, careers, and working conditions, are defined within the realm of the enterprise, and the historical and cultural factors being the enterprise consciousness of workers as they identify with the "enterprise" community.

On the question of whether or not Japanese enterprise unions are bona fide unions, the author stresses three realities: (1) The lack of professional union officers, an alleged defect of enterprise unions, is not a phenomenon unique to Japan; many local union officers in the United States and shop stewards in European countries are paid by the company even while they are engaged in union activities. (2) Union autonomy is rigidly maintained in Japan, in part because union executive officers are granted very little discretionary power. (3) The strike-frequency rate in Japan is approximately equal to that in France and is much higher than rates in Sweden and West Germany, and the duration of strikes in Japan is not really short by international standards, although strikes in the Anglo-Saxon countries do last longer than those in Japan.

In evaluating the strength of Japanese unions, Shirai underlines the danger of using a single "Western" or Anglo-American yardstick, and he suggests the importance of recognizing other virtues. For example, (1) Japanese unions have contributed significantly in narrowing wage and status differentials between blue- and white-collar workers, and (2) each union has secured maximum economic gains for its members by at times cooperating with the management rather than simply stubbornly confronting it, especially in situations and under structural conditions when the interests of union and management in maintaining the prosperity of the enterprise coincide. Although these achievements will not add up to much on the Anglo-American yardstick, the author implies that it is meaningful to have an alternative measure in order to understand the reasons for the survival and the viability of Japanese enterprise unions.

Chapter 6. Trade Union Finance and Administration

Norikuni Naitō reports a number of important facts about the internal administration of Japanese trade unions. The membership fee is exceedingly high by international standards; according to the author, the contribution per member in Japan ranges between 2 and 2.5 percent of a worker's monthly pay, which is nearly ten times the contribution rate of an average British union member. Japanese enterprise unions are generally regarded as relatively weak in comparison with unions in the West, and one is naturally curious to know how this can be, when they collect such a large amount of money in union dues and apparently expend it on union services. How do they use this money, and what kind of services do they provide for union members? The author discloses important aspects of union activities as a key to understanding the apparent paradox of rich and weak Japanese unions.

The major explanations for this paradox are, in order: (1) Japanese unions have a great many full-time union officers—on average one full-time officer paid by the union to 570 members; the ratio increases to about 1:330 when union staff and clerks are included in the count; in contrast, the ratio is one officer to 3,800 members in Britain. Approximately 40–50 percent of the large budget pays the salaries and fringe benefits of union functionaries. In the United States, Britain, and some other advanced countries many full-time union officers at local levels are paid by employers; Japanese unions, in contrast, may be said to pay a high price to maintain their financial independence from employers. (2) Japanese unions hold very frequent conventions or conferences, the cost of which ranges between 10 and 40 percent of the total budget, depending on their frequency. An important explanation for these many conferences may be found in the naive but popular conviction, "the more frequent the conference, the greater the degree of democratic check," which might be labeled "primitive democracy." (3) The bulk of the budget is assigned to publishing periodicals and journals that are distributed on a regular basis to all rank-and-file members. This type of communication between the leadership and the membership is indispensable, the unions believe, in maintaining "democratic" administrations. These aspects inevitably contribute to a highly inefficient union administration characterized by collective leadership, excessively recurrent elections of officers, and, above all, lack of professional leaders. These observations suggest that the weakness of Japanese unions can be attributed to an important extent to administrative inefficiency which, however, is the price that union members apparently are willing to pay as they seek to retain popular control over their union's decision-making.

Chapter 7. The Function of Law in Japanese Industrial Relations

Tadashi Hanami argues that the postwar labor laws, many of which were originally transplanted in whole or part from the United States and some European countries, have come to be interpreted in a uniquely Japanese way in the prevailing culture of Japan. He argues further that the effects upon the growth of unions and the maturing of industrial relations have been disturbing rather than encouraging.

Specifically, the author discusses the legal interpretations, and the consequences of these interpretations, of the right to strike, the right to act collectively, strike votes, and the right to bargain as enforced by the courts. Since the first two rights are guaranteed explicitly in the Constitution and labor lawyers make extensive use of these guarantees, the unions have come to place excessive reliance on these protections while often ignoring the importance of their own organizing efforts. The majority interpretation of the constitutional right of workers to organize, for example, contends that this right is something more positive than the freedom of association guaranteed to ordinary citizens. Since this view implies the encouragement, and perhaps even coercion, of workers to join unions, it tends to neglect any freedom the workers might have to forgo union membership and thus possibly leads the unions to slight the minority of workers who do not agree with the majority leadership within the organization. It is not unusual, therefore, that a legal interpretation of this kind in practice helps to maintain the status quo rather than encouraging unions to broaden their power base and influence, which was the original intention of the interpretation. In a somewhat similar way, an interpretation of the right to act collectively that is excessively permissive and favorable to the unions often goes so far as to regard "violence" as a justifiable use of "power"; thus, the court rulings and even the intentions of the prolabor lawyers, despite their avowed intent, perpetuate the weakness of the unions.

Chapter 8. Conflict Resolution in Japanese Industrial Relations

Yasuhiko Matsuda analyzes the methods and processes by which industrial relations conflicts are resolved; his principal emphasis is on legal procedures. Indeed, industrial relations may be viewed as a constant unfolding of conflict and conflict resolution at various levels and places and over various kinds of issues. Given this broad spectrum, the analysis that Matsuda develops in this chapter clarifies a relatively limited aspect of the entire picture of conflict resolution in Japanese industrial relations. Within this limited sphere, however, the author provides useful information and enlightening insights.

Matsuda discusses four different procedures for conflict resolution and the actual processes employed in each: through the labor relations commissions, through the spontaneous efforts of the parties, through involvement of the courts, and through compromise or conciliation. He describes the processes mainly from a legal viewpoint, emphasizing the practices and problems peculiar to each process. Through his descriptions and analysis, a curious feature of conflict resolution emerges, namely, the excessively legalistic attitudes of the parties, especially the unions, but, at the same time, the frequency with which disputes are spontaneously resolved through compromises.

Chapter 9. The Development of Collective Bargaining in Postwar Japan

Kazutoshi Kōshiro provides a comprehensive and informative explanation of the roles the collective bargaining system plays in Japanese industrial relations and suggests, quite convincingly, the importance of the system as a determinant of the performance of the total Japanese economy.

In developing his argument, Kōshiro first uses the eight criteria proposed by Milton Derber to test the legitimacy of "enterprise-based collective bargaining" and finds that the Japanese system essentially satisfies them. He then examines some of the features unique to Japanese collective bargaining and the context from which they arose.

He presents his discussion in three phases. The first is an exposition of the structure and functioning of Japanese collective bargaining, including detailed descriptions of the structure, historical evolution, and items subject to collective bargaining.

The second is a detailed description and economic analysis of shuntō, the concerted wage negotiations which take place in the spring and which constitute the single most important activity of Japanese collective bargaining. Kōshiro describes the historical development of the Spring Offensive, identifies the factors that determined "pattern setters" in different wage rounds, and highlights the apparent trends towards equalization of negotiated wage settlements among different industries and enterprises. He then presents an intriguing econometric analysis of negotiated wage changes, demonstrating that the seemingly volatile outcomes of Japanese wage negotiations can be consistently explained by what he regards as the principle of economic rationality and responsiveness. He supplements his analysis with an examination of important auxiliary areas of collective bargaining—bonuses, hours of work, employment security, and participation.

In the third phase of his discussion, Kōshiro speculates about how and why a high degree of economic responsiveness became a basic characteristic of Japanese industrial relations, considers several factors that have been hypothesized to be major determinants of the nature of the system, and selects what he calls the hypothesis of the scarcity of well-paid job opportunities as providing the most powerful explanation.

Chapter 10. Labor Relations in Public Enterprises

Kazutoshi Kōshiro supplies institutional information on the structure and functions of a complex system of labor–management relations in Japanese public corporations and national enterprises that operate under a variety of legal restrictions.

Enterprise unions in the public sector in Japan do not conform with the familiar stereotype of organizations that are docile, weak, and cooperative with managements—an image of which the validity is challenged in this book. Public-sector enterprise unions have been quite militant and vigorous in their political activities, and they have frequently engaged in strikes in violation of rigid legal restrictions. As a large proportion of the total number of union members in Japan belong to these unions, they occupy a central position in the complex structure of the Japanese industrial relations system.

It is fair to say, as the author claims, that "without understanding the problems and characteristics of labor–management relations in the public sector, one could not understand industrial relations in Japan." In this chapter, he attempts to provide readers with a stock of basic and yet quite detailed information on the structural, organizational, and legal framework of public-sector industrial relations and how the system actually works.

Kōshiro begins with a description of various concepts of the public enterprises and their historical development. He then explains the various legal restrictions on union activities and labor–management relations in this sector as well as the structure of collective bargaining, employment, and wages. The institutional framework, methods, and process of dispute settlement form another cluster of topics the author discusses. Finally, he reviews a number of contemporary problems such as wage comparability with the private sector, the autonomy of public enterprise authorities, the right-to-strike issue, and union rivalries.

Chapter 11. The Public Sector: Civil Servants

Kōichirō Yamaguchi reports on the historical and legal background of the civil service and its employment relations, union activities, and industrial relations. Although his objective is to provide information on the civil service at all levels—national, provincial, and municipal—he confines his focus to the national level on the ground that activities there are representative of those at the other levels as well. Under the broad heading of conditions of employment, he describes regulations and practices governing appointments, promotions, salaries, hours of work, holidays, discipline and penalties, political neutrality, job security, and retirement. Under the heading of union activities, he discusses the right to organize, collective bargaining, strikes, and concerted actions. In sum, the author provides in this chapter a convenient brief summary of the legal regulations and the realities of the operation of the national civil service. Although he refrains from making explicit value judgments, he hints at some reasons that the union movements in the public sector have been losing public support in recent years.

Chapter 12. A Marxist Interpretation of Japanese Industrial Relations, with Special Reference to Large Private Enterprises

Shigeyoshi Tokunaga presents a view of the majority of the Marxists that is critical of the Japanese union movement and industrial relations system. Let me summarize the major points of his argument.

First, the author emphasizes the importance of recognizing the particular political climate during the first few years of the postwar period. During the late 1940s, that climate changed drastically from one in which the SCAP fully encouraged the union movement to one in which the same SCAP, in the

face of a growing fear of Communism, imposed severely repressive measures, including the denial of the right of public-sector employees to strike.
Therefore, many of the collective bargaining agreements had to be revised to
accord with these new and harsher restraints. These actions provided a
benchmark for postwar Japanese unionism and industrial relations.

Second, calling attention to the bitter labor struggles that occurred during
the years around 1950, the author makes an important point that Japanese
enterprise unions originally were quite militant and uncooperative with management, not tractable and cooperative as they are commonly believed to be
today. Tokunaga attributes the change from militancy to tractability to the
unions' nearly fatal defeat in the struggles of the early 1950s, which was
followed by a vigorous rationalization by the managements. Various new
labor–management policies were introduced, all of which increased labor
intensity, competition among workers, and the emotional dependence of
workers on the employing companies.

Third, given these defects and the weakness associated with enterprise
unionism, even the seemingly successful Spring Offensive has left many
problems unresolved. Also, in spite of their strategic importance, the workshop activities of the unions have failed to develop and capture any substantial control over workshop decision-making. Instead, it is due to the weakness
of union activities at the workshop level that managements were able to
introduce such new policies as ability-based wages and motivation management, utilizing small-group plant organization activities to reinforce labor
intensity schemes and workers' subordination to the managements.

Chapter 13. Japanese Labor Unions and Politics

In his comprehensive exposition of the political aspects of Japanese unionism, Taishiro Shirai provides information on and an explanation of the
unions' political positions, their relationship with political parties, their political ideologies, and the prospects for success of their political activities.

Outside observers get mixed impressions of the relations between Japanese
labor unions and the political structure in Japan. On the one hand, the unions'
political activities seem to be ideologically highly leftist in tone. Yet, in their
dealings with managements, especially at the enterprise level, they appear to
be quite submissive, cooperative, and practical. There is no doubt that Japan
has attained a level of economic maturity that can fully afford and embrace a
pragmatic union movement and endorse collective bargaining as an instrument to determine the workers' fair share of economic growth. Why then do
Japanese unions have to be political? How are they political, if indeed they
are? And what are the prospects of their current political activities?

In an attempt to answer these questions, or to provide information that
would be helpful in evaluating them, Shirai discusses the unions' political

and financial support of political parties, the unions as a pressure group, and political strikes. He also examines thoroughly the single most important ideology, Marxism–Leninism, to analyze why it enjoyed such an overwhelming popularity in the labor movement—at least in the past. His analysis suggests that the prospect for union involvement in politics may well change in the future as the popularity of the Marxist–Leninist ideology declines, a new type of leadership gradually replaces the old, and more fluid and pluralistic relationships develop between unions and political parties.

An Evaluation of the Contribution of this Book

Having reviewed the content of the preceding twelve chapters I turn now to examine what we, the authors, hope this volume will contribute to the stock of knowledge about industrial relations in Japan and to the understanding of the Japanese system among the English-reading audience.

As I stated earlier, we had four objectives in mind as we were planning and writing this book. It would therefore be logical to evaluate what we believe to be the probable contributions in light of these objectives.

The first two are, in fact, interrelated. The first objective was to provide the candid and, we hoped, new ideas of Japanese scholars. The second was to express frankly our heterogeneous views without concealing controversies, which could be a useful and effective means for realizing our first objective. Therefore, let me begin this evaluation of the contributions of the volume by considering these two objectives combined.

The authors of most of the chapters shared a more or less common appraisal of the legitimacy and strength of Japanese enterprise unionism and the related aspects of labor–management relations within enterprises—all essential to an understanding of the nature of Japanese industrial relations. Interestingly, however, their evaluations, viewpoints, and analytical methodologies are quite diverse, even though they employ some common concepts.

They share, for instance, the view that Japanese labor unions have some kind of innate weakness, but their explanations and interpretations are quite different. The most critical appraisal was Tokunaga's (chapter 12). He attributes the weakness of Japanese unionism to the defeat of the labor movement in the late 1940s and early 1950s and the unions' subsequent subordination to management policies, particularly at the workshop level. This view is, in fact, representative of that offered by the majority of Marxist scholars, many of whom were prominent within Japanese academic circles in the fields of economics and industrial relations and whose opinions enjoyed wide popularity. Moreover, although from a different standpoint, the lawyers among the authors present evaluations that resemble this view. Hanami (chapter 7), Matsuda (chapter 8), and Yamaguchi (chapter 11) all imply, though with slightly different emphases, the innate weakness of Japanese unions. A common thread in their arguments is that an important cause of this weakness or immaturity can be found in the unions' tendency to rely almost totally on protections embodied in the law—what might be called their excessively legalistic attitude—rather than to try to develop their own "muscle" to increase their bargaining power.

Although admitting that this weakness exists, the other writers offer rather different interpretations. Naitō (chapter 6) points to administrative inefficiency as an important factor contributing to the weakness of Japanese unions. Shirai (chapter 5) emphasizes the importance of recognizing that the strength and legitimacy of any type of unionism cannot and should not be measured by a single yardstick, particularly of an Anglo-American type. Japanese unionism, according to him, may be viewed as having achieved remarkable results in narrowing status and wage differentials among employees, particularly between blue- and white-collar workers, which may not be adequately appreciated by Anglo-American measures. Kōshiro (chapter 9) contends that modern labor–management policies practiced in large Japanese firms—as an example, the self-actualization philosophy exemplified by the familiar quality-control circle activities—are perhaps the most humane in the world even when evaluated by Western criteria of the quality of working life. Obviously, this is an intentional counterargument to the Marxist preoccupation with the "sophisticated exploitation" thesis. He also argues (chapter 9) that Japanese unionism is perhaps the most efficient and economically rational form of unionism for a late-developed economy dominated by relatively large enterprise organizations. Koike (chapter 2) goes even further to theorize that the rapid development of the internal labor markets of large business organizations granted insufficient time for craft unionism to grow and mature in a rapidly expanding "late-comer" economy. The resulting intensive internalization of labor markets meant that blue- and white-collar workers became almost indistinguishable in their career patterns and motivations. Under such circumstances, the enterprise union turns out to be the most rational and viable form of union organization to represent and protect the workers' common interests. Thus, it is not surprising that Koike, among the authors, shows the least appreciation for the common allegation that Japanese enterprise unions are inherently weak.

Even on the single issue of union strength, the book reveals our various and often conflicting views, and we believe that this forthright expression of our differences on this and other issues will provide the reader with a much truer picture of complex reality than will pseudo-consensus. The Japanese audience is not quite persuaded by—and is frequently dissatisfied with—the simple, classical, culturalist interpretation of Japanese industrial relations as well as the assertions of functional analysis and of the Anglo-American convergence thesis, exemplified, for instance, by Galenson (1976). They are, however, often irritated by their inability to present a clear-cut alternative model. In my view, the reason for this is that the reality is not simple enough to permit easy theorizing. The broad spectrum of different, often conflicting, views in this volume eloquently illustrates this reality. If we are successful in transmitting a picture of the complexity of the real world as well as convincing the reader that there are good reasons for the hesitance of the sensible and traditional Japanese to accept or even propose simple interpretations of complexity, then we feel that this book has made a contribution.

Let me now turn to what may be the most positive contributions of this book. It is important to recognize that most of the chapters are composed as counterarguments or criticisms of the predominant popular views in Japanese academic circles as well as some of the major streams of Western thought on Japanese industrial relations.

Clearly, the chapters by Koike (2 and 4), Kōshiro (3 and 9), Shirai (5), and Naitō (6) can be interpreted as challenging and countering the Marxist interpretation that has been predominant among Japanese scholars in the field of labor and industrial relations. By the same token, the chapters by Hanami (7), Yamaguchi (11), and, to some extent, Matsuda (8) may be read as ironical criticisms of the view held by the majority of Japanese labor lawyers, who seem to believe, happily and naively, that the greater the legal protection a union enjoys, the stronger it will become. Thus, it could be inferred that this is a book of criticism of the predominant and popular views of Japanese academia. It is unfortunate, therefore, that the views that are criticized are only implicitly presented here, except for the neatly organized argument of Tokunaga (chapter 12). Nevertheless, the book does indicate, though indirectly, the notions widely accepted in Japanese academic circles, and it presents quite explicit critiques. Thus the book makes non-Japanese readers aware of the nature of the controversies continuing among Japanese scholars.

Another and still more important contribution is the fact that many of the chapters are written intentionally to dissent from and propose alternatives to some of the major streams of English-language literature on Japanese industrial relations. The chapters by Shirai (5), Koike (2 and 4), and Kōshiro (9) are intended as criticisms of the classical culturalist and the descriptive approaches. Koike (chapter 2) and Kōshiro (chapter 9) offer provocative hypothetical models in an attempt to go beyond the impressionistic approach of the recent intriguing works by foreign observers that I categorized in chapter 1 under the heading of the "neoculturalist synthesis."

When our book is viewed in this way, it certainly fulfills our first two objectives—that is, to provoke new ideas by expressing our diverse and sometimes conflicting opinions.

What about the third objective—to provide information in areas that have been relatively ignored in previous studies? Since the contribution here is more or less self-evident, explanations will be kept to a minimum. On the public sector, Kōshiro (chapter 10) and Yamaguchi (chapter 11) offer ample and useful information. Koike's interpretations of the working conditions and career patterns of workers in small firms and of female workers (chapter 4) are unique and enlightening. Naitō (chapter 6) discloses an important aspect of union activities—the internal administration of enterprise unions. Shirai (chapter 13) presents a comprehensive appraisal of the political activities of Japanese unions. These chapters together will certainly help the English-reading audience to get a more balanced picture of the total system of Japanese industrial relations than was ever available before. However, Koike (chapter 2) adds useful new information on the functioning of the internal labor markets of large Japanese firms, as does Kōshiro (chapter 3) on management's labor policies in the workshop and (chapter 9) on the structure of collective bargaining and, in particular, the concerted wage negotiations known as shuntō. Discussions of the legal aspects of industrial relations by Hanami (chapter 7), Matsuda (chapter 8), and Yamaguchi (chapter 11) certainly contribute useful information on relevant topics. In this sense, we fulfill our third objective.

Our fourth objective was to write manuscripts originally in English in the hope that we would communicate more effectively with the English-reading audience. All of the contributors followed this rule. Whether or not we were successful must be left to our readers to judge.

15 *Taishiro Shirai*

A Supplement:
Characteristics of Japanese Managements
and Their Personnel Policies

Postwar Reforms and the Power Structure of Enterprises

In this chapter we will confine our discussion for the most part to the management organization and practices of large Japanese enterprises, because labor union organization is concentrated in this sector and the system of union-management relations that has evolved over the years between the enterprise unions and the managements of the major corporations has had a strong influence on labor relations in all the other sectors. However, we cannot ignore the management and union structures that prevail in the small and medium-sized enterprises: they employ more than 70 percent of all Japanese workers, and among the difficult problems that remain to be resolved is how to establish and stabilize industrial democracy in this sector. The labor policies of this sector will be described briefly later in this chapter.

It was the large enterprises that commanded the attention of the American Occupation Forces immediately following World War II and a number of reforms were implemented: the zaibatsu were dissolved; the large monopolistic companies were split into smaller units; the stock holdings of these companies were liquidated and stock ownership "democratized"—that is, these stocks became available for purchase on the open market; top company executives who had played leading roles during the war were purged; and property taxes were levied, precipitating the downfall of wartime corporation

369

magnates. All of these reforms had very strong effects on the management structure of large enterprises as well as on their industrial relations philosophy and policies.

One result of these reforms is that the ownership and management of companies in Japan is now more distinctly separate than in most other capitalist countries in the world. "Capitalist control," of course, does not exist in the national enterprises or public corporations (the Postal Service or the National Railways, for example), but it also can be said to be virtually absent in the leading private-sector enterprises. Because company stock is widely dispersed among a large number of owners, each with only a few shares, the stockholders are, in practical terms, virtually deprived of any power over the day-to-day decisions of company managements, and only in extraordinary situations have they had the power to appoint or remove top management personnel. The inevitable consequence is that the general meeting of stockholders has only nominal power and that even the boards of directors of the major corporations have come to be monopolized by the companies' full-time managing directors. Thus, it can be said that a "managerial revolution" has materialized in Japan to the extent that the power of the company management exceeds that of company stockholders.

It may be useful to begin our examination of the management power structure in Japanese companies and the characteristics of their decision-making mechanisms by comparing the functions of inspectors in Japan with those of the West German *Aufsichtsrat*, inspectors' organizations representing shareholders and employees of the company. The German inspectors have the power to appoint members of the board of directors, to control its activities, and to approve or reject some major business decisions. The Japanese inspectors, in contrast, have no such powers and their function traditionally has been limited to auditing a company's accounts. The 1974 revision of the Commercial Law authorized inspectors to review how the executive board members perform their duties, but even here their inspection is confined to whether or not the activities of the board members are legal and does not consider whether they are proper or reasonable. Thus it cannot be said that this change in the law had any visible effect on company power structures. The Commercial Law was again amended in 1981, which further reinforced the authority of the inspectors in that they could ask not only executive board members but also general managers to provide them with necessary information concerning business conditions of the company. This amendment went into effect on October 1, 1982, and the impact on the power balance between inspectors and boards of directors is yet to be seen.

More important than the function of inspectors in any discussion of the management power structure in Japan is the role of the stockholders' general meeting. Its position and power were defined in a 1950 revision of the

Commercial Law as being limited to the determination of conditions fundamental to a corporation's existence, such as its establishment or dissolution, its merger with another company, the appointment or dismissal of executive board members, and changes in the amount of authorized capital. The power to make all strategic business decisions is in the hands of the board of directors. Although the boards do report these decisions at the stockholders' meetings, the meetings themselves are largely ceremonial and it is most unlikely, except in emergency cases, that stockholders would disapprove any decision previously made by a board of directors. As far as appointments or dismissals of board members are concerned, they are usually reported ex post facto and are routinely approved.

The point being emphasized here is that more than merely the law and custom prevail and that control of corporations through a concentration of stock ownership, as is often seen in the United States and Western Europe, operates in only a limited sense in large Japanese enterprises, for the following reasons:

First, as stated earlier, the postwar reforms of the large corporations enabled the "employee managers" to gain the power and authority to function as top management. Another factor that operated to curtail the stockholders' influence and their share of profits was the growth of the enterprise unions.

Second, there has been a great change in the composition of corporation stockholders, with the stock of any one corporation now being owned by a large number of individuals as well as by banks, insurance companies, and other corporations. In 1980, more than 70 percent of the total number of shares of stocks listed on the stock exchange was owned by corporations, and slightly less than 30 percent was owned by individuals. It actually is fairly common in Japan for large corporations to own stock in other large corporations, but that does not mean that any of them will exercise the right to control another's management. Rather, the situation compels them to respect each other's autonomy and to refrain from intervening in the business management. Also, a large corporation may have a considerable number of corporate stockholders who may find it difficult to agree among themselves on the need to intervene or on what type of intervention would be appropriate. Furthermore, many of the corporate stockholders have invested in other corporations only for the profitable utilization of their assets; therefore, their investments may be only on a short-term or temporary basis. Thus, if they are dissatisfied with the management of a particular company, a wiser move would be for them to sell their stock.

Third, the capitalization of large Japanese corporations is probably unique in that owned capital is, on average, no more than 20 percent of total capital. This proportion is lower than that among companies in most developed countries. Thus, a high percentage of a Japanese corporation's financial demands must be met by borrowed capital. So far the corporation managements have been successful in securing the funds they need by persuading the banks to support their long-term investments in plant and equipment. As a result, their need to rely for this capital on stockholders, who are generally concerned with short-term profits, has lessened, and this, in turn, has weakened the stockholders' power to control the corporation managements.

These three factors have worked to expand the scope of top management's discretion in formulating corporate policies and making decisions so that it might be said that large corporations in Japan have realized not only the separation of management from ownership, but also the establishment of a system in which management enjoys almost unrestricted power over the owners.

I should make it clear that when I am speaking about the company's top management, I am referring to a small group of full-time executives, the *Jōmukai*, who actually have the power to make decisions on matters that are discussed by the corporation's board of directors. As a rule, members of this group are the president, the vice-president (unlike U.S. companies, Japanese companies have very few vice-presidents), the senior managing director (*senmu*), and the managing director (*jōmu*). This executive board is kind of an "inner cabinet" of the board of directors which assists the president in the day-to-day operation of the business. The responsibilities vested in this group lead to what we call the "loosening of the checking function of the board of directors" and, consequently, to further concentration and internalization of decision-making power within the corporation.

The Development of Managerial Personnel through "Promotion from Within"

The obvious next questions, then, are: What kinds of people are these top managers, and where do they come from? Generally, the establishment of management control means that professional managers, independent of corporate ownership, come to the fore and assume the responsibility and power to run the business. In the case of Japan, however, it should be noted that when we speak of professional managers, we are referring to something different from what the term means in the United States and other advanced industrialized societies. Top professional managers in the United States frequently move from one company to another, demonstrating their managerial expertise beyond the boundaries of any one corporation. In other words, they are capable of performing their managerial functions as professionals in an open labor market where there is high mobility among firms. As such, they are often scouted and hired away by rival companies. Accordingly, they tend to be free from any commitment to or any identification with a particular corporation, nor do they feel obliged to do more than what is required by their contract.

An overwhelming majority of Japanese managers have advanced to their present positions from the ranks of general employees through the system of internal promotion, or "promotion from within" the particular company.[1] Rather than being a postwar innovation, this system of regular career paths for all employees was well established among large Japanese corporations, both public and private, before World War II. The companies hire groups of new university or college graduates and, as they climb the managerial ladder, they accumulate experience in various jobs, not confined to any specialized field, through job rotation at regular intervals. Finally, those who survive this extensive training and screening process are promoted to top management positions.

The organization of white-collar employees into enterprise unions after the war not only reinforced their employment security, but entrenched more solidly than ever before the practice of developing managers within a particular company by this system of promoting long-service employees. Of course, a system of this kind could not operate successfully in the new and rapidly growing firms, in those companies that have gotten into financial difficulties, or in those companies closely related to public corporations and government agencies. In these latter cases, the probabilities are that they have had to hire managers from outside. These imported managers constitute only a small share of the total in Japan, the overwhelming majority of the managers having been promoted within their particular companies. Support for this statement can be found in data from Keizai Dōyūkai (Japanese Committee for Economic Development), one of the leading associations of managers, collected as part of an international comparative study of boards of directors in nine countries, planned and carried out by The Conference Board.[2]

The origins of 2,636 directors of the 134 member companies that responded to the Japan survey questionnaire are shown in table 15.1. All of the companies have at least some directors who were promoted from the employee ranks, and 91 percent of all full-time directors of the 134 firms surveyed were promoted from within their companies. In The Conference Board final report, only the sources of directors who came to their positions from outside the surveyed companies are tabulated, so these international data provide no conclusive evidence that the Japanese companies are unique in drawing such a large proportion of their full-time directors from within their enterprises.[3] However, the fact that the companies themselves are the source of supply for so many of their directors emphasizes that this internal promotion system is a basic and important characteristic of Japanese management.

Further, the Keizai Dōyūkai survey revealed that 46 of the 134 companies

Table 15.1
Origin of Full-Time Directors of Japanese Companies, 1977

Origin	Companies		Persons	
	N	%	N	%
Employees of the company	134	100.0	2398	91.0
Owner/stockholder	23	17.2	64	2.4
Bank executives	36	26.9	56	2.1
Public officials/government representatives	48	35.8	73	2.8
Others (representatives of manufacturing, trade, insurance corporations, etc.)	36	26.8	45	1.7

Source: Keizai Dōyūkai 1977.

responding to the questionnaire, or 34.2 percent, reported that some member or members of their board of directors had at one time been an executive officer of the company's enterprise union. An even higher percentage of Japanese companies—66.8 percent of the 352 firms responding to a survey by Nikkeiren (Japanese Federation of Employers' Associations) in 1978—reported that former enterprise union officers were currently on their boards of directors.[4] The survey covered 6,457 directors, of whom 1,012 (15.7 percent) had had experience as union officials. Readers should be reminded here that both blue- and white-collar employees of a Japanese company belong to the same enterprise union and that those employees who demonstrate competence and leadership abilities have good prospects of being promoted to top management positions under the internal promotion system. Thus, the appointment of a former union official to a company's board of directors is regarded as a normal progression in Japan's industrial relations system but is considered quite unusual in the industrial societies of the United States and Western Europe. Perhaps this explains why the Conference Board described a Japanese enterprise union as a "company union" in its report.

Management Philosophies and Personnel Policies

The fact that the top management of most Japanese corporations are long-service employees who have been promoted from within their companies undoubtedly affects their management philosophy and especially their industrial relations policies. Five principal features of their philosophy, as it relates to industrial relations, can be summarized: First, their primary concern is the continued existence and further development of their corporation. Second, they regard all company employees, including themselves, as members of the same corporate community. Third, they take an egalitarian view of income distribution between labor and management within the company. Fourth, they are crucially concerned with maintaining stability and peace in the company's industrial relations. In other words, they strive to avoid industrial disputes and strikes, often at any cost. Fifth, they tend to reject the intervention of outside labor groups in any negotiations over internal labor problems, an attitude that might be described as exclusionist. Let me discuss each of these points in more detail.

First, it would seem to be quite natural, and understandable, that the top executives of a Japanese firm would attach the utmost importance to its continued existence and development. This concern is rooted in a sense of identification with the company that results from their own long service with it as well as in a sense of responsibility for the continued employment and improved conditions of their fellow employees. Moreover, only by keeping the company prosperous and expanding can they ensure their own influential positions and prestige both within and outside the corporation. The fact that managers motivated by such a value have been given real power in their companies has contributed to the creation of a highly competitive market economy in Japan, and the positive entrepreneurship of these people is an important factor in the rapid growth of the Japanese economy. These managers have been progressive and enterprising in promoting technological change and innovations, in pioneering in new industrial areas, in adjusting to changing industrial structures, in reorganizing industrial locations, and in expanding international trade and investment overseas as well as in many other corporate activities. Such entrepreneurship is possible only because management has primacy over ownership in Japanese corporations, which enables the managers to make plans and decisions from a long-term perspective, unrestricted by short-term considerations of profits and dividends.

The firm conviction on the part of these managers that company employees are members of a corporate community seems to be quite different from views of employers in the United States and some Western European countries. For those Japanese managers who have climbed the promotion ladder within their companies, it is not extraordinary to consider other employees as colleagues, or subordinates or juniors, in the ranks in which they themselves spent many years. At the same time all these employees belong to the enterprise union of which the managers once were members, and perhaps officers. Since most of the older regular employees have been with the company for most of their working lives and the younger ones expect to follow the same pattern, they and the managers tend to feel that they are "in the same boat." Their relationship, thus, is friendly and respectful rather than formal and contentious. However, it was the bitter labor disputes during the 1950s and first half of the 1960s that firmly established the now prevailing principle that the maintenance and improvement of the employees' working conditions was a more important management responsibility than the maintenance and improvement of stockholders' dividends. The stockholders never benefit at the expense of the employees, but the employees may avoid layoffs at the expense of the stockholders.

When Japanese managers have to deal with redundancy—called an "employment adjustment" in Japan—because of a business slump or a financial problem for the corporation, their first move is to reduce or suspend the payment of dividends and to cut the salaries of the top management. Next, if necessary, they would reduce the salaries of middle management personnel and the amount of the semiannual bonuses that all company employees receive. If further cutbacks are needed, they usually take the form of a reduction in hours of work, termination of the employment contracts of temporary workers, job transfers or rotation of employees,[5] and/or a temporary release from employment.[6] Additional adjustments may include suspension of employees' wage increases, reduction in their monthly compensation or bonuses, and a call for the voluntary retirement of older employees.[7] Management's last resort, if all other efforts fail to solve their problems, would be the dismissal of some employees. Thus, at the heart of management's view of the employees as fellow members of the corporate community is a commitment to provide the regular employees with job security under the so-called lifetime employment system in Japan.

There are at least three factors that underlie the third feature of Japanese management philosophy, the managers' view that income distribution between labor and management should be egalitarian. These factors are (a) that they themselves have come up through the ranks via the system of promotion from within and are familiar with the financial needs of the employees; (b) that both the blue- and white-collar workers belong to the same enterprise union; and (c) that the union, in the collective bargaining process, is able to exert a strong regulatory influence on the distribution of wages and salaries within the company. The result is that over the years the income differentials between labor and management have tended to narrow. As I described in some detail in chapter 5, the enterprise unions have been remarkably successful in reducing the wage and nonwage differentials that formerly existed between blue- and white-collar workers with different educational backgrounds, not only among managers at different levels in the company, but also between the top managers and the rank-and-file union members. Another of Nikkeiren's surveys provides evidence on the latter point: In 1927 the before-tax annual compensation of company presidents in Japan was 110 times the annual starting salaries of new college graduates, but in 1980 the presidents were paid only 14.5 times as much as the newly hired college graduates (see table 15.2).

Table 15.2
Comparison of the Annual Earnings of Company Presidents
and Newly Hired University Graduates, 1927–80
(yen in thousands)

	1927	1963	1973	1980
A Company presidents[a]				
Before tax	165	6,082	15,676.7	23,593
After tax	151	3,013	7,181.4	11,543
B Newly hired employees[b]				
Before tax	1.5	257.9	825.5	1,623
After tax	1.5	252.5	797.4	1,546
A/B				
Before tax	110.0	23.6	19.0	14.5
A/B				
After tax	100.7	11.9	9.0	7.5

Source: Nikkeiren 1982, p.6.

[a]Private industry only. For 1963, 1973, and 1980, the annual earnings of presidents of companies with capital of over ¥500 million.

[b]Male only.

Fourth, it would seem to be almost inevitable that the labor policies of Japanese managers, in keeping with their management philosophies and their attitudes toward their fellow employees, would place primary emphasis on maintaining stability and peace in the labor–management relations within the company. These managers are acutely aware that industrial disputes are most detrimental to the continued existence and progress of any company in a highly competitive market. Needless to say, conflicts of interest between unions and managements do occur in Japan, as elsewhere, and the managers have to deal with them. However, if a strike or other industrial action develops out of one of these conflicts, in Japan it is taken to mean not only that a group of employees has dared to make public their distrust of or hostility toward management within the corporate community, but also that the managers have somehow failed or been clumsy in administering their labor relations policies; this perception will have a decidedly negative effect on their authority and prestige both within and outside the company.

Yet the fact that Japanese managers emphasize the maintenance of industrial peace and stability does not necessarily imply that all of them respect the basic rights of workers and labor union autonomy or that they favor industrial peace based upon the idea of industrial democracy. Like employers in other countries, most Japanese managers would prefer not to have the limits on their decision-making and on management prerogatives that unions and collective bargaining bring to their firms, and Japanese managers generally rate nonunion companies higher than unionized companies. The employers in small and medium-sized companies are the ones who are particularly disconcerted by unions in their establishments, and they often resort to rather extreme measures in their attempts to drive them out.

In postwar Japan, of course, it is unlawful for any employer to deny a labor union recognition or to refuse to bargain, as such actions are unfair labor practices. Therefore, if these employers have to recognize a union as a representative of their employees, they would prefer that it would be one whose membership was confined exclusively to their own employees, and they would make every effort to prevent an outside union from intervening in the labor–management relations within their companies.

Fifth, as has been suggested in the paragraphs above, Japanese managers tend to try to keep their industrial relations with their employees a private affair, confined to the corporation. Such an exclusionist policy takes a variety of forms. For example, managers attempt to avoid any negotiations with a higher labor organization to which their enterprise union might be affiliated, or, if they are forced into such negotiations, they will try to limit the scope of bargaining with that organization. If an outside union does succeed in organizing some of the company employees, the management frequently will try to force those employees to disaffiliate, will deliberately disfavor them on their jobs, or will intervene in the union's affairs. If there are two or more unions representing groups of employees, the management may favor one by taking a moderate approach in dealing with it while adopting a hostile attitude toward the others. All of these actions are unfair labor practices, of course, and are strictly forbidden by law. And, although they seem to be used most frequently and blatantly by the smaller companies, they also can be observed as part of the labor policies of large companies, including those in the public sector.

Even in a company that has one enterprise union representing all of its employees, the management will, as a matter of policy, seek to obtain as much union cooperation as possible and to minimize or eliminate union actions that would intensify labor–management conflict. To accomplish the latter, they might discriminate against union leaders and activists who have taken an antimanagement stance. Because of the structure of enterprise unions in Japan (see chapter 5), the managements find it rather easy to intervene, explicitly or implicitly, in union affairs and to exert pressure, when they find it necessary, on union policy decisions. And since most employees take it for granted that they, as members of the enterprise community, should cooperate with and devote themselves to corporate goals, a relationship between union and management often develops in which each is too dependent upon the other. This dependency status is particularly harmful to a union since it makes that organization very susceptible to an employer's pressure tactics, whether or not those tactics are unfair labor practices.

Management and Industrial Relations in Smaller Enterprises

The employers in the smaller enterprises are the ones who seem to have the most negative views of unions and the most antiunion policies. Of course, there is an infinite variety of such companies and the labor policies of quite a few of them are based on management philosophies and principles of industrial democracy that are even more advanced than those of some of the larger corporations. Generally speaking, however, the management of most of the firms in this sector is not separate from the ownership, as it is in the large stock corporations. Rather, in a typical case, a one-man owner-operator, or his family or relatives, maintain tight control over all company operations. Most of them take a conservative view in their industrial relations because they firmly believe that they cannot afford to do anything else, considering the environmental constraints under which they must operate—an excessively competitive market; heavy dependency on a parent company, client companies, or financial institutions; the relatively low productivity of their employees; their low profits; and the high ratio of their labor costs to total costs, etc. Thus, because they are convinced that they would not be able to survive financially if they had to bargain with representatives of the employees, they may be even reckless at times in their efforts to weaken or destroy unions. Although some of these employers may be ignorant of the law that protects the workers' basic rights and defines unfair labor practices, many of them are entirely familiar with it and pursue their antiunion policies and activities in defiance of it. Thus it is not surprising to find that the overwhelming majority of unfair labor practice cases brought before the Labor Relations Commissions have their source in these smaller companies.

Yet all of the fault cannot be attributed to the policies of the company managers. Because the employees of these small firms find it very difficult to organize and maintain an autonomous enterprise union, they often ask a local industrial or general union to assist them in their organizing efforts. The following is an example of what might happen as a result: Representatives of the so-called gōdō rōso (amalgamated general union), having organized some of a company's employees, suddenly show up one day to notify the company that a union has been organized. They may give the employer no information on how many or who among the company employees are union members, but still they demand immediate collective bargaining, allowing no opportunity for discussion of a mutually acceptable schedule. Most of the group taking part in this confrontation with the company may be union activists from outside and not company employees. If the employer refuses to begin negotiations immediately, or if he fails to respond favorably to what the union representatives are demanding, they will begin industrial actions—strikes, sit-ins, demonstrations, or picketing. Any collective bargaining under such circumstances is highly antagonistic and is likely to lead to violence. The employers, too, often contribute to the antagonism and violence by hiring a gang of racketeers or security guards from outside, by attempting to split the union, or by trying to get rid of it by faking bankruptcy.

Disputes of this kind over union recognition indicate that, on the one hand, in an overwhelming majority of cases the employer is responsible for the union's failure to win recognition as a bargaining representative, but there are also quite a number of instances in which the union is reponsible because its actions are too hasty, too unrealistic, and too threatening for an employer to respond in a positive way toward unionism and collective bargaining. The end result is that labor unions have not been able to expand their coverage among small enterprises.

Employers' Associations and Industrial Relations

The history of employers' associations in Japan can be traced to the Meiji era before World War I, but they did not become concerned with industrial relations until during that war. Even then their involvement in labor–management relations was only indirect. Shōgyō Kaigishō Rengōkai (Federation of Chambers of Commerce) was founded in 1892, Nihon Kōgyō Kurabu (Industry Club of Japan) in 1917, and Zenkoku Sangyō Dantai Rengōkai (National Federation of Industrial Associations) in 1931, but they confined their functions primarily to expressing their opinions to the government and to conducting research on labor problems and labor legislation. The Federation of Chambers of Commerce became a central organization only when it was called upon to elect employers' representatives and advisers to attend the first meeting of the International Labor Organization in 1919. It was Nihon Senshu Kyōkai (Japan Shipowners Association), founded in 1920, that first participated in industry-wide collective bargaining—with the Japan Seamen's Union, the only industrial union at the time.

Since World War II employers' associations have become firmly established at the national, regional, and industrial levels. There are three national federations—Keidanren (Japan Federation of Economic Organizations), established in 1946; Nisshō (Japan Chamber of Commerce and Industry), founded the same year; and Nikkeiren (Japanese Federation of Employers' Associations), formed in 1947. Nikkeiren is the one of the three that has been the spokesman on labor problems, and it is the organization most concerned with industrial relations. It conducts research and publishes the results of industrial relations studies as well as formulating and promoting industrial relations policies and providing guidance to member associations. Part of Nikkeiren's constituency are such regional associations as Kantō Keieisha Kyōkai (Kanto Employers' Association) and Kansai Keieisha Kyōkai (Kansai Employers' Associations) and, under them, the prefectural employers' associations. Employers' associations organized on an industrial basis also belong to Nikkeiren—about 25 in manufacturing and 50 in construction, mining, electric power supply, fishing, transport, finance, insurance and securities, and broadcasting, among other industries.

Even today, so many years after the war, only a limited number of employers' associations are directly involved in labor–management relations as a bargaining agent. In this respect they may be contrasted with employers' associations in some other industrialized countries, particularly in Western Europe, where they are involved directly in collective bargaining on the national and regional levels or on the industry level. As explained in some detail in chapter 5, collective bargaining between an enterprise union and the management of that enterprise is the dominant practice in Japan. Although there are a few employers' associations that are involved as parties in industry-wide negotiations in shipping, mining, textiles, metals, chemicals, private railways, beer brewing, and harbor services, the number of items bargained remains quite limited.[8] The employers' associations may provide leadership or guidance for member companies in their industrial relations, but they have no power to compel those companies to follow their lead. In this sense, the power structure on the employers' side in Japan is as decentralized as it is on the union side.

This does not necessarily mean, however, that Japanese employers are so much more independent than their counterparts in the other industrialized countries that they find it difficult to cooperate in formulating unified labor policies or in making such important decisions as what stand to take with regard to workers' wage levels. As in the case of the labor unions, the success or failure of employers' unified actions depends not only on the organizational structure, the membership coverage, and the decision-making mechanisms of their associations, but also upon the political and economic climate at the time they are seeking these goals. For instance, in a period of economic boom when the supply and demand relationship in the labor market is tight, employers will be in intense competition for workers, and the employers' associations, being able to use only persuasion, will find it difficult both to secure their members' cooperation and to convince them to maintain a unified position. However, when the labor market is loose, individual employers are reluctant to take the social responsibility or to become isolated from other employers by assuming a pattern-setting role, especially if a settlement they reach with their employees might be called inflationary. Therefore, there are particular situations where some employers develop close cooperation, primarily through exchange of information, in formulating policies and making decisions on labor matters, and it tends to be these informal management groups, formed on an ad hoc basis among a limited number of leading corporations in a particular industry rather than the employers' associations that are the actual decision-makers in every Spring Offensive, not only for the industry but, more broadly, for other relevant industries. In recent years the five major steel companies have been the pattern-setters, but in the past several years similar informal groups in ship-building, automobiles, and electrical machinery, equipment, and supplies have played important roles in wage decisions in the Spring Offensive.

Notes

1 See chapter 2 for an elaboration of the system of "promotion from within."
2 This survey was conducted in January–February 1977 by the Japanese Commit-tee for Economic Development and covered 180 companies that employed either the executive officers of the committee or members of its local organizations. A total of 134 companies responded to the survey questionnaire, a response rate of 74.4 percent. These companies represented a variety of industries: 53.7 percent were in manufacturing; 24.6 percent in commerce, finance, insurance, and real estate; 8.2 percent in mining; 7.5 percent in transport, electricity, gas, and services; 6.0 percent in construction and others. Of the total, 60.5 percent of the companies had capital of ¥10 billion or more; 88.8 percent of the companies had 1,000 or more employees.
3 Bacon and Brown 1977. See also The Conference Board, "The Board of Direc-tors in Japan," *Information Bulletin* No. 28, September 1977.
4 *Nikkeiren Times*, October 31, 1978.
5 For an elaboration on the system of rotation and transfer of regular workers to other workshops or even to other companies on a temporary basis, see chapters 2 and 9.
6 Because employees are suspended only temporarily but are not dismissed or terminated, a suspension is different from a layoff in the United States. It would be more accurate to call it "work-sharing."
7 See chapter 9 for a description of the practice of encouraging workers to retire voluntarily, with incentives.
8 With regard to the form of collective bargaining in which an employers' associ-ation or a group of employers is a party, see Shirai et al. 1977, ch. 5.

Reference Material

Glossary

Government and Business Organizations

Chirōi (*Chihō Rōdō Iinkai*): Local Labor Relations Commission in each prefecture

Chūrōi (*Chūō Rōdō Iinkai*): Central Labor Relations Commission for private sector industries.

Gaikō Rōmu Kyōkai: Association of Ocean–Going Maritime Companies for Labor Affairs

Keidanren (*Keizai Dantai Rengōkai*): Japan Federation of Economic Organizations

Keizai Dōyūkai: Japanese Committee for Economic Development (JCED)

Kōrōi (*Kōkyō Kigyōtai Tō Rōdō Iinkai*): Public Corporation and National Enterprise Labor Relations Commission (PCNELR Commission)

Nihon Kōgyō Kurabu: Industry Club of Japan

Nihon Men Sufu Orimono Kōgyō Kumiai Rengōkai: Association of Cotton and Staple Fiber Textile Industries

Nihon Sekitan Kōgyō Renmei: Japan Coal Mining Association

Nihon Senshu Kyōkai: Japan Shipowners' Association

Nikkeiren (*Nihon Keieishadantai Renmei*): Japan Federation of Employers' Associations

Nisshō (*Nihon Shōkō Kaigisho*): Japan Chamber of Commerce and Industry

Sampō (*Sangyō Hōkokukai*): "Association for Service to the State through Industry"—a wartime patriotic labor organization

Shōgyō Kaigisho Rengōkai: Federation of Chambers of Commerce

Tekken Kōdan (*Nihon Tetsudō Kensetsu Kōdan*): National Railways Construction Public Corporation

Zenkoku Sangyō Dantai Rengōkai: National Federation of Industrial Associations

Unions and Union Organizations

Chūritsurōren (*Chūritsu Rōdō Kumiai Renraku Kaigi*): Federation of Independent Unions of Japan—one of the four national centers

Denkirōren (*Zen Nihon Denkikiki Rōdō Kumiai Rengōkai*): All Japan Federation of Electric Machine Workers' Unions (Chūritsurōren)

Dentsūkyōtō (*Denki Tsūshinsangyō Rōdō Kumiai Kyōtōkaigi*): Joint Council of Telecommunication Industry Trade Unions (Sōhyō)

Dōmei (*Zen Nihon Rōdō Sōdōmei*): Japanese Confederation of Labor—one of the four national centers

Dōryokusha *(Kokutetsu Dōryokusha Rōdō Kumiai)*: National Railway Locomotive Engineers' Union (Sōhyō)

Gōkarōren *(Gōseikagakusangyō Rōdō Kumiai Rengō)*: National Federation of Synthetic Chemical Industry Workers' Unions (Sōhyō)

Jichirō *(Zen Nihon Jichidantai Rōdō Kumiai)*: All Japan Prefectural and Municipal Workers' Unions (Sōhyō)

Jidōsharōren *(Nihon Jidōshasangyō Rōdō Kumiai Rengōkai)*: Federation of Japan Automobile Workers' Unions (Dōmei)

Jidōshasōren *(Zen Nihon Jidōshasangyō Rōdō Kumiai Sōrengōkai)*: Confederation of Japan Automobile Workers' Unions (Independent)

Kagaku Enerugī Rōkyō *(Nihon Kagaku Enerugī Rōdō Kumiai Kyōgikai)*: Japan Council of Chemical and Energy Workers (Independent)

Kaiin *(Zen Nihon Kaiin Kumiai)*: All Japan Seamen's Union (Dōmei)

Kokurō *(Kokutetsu Rōdō Kumiai)*: National Railway Workers' Union (Sōhyō)

Kōrōkyō *(Kōkyō Kigyōtai Tō Rōdō Kumiai Kyōgikai)*: Joint Council of the Public Enterprise Unions

Kōtsurōren *(Zenkoku Kōtsū Unyu Rōdō Kumiai Sōrengō)*: Japan Federation of Transport Workers' Unions (Dōmei)

Nichirinrō *(Nihon Ringyō Rōdō Kumiai)*: Japan National Forest Workers' Union (Sōhyō)

Nikkyōso *(Nihon Kyōshokuin Kumiai)*: Japan Teachers' Union (Sōhyō)

Sanbetsu Kaigi *(Zen Nihon Sangyōbetsu Kumiai Kaigi)*: All Japan Congress of Industrial Unions

Seisaku Suishin Rōsō Kaigi: Trade Union Council for Policy Formulation—a non-affiliated national center for concerted action

Shinsanbetsu *(Zenkoku Sangyōbetsu Rōdō Kumiai Rengō)*: National Federation of Industrial Organizations—one of the four national centers

Shitetsusōren *(Nihon Shitetsu Rōdō Kumiai Sōrengō)*: General Federation of Private Railway Workers' Unions of Japan (Sōhyō)

Shuntō Kyōtō Kaigi: Joint Struggle Committee of Unions for the Spring Offensive

Shuppanrōren *(Nihon Shuppan Rōdō Kumiai Rengōkai)*: Japan Federation of Publishing Workers' Unions (Independent)

Sōdōmei *(Nihon Rōdō Kumiai Sōdōmei)*: Japan Confederation of Trade Unions, forerunner of present Dōmei

Sōhyō *(Nihon Rōdō Kumiai Sōhyōgikai)*: General Council of Trade Unions of Japan— one of the four national centers

Tanrō *(Nihon Tankō Rōdō Kumiai)*: Japan Coal Miners' Union (Sōhyō)

Tekkōrōren *(Nihon Tekkōsangyō Rōdō Kumiai Rengōkai)*: Japanese Federation of Iron and Steel Workers' Unions (Sōhyō)

Tetsurō *(Tetsudō Rōdō Kumiai)*: Japan Railway Workers' Union (Dōmei)

Tōitsurōsokon *(Toistusensen Sokushin Rodokumiai Kondankai)*: Conference of Trade Unions for the Promotion of a United Front

Unyuippan *(Zen Nihon Unyusangyō Ippan Rōdō Kumiai)*: All Japan Transport and General Workers' Union (Sōhyō)

Zendentsū (*Zenkoku Denki Tsūshin Rōdō Kumiai*): Telecommunication Workers' Union of Japan (Sōhyō)

Zenkankō (*Zen Nihon Kankō Shokurō Kyōgikai*): All Japan Council of Public Employee Unions (Dōmei)

Zenkokuippan (*Sōhyō Zenkoku Ippan Rōdō Kumiai*): National Union of General Workers (Sōhyō)

Zenrinya (*Zenrinya Rōdō Kumiai*): National Forest Workers' Union of Japan (Sōhyō)

Zenrō —old name for Dōmei until 1962

Zensekiyu (*Zenkoku Sekiyusangyō Rōdō Kumiai Kyōgikai*): All Japan Oil Workers' Union (Chūritsurōren)

Zensendōmei (*Zenkoku Sen'isangyō Rōdō Kumiai Dōmei*): Japanese Federation of Textile Industry Workers' Unions (Dōmei)

Zensonpo (*Zen Nihon Songai Hoken Rōdō Kumiai*): All Japan Property Insurance Labor Union (Independent)

Zentei (*Zenteishin Rōdō Kumiai*): Japan Postal Workers' Union (Sōhyō)

Zenyūsei (*Zen Nihon Yūsei Rōdō Kumiai*): All Japan Post Office Workers' Union (Dōmei)

Zōsenjūkirōren (*Zenkoku Zōsen Jūkikai Rōdō Kumiai Rengōkai*): National Federation of Shipbuilding and Heavy Machinery Workers' Unions (Dōmei)

References

Abegglen, James C. 1958. *The Japanese Factory: Aspects of Its Social Organization.* Glencoe, Ill.: Free Press.
————. 1969. "Organizational Change." In Ballon, ed., 1969.
————. 1973. *Management and Worker: The Japanese Solution.* Tokyo: Sophia University Press.
Akita Joju. 1977. "Sōgiken no Genjō Iji mata wa Tōketsu no Kinō ni tsuite" [The function of policies to maintain the status quo or freeze the right to strike]. In Hyōdō Tsutomu et al., eds., *Kōkyō Bumon no Sōgiken* [The right to strike in the public sector]. Tokyo: Tokyo University Press.
Ariizumi Tōru. 1963. *Rōdō Kijun Hō* [The Labor Standards Law]. Tokyo: Yūhikaku.
————. 1973. "The Legal Framework: Past and Present." In Ōkōchi, Karsh, and Levine, eds., 1973.
Asahi Shimbun. 1969, 1971-72, 1974, 1976-77, 1979. *Asahi Nenkan* [Asahi yearbook]. Tokyo: Asahi Shimbunsha.
Asia Shakai Mondai Kenkyūjo (Asian Institute for Social Problems). 1978. *Nihon no Rōdō Kumiaihi ni kansuru Chōsa Hōkoku* [Survey report on Japanese trade union dues]. Tokyo: Asia Shakai Mondai Kenkyūjo.

Bacon, Jeremy, and Brown, James K. 1977. *The Board of Directors: Perspectives and Practices in Nine Countries.* Research Report from The Conference Board Division of Management Research. New York: The Conference Board.
Bain, George S., and Price, Robert. 1972. "Union Growth and Employment Trends in the UK." *British Journal of Industrial Relations* 10:366-81.
Bairy, Maurice. 1969. "Motivational Forces in Japanese Life." In Ballon, ed., 1969.
Ballon, Robert J. 1969a. "The Japanese Dimensions of Industrial Enterprise." In Ballon, ed., 1969.
————. 1969b. "Lifelong Remuneration System." In Ballon, ed., 1969.
————, ed. 1969. *The Japanese Employee.* Tokyo: Sophia University Press and Charles Tuttle Co.
Bauman, Alvin. 1970. "Measuring Employees' Compensation in U.S. Industry." *Monthly Labor Review* 93, No. 10 (October), pp. 17-24.
Becker, Gary S. 1964. *Human Capital: Theoretical and Empirical Analysis with Special Reference to Education.* First ed., New York: National Bureau of Economic Research. Second ed., New York: Columbia University Press, 1975.

Benedict, Ruth. 1946. *The Chrysanthemum and the Sword*. New York: Houghton Mifflin.

Bennett, John W. 1967. "Japanese Economic Growth: Background for Social Change." In Dore, ed., 1967.

———, and Levine, Solomon B. 1976. "Industrialization and Social Deprivation: Welfare, Environment and the Postindustrial Society in Japan." In Patrick, ed., 1976.

Boraston, Ian; Clegg, Hugh; and Rimmer, Malcolm. 1975. *Workplace and Union: A Study of Local Relationships in Fourteen Unions*. London: Heinemann Educational Books.

Brooks, G. W., and Gamm, S. 1955. "The Practice of Seniority in Southern Pulp Mills." *Monthly Labor Review* 78, No. 7 (July), pp. 757–65.

Brown, William, 1969. "Japanese Management: The Cultural Background." In Ross A. Webber, ed., *Culture and Management*. Homewood, Ill.: Richard D. Irwin.

CKKT: Japan, Rōdōshō, Tōkei Jōhōbu (Ministry of Labor, Department of Statistics and Information). 1954–76. *Chingin Kōzō Kihon Tōkei Chōsa Hōkoku* [Report on the basic statistical survey of the wage structure]. This series of surveys was published under different names between 1954 and 1963:

> 1954. *Shokushubetsu tō Chingin Jittai Chōsa. Kōjinbetsu Chingin Chōsa Kekka Hōkukusho.*
> 1955–57. *Shokushubetsu tō Chingin Jittai Chōsa Kekka Hōkokusho.*
> 1958–60. *Chingin Kōzō Kihon Chōsa Kekka Hōkokusho.*
> 1961. *Chingin Jittai Sōgō Chōsa Kekka Hōkokusho.*
> 1962–63. *Tokutei Jōken Chingin Chōsa Kekka Hōkoku.*

Chang, Paul T. 1969. "The Labor Movement." In Ballon, ed., 1969.

Chūbachi Masayoshi, and Taira, Koji. 1976. "Poverty in Modern Japan: Perceptions and Realities." In Patrick, ed., 1976.

Chūō Rōdō Iinkai. *See* Japan, Chūō Rōdō Iinkai.

Cochrane, James L. 1979. *Industrialism and Industrial Man in Retrospect*. New York: Ford Foundation.

Cole, Robert E. 1971a. *Japanese Blue Collar: The Changing Tradition*. Berkeley: University of California Press.

———. 1971b. "The Theory of Institutionalization: Permanent Employment and Tradition in Japan." *Economic Development and Cultural Change* 20:47–70.

———. 1972. "Permanent Employment in Japan: Facts and Fantasies." *Industrial and Labor Relations Review* 26:615–30.

———. 1979. *Work, Mobility and Participation: A Comparative Study of American and Japanese Industry*. Berkeley: University of California Press.

———, and Tominaga, Ken'ichi. 1976. "Japan's Changing Occupational Structure and Its Significance." In Patrick, ed., 1976.

Commons, John R. 1913. *Labor and Administration*. New York: Macmillan Co.

Cook, Alice H. 1966. *An Introduction to Japanese Trade Unionism*. Ithaca, N.Y.: Cornell University Press.

Delamotte, Yves, and Walker, Kenneth F. Undated. "The Humanization of Work and the Quality of Working Life—Trends and Issues." Series No. 11. Geneva: International Institute for Labor Studies.

Derber, Milton. 1970. *The American Idea of Industrial Democracy, 1865–1965.* Urbana: University of Illinois Press.

———. 1979. "Recent Developments in Collective Bargaining and Industrial Democracy in the United States and Canada." Paper presented to the International Symposium on Collective Bargaining and Industrial Democracy sponsored by the Center for International Communication, Hōsei University, September 5–6, 1978. The Japanese proceedings are published in *Dantai Kōshō to Sangyō Minshūsei.* Tokyo: Bokutakusha.

Doeringer, Peter B., and Piore, Michael J. 1971. *Internal Labor Markets and Manpower Analysis.* Lexington, Mass.: D.C. Heath.

De Vos, George. 1974. "Achievement Orientation, Social Self-Identity, and Japanese Economic Growth." In Irvin Scheiner, comp., *Modern Japan.* New York: Macmillan.

———, and Wagatsuma, Hiroshi. 1973. "The Entrepreneurial Market of Lower Class Urban Japanese in Manufacturing." In George De Vos, ed., *Socialization for Achievement: Essays in the Cultural Psychology of the Japanese.* Berkeley: University of California Press.

Doi, Takeo. 1962. "*Amae:* A Key Concept for Understanding Japanese Personality." In Robert J. Smith and Richard K. Beardsley, eds., *Japanese Culture.* Chicago: Aldine.

———. 1967. "Giri-Ninjō: An Interpretation." In Dore, ed., 1967.

———. 1978. *Anatomy of Dependence.* Tokyo: Kodansha-International.

Dōmei (Japanese Confederation of Labor). 1974. *Rōdō Jōken to Chōsa Hōkoku Tokushū* [Special report on working conditions]. Shiryō Series No. 22 (February). Tokyo: Dōmei.

———. 1975. *Sanka Keizai Taisei no Jitsugen no tame ni* [For achieving the participatory economic system]. An Interim Report of the Task Force of the Union. Shiryō Series No. 26 (March). Tokyo: Dōmei.

Dore, Ronald P. 1958. *City Life in Japan.* Berkeley: University of California Press.

———. 1969. "The Modernizer as a Special Case: Japanese Factory Legislation, 1882–1911." *Comparative Studies in Society and History* 5:433–50.

———. 1971. "Commitment—to What, by Whom and Why." In *Social and Cultural Background of Labor-Management Relations in Asian Countries.* Tokyo: Japan Institute of Labor.

———. 1973. *British Factory—Japanese Factory: The Origins of National Diversity in Industrial Relations.* Berkeley: University of California Press.

———, ed. 1967. *Aspects of Social Change in Modern Japan.* Princeton, N.J.: Princeton University Press.

Dōryokusha Undōshi Hensan Iinkai (National Railway Locomotive Engineers' Union History Compilation Committee). 1973. *Dōryokusha 20 Nen Shi* [The 20-year history of the locomotive union of the Japan National Railway]. Tokyo: Dōryokusha.

Dunlop, John T. 1958. *Industrial Relations Systems.* New York: Henry Holt.
———, Harbison, Frederick; Kerr, Clark; and Myers, Charles A. 1975. *Industrialism and Industrial Man Reconsidered: Some Perspectives on a Study over Two Decades of the Problem of Labor and Management in Economic Growth.* Princeton, N.J.: Inter–University Study of Human Resources in National Development.

Economic Planning Agency. *See* Japan, Economic Planning Agency.
European Community (EC). 1972–75. *Labor Costs in Industry.* Brussels: EC.
———. *Structure of Earnings in Industry. See* SEI.
———. 1974. *Jahrbuch Sozialstatistik.* Brussels: EC.
Evans, Robert, Jr. 1971. *The Labor Economies of Japan and the United States.* New York: Praeger.

Fellner, William. 1979. *Contemporary Economic Problems.* Washington: American Enterprise Institute.
Feringa, Bert. 1976. "Permanent Employment in the Netherlands: The Dutch Employment Relationship in a Japanese Perspective." Mimeo.
Finegan, T. Aldrich. 1962. "Hours of Work in the United States: A Cross-Sectional Analysis." *Journal of Political Economy* 70 (October):452–70.
Fujita, Wakao. 1973. "Labor Disputes." In Ōkōchi, Karsh, and Levine, 1978.
Fukada Shunsuke. 1971. *Shinnittetsu no Teihen kara* [From the bottom of the Japan Steel Corporation]. Tokyo: San'ichi Shobō.
Funahashi, Naomichi. 1973. "The Industrial Reward System: Wages and Benefits." In Ōkōchi, Karsh, and Levine, 1973.

Galenson, Walter, with the collaboration of Odaka, Konosuke. 1976. "The Japanese Labor Market." In Patrick and Rosovsky, eds., 1976.
Glazer, Herbert. 1969. "The Japanese Executive." In Ballon, ed., 1969.
Glazer, Nathan. 1976. "Social and Cultural Factors in Japanese Economic Growth." In Patrick and Rosovsky, eds., 1976.
Great Britain, Department of Employment. 1960, 1965, 1970, 1975. *Gazette.*
———. *New Earnings Survey. See* NES.
Great Britain, Royal Commission on Trade Unions and Employers' Associations. 1965–68. *Report Cmnd. 3623.* London: Her Majesty's Stationery Office.
Guest, Robert H. 1954. "Work Careers and Aspirations of Automobile Workers." *American Sociological Review* 19, No. 2 (April), pp. 155–63.
Gusfield, Joseph. 1967. "Tradition and Modernity: Misplaced Polarities in the Study of Social Change." *American Journal of Sociology* 72:351–62.
Gyōsei Kanrichō. *See* Japan, Gyōsei Kanrichō.

Hagisawa Kiyohiko. 1968. "Saikin no Rōdōkarishobun o meguru Mondaiten" [On recent labor provisional dispositions]. *Nihon Rōdōhō Gakkaishi Rōdōsōshō* 32:5.
Hall, John. 1962. "Feudalism in Japan: A Reassessment." *Comparative Studies in Society and History* 5:15–51.

Hamel, Harvey R. 1967. "Job Tenure of Workers, January 1966." *Monthly Labor Review* 90, No. 1 (January), pp. 31–37.

Hanami Tadashi. 1963. *ILO to Nihon no Danketsuken* [ILO and the right to organize in Japan]. Tokyo: Daiyamondosha.

————. 1967. "Kankō Rōdōsha no Sōgiken" [Public employees' right to strike]. *Nihon Rōdō Kyōkai Zasshi* 95 (February):2.

————. 1969. "Labor Disputes and Their Settlement." In Ballon, ed., 1969.

————. 1972. "Kankōrō no Sōgikoi to Saikin no Hanrei" [Recent court decisions in dispute practices and public worker unions]. *Kōrōi Kihō*, No. 11 (April).

————.1973. "Labor Relations in the Public Sector." *Japan Labor Bulletin* 12, No. 7 (July), pp. 6–8.

————. 1979a. *Labour Law and Industrial Relations in Japan*. Deventer, The Netherlands: Kluwer.

————. 1979b. *Labour Relations in Japan Today*. Tokyo: Kodansha-International.

Harari, Ehud. 1973. *The Politics of Labor Legislation in Japan*. Berkeley: University of California Press.

Hashimoto, Masanori. 1979. "Bonus Payments, On-the-Job Training, and Lifetime Employment in Japan." *Journal of Political Economy* 87:5.

Hazama, Hiroshi. 1976. "Historical Change in the Life Style of Industrial Workers." In Patrick, ed., 1976.

————. 1971. "Igirisu Kōjōnai Rōshi Kankei" [Industrial relations at the plant level in England]. *Tokyo Kyōiku Daigaku Shakai Kagaku Ronshū*, vol. 18.

Herrick, Neal Q., and Maccoby, Michael. 1975. "Humanizing Work: A Priority Goal of the 1970s." In Louis E. Davis, Albert B. Cherns, et al., eds., *The Quality of Working Life*, Vol. 1. New York: Free Press.

Hines, A. G. 1964. "Trade Unions and Wage Inflation in the United Kingdom, 1893–1961." *Review of Economic Studies* 31 (October):221–52.

Hirano Yoshitarō. 1934. *Nihon Shihonshugi Shakai no Kikō* [The structure of Japanese capitalistic society]. Tokyo: Iwanami Shoten.

Hodgson, James D. 1978. *The Wondrous Working World of Japan*. Reprint No. 81. Washington, D.C.: American Enterprise Institute.

Hyōdō Tsutomu. 1971. *Nihon ni okeru Rōshi Kankei no Tenkai* [The development of labor–capital relations in Japan]. Tokyo: University of Tokyo Press.

————. 1977. "Rōdō Kumiai Undō no Hatten" [The development of the trade union movement]. In *Kōza Nihon Rekishi: Gendai* [Lectures on the history of Japan: the modern period]. Tokyo: Iwanami Shoten.

ILO Yearbook. *See* International Labor Office. 1955–79.

Ichino, Shōzō. 1980. "The Structure of the Labor Force and Patterns of Mobility 1950–1965." In Nishikawa, ed., 1980.

Ichinose Tomoji et al., eds. 1977. *Kōkyōkigyōron* [On public enterprises]. Tokyo: Yūhikaku.

IMF–JC. *See* International Metalworkers Federation—Japan Council.

Inoue Shōzō. 1969. "Kigyōnai Rōdō Shijō no Kōzō ni tsuite" [The structure of internal labor markets]. Keio University, *Mitagakkai Zasshi* 62, No. 9 (September), pp. 26–43.

International Council for the Quality of Working Life. 1973. *News Letter* (Mimeo).

International Labor Office (ILO). 1955–79. *Yearbook of Labor Statistics*. Geneva: ILO.

———. 1966. *Report of the Fact-Finding and Conciliation Commission on Freedom of Association Concerning Persons Employed in the Public Sector in Japan*. ILO Official Bulletin, Supplement, Vol. 49, No. 1 (January). Geneva: ILO.

International Metalworkers Federation—Japan Council (IMF–JC). 1978. *Rōdō Kumiai Zaisei no Chūchoki Seisaku to Tembō* [A medium- and long-term policy and prospect for union finance]. Tokyo: IMF–JC.

Ishida Hideo. 1976. *Nihon no Rōshi Kankei to Chingin Kettei* [Japanese industrial relations and wage determination]. Tokyo: Tōyō Keizai Shimpōsha.

Ishikawa Akihiro. 1975. *Shakai Henka to Rōdōsha Ishiki* [Social change and workers' consciousness]. Tokyo: Nihon Rōdō Kyōkai.

Ishikawa Kichiemon. 1974. "Kōrōhō chū Sōgikōi ni kansuru Kitei no Kaisei Shiron" [A private view on revision of the provisions of the PCNELR Law concerning acts of dispute]. In Tōdai Rōdōhō Kenkyūkai, ed., *Rōdōhō no Shomondai* [Problems of labor law]. Tokyo: Keisō Shobō.

———. 1978. *Rōdō Kumiai Hō* [Trade union law]. Tokyo: Yūhikaku.

Isomura, Motoshi. 1969. "Private Pension Plans." In Ballon, ed., 1969.

Iwata Makoto. 1977. "Iwayuru Nagoya Chūō Yūbinkyoku Jiken no Saikō Saibansho Daihōtei Hanketsu ni tsuite" [On the full bench decision of the Supreme Court on the so-called Nagoya Central Post Office Case]. *Hanrei Jiho,* No. 848 (July 11), pp. 3–5.

Jacoby, Sanford. 1979. "The Origins of Internal Labor Markets in Japan." *Industrial Relations* 18, No.2, pp. 184–96.

Japan, Chūō Rōdō Iinkai, Jimukyoku (Central Labor Relations Commission, Executive Office). 1970, 1974a. *Rōdō Kyōyaku Chōsa* [Survey of collective bargaining agreements]. Tokyo: Chūō Rōdō Iinkai.

———. 1974b, 1975–80. *Rōdō Iinkai Nempō* [Annual report of labor relations commissions]. Tokyo: Rōi Kyōkai.

Japan, Economic Planning Agency. 1975, 1977. *White Paper on National Life* (original Japanese title: *Kokumin Seikatsu Hakusho*). Tokyo: Overseas Data, Ltd.

———. 1979. *Economic Survey of Japan* (original Japanese title: *Keizai Hakusho*). Tokyo: Japan Times, Ltd.

Japan, Gyōsei Kanrichō (Administrative Management Agency). 1976, 1978. *Tokushu Hōjin Sōran* [Directory of special juridical persons]. Tokyo: Ōkurashō Insatsukyoku, 1976; Gyōsei Kanri Kenkyū Sentā, 1978.

Japan, Jichishō (Ministry of Local Autonomy). 1976. *Chihō Kōei Kigyō Nenkan* [Yearbook of local public enterprises]. Vol. 28. Tokyo: Chihō Zaimu Kyōkai.

Japan, Jinjiin (National Personnel Authority). 1978. *Jinjiin Geppō* [Monthly review of the National Personnel Authority]. No. 319 (September).

Japan, Keizai Kikakuchō (Economic Planning Agency). 1968. *Bukka Antei to Sho-toku Seisaku* [Price stabilization and income policy]. Report of the Study Commit-tee on Prices, Wages and Incomes, Kumagaya Hisao, Chairman. Tokyo: Keizai Kikaku Kyōkai.

———. 1972. *Gendai Infure to Shotoku Seisaku* [Modern inflation and income pol-icy]. Report of the Committee on Prices, Incomes and Productivity, Sumiya Mikio, Chairman. Tokyo: Keizai Kikaku Kyōkai.

———. 1975. *Shotoku Shisan Bunpai no Jittai to Mondaiten* [The practice and problems of income and assets distribution]. Report of the Study Committee on Income Distribution, Baba Keinosuke, Chairman. Tokyo: Ōkurashō Insatsukyoku.

———. 1976. *Kokumin Seikatsu Senkodo Chōsa* [Survey of people's needs, satisfac-tion and dissatisfaction]. Tokyo: Ōkurashō Insatsukyoku.

Japan, Kōkyō Kigyōtai Shingikai (Deliberating Council on Public Enterprises). 1957. *Tōshin* [Report to the Cabinet]. Tokyo, December.

Japan, Kōmuin Seido Shingikai (Deliberating Council on the Civil Service System). 1973. *Kampō* [Official gazette]. Appendix to No. 14038, October 11.

Japan, Kōseishō (Ministry of Health and Welfare). 1978. *Kōsei Hakusho* [White paper on health and welfare]. Tokyo: Ōkurashō Insatsukyoku.

Japan, Ministry of International Trade and Industry. 1960, 1965-74. *Census of Manufacturers* (original Japanese title: *Kōgyō Tōkei Hyō*). Tokyo: Tsūshō San-gyōshō.

Japan, Ministry of Labor. 1968. *Japan Labour Laws 1968.* Tokyo: Rōmu Gyōsei Kenkyūsho.

Japan, Ministry of Labor, Department of Statistics and Information. 1977. *Monthly Labor Statistics and Research Bulletin,* September (original Japanese title: *Rōdō Tōkei Chōsa Geppō)*. Tokyo: Rōmu Gyōsei Kenkyūsho.

Japan, Prime Minister's Office, Bureau of Statistics. 1962, 1971. *Employment Status Survey* (original Japanese title: *Shūgyō Kōzō Kihon Chōsa)*. Tokyo: Nihon Tōkei Kyōkai.

———. 1920, 1930, 1970. *Population Census of Japan* (original Japanese title: *Kokusei Chōsa)*. Tokyo: Nihon Tōkei Kyōkai.

———. 1975. *Japan Statistical Yearbook* (original Japanese title: *Nihon Tōkei Nen-kan)*. Tokyo: Nihon Tōkei Kyōkai.

Japan, Rinji Gyōsei Chōsakai (Temporary Research Council on Administration). 1964. *Tōshin* [Report to the Cabinet]. Tokyo, September.

Japan, Rinji Kōkyō Kigyōtai Gōrika Shingikai (Temporary Deliberating Council on Rationalizing Public Enterprises). 1954. *Tōshin* [Report to the Cabinet]. Tokyo, November.

Japan, Rōdōshō (Ministry of Labor). 1956-78, 1979a, 1980-81. *Rōdō Hakusho* [White paper on labor]. Tokyo: Ōkurashō Insatsukyoku.

———. 1979b. "Minkan Shuyō Kigyō ni okeru Shuntō Chinage Jyōkyō no Suii" [Changes of wage increase in the major private companies due to the Spring Offensive]. June 15. Mimeo.

Japan, Rōdōshō, Rōseikyoku (Ministry of Labor, Bureau of Labor Policy). 1945–46, 1951, 1959, 1961, 1971. *Shiryō Rōdō Undō Shi* [Documentary history of the labor movement]. Tokyo: Rōmu Gyōsei Kenkyūsho.

———. 1964, 1969, 1974. *Rōdō Kyōyaku tō Jittai Chōsa Hōkokusho* [Report on the survey of practices of collective bargaining agreements]. Tokyo: Rōdō Hōrei Kyōkai.

———. 1979. *Saishin Rōdō Kyōyaku no Jittai* [Recent collective bargaining agreements in practice]. Tokyo: Rōmu Gyōsei Kenkyūsho.

Japan, Rōdōshō, Rōshi Kankeihō Kenkyūkai (Ministry of Labor, Study Group on Industrial Relations Law). 1967. *Rōshi Kankeihō Unyō no Jitsujō oyobi Mondaiten* [The actual application and problems of industrial relations law.] Tokyo: Nihon Rōdō Kyōkai.

Japan, Rōdōshō, Tōkei Jōhōbu (Ministry of Labor, Department of Statistics and Information), formerly Rōdō Tōkei Chōsabu. 1968. *Rōdōhiyō Chōsa Hōkoku* [Report on the labor cost survey]. Tokyo: Rōdōshō, Tōkei Jōhōbu.

———. 1970. *Koyō Dōkō Chōsa Hōkoku* [Report on the labor mobility survey]. Tokyo: Rōdōshō, Tōkei Jōhōbu.

———. 1972. *Kinrōsha Seikatsu Ishiki Chōsa Hōkoku* [Report on opinion survey of working life]. Tokyo: Rōdōshō, Tōkei Jōhōbu.

———. 1975. *Okugai Rōdōsha Chingin Jittai Chōsa* [Wage survey of building, trucking and longshoremen's trades]. Tokyo: Rōdōshō, Tōkei Jōhōbu.

———. 1976. *Rōdō Keizai Dōkō Chōsa Hōkoku* [Report on the survey of the changing situation of the labor economy]. Tokyo: Rōdōshō, Tōkei Jōhōbu.

———. 1977. *Rōshi Komyunikeishon Chōsa* [Survey on communication between labor and management]. Tokyo: Rōdōshō, Tōkei Jōhōbu.

———.1979. *Rōdō Kankei Kokusai Hikaku Shiryōshū* [Document for international comparison of labor relations]. Tokyo: Rōdōshō, Tōkei Jōhōbu.

———. 1980a. *Rōdō Tōkei Yōran* [Handbook of labor statistics]. Tokyo: Ōkurashō Insatsukyoku.

———. 1980b. *Rōdō Undō Hakusho* [White paper on the labor movement]. Tokyo: Nihon Rōdō Kyōkai.

———. *Chingin Kōzō Kihon Tōkei Chōsa* [Basic survey of the wage structure]. *See* CKKT.

———. *Maigetsu Kinrō Tōkei Chōsa* [Monthly labor statistics survey]. *See* MKTC.

———. *Rōdō Kumiai Kihon Chōsa* [Basic survey of trade unions]. *See* RKKC.

Japan, Senmoniin Kondankai (Expert Committee of the Conference of Ministers Concerned with Public Corporations and National Enterprises). 1975. *Sankōsha Gogengyō Tō no Arubeki Seikaku to Rōdō Kihonken Mondai ni tsuite* [On the desirable nature of the three public corporations and five national enterprises and the right to strike). Tokyo: Sōrifu.

Japan, Sōrifu, Tōkeikyoku (Prime Minister's Office, Bureau of Statistics). 1920, 1930. *Kokusei Chōsa.* [Population census]. Tokyo: Sōrifu.

———. 1971. *Kinrōsha no Ishiki Chōsa* [Survey of workers' opinions and attitudes]. Tokyo: Sōrifu (mimeo).

———. 1978. *Kinrō Ishiki ni kansuru Yoran Chōsa* [Survey of workers' consciousness]. Tokyo: Sōrifu (mimeo).

Japan, Tsūshō Sangyōshō (Ministry of International Trade and Industry). 1976. "Shinkokuna Jukyū Gyappu ni nayamu Zōsen Gyōkai" [The ship-building industry worries about a serious supply-demand gap]. *Nihon Keizai Shimbun*, November 2.

Japan, Yūseishō (Ministry of Posts and Telecommunications). 1976a. *Chitsujo Aru Rōshi Kankei no tame ni* [For orderly labor-management relations]. Tokyo: Kangyō Rōdō Kenkyūjo.

———. 1976b. *Rōdō Kihonken Mondai no Rikai no tame ni* [Understanding the right to strike issue]. Tokyo: Yūseishō.

Japan Institute of Labor. *See* Nihon Rōdō Kyōkai.

Japan Productivity Center. *See* Nihon Seisansei Honbu.

Japan QWL Committee. 1974. *Oubei Shokoku ni okeru QWL Mondai* [QWL problems in the United States and European countries]. QWL Report No. 1. Tokyo: Japan QWL Committee.

Jichishō. *See* Japan, Jichishō.

Jinjiin. *See* Japan, Jinjiin.

Johnson, Richard T. 1976. *Employment Practices and Employee Attitudes: A Study of Japanese and American Managed Firms in the United States*. Research Paper no. 349. Stanford, Cal.: Stanford University, Graduate School of Business.

———, and Ouchi, William. 1974. "Made in America (under Japanese Management)." *Harvard Business Review* 52:61–69.

Kamata Satoshi. 1973. *Jidōsha Zetsubō Kōjō* [A despairing auto works]. Tokyo: Gendai Shuppankai.

Kaneko, Yoshio. 1980. "The Future of the Fixed-Age Retirement System." In Nishikawa, ed., 1980.

Karsh, Bernard, and Cole, Robert E. 1968. "Industrialization and the Convergence Hypothesis: Some Aspects of Contemporary Japan." *Journal of Social Issues* 24:45–64.

Katō Kan. 1966. *Kōkigyō no Keizaigaku* [Economics of public enterprises]. *Sōsho* series, No. 5. Tokyo: Nihon Keizai Kenkyū Sentā.

———. 1976. *Gendai Nihon no Kōkigyō* [Public enterprises in modern Japan]. Tokyo: Nihon Keizai Shimbunsha.

———, ed. 1968. *Nihon no Kōkigyō* [Public enterprises in Japan]. Tokyo: Nihon Keizai Shimbunsha.

Kawada, Hisashi. 1973. "Workers and Their Organizations." In Ōkōchi, Karsh, and Levine, eds., 1973.

Kawanishi Hirosuke. 1978. *Shōsūha Kumiai Undō Ron* [The minority trade union movement]. Tokyo: Kaien Shobō.

Kawashima Takeyoshi. 1967. *Nihonjin no Hōishiki* [Legal consciousness of the Japanese]. Tokyo: Iwanami Shoten. Published in English as "The Legal Consciousness of Contract in Japan." *Law in Japan* 7:1 (1974).

——. 1964. "Dispute Resolution in Contemporary Japan." In Arthur Taylor von Mehren, ed., *Law in Japan*. Cambridge, Mass.: Harvard University Press.

Keizai Dōyūkai (Committee for Economic Development). 1977. *Torishimariyakukai ni kansuru Jittai Chōsa Shūkei Kekka* [Report on a survey of boards of directors]. Tokyo: Keizai Dōyūkai.

Keizai Kikakuchō. *See* Japan, Keizai Kikakuchō.

Kenkō Hoken Rengōkai (Health and Hygiene Insurance Association). 1978. *Shakai Hoshō Nenkan* [Social Security yearbook]. Tokyo: Tōyō Keizai Shimpōsha.

Kerr, Clark; Dunlop, John T.; Harbison, Frederick; and Meyers, Charles A. 1960. *Industrialism and Industrial Man*. Cambridge: Harvard University Press.

King, Carl B., and Risher, Howard W., Jr. 1969. *The Negro in the Petroleum Industry*. Philadelphia: University of Pennsylvania Press.

Knowles, K. J.; Ostry, S. W.; and Cole, H. T. 1958. "Wage Differentials in Large Steel Firms." Oxford University, Institute of Statistics, *Bulletin*, Vol. 20, No. 3.

Kobayashi Shigeru. 1966. *Sony wa Hito o Ikasu* [Sony revitalizes its employees]. Tokyo: Nihon Keiei Shuppankai.

Koga Makoto et al. 1974. "Rōdō Jikan no Kettei Yōin to Jikan Tanshuku ga Seisan ni oyobosu Kōka" [Factors determining hours of work and the impact of shorter hours on output]. *Keizai Bunseki* 47 (July).

Koike Kazuo. 1962. *Nippon no Chingin Kōshō* [Wage bargaining in Japan]. Tokyo: Tokyo University Press.

——. 1977. *Shokuba no Rōdō Kumiai to Sanka: Rōshi Kankei no Nichibei Hikaku* [Trade unions on the shop floor: A comparative study of industrial relations in the U.S. and Japan]. Tokyo: Tōyō Keizai Shimpōsha.

——. 1978a. "Japan's Industrial Relations: Characteristics and Problems." *Japanese Economic Studies* 7, No. 1 (Fall), pp. 42–90.

——. 1978b. *Rōdōsha no Keieisanka: Seiō no Keiken to Nippon* [Workers' participation in management: the Western experience and Japan]. Tokyo: Nihon Hyōronsha.

——. 1979. "Employment in Japan, a 'Superdeveloped Country'." *Japan Echo* 6, No. 3, pp. 34–47.

——. 1981. *Chūshō Kigyō no Jukuren* [Skill formation in small business]. Tokyo: Dōbunkan.

Kōkyō Kigyōtai Shingikai. *See* Japan, Kōkyō Kigyōtai Shingikai.

Komatsu Ryūji. 1971. *Kigyōbetsu Kumiai no Keisei* [Development of enterprise unionism]. Tokyo: Ochanomizu Shobō.

Komiya Ryūtarō. 1975a. "Kōkyō Bumon no Sutoken to Kokumin Fukushi" [The right to strike in the public sector and national welfare]. *Nihon Keizai Shimbun*, October 1 and 2.

——. 1975b. "Kōkyō Bumon no Sutoraiki" [Strikes in the public sector]. *Shyūkan Tōyō Keizai*, November 1.

Kōmuin Seido Shingikai. *See* Japan, Kōmuin Seido Shingikai.

Kōreika Mondai Kondankai (Conference on the Problems of Aging). 1980. "Kōreika Shakai ni okeru Rōdō Keizaiteki Shomondai no Chōki Tembō" [A long-term outlook of labor economic problems in the aging society]. *Rōdō Tokei Chōsa Geppō*, August 1980, pp. 4–18.

Kōseishō. *See* Japan, Kōseishō.

Kōshiro Kazutoshi. 1959. "Nōritsukyu to Kanri Soshiki" [Payment by results and management organizations]. In Ōkōchi, Ujihara, and Fujita, eds., 1959.

———. 1973. *Nihon no Chingin Kettei Kikō* [The structure of wage determination in Japan]. Tokyo: Nihon Hyōronsha.

———. 1975a. "Haichitenkan ni kansuru Rōdō Kumiai no Seisaku" [Trade union policies concerning job transfers]. In Nihon Rōdō Kyōkai, ed., 1975.

———. 1975b. "Kōsha no Tōjisha Nōryoku" [Managerial autonomy of public corporations]. *Kōkirō Kenkyū* No. 22 (April).

———. 1975c. "Kumiai Kōshōryoku to Sōgi Shihyō" [Bargaining power of unions and the index of labor disputes]. In Kōshiro, Sano, and Shimada, eds., 1975.

———. 1975d. "Wage Determination in the National Public Service in Japan: Changes and Prospects." In Charles M. Rehmus, ed., *Public Employment Labor Relations: An Overview of Eleven Nations*. Ann Arbor: University of Michigan—Wayne State University, Institute of Labor and Industrial Relations.

———. 1977a. "Dantai Kōshō" [Collective bargaining]. In Shirai et al., eds., 1977.

———. 1977b. "Humane Organization of Work in the Plants: Production Techniques and the Organization of Work in Japanese Factories." Paper presented at 6th Japanese–German Economic and Social Conference, Düsseldorf, Germany, October 3–9.

———. 1977c. "Kōkigyō no Rōdō Mondai" [Labor problems in public enterprises]. In Ichinose et al., eds., 1977.

———. 1977d. "Nihon no Chingin Kettei to Kokusai Hikaku" [Wage determination in Japan and international comparison]. In Ujihara Shōjirō et al., eds., *Gendai Nihon no Chingin* [Wages in contemporary Japan]. Tokyo: Shakai Shisōsha.

———. 1977e. "Rōdō Kumiai to wa Nani ka?" [What are trade unions for?] In Shirai, Hanami, and Kōshiro, eds., 1977.

———. 1978a, 1979. "Labor Productivity and Recent Employment Adjustment Programs in Japan: Are We Workaholics?" *Japan Labor Bulletin* 17 (December):8–10; 18 (January):4–8.

———. 1978b. *Tenkanki no Chingin Kōshō* [Wage negotiations at the turning point]. Tokyo: Tōyō Keizai Shimpōsha.

———. 1980a. "Dainiji Sekiyu Kiki Ka no Chingin Kettei" [Wage determination under the second oil crisis]. *Nihon Rōdō Kyōkai Zasshi*, No. 254 (May), pp. 2–13.

———. 1980b. "The Economic Impact of Labor Disputes in the Public Sector." In Nishikawa, ed., 1980.

———. 1980c. "Nihon ni okeru Rōdō Seikatsu no Shitsu" [Quality of working life in Japan]. *Nihon Rōdō Kyōkai Zasshi* No. 255 (June), pp. 15–23.

———. 1980d. "Perceptions of Work and Living Attitudes of the Japanese." *Japan Quarterly* 27 (January–March): 46–55.

———, ed. 1973. *Nihon no Chingin Kettei Kikō* [Mechanisms of wage determination in Japan]. Tokyo: Nihon Hyōronsha.

Kōshiro Kazutoshi, Sano Yōko, and Shimada Haruo. 1975. *Shuntō Chinage ni oyobusu Kankōrō no Eikyō no Sūryōteki Kenkyū* [A quantitative analysis of the impact of public employee unions upon wage determination by the spring offensive]. Tokyo: Tōkei Kenkyūkai.

Kubo Keiji. 1963. "Kujō Shori" [Grievance settlements]. In Ishii Teruhisa and Ariizumi Tōru, eds., *Rōdōhō Taikei* [A comprehensive series on labor laws]. Tokyo: Yūhikaku.

Kuratani, Masatoshi. 1973. "A Theory of Training, Earnings and Employment: An Application to Japan." Ph.D. Thesis, New York: Columbia University.

Laidler, D., and Purdy, D. L., eds. 1974. *Inflation and the Labour Market*. Manchester: Manchester University Press.

Leibenstein, Harvey. 1976. *Beyond Economic Man*. Cambridge, Mass.: Harvard University Press.

Lerner, Shirley, et al. 1969. *Workshop Wage Determination in a System of National Bargaining*. New York: Pergamon Press.

Levine, Solomon B. 1958. *Industrial Relations in Postwar Japan*. Urbana: University of Illinois Press.

———. 1967. "Postwar Trade Unionism, Collective Bargaining, and Japanese Social Structure." In Dore, ed., 1967.

———, and Kawada, Hisashi. 1980. *Human Resources in Japanese Industrial Development*. Princeton, N.J.: Princeton University Press.

———, and Taira, Koji. 1977. "Labor Markets, Trade Unions and Social Justice: Japanese Failures?" *Japanese Economic Studies* 5, No. 3 (Spring), pp. 66–95.

———, and Taira, Koji. 1978. "Interpreting Industrial Conflict: The Case of Japan." In Benjamin Martin and Everett Kassalow, eds., *Labor Relations in Advanced Industrial Societies: Issues and Problems*. Washington, D.C.: Carnegie Endowment for International Peace.

Levinson, Charles. 1974. *Industry's Democratic Revolution*. London: George Allen and Unwin.

Lockwood, William W. 1968. *The Economic Development of Japan* (Expanded edition.) Princeton, N.J.: Princeton University Press.

Lupton, Tom. 1962. *On the Shop Floor*. Elmswood, N.Y.: Pergamon Press.

MKTC: Japan, Rōdōshō, Tōkei Jōhōbu (Ministry of Labor, Department of Statistics and Information). 1955–1980. *Maigetsu Kinrō Tōkei Chōsa Sōgō Hōkokusho* [Report on monthly labor statistics surveys]. Tokyo: Rōdō Hōrei Kyōkai.

McCabe, David A. 1952. "Union Policies as to the Area of Collective Bargaining." In George W. Brooks, Milton Derber, David A. McCabe, and Philip Taft, eds., *Interpreting the Labor Movement*. Madison, Wis.: Industrial Relations Research Association.

Macrae, Norman. 1980. "Must Japan Slow? A Survey." *Economist*, February 23.

Marsh, Robert M., and Mannari, Hiroshi. 1971. "Lifetime Employment in Japan: Roles, Norms and Values." *American Journal of Sociology* 76:795–812.

———. 1976. *Modernization and the Japanese Factory.* Princeton, N.J.: Princeton University Press.

Matsuda, Yasuhiko. 1966. "Government Employees in Japan." *Japan Labor Bulletin* 5, No. 10 (October), pp. 4–11 and 5, No. 11 (November), pp. 4–8.

———. 1980. "Industrial Conflict Resolution: Social Tensions and Industrial Relations Arising in the Industrialization Processes of Asian Countries." In *Proceedings of the 1979 Asian Regional Conference on Industrial Relations.* Tokyo: Japan Institute of Labor.

Matsuzaki Yoshinobu. 1952. *Kaisei Kōkyō Kigyōtai Rōdō Kankeihō no Kaisetsu* [Commentary on the amended PCNELR Law]. Tokyo: Jiji Tsūshinsha.

Minami, Ryōshin. 1968. "The Turning Point in the Japanese Economy." *Quarterly Journal of Economics* 52:38–42.

———. 1971a. *Nihon Keizai no Tenkanten* [The turning point in the Japanese economy]. Tokyo: Sōbunsha.

———. 1971b. *The Turning Point of Japanese Economy.* Tokyo: Kinokuniya.

Minemura Teruo. 1969. *Kōkyō Kigyōtai tō Rōdō Kankeihō* [The PCNELR Law]. *Hōritsugaku Zenshū* series, No. 48. Tokyo: Yūhikaku.

———. 1971. *Kōrōhō—Chikōrōhō* [The PCNELR Law and the LPELR Law]. Tokyo: Nihon Hyōronsha.

Ministry of International Trade and Industry. *See* Japan, Ministry of International Trade and Industry.

Ministry of Labor. *See* Japan, Ministry of Labor.

Mouer, Ross E. 1979. "A Methodological Investigation of Nakane Chie's *Japanese Society* and Some Comments on the Uses of Her Non-Scientific Exposé." Paper presented at the 3rd New Zealand Asian Studies Conference, University of Aukland, New Zealand, May 13–16.

Murphy, Betty Southard. 1975. "The NLRB in Its Fortieth Year." *Labor Law Journal* 26 (September):551–58.

NES: Great Britain, Department of Employment and Productivity. 1975. *New Earnings Survey.* London: Her Majesty's Stationery Office.

Nakamura, Atsushi. 1980. "Intra-Firm Wage Differentials." In Nishikawa, ed., 1980.

Nakamura Hiroshi. 1971. *Kōmuin no Sōgikōi to Shobun* [Acts of dispute by civil service and disciplinary actions]. Tokyo: Chūō Keizaisha.

———. 1972. *Kōmuinhō no Riron to Jissai* [Theory and practice of the Civil Service Law]. Tokyo: Chūō Keizaisha.

———. 1972b. *Kōmuin no Sōgikoi* [Acts of dispute by the civil service]. Tokyo: Nihon Rōdō Kyōkai.

Nakane Chie. 1967. *Tate Shakai no Ningen Kankei* [Human relations in a vertical society]. Tokyo: Kodansha.

———. 1970. *Japanese Society.* Berkeley: University of California Press.

Nakaoka Tetsurō. 1971a. *Gijutsu no Ronri—Ningen no Tachiba* [The logic of technology—from the standpoint of human beings]. Tokyo: Chikuma Shobō.

———. 1971b. *Kōjō no Tetsugaku* [A philosophy of factories]. Tokyo: Heibonsha.

Nakayama, Ichiro. 1975. *Industrialization and Labor-Management Relations in Japan*. Tokyo: Japan Institute of Labor.

National Union of Railwaymen. 1976. *Rules*. London: National Union of Railwaymen.

Nihon Chingin Kenkyū Sentā (Japan Wage Research Center). 1976. *Shinki Chingin Kōshō Shiryō* [Data for spring wage bargaining]. Tokyo: Sangyō Rōdō Chōsajo.

Nihon Kikanshi Kyōkai (Japan Association of Union Journals). 1977. *Kikanshi to Senden* [Union journals and propaganda]. November, pp. 22–23.

Nihon Rōdōhō Gakkai (Japan Labor Law Research Association). 1966. *Kankō Rōdōsha no Rōdō Kihonken* [Basic rights of public employees]. *Nihon Rōdōhō Gakkaishi* series, No. 27. Tokyo: Sōgō Rōdō Kenkyūjo.

————. 1972. *Kankō Rōdō Kankei to Rōdōhō* [Labor relations in the public sector and labor laws]. *Nihon Rōdōhō Gakkaishi* series, No. 39. Tokyo: Sōgō Rōdō Kenkyūjo.

Nihon Rōdō Kyōkai (Japan Institute of Labor). 1969. *Sankōsha Gogengyō Chingin Funsō Chōsei Jittai no Kenkyū* [A study of adjustments in wage disputes in the three public corporations and five national enterprises]. Tokyo: Nihon Rōdō Kyōkai.

————, ed. 1975. *Haichitenkan o Meguru Rōshi Kankei* [Labor-management relations concerning job transfers]. Tokyo: Nihon Rōdō Kyōkai.

Nihon Seisansei Hombu (Japan Productivity Center). 1972. *Chingin Hakusho* [White paper on wages]. Tokyo: Nihon Seisansei Hombu.

————. 1973. *Sanka Jidai no Rōshi Kankei: Rōshi Kankei Seido Jittai Chōsa Hōkoku* [Industrial relations in the age of participation: a report on the practice of the industrial relations system]. Tokyo: Nihon Seisansei Hombu.

————. 1977, 1979, 1980. *Katsuyō Rōdō Tōkei* [Applied labor statistics]. Tokyo: Nihon Seisansei Hombu.

Niinuma Takashi. 1977. "Rōdō Kumiai no Koyō Seisaku" [Employment policies of labor unions]. In Nihon Rōdō Kyōkai, Koyō Kenkyūkai (Japan Institute of Labor, Study Group on Employment), ed., *Teiseichōka no Koyō Mondai* [Employment problems under low growth]. Tokyo: Nihon Rōdō Kyōkai.

Nikkeiren (Japan Employer's Association). 1969. *Nōryokushugi Kanri* [Full-ability management]. Tokyo: Nikkeiren.

————. 1971. *Wagakuni Rōmu Kanri no Gensei* [The present condition of labor management]. Third Report. Tokyo: Nikkeiren.

————. 1975. *Wagakuni Jinji Rōmu Kanri no Gensei* [The present conditions of personnel and labor management]. Fourth Report. Tokyo: Nikkeiren.

————. 1982. *Rōdō Mondai Kenkyū Iinkai Hōkoku* [Research report of the study group on labor problems]. Tokyo: Nikkeiren.

Nishikawa, Shunsaku, ed., 1980. *The Labor Market in Japan: Selected Readings*. Tokyo: Japan Foundation.

————, and Shimada, Haruo. 1980. "Employment and Unemployment: 1970–1975." In Nishikawa, ed., 1980.

Nomura Heiji and Ujihara Shōjirō. 1961. *Chūshōkigyō no Rōdō Kumiai* [Labor unions in small and medium-sized firms]. Tokyo: Nihon Hyōronsha.

Northrup, Herbert R., et al. 1970. *Negro Employment in Basic Industry.* Philadelphia: University of Pennsylvania Press.

Numata Inejirō, ed. 1963. *Gōdō Rōso no Kenkyū* [A study on amalgamated regional unions]. Tokyo: Sōgō Rōdō Kenkyūjo.

OECD. *See* Organization for Economic Cooperation and Development.

Obi, Keiichirō. 1980. "The Theory of Labor Supply: Some New Perspectives and Some Implications." In Nishikawa, ed., 1980.

Obuchi, Hiroshi. 1976. "Demographic Transition in the Process of Japanese Industrialization." In Patrick, ed., 1976.

Ohkawa Kazushi. 1962. *Nihon Keizai Bunseki* [Analysis of the Japanese economy]. Tokyo: Shunjūsha.

———, and Rosovsky, Henry. 1973. *Japanese Economic Growth.* Stanford: Stanford University Press.

Ohta Kaoru. 1961. *Rōdō Kumiairon* [On trade unions]. Tokyo: Rōdō Keizaisha.

Oi, Walter. 1962. "Labor as a Quasi-Fixed Factor." *Journal of Political Economy* 70:538–55.

Okamoto, Hideaki. 1973. "Management and Their Organizations." In Ōkōchi, Karsh, and Levine, eds., 1973.

———. 1975. "Haichitenkan to Rōdōsha" [Job transfers and workers]. In Nihon Rōdō Kyōkai, ed., 1975.

Ōkōchi Kazuo. 1952. *Reimeiki no Nihon Rōdō Undō* [The dawn of the Japanese labor movement]. Tokyo: Iwanami Shoten.

———. 1958a. *Gijutsu Kakushin to Rōdō Mondai* [Technological innovations and labor problems]. Tokyo: Nihon Seisansei Hombu.

———. 1958b. *Labor in Modern Japan.* Tokyo: Science Council of Japan.

———. 1965. "The Characteristics of Labor-Management Relations in Japan." *Journal of Social and Political Ideas in Japan* 3:44–49.

———, ed. 1965. *Sangyōbetsu Chingin Kettei no Kikō* [The structure of industrial wage determination]. Tokyo: Nihon Rōdō Kyōkai.

Ōkōchi, Kazuo; Karsh, Bernard; and Levine, Solomon B., eds. 1973. *Workers and Employers in Japan: The Japanese Employment Relations System.* Tokyo: Tokyo University Press and Princeton: Princeton University Press.

Ōkōchi Kazuo, Ujihara Shōjirō, and Fujita Wakao, eds., 1959. *Rōdō Kumiai no Kōzō to Kinō* [The structure and functions of labor unions]. Tokyo: Tokyo University Press.

Ono Akira. 1972. "Rōdō Kumiai no Kōshōryoku to Chingin—Bukka" [The collective bargaining power of labor unions and wages—prices]. *Keizai Hyōron* (February), pp. 20–31.

———. 1973. *Sengo Nihon no Chingin Kettei* [Wage determination in postwar Japan]. Tokyo: Tōyō Keizai Shimpōsha.

———, and Watanabe, Tsunehiko. 1976. "Changes in Income Inequality in the Japanese Economy." In Patrick, ed., 1976.

Organization for Economic Cooperation and Development (OECD). 1973. *Manpower Policy in Japan.* Paris: OECD.

————. 1977. *The Development of Industrial Relations Systems: Some Implications of Japanese Experience.* Paris: OECD.

Orii Hyūga. 1973. *Rōmu Kanri Nijūnen* [Twenty years of labor management]. Tokyo: Tōyō Keizai Shimpōsha.

Patrick, Hugh, ed. 1976. *Japanese Industrialization and Its Social Consequences.* Berkeley: University of California Press.

————, and Rosovsky, Henry. 1976. "Japan's Economic Performance: An Overview." In Patrick and Rosovsky, eds., 1976.

————, eds., 1976. *Asia's New Giant: How the Japanese Economy Works.* Washington: Brookings Institution.

Prime Minister's Office. *See* Japan, Prime Minister's Office.

RKKC: Japan, Rōdōshō, Tōkei Jōhōbu (Ministry of Labor, Department of Statistics and Information). 1945–61, 1964, 1971, 1975–76, 1978. *Rōdō Kumiai Kihon Chōsa* [Basic survey of trade unions in Japan]. Tokyo: Ōkurashō Insatsukyoku.

Reder, Melvin W. 1955. "The Theory of Occupational Wage Differentials." *American Economic Review* 45 (December):833–52.

Reischauer, Edwin O. 1977. *The Japanese.* Cambridge, Mass.: Harvard University Press.

Rinji Gyōsei Chōsakai. *See* Japan, Rinji Gyōsei Chōsakai.

Rinji Kokyō Kigyōtai Gorika Shingikai. *See* Japan, Rinji Kokyō Kigyōtai Gorika Shingikai.

Rōdōshō. *See* Japan, Rōdōshō.

Rōdō Sōgi Chōsakai (Research Council on Labor Disputes). 1956–58. *Sengo Rōdō Sōgi Jittai Chōsa* [Surveys of postwar labor dispute practices]. Tokyo: Chūō Kōronsha.

Vol. I, *Sekitan Sōgi* [Coal labor disputes], 1957.

Vol. II, *Densan Sōgi* [Labor disputes in the electric power generating industry], 1957.

Vol. III, *Kōtsū Bumon ni okeru Sōgi* [Labor disputes in the transportation industry], 1957.

Vol. IV, *Sen'i Rōdō Sōgi to Kumiai Undō* [Labor disputes and trade union movements in the textile industry], 1956.

Vol. VII, *Tekkō Sōgi* [Labor disputes in the iron and steel industry], 1958.

Vol. VIII, *Kagaku Kōgyō no Rōdō Sōgi to Kumiai Undō* [Labor disputes and trade union movements in the chemical industry], 1958.

Rohlen, Thomas. 1974. *For Harmony and Strength.* Berkeley: University of California Press.

————. 1975. "The Company Work Group." In Vogel, ed., 1975.

————. 1979. "Permanent Employment Faces Recession, Slow Growth, and an Aging Workforce." *Journal of Japanese Studies* 5:2.

Rōshi Kankeihō Kenkyūkai. *See* Japan, Rōdōshō, Rōshi Kankeihō Kenkyūkai.

Royal Commission on Trade Unions. *See* Great Britain, Royal Commission on Trade Unions.

SEI: European Community (EC). 1972. Structure of Earnings in Industry. Brussels: EC.

Saitō Shigeo. 1974. Waganaki ato ni Kōzui wa Kitare! [After us comes the flood] Tokyo: Tokuma Shoten.

Sakata Tokio. 1976. Chihō Kōei Kigyō [Local public enterprises]. Tokyo: Daiichi Hōki Shuppan.

Sakisaka Itsuro. 1937, 1947. Nihon Shihonshugi no Shomondai [The problems of Japanese capitalism]. Tokyo: Ōdosha.

Sakurabayashi, Makoto. 1969. "Enterprise Unionism and Wage Increase." In Ballon, ed., 1969.

Sano Yōko. 1970. Chingin Kettei no Keiryō Bunseki [A quantitative analysis of wage determination]. Tokyo: Tōyō Keizai Shimpōsha.

———. 1980. "A Quantitative Analysis of Factors Determining the Rate of Increase in Wage Levels during the Spring Wage Offensive." In Nishikawa, ed., 1980.

———, ed. 1972. Joshi Rōdō no Keizaigaku [Economics of female workers]. Tokyo: Nihon Rōdō Kyōkai.

———, Koike Kazuo, and Ishida Hideo, eds., 1969. Chingin Kōshō no Kōdō Kagaku [The behavioral science of wage negotiations]. Tokyo: Tōyō Keizai Shimpōsha.

Scott, W. H., et al. 1956. Technical Change and Industrial Relations. Liverpool: Liverpool University Press.

Senmoniin Kondankai. See Japan, Senmoniin Kondankai.

Shiba, Shōji. 1973. A Cross-National Comparison of Labor Management with Reference to Technology Transfer. IDE Occasional Papers Series, No. 11. Tokyo: Institute of Developing Economies.

Shimada, Haruo. 1970. "Japanese Labor's Spring Wage Offensive and Wage Spill Over." Keio Economic Studies 7, No.2, pp. 33–61.

———. 1974. "The Structure of Earnings and Investments in Human Resources: A Comparison between the United States and Japan." Ph.D. dissertation, University of Wisconsin–Madison.

———. 1976. "Kajō Koyōron o Kangaeru" (A Comment on Opinion Alleging a Surplus in Employment), Nihon Keizai Shimbun, April 11, 12.

———. 1977. "The Japanese Labor Market after the Oil Crisis: A Factual Report." Keio Economic Studies 14, No. 1, pp. 49–65 and No. 2, pp. 37–59.

———. 1978. "Are Japanese Industrial Relations So Mysterious?" Look Japan, May 10.

———. 1980. The Japanese Employment System. The Japanese Industrial Relations Series No. 6. Tokyo: Japan Institute of Labor.

———, and Nishikawa, Shunsaku. 1979. "An Analysis of Japanese Employment System and Youth Labor Market." Keio Economic Studies 16, Nos. 1 and 2, pp. 1–16.

Shinozuka Eiko and Ishihara Emiko. 1977. "Oil Shock ikō no Koyō Chōsei: 4 ka Koku Hikaku to Nihon no Kibokan Hikaku" [Adjustment in employment after the oil shock: A comparative study of four countries and of different sized firms in Japan]. Nihon Keizai Kenkyū (August).

Shinozuka Eiko. 1978. "Koyō Chōsei no Mondaiten" [Problematic points concerning employment adjustment]. Keizai Kikakuchō, *ESP* 72 (April).

Shirai, Taishiro. 1965. "Changing Patterns of Collective Bargaining in Japan." In Japan Institute of Labor, ed., *The Changing Patterns of Industrial Relations.* Tokyo: Japan Institute of Labor.

———. 1973. "Collective Bargaining." In Ōkōchi, Karsh, and Levine, eds., 1973.

———. 1975. "Decision-Making in Japanese Unions." In Vogel, ed., 1975.

———, Hanami Tadashi, and Kōshiro Kazutoshi, eds. 1977. *Rōdō Kumiai Dokuhon* [Readings on labor unions]. Tokyo: Tōyō Keizai Shimpōsha.

———, and Kōshiro Kazutoshi. 1960. *Kinzoku Kikai Sangyō ni okeru Kumiai Soshiki to Rōdō Kyōyaku* [Union organization and collective bargaining agreements in the metal and machinery industries]. Tokyo: Nihon Rōdō Kyōkai.

———, and Shimada, Haruo. 1978. "Japan." In John T. Dunlop and Walter Galenson, eds., *Labor in the Twentieth Century.* New York: Academic Press.

Smith, Thomas C. 1955. "Old Values and New Techniques in the Modernization of Japan." *Far Eastern Quarterly* 45:355–63.

———. 1964. "Japan's Aristocratic Revolution." *Yale Review* 50:370–83.

Somers, Gerald, and Tsuda, Masumi. 1966. "Job Vacancies and Structural Change in Japanese Labor Markets." In *The Measurement and Interpretation of Job Vacancies: A Conference Report,* National Bureau of Economic Research, ed., New York: Columbia University Press.

Sōrifu. *See* Japan, Sōrifu.

Sturmthal, Adolf. 1963. "Some Thoughts on Labor and Political Action." *University of Illinois Bulletin* 60, No. 51, Institute of Industrial and Labor Relations.

———. 1972. *Comparative Labor Movements: Ideological Roots and Institutional Development.* Belmont, Cal.: Wadsworth.

Sumiya, Mikio. 1963. *Social Impact of Industrialization in Japan.* Tokyo: Japanese Commission for UNESCO.

———. 1966a. "The Development of Japanese Labor Relations." *Developing Economies* 4:449–518.

———. 1966b. *Nihon Rōdō Undōshi* [History of the labor movement in Japan]. Tokyo: Yūshindo.

———. 1973a. "The Emergence of Modern Japan." In Ōkōchi, Karsh, and Levine, eds., 1973.

———. 1973b. "Comtemporary Arrangements: An Overview." In Ōkōchi, Karsh, and Levine, eds., 1973.

———. 1976. *Nihon Chinrōdō no Shiteki Kenkyū* [A historical study of Japanese wage labor]. Tokyo: Ochanomizu Shobō.

———. 1981. "Japan: A Survey of Industrial Relations Theories." In Peter B. Doeringer, *Industrial Relations in International Perspective.* London: Macmillan Co.

Taira, Koji. 1962. "The Characteristics of Japanese Labor Markets." *Economic Development and Cultural Change* 10:150–68.

————. 1970. *Economic Development and the Labor Market in Japan.* New York: Columbia University Press.

————. 1977. "Nihongata Kigyōbetsu Rōdō Kumiai Sambiron." *Chūō Kōron* (March). The translated version of this paper, "In Defense of Japanese Enterprise Unions," appeared in *Japan Echo* 4, No. 2, pp. 98–109.

Takahashi Kō. 1965. *Nihonteki Rōshi Kankei no Kenkyū* [A study of Japanese labor and industrial relations]. Tokyo: Miraisha.

Takahashi, Takeshi. 1973. "Social Security for Workers." In Ōkōchi, Karsh, and Levine, eds., 1973.

Takahashi Tatsuo. 1956. "Kōkyō Kigyōtairon Hihan" [Criticism of views on public enterprises]. *Denshin Denwa Keiei Geppō,* No. 85 (October), pp. 11–18.

Takanashi Akira. 1965. "Tekkō" [The iron and steel industry]. In Ōkōchi, ed., 1965.

Takemae Eiji. 1970. *Amerika Tainichi Rōdō Seisaku no Kenkyū* [A study of the American Occupation policy toward labor in Japan]. Tokyo: Nihon Hyōronsha.

Takezawa, Shin'ichi, and Asazawa, Nobuo. 1977. "Trends in Improvements in the Quality of Working Life in the Shipbuilding Industry." Report presented to the International Labor Organization, November 8, 1977. Tokyo: Japan Institute of Labor, June. Mimeo.

Tan, W. Hong. 1980. "Human Capital and Technical Change: A Study of Wage Differentials in Japanese Manufacturing." Ph.D. dissertation, Yale University.

Tanaka, Hirohide. 1980. "An Analysis of Factors Determining Starting Pay." In Nishikawa, ed., 1980.

Tanaka Manabu. 1976. "Nihon Shihonshugi no Kaikyū Kankei" [Class relations in Japanese capitalism]. *Keizaigaku Hihan* [Critique of economics], No. 1. Tokyo: Shakai Hyōronsha.

Tanaka Tsunemi. 1971. "Tekkōgyō no Yonkumi Sankōtaisei ni tsuite" [On the system of three shifts by four crews in the iron and steel industry]. *Nihon Rōdō Kyōkai Zasshi,* No. 150 (September), pp. 40–48.

Taylor, Robert. 1978. *The Fifth Estate: Britain's Unions in the Seventies.* London: Routledge and Kegan Paul.

Tekkōrōren (Federation of Iron and Steel Workers' Unions). 1971. *Tekkō Sangyō Niokeru Rōshi Kankei Ishiki no Mensetsu Chōsa* [A report of interview research on industrial relations in the steel industry]. Tokyo: Tekkōrōren.

————. 1977. *Ōte Seitetsusho no Rōdōsha to Rōdō Kumiai* [A report on workers and trade unions in the big steel companies]. Tokyo: Tekkōrōren.

————. 1978. *Yōkyū Daketsumen kara mita '78 Shuntō no Chūkan Sōkatsu* [An interim report on the 1978 spring offensive wage demands and the negotiated results]. Tokyo: Tekkōrōren.

Tōkei Shiryō Kenkyūkai (Institute for Statistical Documents Research). 1978. *Tōkei Nihon Keizai Bunseki* [Statistical analysis of the Japanese economy]. Tokyo: Tōkei Shiryō Kenkyūkai.

Tokunaga Shigeyoshi. 1970. *Rōdō Mondai to Shakai Seisakuron* [Labor problems and social policy]. Tokyo: Yūhikaku.

408

Tokyo Daigaku Shakai Kagaku Kenkyūjo (Tokyo University, Institute of Social Sciences). 1950. *Sengo Rōdō Kumiai no Jittai* [The practices of postwar labor unions]. Tokyo: Nihon Hyōronsha.

Tominaga, Ken'ichi. 1962. "Occupational Mobility in Japanese Society: Analysis of the Labor Market in Japan." *Journal of Economic Behavior* 2:1–37.

Tomita, Iwao. 1969. "Labor Cost Accounting." In Ballon, ed., 1969.

Totsuka H.; Nakanishi Y.; Hyōdō T.; and Yamamoto, K. 1976. *Nihon ni okeru "Shin Sayoku" no Rōdō Undō* [The labor movement of the "New Left" in Japan]. 2 vols. Tokyo: Tokyo University Press.

Totten, George O. 1967. "Collective Bargaining and Works Councils as Innovations in Industrial Relations in Japan during the 1920's." In Dore, ed., 1967.

Tsuda, Masumi. 1973. "Personnel Administration at the Industrial Plant Level." In Ōkōchi, Karsh, and Levine, eds., 1983.

———. 1977. "Study of Japanese Management Development Practices." *Hitotsubashi Journal of Social Studies* 9:1–12.

Tsujimura, Kōtarō. 1980. "The Effect of Reductions in Working Hours on Productivity." In Nishikawa, ed., 1980.

Tsūshō Sangyōshō. *See* Japan, Tsūshō Sangyōshō.

Turner, H. A. 1966. *Labor Relations in the Motor Industry.* London: G. Allen and Unwin.

Ujihara Shōjirō. 1955. "Keihin Kōgyō Chitai ni okeru Daikōjō Rōdōsha no Seikaku" [Characteristics of workers in big factories in the Tokyo-Yokohama area]. In *Nihon Rōdō Mondai Kenkyū* [Research in Japanese labor problems], Part III. Tokyo: University of Tokyo Press, 1966.

———. 1973. "The Labor Market." In Ōkōchi, Karsh, and Levine, eds., 1973.

———. 1979. "Dantai Kōshō to Rōshi Kyōgisei" [Collective bargaining and joint consultation]. *Chūō Rōdō Jihō* (April).

Umemura Mataji. 1964. *Sengo Nihon no Rōdōryoku* [The labor force in postwar Japan]. Tokyo: Iwanami Shoten.

———. 1971. *Rōdōryoku no Kōzō to Koyō Mondai* [The structure of the labor force and problems of employment]. Tokyo: Iwanami Shoten.

———. 1980. "The Seniority-Wage System in Japan." In Nishikawa, ed., 1980.

United States, Department of Commerce, Bureau of the Census. 1960. *Census of Population, 1960, Occupations by Earnings and Education,* Census Report PC (2) 7B, Washington, D.C.: Government Printing Office.

United States, Department of Labor, Bureau of Labor Statistics. 1954. *Techniques of Preparing BLS Statistical Series.* New York: Greenwood Press.

———. 1970. *Bulletin* No. 1425–11. Washington, D.C.: Government Printing Office.

———. 1975. *Handbook of Labor Statistics 1975.* Washington, D. C.: Government Printing Office.

United States, Federal Mediation and Conciliation Service. 1963–76. *Annual Report.* Washington, D.C.: Government Printing Office.

Urabe Kuniyoshi. 1949. *Kōkyō Kigyōtairon* [On public enterprises]. Tokyo: Moriyama Shoten, 1949; second ed., 1969.

Vogel, Ezra F. 1963. *Japan's New Middle Class*. Berkeley: University of California Press.

——. 1967. "Kinship Structure, Migration to the City, and Modernization." In Dore, ed., 1967.

——. 1979. *Japan as Number 1*. Cambridge, Mass.: Harvard University Press.

——, ed. 1975. *Modern Japanese Organization and Decision-Making*. Berkeley: University of California Press.

Walton, Richard E. 1975. "Criteria for the Quality of Working Life." In Louis E. Davis, Albert B. Cherns, et al., eds., *The Quality of Working Life*, Vol. 1. New York: Free Press.

Watanabe Tsunehiko. 1966. "Chingin Kakaku no Kankei to Sono Seisakuteki Imi" [The relationship between wages and prices and their policy implications]. In Kumagaya Hisao and Watanabe Tsunehiko, eds., *Nihon no Bukka* [Prices in Japan]. Tokyo: Nihon Keizai Shimbunsha.

Webb, Sidney and Beatrice. 1920. *Industrial Democracy*. New York: Augustus M. Kelley. Originally published in 1897. The Japanese translation, *Sangyō Minshūsei Ron* by Takano Iwasaburō, is based on the 1920 edition. Tokyo: Dōjinsha, 1927.

Whitehill, Arthur, and Takezawa, Shin'ichi. 1968. *The Other Worker*. Honolulu: East-West Center Press.

Windmuller, John P., ed. 1974–75. "European Labor and Politics: A Symposium (I and II)." *Industrial and Labor Relations Review* 28, Nos. 1 and 2 (October 1974 and January 1975).

Yamada Moritarō. 1934. *Nihon Shihonshugi Bunseki* [An analysis of Japanese capitalism]. Tokyo: Iwanami Shoten.

Yamada Yukio. 1957. *Kōkigyōhō* [Public enterprises and the law]. *Hōritsugaku Zenshū* series, No. 13. Tokyo: Yūhikaku.

Yamaguchi Kōichirō. 1971. "Giseisha Kyūen Hoshō o meguru Shomondai" [Problems concerning the relief fund for victimized members]. *Rōdōhō*, No. 38, pp. 102–118.

——. 1976a. "Right to Strike Issues in the Public Sector." *Japan Labor Bulletin* 15, No. 2 (February), pp. 6–8.

——. 1976b. "Strikes and Liability for Strike-Related Damage." *Japan Labor Bulletin* 15, No. 7 (July), pp. 6–8.

——. 1977. "Hōritsu Seisaku toshite no Sōgiken Mondai" [Problems of the right to strike as legal policy]. In Tsutomu Hyōdō et al., eds., *Kōkyō Bumon no Sōgiken* [The right to strike in the public sector]. Tokyo: Tokyo University Press.

——. 1978. "The Right to Strike in the Public Sector." *Japan Labor Bulletin* 17, No. 9 (September), pp. 5–8.

Yamamoto Kiyoshi. 1978. "Jidōsha Kōgyō ni Okeru Chingin Taikei" [Wage systems in the automobile industry]. *Tōkyō Daigaku Shakai Kagaku Kenkyū* 30, No. 1 (July), pp. 176–205.

Yamamura, Kōzō. 1967. *Economic Policy in Postwar Japan: Growth versus Economic Democracy*. Berkeley: University of California Press.

————. 1976. "General Trading Companies in Japan—Their Origins and Growth." In Patrick, ed., 1976.

Yamashita Fujio. 1973. "Sankōsha Gogengyō no Chingin Kettei" [Wage determination in the three public corporations and five national enterprises]. In Kōshiro, ed., 1973.

Yanagawa Noboru, ed. 1956. *Kōkyō Kigyōtai no Kenkyū* [A study of public enterprises]. Tokyo: Yūhikaku.

Yasuba, Yasukichi. 1975. "Anatomy of the Debate on Japanese Capitalism." *Journal of Japanese Studies* 2:1.

————. 1976. "The Evolution of Dualistic Wage Structure." In Patrick, ed., 1976.

Yoshikawa Daijiro. 1968. *Karishobun no Shomondai* [Problems of provisional disposition]. Tokyo: Yūhikaku.

Yoshino, Michael. 1968. *Japan's Managerial System.* Cambridge, Mass.: MIT Press.

Yoshitake, Kiyohiko. 1973. *Public Enterprises in Japan.* Tokyo: Nihon Hyōronsha.

Yūseishō. *See* Japan, Yūseishō.

Index

Abegglen, James C., 7-8, 9, 10, 14, 79
Absenteeism, 64-66, 68, 69, 74, 85, 356
Accidents, 73, 86-87n6; zero, 72, 73. See
    also Safety
AFL-CIO, 331, 349
Age: as factor of unemployment, 49; of labor
    force, 134, 247; retirement, 247-48, 303-4;
    and separation rates, 40-42; -wage profiles,
    9, 15, 30-33, 50, 90, 109, 111-15
Akita Joju, 277
Alcohol Monopoly, 261, 265, 288
All Japan Seamen's Union. See Kaiin
Allowance: dismissal, 217; family, 38, 40,
    240, 298; good-result, 298 (see also
    Bonuses); regional, 298; retirement, 38,
    131, 217, 247, 298, 304; seasonal, 298
Apprenticeship, 42, 58, 128
Arbitration, 196, 217, 233, 260, 273, 275;
    binding, 288; compulsory, 193, 266; griev-
    ance, 180, 181, 190, 191, 201; nonbinding,
    272; in PCNE, 269-70, 271, 281, 288; in
    Western countries, 190, 201
Ariizumi Tōru, 12
Asazawa, Nobuo, 74
Attrition, 68, 75
Aufsichtrat, 370

Bain, George S., 96
Bank of Japan, 262, 267
Banks, 262, 264, 267
Bargaining. *See* Collective bargaining
Basic Survey of the Wage Structure (CKKT),
    54, 109
Basic Survey of Trade Unions (RKKC), 121
Becker, Gary S., 59, 76
Benedict, Ruth, 7
Bonuses, 15, 38, 130, 135, 217, 240, 241-42,
    298, 362, 376; based on productivity, 173;
    semiannual, 146

Boraston, Ian, 150

Capital: human, 14, 15, 52, 57-58, 252;
    intensity, 251, 252; in Japanese firms, 59,
    138, 371-72
Career patterns: internal promotion as, 50-60,
    90, 97, 115, 138-39, 355, 357, 366,
    372-74, 376; management, 138, 372-74,
    375, 376; in process industries, 59; in small
    v. large firms, 55, 97-103; in U.K., 55,
    59; in U.S., 55, 59
Christianity, 339
Chūritsurōren (Federation of Independent
    Unions of Japan), 219, 249, 336
Civil service, 295-311, 363; acts of dispute
    in, 308-9; appointment in, 297; collective
    bargaining in, 305-6; Constitution on, 296;
    courts on, 300, 302, 307-8, 309; discipline
    in, 300-302; dismissal in, 304; employ-
    ment conditions in, 296-304; fringe bene-
    fits in, 298-300; government control of,
    298; grievances in, 297, 302; history of,
    296; job security in, 302-4; law, 266, 279,
    296, 297, 300, 302, 304, 305, 306, 309;
    legal determinism in, 298, 305; local, 267,
    271, 295, 298, 308; moonlighting prohib-
    ited in, 300-302; v. PCNE, 266-67,
    270-71; pensions in, 298-99; political neu-
    trality of, 302; promotion in, 297-98;
    retirement in, 303-4, 309; right to organize
    in, 304-5; strike rights in, 306-8, 309, 332;
    unions in, 304-5, 363; wages in, 298-99;
    workweek in, 299
Class consciousness/structure, 130, 154, 253,
    255, 341-42, 348
Cole, Robert, 15-16, 17-18, 21, 68, 79, 124,
    253-54
Collective action, 161, 180, 309; Constitution
    on, 206, 207, 283, 304, 338; right of, 162,
    163, 166, 168, 172, 174, 360, 361

411

JACKET DESIGNED BY MIKE JAYNES
COMPOSED BY LANDMANN ASSOCIATES, INC., MADISON, WISCONSIN
PRINTED BY FAIRFIELD GRAPHICS, FAIRFIELD, PENNSYLVANIA
TEXT AND DISPLAY LINES ARE SET IN TIMES ROMAN

Library of Congress Cataloging in Publication Data
Main entry under title:
Contemporary industrial relations in Japan.
Bibliography: pp. 389–410.
Includes index.
1. Industrial relations—Japan—Addresses, essays,
lectures. I. Shirai, Taishirō.
HD8726.5.C65 1983   331'.0952   83-47770
ISBN 0-299-09280-1